Benjamin Britten

a Commentary
on his works
from a group of specialists

Edited by

DONALD MITCHELL
and HANS KELLER

GREENWOOD PRESS, PUBLISHERS
WESTPORT, CONNECTICUT

Library of Congress Cataloging in Publication Data

Mitchell, Donald, 1925–   ed.
    Benjamin Britten.

    Bibliography: p.
    1. Britten, Benjamin, 1913–   Works. I. Keller,
Hans Heinrich, 1919–   ed. II. Title.
ML410.B853M5   1972   780'.924   70-138166
ISBN 0-8371-5623-8

Originally published in 1952 by Rockliff Publishing Corporation Limited, London

Reprinted with the permission of Philosophical Library, Inc., New York

Reprinted in 1972 by Greenwood Press, Inc.
51 Riverside Avenue, Westport, CT 06880

Library of Congress catalog card number 70-138166
ISBN 0-8371-5623-8

Printed in the United States of America

10 9 8 7 6 5 4 3

BENJAMIN BRITTEN

I

PREFACE TO THE REPRINT EDITION

This is a reprint (with some factual corrections), not a new edition. *Tempora mutantur,* and so do even editors: to measure the unchanged text against the change of time is not, perhaps, altogether their task. But they feel that so far as Britten's present position in the musical world is concerned, this symposium has itself contributed towards a change in evaluation.

About the chapters they themselves wrote they occasionally differ. Donald Mitchell thinks that what seems to have been an unsympathetic response to Stravinsky would require serious revision today. Hans Keller, in his turn, thinks he has no right to criticize the Hans Keller of eighteen years ago: the latter is not around to defend himself. In any case, we owe it to Britten's music that our specific observations on it are not out of date. A genius is never up to date in the first place: he is up to other things, and hence never dates. In this sense, the book remains as topical as ever.

It does not, of course, cover any of the works Britten has composed since 1952, but there have been several studies of his music published in the intervening period. We cannot recommend Patricia Howard's survey of Britten's operas (*The Operas of Benjamin Britten*, Barrie and Rockliff, London: Praeger, New York, 1969) and would suggest that for the best documented account of Britten's life and operatic works readers should turn to the re-issue of Eric Walter White's *Benjamin Britten: His Life and Operas* (Faber, London: University of California Press, 1970). A less ambitious book is Imogen Holst's *Britten* (Faber, London: Crowell, New York, 1966), a study designed for the younger reader but one which is informed by a close acquaintance with the composer's personality and his art.

D.M., H.K.

London, 1971

PREFACE

THE help of all who have assisted us is acknowledged on pages viii and ix . It remains for us to thank ourselves for not giving up half way through, but only shortly before publication day, when we realized that the book had to be given up if it were ever to be published.

Any instance of the contributors' opinions coinciding with the Editors' is purely coincidental.

DONALD MITCHELL   HANS KELLER

Mondsee,
August, 1952.

ACKNOWLEDGEMENTS

Our thanks are due

to Messrs. Boosey and Hawkes, Britten's publishers, for putting their services so liberally at our disposal;

to the Oxford University Press, for permission to quote from works of Britten's published by them;

to Messrs. Faber and Faber, for permission to quote from Mr. T. S. Eliot's essay "Tradition and the Individual Talent", published in *Selected Essays*, 3rd edn., London, 1951;

to the Editors of *Hallé, Journal des Jeunesses Musicales de France, The Listener, London Musical Events, Musical Opinion, The New Statesman and Nation, Philharmonic Post*, and *La Rassegna Musicale*, for bibliographical assistance;

to the Editor of *Music and Letters*, for permission to make use of Hans Keller's "Britten and Mozart" [136];

to the Editor of *Tempo*, for permission to reproduce part of Erwin Stein's "Opera and 'Peter Grimes' " [287], and Hans Keller's "Britten's Second Quartet" [132];

to the Librarians of *Picture Post* and the Central Music Library, Westminster, for bibliographical assistance;

and to the following individuals:

Miss Grace Bennet of the B.B.C., and Mr. Lionel Bradley of the London Library, for bibliographical assistance;

Mr. and Mrs. Alec Bristow, for assistance in the preparation of copy and proofs;

Mr. Benjamin Britten, for the loan of photographs and checking certain music examples;

Mr. John Coombs of Boosey and Hawkes, for prolonged and invaluable bibliographical assistance;

Mr. Anthony Gishford of Boosey and Hawkes, for many a courtesy;

The Earl of Harewood, for help in selecting the photographic illustrations;

Mr. Jack Henderson of Boosey and Hawkes, and Miss Anna Instone of the B.B.C., for bibliographical assistance;

Mrs. Kathleen Livingston, for aid in preparation of copy;

Miss Phyllis Long, formerly of the Central Office of Information, and Miss Renée Oliver of the B.B.C., for bibliographical assistance;

Mr. Erwin Stein of Boosey and Hawkes, for clearing up some textual points;

Mr. Denis Stevens, for bibliographical assistance;

Mr. Eric Walter White, for prolonged bibliographical assistance on a most generous scale.

D.M., H.K.

CONTENTS

		Page
Preface to the Reprint Edition		v
Preface		vii
Acknowledgments		viii
THE EARL OF HAREWOOD	*The Man*	1
DONALD MITCHELL	*The Musical Atmosphere*	9
PETER PEARS	*The Vocal Music*	59
GEORGE MALCOLM	*The Purcell Realizations*	74
H. F. REDLICH	*The Choral Music*	83
ARTHUR OLDHAM	*Peter Grimes* I. THE MUSIC; THE STORY NOT EXCLUDED	101
HANS KELLER	*Peter Grimes* II. THE STORY; THE MUSIC NOT EXCLUDED	111
ERWIN STEIN	*Peter Grimes* III. OPERA AND PETER GRIMES	125
NORMAN DEL MAR	*The Chamber Operas* I. THE RAPE OF LUCRETIA II. ALBERT HERRING III. THE BEGGAR'S OPERA	132 146 163
GEORGE MALCOLM	*Dido and Aeneas*	186
ERWIN STEIN	*Billy Budd*	198
PAUL HAMBURGER	*The Chamber Music*	211
BOYD NEEL	*The String Orchestra*	237
ERWIN STEIN	*The Symphonies*	245
JOAN CHISSELL	*The Concertos*	257

Page

GEORGES AURIC · *The Piano Music*
I. ITS PLACE IN BRITTEN'S
DEVELOPMENT · 266

A. E. F. DICKINSON · *The Piano Music*
II. CRITICAL SURVEY · 269

IMOGEN HOLST · *Britten and the Young* · 276

LENNOX BERKELEY · *The Light Music* · 287

WILLIAM MANN · *The Incidental Music* · 295

ERIC WALTER WHITE · *Bibliography of Benjamin Britten's
Incidental Music* · 311

PAUL HAMBURGER · *The Pianist* · 314

HANS KELLER · *The Musical Character* · 319

DESMOND SHAWE-TAYLOR · *Discography* · 352

Chronological Catalogue of Works · 361

Bibliography · 368

Index to Britten's Music · 389

Index of Works other than Britten's · 399

Index of Names and Places · 402

Index of Music Examples · 409

ILLUSTRATIONS

I   Benjamin Britten   *Frontispiece*

II   Benjamin Britten at seven   *facing page* 4

III   E. M. Forster and Benjamin Britten   4

IV   Benjamin Britten with Mr. and Mrs. Frank Bridge   5

V   Benjamin Britten and Frank Bridge   5

VI   Benjamin Britten and Peter Pears   5

VII   Benjamin Britten   20

VIII   A page from the autograph score of the *Spring*   245
      Symphony

COLLOTYPE PLATES FROM DRAWINGS BY MILEIN COSMAN

BETWEEN PAGES 108 AND 109
Peter Grimes
Peter Pears as Peter Grimes

xii

The Beggar's Opera
Catherine Lawson as Mrs. Coaxer
Nancy Evans as Polly
Otakar Kraus as Lockit
Nancy Evans as Polly
Rose Hill as Lucy
Gentlemen of the Road
Peter Pears as Captain Macheath

BETWEEN PAGES 140 AND 141
The Rape of Lucretia
Act I Scene 1 from the Salzburg 1950 production
Elisabeth Höngen as Lucretia

Albert Herring
Richard Lewis as Albert Herring
Margaret Ritchie as Miss Wordsworth
Joan Cross as Lady Billows

Billy Budd
Peter Pears as Captain Vere
Theodor Uppman as Billy Budd
Billy Budd aboard the "Indomitable" before his execution

EDITORS' NOTES

THERE are three ways of referring to music examples in this book:

'Ex. 0' means that the passage discussed appears as a music example; 'See Ex. 0' means that the musical concept discussed appears as part of the music example in question; 'cf. Ex. 0' means what it says.

All square-bracketed numbers refer to the *Bibliography* (pp. 368-388).

Musical terms are italicized where they represent quotations from the score.

ERRATA

p. 141, Ex. 9, bar 4/2/4: G *natural*.

p. 142, Ex. 12, bar 4/8: *semiquaver* E♯, *semiquaver rest*.

p. 143, Ex. 13, bar 1/1/4: *semiquaver* F♯.

p. 143, Ex. 14: respective key signatures.

p. 153, Ex. 5, bar 3/4: *dotted quaver* A♭.

p. 158, Ex. 14, bar 4/2: a', not c''.

p. 161–2, Ex. 17, harp: (1) bar 1/1: *octave* A (no B) and crush-note a''';
                      (2) bar 2: for values, see bar 3;
                      (3) bar 5: G *natural*;
    voice, bar 4: *quaver* on "glass";
    'cello, bar 4/3: G *natural*.

p. 172, Ex. 2, voice, bar 1/2–3: *dotted crotchet* f' and *quaver* g';
    oboe, bar 8: see p. 183, Ex. 11, bar 2.

p. 180, Ex. 9, chords, bar 2/6: A♭–E;
    bar 2/7: A *flat* (not A).

Collotype plate between pages 108 and 109: for "Ottokar Kraus" read "Otakar Kraus".

SUPPLEMENTARY ERRATA LIST

p. 2, line 24: The first public performance of Britten's music took place in fact on 12th December, 1932, when the unpublished *Phantasy for String Quintet* in one movement and Three Two-Part Songs for female voices to words by Walter de la Mare were given at a Macnaghten-Lemare concert in London.

p. 9, line 8: See *Pears* p. 63, not p. 163.

p. 26, footnote, line 1: p. 292, not p. 278.

p. 38, line 15: Two pianos in Stravinsky's *Symphony of Psalms* but piano duet in Britten's *St. Nicolas.*

p. 50, footnote 1: This should read: Not to speak of equally un-English funeral marches and waltzes.

p. 55, line 9: p. 293, not p. 294.

p. 95, line 15: Robert Herrick, not George Herrick (and correct Index accordingly, p. 204).

p. 115, footnote 2, line 3: Delete Eds.

p. 143, footnote 1, line 3: Should read: The basic, falling third . . .

p. 196, Ex. 14, bar 3: The last quaver (eighth-note) in the voice part should read E natural.

p. 207, Ex. 12, bar 1: See Ex. 21, p. 27, for the correct rhythmic pattern of the ostinato and also for the correct synchronisation of the ostinato with the chorus.

p. 221, line 13: *Allegretto con slancio,* not *Allegro con slancio.*

p. 222, line 9: The diagram should read A^1-A^2-B-A^2.

p. 222, line 10: A^1, not A^2.

p. 222, line 11: Bars 352, not bars 325.

p. 247, Ex. 2, bass system, bar 6: The second crotchet (quarter-note) should read A, not B flat.

p. 263, last line *et seq.*: The Diversions underwent a further revision by the composer in 1954.

p. 299, line 18 *et seq.*: It should be remembered however that Britten's Rossini arrangements for *The Tocher* were probably composed in 1936. It was the film that was not completed until 1938.

pp. 311/312, section (b) for radio: Add THE COMPANY OF HEAVEN: radio feature (?), Michaelmas, 1937; and THE WORLD OF THE SPIRIT, radio feature (?), Whitsun, 1938 (?).

p. 312, section (c) for cinema: Add PEACE FILM: 1936.

p. 323, line 36: 'Listener' not 'listeners'.

p. 338, line 9: Close bracket after 'method'.

p. 344, line 14: 'Creative act' not art'.

p. 346, line 14: Insert full stop after '(*Pears*, p. 62)'.

p. 361, *et seq.*: The Chronological Catalogue of Works should now be used with caution. We have only amended below those years or months in the dates of composition which have since proved to be erroneous. For further information, readers should refer to the Complete Catalogue of Britten's Works published in November, 1963, by Boosey & Hawkes Ltd., and the current Britten catalogues issued by the same publishers. Since 1964, all Britten's works have been published by Faber Music Ltd. (London), whose complete catalogue should also be consulted.

p. 362, Op. 2: Date of composition should read October, 1932.

p. 362, Op. 3: Date of composition should read May, 1933, and add: revised 1955.

p. 362, *Te Deum in C major*: Date of composition should read 17th July, 1934.

p. 363, Op. 13: Date of composition should read 26th July, 1938 (revised 1945).

p. 363, Op. 14: Date of composition should read 29th March, 1939.

p. 363, Op. 15: Revised 1950 and 1958.

p. 363, Op. 19: Date of composition should read 10th December, 1939.

p. 363, Op. 21: Add: revised 1951 (not 1950) and 1954.

p. 364, Op. 22: Date of composition should read 30th October, 1940.

p. 364, Op. 26: Date of composition should read 27th October, 1941.

p. 365, Op. 32: Date of composition should read 9th November, 1944.

p. 365, Op. 33: Date of composition should read February, 1945.

p. 365, Op. 34: Date of composition should read 1946.

p. 366, *Prelude and Fugue*: Date of composition should read 18th September, 1946.

p. 367, Op. 50: Add: revised 1960.

p. 367, Op. 51: Add date of publication: 1953.

p. 367, Op. 41: Add date of publication: 1953.

p. 382, line 14: For Ottoway, read Ottaway.

p. 388, Addenda, line 7: Delete 'X'.

The Man

THE facts of Britten's life are simple. He was born an East Anglian, he wandered away from home and gained a variety of experience, and he returned to resume his creative life in his natural surroundings. Like Peter Grimes, he could say:

> I am native, rooted here . . .
> By familiar fields,
> Marsh and sand,
> Ordinary streets,
> Prevailing wind.

He was born at Lowestoft, in Suffolk, on St. Cecilia's Day (November 22nd), 1913, the youngest of a family of four. His mother was secretary of the Lowestoft Choral Society, and his own precocious musical talents had their first contact with the outside musical world through the visiting soloists who were invited to stay in the house[1]. Composition seems to have come to him naturally as soon as he felt the need to make music (at the age of about five). Initially, his music took the form of commentary on the great events of the household, but before long was diverted from such emotional inspirations towards more abstract forms. He received nothing but encouragement from his family in his musical aspirations, at all events as long as there was need for encouragement. I well remember his delight when a respected relation quite recently heard *The Rape of Lucretia* for the first time and produced the unanswerable comment: "What could you expect from someone who kept the servants up so late?"

Life at his preparatory school, South Lodge, seems to have been

[1]See also *The Vocal Music*, p. 59.—EDS.

I

congenial. It was at the age of twelve that he met for the first time
Frank Bridge, his principal teacher and in many ways the biggest single
influence on his musical life. He went regularly up to London to work
with him in the school holidays, and continued his lessons until Bridge
encouraged him to try for a scholarship at the Royal College of Music.
Though Bridge seems to have made no concessions to his pupil's
youth where composition lessons were concerned, his friendship and
enthusiastic direction were obviously of the greatest benefit to Britten,
whose devotion to Bridge's memory is very strong today, and shows
itself not least in his advocacy and performance of his music. Bridge
insisted on a thorough knowledge of the craft as well as of the art of
composition; he influenced the direction of his pupil's curiosity about
other music, but never at any time attempted to alter the natural course
of his musical inclination. Perhaps no teacher can have a strong
adverse effect on his pupil; perhaps such a combination of pupil and
teacher occurs more frequently than one is inclined to believe; but
when one talks to Britten nowadays it is difficult to avoid the conclusion
that Bridge was the ideal teacher.

After two years at Gresham's School, Holt, he left at the age of
sixteen and won a scholarship to the Royal College of Music, London,
where, on Bridge's recommendation, he studied composition with John
Ireland and the piano with Arthur Benjamin. While at the College, he
wrote the oboe Quartet, the *Sinfonietta*, and the choral variations *A
Boy was Born*. The first public performance of his music took place
a couple of months after his nineteenth birthday when the *Sinfonietta*
(actually written soon after he was eighteen) was given on January
31st, 1933, at one of Iris Lemare's concerts of contemporary music.
Probably the main advantage he gained from his time at the College
was his contact with the larger musical scene, with other musicians,
and with the most important contemporary music—or so one might
deduce from such small but not insignificant facts as the peremptory
refusal of the College Library authorities to buy the score of Schoenberg's *Pierrot lunaire* which Britten had put into the suggestion book.
A curious incident occurred when Britten won a College award which
carried enough money to maintain a stay abroad of about six months.
He decided to go to Vienna to study with Alban Berg, and broached
the subject to the authorities. He later discovered that academic suspicion had supervened with objections, and, much to his own dis-
appointment (and the fury of Frank Bridge), his family did not allow

him to go. History is full of 'might-have-beens'; perhaps the fairest comment is Britten's own: "It might have taught me how to unlock gates I did in fact have to climb over."

When he left the College, the most lucrative alternative to work as a teacher or accompanist seemed to lie in the films, and Britten joined a company specializing in documentaries. Although he produced work of considerable importance in itself, no less important was the opportunity it gave him for his first collaboration with W. H. Auden, whom he had met as long before as 1931. Auden's strong influence on his own generation extended to Britten, and he was to play a considerable part in the composer's life during the seven years which followed their first collaboration in 1935. Between 1935 and 1939, Britten worked with Auden on the films *Coal Face* and *Night Mail*; he wrote incidental music to *The Ascent of F6* and *On the Frontier*; they collaborated on radio features; and Auden provided the lyrics for *Our Hunting Fathers*, *On This Island* and (with Swingler) the *Ballad of Heroes*. The last-named was written for a special Festival of Music for the People; dedicated to the men of the British Battalion of the International Brigade who fell in Spain, it provides a clue, if not to Britten's musical personality at the time, at least to his political sympathies. During this phase of his career, Britten was enormously helped and encouraged by the practical confidence of his publisher Ralph Hawkes, who gave him a contract the moment he had finished at the College, and whose belief in Britten's future was quite undiminished by the slow speed at which his early music sold. He was no doubt lucky to have secured Britten's contract; the converse is equally true.

A few weeks after the *première* of the *Ballad of Heroes*, Britten left England for the United States, influenced in his decision both by Auden's departure for America and by depression at the prevalent handling of the rapidly darkening political situation in Europe. It would be wrong to imply that Britten left Europe with his mind firmly made up that he would settle in America; but the trip was at least in the nature of a trial, and emigration was the end in view. Looking back on his career prior to his departure for America, it is easy now to exaggerate the success his music had enjoyed. Conditions then, as today, were hardly favourable to a young composer, who might well be forgiven if the grudging reception habitually given to his music resulted in an impatient attitude of mind. Certainly, there was a feeling amongst Britten's friends that he was restricted in England. As it turned out,

probably nothing could have been better for his career than his stay
in America. Negatively, it threw him back on Europe and particularly
England; positively, it broadened his horizon, and provided a stimulus
(whether the challenge of novelty or a reaction to more appreciative
surroundings) which was to result in a short space of time in, amongst
others, such works as the violin Concerto, *Les Illuminations*, the first
string Quartet, the two pieces for two pianos, and above all the *Sinfonia
da Requiem* and the *Michelangelo Sonnets*. As a composer, he came to
maturity in America: there can be little doubt that the works he wrote
there show, not perhaps a new, but at least a more consistent sensitivity
and depth.

After a holiday in Canada, Britten visited friends in Amityville,
Long Island, and there he stayed intermittently for the next two and
a half years. During February and March 1940, he lay seriously ill in
New York, but before that he and Peter Pears had gone to live in an
artistic colony in Brooklyn, which was headed by W. H. Auden.
Britten's collaboration with Auden continued while he was in America
and resulted in his first operatic essay, *Paul Bunyan,* and the *Hymn to
St. Cecilia*. Perhaps no less important for the future was the beneficial influence Auden all this time exercised on Britten's natural liking
and understanding for poetry.

It is odd, but I think altogether appropriate, that what gave the
final impetus to Britten's decision to come back to an England which
was torn by the blitz and which had not yet turned the corner of
Alamein, should have been a reading in *The Listener* of an article by
E. M. Forster on George Crabbe, the poet of East Anglia and more
particularly of Aldeburgh; appropriate, and certainly no mere coincidence. He made up his mind to return to England, but it was anything
but easy to secure a passage at that stage of the war, and he and Peter
Pears waited six months on the East Coast of America before they were
able to leave in March, 1942. As it happened, the delay had its compensa-
tions. After a performance of the *Sinfonia da Requiem* in Boston, Britten
was asked by Koussevitzky why a composer with his natural feeling for
drama had not yet written an opera. Britten explained that there were
financial reasons why a young composer found it difficult to tackle
something so long, but told the conductor that he was thinking of a
subject taken from Crabbe. A few weeks later he heard that the Koussevitzky Music Foundation was prepared to put up the money he would
need if he were to set aside sufficient time in which to write an opera.

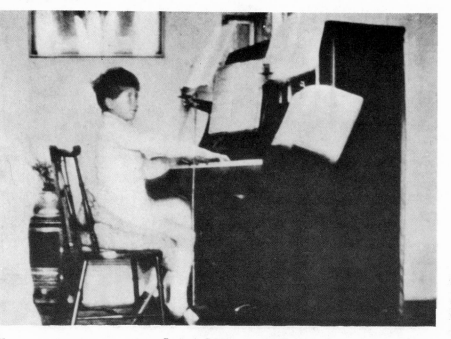

II   Benjamin Britten at seven

III   E. M. Forster and Benjamin Britten   [*Picture Post*]

IV   Benjamin Britten with Mr. and Mrs. Frank Bridge

V   Benjamin Britten and Frank Bridge   VI   Benjamin Britten and Peter Pears

[*British I.S.B.*]

Britten brought back with him to England a quantity of music which had not been heard here before, and as a result his reception by musicians was little short of enthusiastic. While he was in America, he had realized that his belief that violence can breed nothing but violence, and his fundamental objection to meet hatred with hatred, would make acceptance in war-time England a difficult matter for him. He was exempted from military service, and, like musicians in other countries, was allowed to continue his life as a composer and as a performing musician. Most readers will not need any reminder that the rôle of a conscientious objector, though more widely understood in the last world war than in the first, was not an easy one. For a musician, the possibility existed of continuing a peace-time career in the excellent orchestra of the R.A.F., and Britten's decision to sacrifice the easier way to scruples of conscience is not one I, personally, would be inclined to underestimate.

In 1938, after the death of his mother (his father had died a few years earlier), he had bought a disused mill at Snape, near Aldeburgh, and it was there that he wrote *Peter Grimes* in the intervals of his concert tours for C.E.M.A. The first performance of this work on 7th June, 1945, marked in many people's opinion the turning of the tide for British music: it certainly established Britten in public estimation as a major composer, and it was the first of a series of operas which have subsequently appeared (apart from 1950) at the rate of one a year. Britten's career in the years since the war is public property: it is one of unremitting composition and performance. In 1946, with the composition of *The Rape of Lucretia* and the formation of the English Opera Group, his career as a performer entered a new phase. He had always been interested in music written for smaller combinations, but now he became more intimately concerned as the musical leader and dominating personality of a group which was to specialize in such music and give performances of it all over England and Europe.[1] Its formation inevitably added to Britten's commitments as a performer, as did the foundation of the Aldeburgh Festival in 1948.

If there were not such strong evidence to the contrary, the diversity of Britten's activities might blind one to his intensely professional

---

[1] The orchestration of the *Spring Symphony* and of *Billy Budd*, with its tendency towards clearly differentiated textures and away from what Britten has described as "the luscious *tutti* effect" of a large orchestra, is only a logical musical development from his work with a chamber orchestra of solo instruments; it might have taken longer to evolve without this practical experience.

attitude towards music in particular and art in general. This is something one cannot emphasize too strongly. It was evolved in the teeth of opposition from every tenet of birth, upbringing, and environment, and it had to contend not only with the Englishman's innate lack of seriousness in his attitude towards the arts, but also with the determined amateurism fostered in the public schools, and supported by every form of pressure, social and moral, at their command. Britten's professionalism is responsible for his own scrupulous attention to detail and his very great understanding for other men's music. It also accounts for his acute impatience of hostile criticism; to feel his own (or someone else's) *motives* misunderstood and to be therefore criticized (or praised) on a basis which does not in his view exist, is to him the most exasperating aspect of a press notice. Professionally, he is easily bored, quickly aggravated, by incompetence in his fellow professionals, by lack of knowledge—more still by pretence—on the part of anyone performing music or writing or talking about it. This is not the boredom or the anger of the self-centred man: it extends far beyond things which concern him personally. To take two random examples: a slighting reference to Purcell will make him genuinely angry, and he was saddened and taken aback at the deprecatory tone of some of the so-called 'appreciative' notices which appeared after the death of Artur Schnabel. Britten is a professional and in earnest, and he makes such things a personal matter: "I have nothing against him," he will say of the writer of such an article, "I just don't want to see him." His own performances, or those he is connected with, he will criticize unmercifully; he can be partially consoled, but not convinced, by a less stringent view.

His likes and dislikes are based on an extraordinarily detailed knowledge of his subject, and it is from them that the external influences on his music are derived. His extreme dissatisfaction with Brahms's music (which he once admired) is supported by his thorough acquaintance with it: "I play through all his music every so often to see if I am right about him; I usually find that I underestimated last time how bad it was!" When choosing music for the Aldeburgh Festival, he will suggest pieces by composers in whom one might have thought him uninterested, but his predilections are for what he has described as "the clear and clean—the 'slender' sound of, say, Mozart or Verdi or Mahler— or even Tchaikovsky, if he is played in a restrained, though vital way." He was referring to the sound of their orchestration, but his attitude to all music and not just to orchestration could be described in similar terms. His passion for Elizabethan music is only exceeded by his devotion to Purcell, of whom he has an unrivalled understanding as performer. To these add the names of Monteverdi and Bach, Gluck and Weber, Schubert and Berg and you have a collection of composers whose music delights Britten, and whose techniques and values appear in his own music, digested and assimilated to be sure, but still often discernible. His dislike of so many aspects of romanticism has not led him to adopt the neo-classicism of Strawinsky in spite of his enthusiasm for the early music of that composer, any more than his present reaction against Strawinsky's more recent music (and also his writings) causes him to refer to him as anything but a master. He has been able to choose his own path regardless of fashionable reactions.

His vital impulsive sympathy for the struggle of the human being against the mass—it can be seen in many of his compositions, particularly the operas—matches his own individualism. It also indicates a social conscience which is tied to no '-ism', but has been active since he was at his preparatory school. The various compositions which reflected a left wing ideology at about the time of the Spanish Civil War were straws in a wind which has not changed its direction, however much it may have come to blow with an increased economy and discrimination. His vigorous reaction against restrictive practices, whether of right or left wing origin, is sufficient proof that the pattern of his political beliefs has not materially changed.

I have indicated that Britten's excursion to America was not least important in the effect it had of focusing his desire to return to his native Suffolk. In the summer of 1947 he bought a house in the small fishing town of Aldeburgh, which he had known from his earliest youth, and since August of that year this has been his home. His love for Aldeburgh is shown in his unceasing work for its Festival, which has grown, largely through his efforts and those of Peter Pears, into something of an institution with ramifications far beyond the confines of Suffolk. But there is more to it than that; at Aldeburgh he can work as nowhere else. He will get up early to write—say, at six o'clock or half-past—and continue all morning with only a few minutes for breakfast, and have finished work for the day by luncheon. To interrupt him in the morning is to risk assuming the mantle of Coleridge's 'person from Porlock'. His afternoon may be spent in any number of ways, but he will probably not put pen to paper again until next day, by which time he will have completed in his mind what he is going to write. Isolation at Aldeburgh has not made Britten into an 'ivory tower' composer. He goes out to sea to fish, he plays tennis, he watches birds, he is by no means an unsociable neighbour, and he entertains frequently. He is unhappy in London, which he associates with concert-giving and visits to the dentist, with meetings and being rung up on the telephone, with auditions and having to see people on business—with anything in fact except composing. And that which he does at Aldeburgh is, after all, his life.

DONALD MITCHELL

The Musical Atmosphere

"Home is where one starts from . . ." T. S. ELIOT, *East Coker.*

I. *A BOY WAS BORN*; EARLY MANIFESTATION OF BRITTEN'S ENGLISHRY

HOW closely related is Benjamin Britten to the English tradition?

Many will argue that he isn't; that lying outside nationalist musical considerations he fails to secure a place for himself in our affections; that he is too clever, too sophisticated, too eclectic, too polished, too heartless even—a list of adjectives the opposites of which might add up to the average Englishman's conception of the national character (see *Pears*, p. 163).

Mannerisms may sustain a tradition but can never make one; the great composer will largely create a tradition of his own. It is the composer of minor gifts who has to rely stylistically on his native musical tradition. Therefore to discuss Britten—whom I judge a great composer—partly in terms of his Englishry (see *Berkeley*, pp. 293f.), may not appear to be a very valuable critical enterprise; but one finds that it reveals aspects of his musical character which might otherwise remain hidden, and, as with all the few great composers, 'local' characteristics are often of universal import. As I hope to show (Section VII, *The English Synthesis*, pp. 46–58) Britten's Englishry is of the profoundest significance for the musical culture of Europe and ourselves.

Britten's early Englishry established itself with *A Boy was Born*, written in 1932. A choral work, the choice of its texts indicated a discriminating literary taste. In view of Britten's later development (the

9

Serenade, Spring Symphony, Five Flower Songs, etc.), this now causes us no surprise. But those traditionalists of the 'thirties' English school who were aware of the achievements of Parry, Stanford and Vaughan Williams in their care for, and cultivation of, the English language's relation to English music, must have realized that here was a new composer with an exceptional sensibility to his mother tongue. So far, so English; and while *A Boy was Born*'s form was unorthodox— a theme and six variations, the last being an extended finale—it was not so in a manner that militated against traditional acceptance.

In the fortunate position of the critic with hindsight, one is not astonished at this early use of variation form—it has remained one of Britten's favourite procedures. Nevertheless, choral variations were uncommon enough for *A Boy was Born* to have made an impression with its formal innovation, and the deployment of a boys' choir was a momentous sign of Britten's awakening interest in the musical possibilities of children's voices. Thus *A Boy was Born* presents not only aspects of Britten's Englishry, but sure evidence of stylistic, textural and aesthetic trends now accepted as characteristics of his music. A common complaint—Britten's lack of a 'personal idiom' and/or too masterful a grasp of every other composer's—seems to be a misconception based on inadequate knowledge of his output; a thorough examination from Op. 1 onwards would disclose a consistently developing and integrated musical personality, with finger-prints as recognizable in their musical youth as in their full maturity (see *Auric,* pp. 266ff.). Those misguided well-wishers who imagine Britten to be an eclectic, but to have made a virtue of his eclecticism, betray the eclecticism of ears which have heard too much music and ceased to discriminate; a generous tolerance of eclecticism is hardly proof of penetrating understanding of the historical content of Britten's style.

A detailed musical analysis of *A Boy was Born* could have done little to disturb the English conservatives, though had they recalled the powerful European inflections of the *Sinfonietta* their faith might have been a little less secure. Perhaps it was imagined that Britten had left his Europeanism behind him (as, in a sense, he was to do, but some ten years later). Yet to compare the Englishry of *A Boy was Born* with that of the *Spring Symphony* is to see that our English traditionalists could have been none too sure what that English tradition was. Even a very acute critic, Wilfrid Mellers, rather overstates the case when he writes that *A Boy was Born* was "directly in the English line bequeathed to our composers by the work of Vaughan Williams . . ." [202]. Of course Britten's piece owes something to Vaughan Williams's clarifying spirit, but harmonically it was biased rather in favour of a mild cosmopolitanism reminiscent of the more sophisticated idiom of John Ireland, one of Britten's teachers at the R.C.M. (see Ex. 1):

Ex.1

That Britten should have chosen for the most English of his early works the most European of then available English styles was prophetic of the synthesis to come.

II. THE EUROPEANISM OF THE *FRANK BRIDGE VARIATIONS*; PARODY AND SATIRE; *OUR HUNTING FATHERS*

Although *A Boy was Born* had a marked European feature, if not nearly so marked as the earlier chamber *Sinfonietta* or *Phantasy* Quartet, the *Variations on a Theme of Frank Bridge* for string orchestra were almost stressedly European and showed a number of European influences which had come to stay. First and foremost that of Mahler and the late Viennese school. It would be a mistake to imagine that Britten's parodistic talents, as apparent in these variations, very seriously mock the Viennese tradition—in relation to which Britten stands in many ways as English inheritor and innovator. Indeed the satire may be taken rather as a measure of his underlying respect[1]. In the acid yet affection-

---

[1] I have written elsewhere [221]: "Parody, in the deepest sense, is one of Britten's major gifts—these [*Frank Bridge*] variations were an early but exceptionally accomplished manifestation of it. Why does parody, as such, concern us here? Because very often *the style a composer parodies is a style which holds for him the greatest possible attraction and by which he has been and will be influenced.* Parody (using the term in its widest meaning) is frequently a symptom of strong affection for a style and a powerful desire for self-identification with it." [A striking parallel in human affairs may be found in the child who 'makes fun' of his parents; his 'imitations' will be based on both admiration and hostility. It seems probable that this child-parent relationship is the origin of most parody in the arts, not to speak of the fact that creative artists inevitably begin by imitating. While parody does not exclude this dependent attitude, it is also an assertion of individuality, a gesture of freedom. In music it might be looked upon as a rather back-handed way of paying compliments to one's musical parents.] "The parodistic variations in the *Bridge* set—all based on European models; there is no parody of an English folk song for instance—give us a series of clues to Britten's European inflections

ate *Wiener Walzer*, in the *Funeral March* and *Chant*, the current of musical feeling seems to run deepest where Vienna is directly or indirectly involved; a symptom of particular interest, since the whole work is a pocket anthology of foreign styles—the Rossinian *Aria Italiana*, the Viennese *Walzer*, the Gallic *Bourrée Classique*, the neo-classical, cosmopolitan *Romance*. The variations could hardly have been more frankly European, more recognizably Britten, yet less stemming from the tentative European inflections of *A Boy was Born*. By means of the intervening *Our Hunting Fathers*, Britten had travelled a long way towards Europe since 1932.

The *Frank Bridge Variations* were written in 1937, at a time when Britten was closely associated with W. H. Auden, the novelist Christopher Isherwood, and the work of the Experimental Theatre Group. The *Variations'* predominantly satirical mood, quite apart from their skilful parodying, reflects their period as accurately as the joint dramatic productions of Auden and Isherwood. Not that Britten has ever lost his gift for satire or his powerful social conscience—it is odd that Ex. 2 from the *Spring Symphony* (Part II, No. 3)

Ex.2

Nor ask what doubt-ful act al -
-lows Our free - dom — in this Eng - lish house, Our pic-nics in the sun.

(Footnote continued from page 11.)

in a most compact and assimilable manner. This applies not only to the light-hearted *Aria Italiana* but to the well-nigh broken-hearted *Funeral March*."

In view of Britten's subsequent operatic career, the *Aria Italiana* is of special significance. That piece of Rossinian fun has proved to be highly prophetic.

has been little remarked upon from this point of view—but Britten's music is witness to a satire always informed by a deep compassion (*Albert Herring*), and, in *Peter Grimes*, or even *The Little Sweep*, a discriminating social conscience that had been more rawly expressed in the earlier *Our Hunting Fathers* and the *Ballad of Heroes*.

But *Our Hunting Fathers* is not to be musically underestimated for all the fact that, in Scott Goddard's words, "at the Norwich Festival in 1936 [it] . . . scandalized those among the gentry who caught Auden's words" [100]. A *succès de scandale*, it doubtless prevented our musical prophets from evaluating the worth of the music itself and the sign-post significance of its sub-title, a 'Symphonic Cycle for High Voice and Orchestra'. Symphonic song cycles of such instrumental resource and ambition are rarely enough met with, and *Our Hunting Fathers* was the first of Britten's long series of similar works.

Our Hunting Fathers, *Les Illuminations* and the *Serenade* are interesting descendants of a tradition initiated by Mahler[1] with the *Kindertotenlieder* and the *Lieder eines fahrenden Gesellen*, but it was the *Frank Bridge Variations* which first revealed to English ears Mahler's influence on Britten, a revelation in itself somewhat retarded by English musicians' ignorance of Mahler's status as a composer. Very little Mahler was to be heard in this country before 1939; Britten's re-scoring (in the 1940's) for reduced orchestra of a movement from Mahler's Third Symphony (the minuet *What the wild flowers tell me*) is thus of special interest, showing his practical insight into Mahler's music and a desire to see it more widely performed. Mellers writes as follows upon the Mahlerian aspects of the *Frank Bridge Variations*:

> The influences in Britten's music may seem odd for a British composer—particularly that of late Mahler which with its widely leaping melodies and translucent orchestration is noticeable not only in the *Sinfonia da Requiem* but as early as the slow sections of the string orchestra *Variations*[2] [202].

This is a correct enough observation but, while taking note of Mahler, it would be unreasonable to lose sight of the characteristic Britten who, far from hiding his light under a European bushel, shone it in no uncertain manner in the *Variations*' very first bars (Ex. 3):

[1] Certainly as far as Britten is concerned. Mahler, no doubt, found his precedents in Beethoven and Schubert, and perhaps in Berlioz's *Les Nuits d'été*. Redlich (pp. 83f.) suggests even earlier examples of the song cycle principle.

[2] And as late as the impassioned orchestral meditation which immediately precedes Billy's trial in *Budd*'s Act III, Sc. 2: incidentally, a remarkable and mature example of Britten's 'rhetoric' (see my remarks on p. 14).

Ex.8

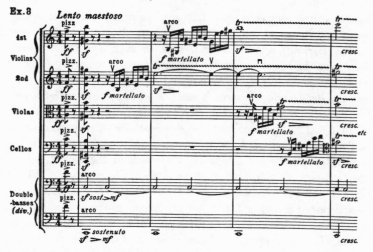

The incisive E major semiquaver figures, which struggle hard against the pull of a stubbornly prolonged pedal on C, foreshadow many like rhetorical passages in later works; the semiquavers' quasi-fanfare character may be compared with Exx. 4, 22, 26 and 52d. Mahler's lavish use of fanfares is inevitably recalled.

Mellers views Britten as "essentially a rhetorical[1] composer, bringing our seventeenth century rhetorical period to a belated consummation" [202]. But the late 19th century Viennese school (Mahler to Berg) was equally rich in rhetorical, often theatrical content, and Britten is as much a consummation of that distinctly European tradition as he is of 17th century England's. This double historical function is of unique significance. The rhetorical, dramatic elements, derived from both European and English sources, indicate why *A Boy was Born* was less influenced by Vaughan Williams than might reasonably have been predicted. Britten knew instinctively what he was about when he chose the more latently and potentially European of available English styles, a judgment Mellers would seem to confirm: "Neither the pure polyphonic conception, nor the idea of dramatic tonal conflict plays much part in his music" [202]. At least, Mellers is right about the polyphony[2] and misleading when he posits the

---

[1] *Chissell* (p. 263) obviously uses 'rhetorical' in its other sense.—EDS.

[2] On the other hand the passacaglia finale of the violin Concerto shows what Britten might have done with a solely polyphonic idiom had he chosen to pursue that stylistic path.

absence of tonal conflict—he can't, in my view, have thought over-much about the dramatic use of tonality in Britten's operas[1] [150]. But there is no doubt that whereas Vaughan Williams's style is very closely associated with 16th century polyphony—the 5th Symphony for instance—Britten owes much more to the dramatic, rhetorical stylization of the 17th century, especially to Purcell.

The *Frank Bridge Variations* were the first work of Britten's which enabled the not so perspicacious to babble freely of the young composer's precocious technique—a form of disparaging compliment which precluded any genuine understanding of the music. Mellers proves himself a substantial historian when he points out that

> Britten's professional competence . . . his virtuoso qualities were important at a time when these things were hard to come by in English music . . . [202]

—qualities which might be said to be yet further examples of his un-Englishness, for Britten's 'technical facility' has contributed as much as anything to the atmosphere of suspicion with which so many of his works have been received[2]. In an age not too generously furnished with genius, the fertility of genius has become confused, or even identified, with the facility of talent; and the old English custom of only encouraging the composer who has had to fight visibly for his technique can be a positive hindrance when estimating works of art as highly accomplished as Britten's (cf. [159]).

At this stage in Britten's career the *Frank Bridge Variations* represented an Englishry more negative than positive, and the satire of *Our Hunting Fathers* must have been considered as very convincing evidence of Britten's revolt not only against English musical habits, but also against his English environment. It would have been advisable to remember that satire does not exclude a very deep care for its target,

---

[1] And *Billy Budd* (written, of course, some years after Mellers's book) only serves to confirm this opinion.

[2] An illustrative example from 1951: after *Billy Budd*'s first performance, Mosco Carner wrote in *Time and Tide* of December 8th:

". . . the whole organization of the score evinces a sovereign command of technical resources and an intuitive grasp of a complex medium. But there is too often the impression that cleverness and facile fluency take the place of a more profound idea, that 'tricks' are made to serve where intrinsic invention is required and that interpretation from within is shirked by description from without. For example, is Claggart's monologue *musically* a complete revelation of the man, as it ought to be? Does not the handling of the execution scene or of the naval action smack of slick and no more than adequate film music?"

It is noteworthy that critics who adopt this attitude always leave the " 'tricks' " unspecified, nor do they concretely indicate "the more profound idea" that has been displaced by "cleverness and facile fluency".

and that responsible satire is more the result of outraged affection than the desire to upset established conventions. While not ignoring the youthful and provoking ebullience of *Our Hunting Fathers,* one should not have underrated its adult (and even English) seriousness of motive.

III. *ON THIS ISLAND*; POINTS OF STYLE; BRITTEN'S COUNTERPOINT, PUBLIC AND PRIVATE; ORDER, DIS-ORDER, AND THEMATIC ORGANIZATION; HIS PERSON-ALITY IN- AND OUT-TURNED

Hard on the heels of the *Frank Bridge Variations* followed five songs for high voice and piano, *On This Island,* composed in 1937 to poems by W. H. Auden[1]. The first song shares some of its rhetoric with the introduction of the *Variations* (see Ex. 3). Auden's text,

> Let the florid music praise,
> The flute and the trumpet,
> Beauty's conquest of your face . . .

demands and receives Britten's quasi-fanfare treatment (Ex. 4):

Ex.4 *Maestoso— non troppo presto*

Let the flo-rid mu-sic praise,

---

[1] Strictly speaking, *On This Island* (op. 10) was composed both before and after the *Frank Bridge Variations* (op. 11). Two of the songs (Nos. 2 and 4) were written in May, 1937, the remainder in October. The *Variations* were completed in July of the same year.

But whereas the *Frank Bridge Variations* were distinctly European, in *On This Island* Britten's English stylization begins to make itself substantially felt. The first song's *bravura* cadenza (Ex. 5) clearly indicates in which direction the English wind will eventually blow:

Subsequent sequential writing in *Let the florid music praise!* betrays a certain stylistic hesitancy; the sense of pastiche, not of a thoroughly assimilated style, persists (see Ex. 6):

Whereas Ex. 6 is faulty, Ex. 7 from *The Little Sweep* (No. XV, *Aria*) shows how Britten's developed style can accommodate a similar 'cliché' without strain:

On This Island provides ample evidence of Britten's already fastidious musical imagery—as in the sharp melodic curve (see Ex. 8) of the gull's flight which succeeds a just previous and stubborn lodgement on a repeated E♭ (No. 3, *Seascape*):

The last song, *As it is, plenty*, is of particular interest since it displays Britten's partiality for dotted rhythm in an odd guise. The song is a rare instance of Britten's making highly ironical use of a fairly straight-faced jazz idiom (Ex. 9):

Dotted rhythm crops up continuously throughout Britten's music, though elsewhere in more characteristic and Purcellian dress. Ex. 10 is from the Cantata *Rejoice in the Lamb* (organ part excluded):

Perhaps Britten's most subtle employment of dotted rhythm occurs in the *Spring Symphony*'s vocal and orchestral canon *Fair and fair* (Part III, No. 2; Ex. 11):

Ex.11

But apart from these mature fulfilments of *On This Island*'s stylistic promises, the second song, *Now the leaves are falling fast*, contains a *tranquillo* coda of immense import. Exactly matching the visionary quality of Auden's verse, it has about it that air of tense beauty which is so marked an aspect of many like passages in Britten's later music. The harmonic structure is simple, yet deceivingly encloses the deepest feeling (Ex. 12):

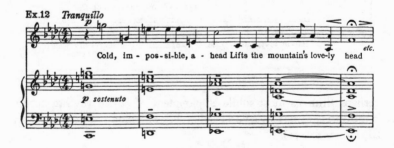

VII

The coda (Ex. 12) is not only an augmented version of the song's two introductory bars (Ex. 13),

but, in its four final bars (Ex. 14a), an augmentation of the bar (Ex. 14b) at which the voice first enters:

These examples are not only symptomatic of Britten's habitual economy of form, but the coda in particular is a striking forerunner of things to come—for instance, "Quel che nel tuo bel volto bramo e 'mparo" (Ex. 15) from the *Michelangelo* cycle's *Sonetto LV*. The expression is more personal, the experience deeper, yet it is obvious that in both examples the same musical mind is at work.

Exx. 12 and 15 point to Britten's achievement of extreme tension by the simplest harmonic means, a judgment confirmed by Albert's passionate and uncomplicated G major song "It seems as clear as clear can be" (*Herring*, Act I, Sc. 2; see Ex. 16),

or Grimes's "Now the Great Bear and Pleiades" (*Grimes*, Act I, Sc. 2;
see Ex. 17), which ponders on an almost undisturbed E major:

The structure of this piece reminds us that canon is a constant
feature of Britten's music: *Fair and Fair* from the *Spring Symphony*
(Ex. 11); *This little Babe* (No. 6, *A Ceremony of Carols*); the middle
section of the *Spring Symphony*'s Finale (at figure 14 "Now little
fish on tender stone begin to cast their bellies"); the soprano-tenor
duet in the *Wedding Anthem*; the Novice's flogging ensemble in
Billy Budd, Act I (at figure 42); and, in *Herring* (Act I, Sc. 2),
Sid's and Nancy's unison "We'll walk to the spinney" (Ex. 18),

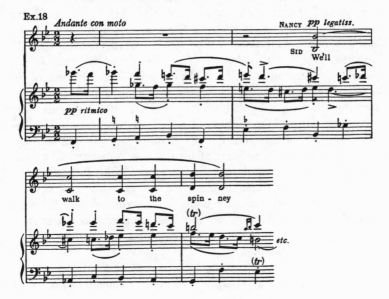

accompanied by an unobtrusive, close-fitting canon at the octave which consolidates the unity of their love.

Britten's contrapuntal art makes itself known in the best of all possible ways: it makes itself *felt*, is emotionally experienced, prior to its formal recognition. One suspects that Ex. 18 was written without a conscious thought as to its technical implications. On the other hand, when the musical or dramatic situation demands that the counterpoint shall obtrude, when the display of artifice is an aesthetic necessity, Britten is capable of ostentatious counterpoint without ever becoming a bore or pedant. *The Young Person's Guide* (see *Holst*, pp. 276ff.) being something of a textbook, its concluding fugue, which spotlights the orchestra individually, sectionally and *tutti*, must be bold in advocating its function. It would fail in its purpose if fugue were not writ large upon it. Britten does not falter—a full-blooded fugue it is; and that it happens to be a remarkable culmination to a rare musical event is not incidental but of great importance to the true understanding of Britten's style. The 'committed' craft is in no way antagonistic to the art.

Another example—dramatic not educative—of Britten's explicitly contrapuntal counterpoint occurs in *Herring*, Act I, Sc. 1—"We've made our own investigations", the fugue addressed to Lady Billows. Britten's fugue subject wears a public face which matches the self-importance of the participants, while the formal structure of the *ensemble* both parodies itself and the absurdly formal method of the investigators' delivery. Moreover, the counterpoint indicates the remorseless burrowing by each of these self-appointed busybodies into the private affairs of the citizens of Loxford—a present musical realization of bygone activities; it is quite extraordinary how Britten's operatic characterizations take account of his characters' pasts; their musical histories extend backwards as well as forwards. In fact Britten can be a merciless investigator himself; hence Ex. 19. To make their operatic point clear the rather clumsy boots of Superintendent Budd must make themselves well and truly heard. The theme must be correspondingly sure-footed, and the fugue's working out correspondingly 'obvious' in its counterpoint.

The investigation fugue may raise a legitimate enough laugh, but we

must puzzle out for ourselves how it is that Britten can convey such bumbledom in music so precise. One thing is certain. A composer who sets out to satirize the muddle-headed or heavy-handed cannot afford to suffer from the vices of those whom he satirizes. Even where the dramatic situation demands confusion, musically speaking the art must be as ordered and as highly organized as ever.

That Britten has solved this seeming paradox with exceptional deftness may be clearly seen by reference to the third of *The Little Sweep*'s audience songs—the *Night Song*. The four bird calls, each of which has been presented separately by a section of the audience, are, between the song's last stanzas, combined in a motley, but not cacophonous, cadenza[1] (Ex. 20):

[1] At public performances in my experience this part of the *Night Song* and its subsequent repetition have never been sufficiently rehearsed with the audience. As a result, they have all too often deteriorated into cacophonous cadenzas which contradict the intentions of the score.

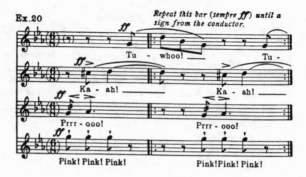

A repetition of the cadenza, *pianissimo* and "dying away to nothing", forms the song's final bars. As Ex. 20 illustrates, strict musical order underpins the language of the aviary, however improvisatory the mingling of feathered tongues may sound.

This fondness for vocal cadenzas shows itself in many shapes, sizes and guises throughout Britten's operas—for instance at the end of the *Threnody* in *Albert Herring* (Act III, figure 57) where the nine participants simultaneously deliver their characteristic and characterizing vocal lines (previously heard soloistically against the *Threnody*'s chant) over a bass pedal.

A rather different example of this planned confusion—but one very well worth remarking—is the beautifully conceived recitativic chatter of the Loxford committee which preludes Lady Billow's entry in *Herring*, Act I, Sc. 1. In *Lucretia*, the cadenza principle is evident on a smaller scale in the "Good night!" ensemble which closes Act I (Sc. 2, from figure 97) and, rather more remotely and monumentally, in the passacaglia from Act II, Sc. 2. The tradition[1], so to speak, is maintained in *Billy Budd*, Act III, Sc. 1, where the *Indomitable*'s crew —Gunners, Seamen, Marines, Powder Monkeys and so forth— assembles soloistically (each section to its own motive), and finally (five bars after figure 20) unites in a complex combination of all the crew's character-motives. Meanwhile the battle-scene's 'ostinato'—either the

---

[1] See also *The Light Music*, p. 278, Ex. 3, *The Incidental Music*, p. 306 (the description of the Antimasque's Trio from *This Way to the Tomb*), and—a very different context— *The Chamber Music*, p. 230, Ex. 12.

theme itself (Ex. 21 (x)) or the associated, dominating rhythm (Ex. 21 (y))—has never long been absent, either vocally or instrumentally:

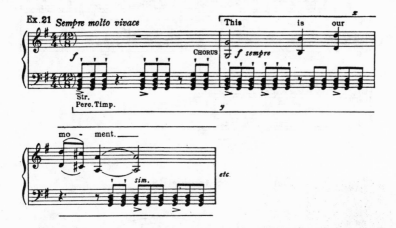

The scene in its musical entirety provides the exactest possible representation of the naval hurly-burly which precedes the firing of a 'long eighteen'.

In this case Britten makes brilliant use of the crew's character-motives by reintroducing them in the orchestral execution 'march' (Act IV, Sc. 2) across a fugally treated ostinato rhythm;

Each department of the crew takes up its position on the main deck as the relevant motive appears in the orchestra.

Any inquiry into Britten's ability to encompass a variety of musical ideas and swiftly changing action within a very tight musical structure can hardly fail to take note of *Billy Budd*'s Act I, particularly the act's first 'part' (from figures 4 to 15) which establishes the energetic bustle of a man-o'-war's main deck primarily by means of the following material:

The fanfare-like Ex. 22 (Motive A):

Ex.22

The working shanty (Ex. 23; motive B):

Ex.23

The jaunty tune (Ex. 24; motive C) linked with the Sailing Master, taken up by the Midshipmen, and later parodied by Donald:

Ex.24

and the string of major seconds (Ex. 25; motive D_1) which accompanies its vocal equivalent as the crew hoists the yards (Ex. 25; motive D_2):

How subtly · Britten has organized his motives into a perfectly balanced formal scheme can be conveniently exposed by means of a simple diagram. The first 'part' of the act falls into five 'sections':

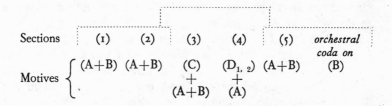

Sections	(1)	(2)	(3)	(4)	(5)	*orchestral coda on*
Motives	(A+B)	(A+B)	(C) + (A+B)	(D₁, ₂) + (A)	(A+B)	(B)

By treating sections (1) and (2) as an 'exposition' with repeat (motives A and B acting as strongly contrasted 'first and second subjects'), the 'expansions' (3) and (4) as a 'development' (introducing the new motives C and $D_{1,2}$ in combination with thematic elements of A and B), and (5) as a 'recapitulation' with 'coda', this thematic analysis automatically assumes sonata shape: an obvious analytical exaggeration, but it does, at the very least, hint at the minute organization beneath the surface of the dramatically indispensable turmoil of *Budd*'s opening scene[1].

[1] Needless to say, Captain Vere's despairing lament in the immediately preceding *Prologue*

—is opposed at every turn by the opera's organic structure.

To return to Britten's counterpoint, the alternative uses—public and private—to which he puts it (see Exx. 18 and 19) give us a clue to another aspect of his music. On the one hand its extreme solitariness, its inwardness, and on the other, its extreme sociability, a turning outwards to the world [112], the latter resulting in a genuinely popular style which is often misunderstood as Britten's eclecticism. This fact suggests that his popularity is frequently based on a stylistic misconception, but it would be an error to suppose that Britten's sociability is not a strong determining factor in his musical character. Certainly it accounts for his very vigorous efforts to bridge the gap between the artist and his audience (see Section VII, pp. 46–58).

Our Hunting Fathers, the *Ballad of Heroes,* the part song *Advance Democracy,* were early proof of Britten's response to society. While recently his sociability has become less particularized and didactic, the *Holy Sonnets of John Donne* indicate an inwardness, a turning in on himself, a revulsion even from the world, which reaches a frightening pitch of intensity. The *John Donne Sonnets* make the least concessions to Britten's own social, out-turning tendencies. A song cycle which seems to be the declaration of a creative loneliness finding no remedy or relief in the act of creation, the music at times appears to underline its own withdrawal from humanity and the consolations of human sorrow. This in-turned contemplation is to be found throughout Britten's music, rubbing neighbourly shoulders with his more extrovert tendencies—in *Grimes, Herring,* or the *Spring Symphony* even; but such is Britten's rigorous control over his musical material that there is no consequent disparity of style. Perhaps the *John Donne Sonnets* represent the extremest limits to this kind of personal withdrawal. It is meaningful that they have never attained the same degree of popularity as the *Michelangelo* set.

IV. THE EUROPEAN STYLIZATION OF *LES ILLUMINATIONS*; BRITTEN'S HARMONIC ASSURANCE; HIS CHROMATICISM; HIS CLASSICISM

But fully to understand the *Michelangelo Sonnets* it is necessary to come to them (as Britten himself did) by way of the song cycle for high voice and string orchestra, *Les Illuminations,* and with a further backward glance or two at *On This Island.* Whereas *On This Island* showed some signs of an English stylization, *Les Illuminations* are as

European as they might be—or, more decisively, as French as their title.
Not only were Rimbaud's prose poems the first continental text Britten
set[1], but Rimbaud himself was something of a curious poet for an
English composer to choose, particularly from the view-point of the
work's contemporary audiences. In 1939 it was less generally recognized
than now that Auden's verse was as much influenced by the French
poet as it was by the German Rainer Maria Rilke; no doubt it was this
cosmopolitan, European aspect of Auden's poetry which had throughout appealed to Britten's imagination. The step to a poet of exclusively
European origin was not surprising. What astonished the contemporary
listeners to *Les Illuminations*, and what continues to amaze, was the
consummate artistry with which Britten handled the French language.
As an English critic has remarked, *Les Illuminations* prove one need not
be a French chef to dish up perfect French cooking. But more remarkable than Britten's absorption of a European style (very different from
a European style's absorption of Britten) was his success in presenting
highly abstruse poetic contents in music which is at once intelligible
and yet free of any over-simplification of the subtleties of the text. This
could only be achieved by the adoption of an already highly developed
stylization—a style which both reveals and conceals; a system of musical
manners which nevertheless permits the greatest freedom of speech.
It was the sole musical solution to the civilized complexity of Rimbaud's
verse. The style of *A Boy was Born* could not have sustained the weight
of Rimbaud's imagery; the more fruitful stylization of *On This Island*
was as yet insufficiently integrated; and Britten was too responsible
a composer to allow any stylistic ambiguity to obscure his intentions.
Les Illuminations, moreover, were the first of his whole-hearted
European stylizations and represented frankly, if momentarily, a
conscious abandonment of the English tradition. Britten was to fulfil
this Europeanism in *Les Illuminations*, the *Sinfonia da Requiem*, and the
Michelangelo Sonnets, before concerning himself again with matters
more recognizably English.

Although Britten's European excursion was so completely accomplished, it would be an error to suppose that *Les Illuminations* are un-
characteristic Britten. On the contrary, they signify a further clarifica-
tion and intensification of his style. The quasi-fanfare violin figure in
the work's *maestoso* opening (Ex. 26) bears an obvious relation to the

[1] See, however, *Pears*, p. 60, on Britten's youthful and unpublished settings of
Verlaine.

rhetorical semiquavers in the *Frank Bridge Variations'* *lento* introduction (Ex. 3):

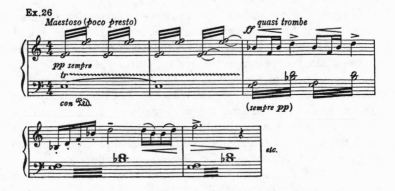

Antique (*No. 3b*) yet further refines on the *Variations'* *Romance*—the rhythms are subtler, and the melodic structure is not only more complex, but, rather interestingly, almost independent of the vocal line (see Ex. 27):

This highly formalized *cantabile* style occurs again and again in
Britten's music (see Ex. 37), perhaps at its maturest in *Herring*, for
instance, in Albert's last act song "And I'm more than grateful to you
all" (Ex. 28):

Ex.28 *Amabile (molto moderato)*

The vocal line of *Les Illuminations*, unlike *On This Island*'s, is free
of ornaments except in *Marine* (No. 5)[1], but the thematic invention is
personal and occasionally prophetic. The festive melody of *Royauté*
(No. 4; Ex. 29a) is of the same 'public' category as Ex. 29b from
Herring, Act I, Sc. 1:

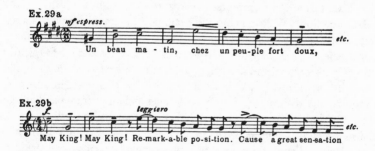

Ex.29a

Ex.29b

Apart from their European stylization, the most important aspect of
Les Illuminations was their lucid diatonicism, and nowhere was
Britten's harmonic assurance more evident than in *Départ*'s (No. 9's)
slow rate of harmonic change, which gives this last song its feeling
of spaciousness and long farewell (see Ex. 30):

[1] And in *Being Beauteous* (No. 7), on the word "chargeant": an expansion which is,
however, more thematic than decorative.

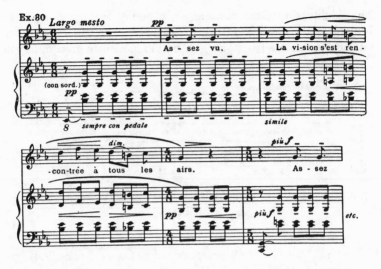

The prolonged C major unfolding of *Being Beauteous* (No. 7) indicates Britten's harmonic poise—a refusal to be harried by a 'modern' conscience into nervous rhythms or a debilitating chromaticism. One of the main problems of the contemporary (but not just English) composer has been this inhibited attitude towards, or downright fear of, a largely diatonic idiom. Walton is a good example of a composer who almost aggressively attempts to suppress, or at least disguise, his diatonic tendencies—hence his often self-destructive rhythms and his frequently cloying chromaticism[1]. Britten's poise must not be taken to imply that he is incapable of rhythmic energy or exciting modulations, nor that his diatonicism is not sometimes enlarged into pandiatonic spheres; but bearing in mind the contemporary attitude towards harmony which puts a premium on restlessness, Britten's harmonic long-term policy is something of a phenomenon. Generally speaking, his harmonic poise is refreshingly unsymptomatic of his time—a case of the composer creating his time rather than being created by it. In addition, Britten is harmonically extremely versatile. I do not mean in this connection that he commands many harmonic styles (though that would also be true), but rather that he can use the same harmonic device for diverse purposes. In *Herring* for instance the expansive B♭

[1] I have elaborated this point in "Some Observations on William Walton", *The Chesterian*, January and April, 1952.

opening to the Vicar's homily on virtue (Act I, Sc. 1; figure 39) serves to emphasize not only Mr. Gedge's endless platitudes but also the awkward pauses which punctuate his sermon while he searches for the next *bon mot*; each modulation, perfectly timed, signifies a further verbal inspiration on the part of the Vicar ("Rarer than . . . pearls . . . rubies . . . amethyst, Richer than . . . wealth . . . wisdom . . . righteousness!") and just saves him (and us) from acute musical embarrassment.

It would, however, be a gross error to overlook Britten's chromaticism, since his use of it gives us a deep insight into his musical character. Never is it subjectively either pathetic or self-pitying; his chromaticism is so far projected that any element of compositional pathos is entirely expunged. Take, as an instance, the clarinet obbligato which comments on Nancy's lament in Act III of *Herring* (Ex. 31),

or Mum's part (see Ex. 32) in the subsequent quartet (Mum, Nancy, the Vicar and Miss Wordsworth),

Ex. 32

where the chromaticism is so formalized (an impression confirmed by the nature of the theme which continuously folds back on itself and returns to its point of departure) that there is no danger of its expressiveness swamping either the style or the dramatic moment. Britten's proportioned and projected chromaticism is evidence of the truly classical spirit[1] which informs so much of his music and underlies his aristocratic attitude to style. On occasions such as Ex. 32, his stylization represents an intensification of feeling rather than a suppression of it. It is easy enough to feel deeply, but less easy to feel deeply to some formal purpose[2].

---

[1] Britten's 'detachment' is often misunderstood as a kind of heartlessness, an inability to feel profoundly. Wrote St. John of the Cross:
"Love consists not in feeling great things, but in having great detachment and in suffering for the Beloved"
—a thought sharing much in common with the classical spirit which is particularly characteristic of Britten's dramatic approach. It is interesting that in two of his operas he makes use of a device which lends 'distance' (psychic and physical) to the action: the *Prologue* and *Epilogue* in *Billy Budd* [226], the Male and Female Chorus in *Lucretia* (see *Del Mar*, p. 133), or even the Beggar in *The Beggar's Opera*.

[2] A perfect example of this crystallization of extreme feeling into form occurs in *Billy Budd*, Act I, i.e. the Novice's flogging ensemble, one of the most deeply felt, hence one of the most highly formal, passages in the whole opera.

V. EUROPEAN INTERLUDE

"... *I do not see why I should lock myself inside a narrow personal idiom.*"—BENJAMIN BRITTEN[1]

The *Seven Sonnets of Michelangelo* are, without doubt, the best known examples of Britten's Europeanism. If *Les Illuminations* were substantially French in character, the *Sonnets* are substantially Italian. That the major intervening work between *Les Illuminations* and the *Sonnets* was the Italian-titled *Sinfonia da Requiem* seems to be of little moment except to Scott Goddard who has declared, "the Italian title is significant. Britten is the least national of composers and directs his work to whatever quarter of the world will receive it" [100]. As far as is ascertainable the piece has not been specially adopted by the Italians, and Goddard's estimate of Britten "as the least national of composers" proves that even as late as 1946 the real importance of Britten's European stylizations and their relation to, or reaction from, the English tradition was still far from being understood. The *Sinfonia* itself is discussed in detail elsewhere (see *Stein*, pp. 249ff.).

What is more important for an historical character study of Britten's music is his enormously resourceful handling of a very large orchestra. The *Sinfonia* remains an orchestral *tour de force*: a wonderfully effective deterrent at the time to sensible comment on its structure and content. Britten's first large-scale extended orchestral piece, it represents a highly ingenious by-passing of, yet nowise cowardly retreat from, the contemporary symphonic problem. Britten is one of the few contemporary composers who has had the courageous intelligence to resist having likely failures forced upon him by a false sense of historical obligation—sonata form was not dealt with exhaustively until the second string Quartet's first movement[2]. While it would be misleading to suggest a strict correspondence between the Quartet's three movements—*Allegro, Scherzo, Chacony*—and the *Sinfonia*'s three-in-one—*Lacrymosa, Dies Irae, Requiem Aeternam*—it should not be overlooked that Britten in both works employs the Mahlerian device of placing his slow movements last (both *are* movements and not simply epilogues), a structural tendency which shows Britten's acute awareness of the historical problem of writing a last movement, either to the orchestral symphony or the symphonic quartet. If the opening funeral march

[1] [322].
[2] See, however, Hamburger's formal analyses of the *Phantasy* Quartet and the first string Quartet in *The Chamber Music*, pp. 211–233.

of the *Sinfonia da Requiem* immediately establishes a link with Mahler—
funeral marches (see *Redlich*, pp. 97f.) being a more or less constant
factor in the Austrian composer's music—the *Sinfonia*, at the very least,
displays an equal assimilation of the influential Strawinsky, a composer
from whom Britten has learned much, and whose earnest stylistic
explorations must have proved both stimulating and alluring to Britten's
creativity. It may be added that in some respects Strawinsky's experiments have remained experimental and less artistically fruitful than
Britten's; the triumph of ultimate fulfilment is sometimes lacking (cf.
Pears, p. 64). Strawinsky affected more than the instrumental technique of the *Sinfonia da Requiem*—he took a guiding hand in the con-
soling flute trio from the *Sinfonia*'s finale (see Ex. 8 in *Stein*, p. 251),
and his subsequent influence on Britten's texture has been substantial—
compare for instance *St. Nicolas* with the *Symphony of Psalms*; the
striking use of two pianos is by no means the most compelling textural
affinity between the two works. How much Britten owes to Strawinsky's
innovatory handling of small chamber-orchestral groups (in *Herring*
or *Lucretia* for instance, or the sectional instrumental treatment of the
Spring Symphony) would be too laborious a task to describe and not
a very profitable one as far as a study of Britten is concerned. It would
be more valuable for the chronicler of Strawinsky, since the composers
influenced by a genius will often reveal to us fresh aspects of the genius
by whom they are influenced; Britten, as it were, would tell us something about Strawinsky[1]. But while talent can almost always be satisfactorily defined in terms of influence and historical necessity alone,
genius, either of teacher or pupil (and the two are not interdependent)
is finally unaccountable: it can only be accepted or (more probably)

[1] Similarly Britten's *Peter Grimes* throws fresh light on Berg's *Wozzeck*. This changing
relationship between works of art has been very profoundly stated by T. S. Eliot in his
"Tradition and the Individual Talent" (*Selected Essays*, 3rd edn., London, 1951, p. 15):
"No poet, no artist of any art, has his complete meaning alone. His significance, his
appreciation is the appreciation of his relation to the dead poets and artists. You cannot
value him alone; you must set him, for contrast and comparison, among the dead.
I mean this as a principle of aesthetic, not merely historical, criticism. The necessity
that he shall conform, that he shall cohere, is not onesided; what happens when a new
work of art is created is something that happens simultaneously to all the works of
art which preceded it. The existing monuments form an ideal order among themselves,
which is modified by the introduction of the new (the really new) work of art among
them. The existing order is complete before the new work arrives; for order to persist
after the supervention of novelty, the *whole* existing order must be, if ever so slightly,
altered; and so the relations, proportions, values of each work of art toward the whole
are readjusted; and this is conformity between the old and the new. Whoever has
approved this idea of order, of the form of European, of English literature will not
find it preposterous that the past should be altered by the present as much as the present
is directed by the past."

rejected. The most a discussion of Strawinsky's influence on Britten could accomplish is to further our historical awareness, and, with luck, increase our potential insight into Britten's style and beyond it. Final appreciation—perhaps for all composers and for all music—must remain an act of faith between the creator (or the creator's creator) and his audience.

Perhaps not *'how* Strawinsky?' but *'why* Strawinsky?' is the more relevant question. Bearing in mind Britten's own search for a European stylization and Strawinsky's patent and potent Europeanism, the choice, conscious or unconscious, was an obvious one. Quite apart from Strawinsky's immense competence and musical virtuosity, he straddles the contemporary scene as a modern Colossus. The popular (if slightly derogatory) judgment of Strawinsky as the 'modern' composer *par excellence* has a grain of truth in it. Strawinsky represents within a single life's span the sum total of almost half a century's European exploration and experimentation—his failures have been as pregnant as his successes. From this point of view Strawinsky's supra-nationalism (his 'eclecticism' even) and above all his essentially extrovert personality must have constituted an extraordinarily powerful appeal to Britten's imagination, and coincided with his own desire for a widely-based 'contemporary' style uninhibited by purely nationalist considerations. I use the term 'contemporary' in the sense of 'generally recognized as of our time'[1]. Of particular importance is Britten's fondness for ostinatos of all kinds, the ground bass and the passacaglia—a fondness he shares with Strawinsky. While Britten's partiality for these formal devices obviously derives partly from his sympathy with 17th century English music, it seems likely that this element in Strawinsky (more primitively expressed and with earlier than 17th century affiliations) was of special significance for Britten since it corresponded to a 'primitivity' *already achieved on a European level.* Whereas the English school returned to the polyphonic Englishry of the 16th century, Britten responded to the rhetorical Englishry of the 17th and a 'primitivity' already absorbed within Strawinsky's European stylizations. On the other hand it is impossible to underrate the melodic and sensuous contribution made to Britten's texture and style by Mahler and the Viennese school[2], which, in many ways, seems to conflict cul-

[1] I must point out that this passage was written before the first performance of *The Rake's Progress,* an experiment in retrogression which is a symptom of our time rather than a genuine contribution to it.
[2] Alban Berg above all.

turally and historically with Strawinsky's aggressive and percussive 'primitivity'. The paradox is resolved, however, if we recall that Mahler also was something of a supra-nationalist in his eclecticism (albeit an eclecticism frequently misunderstood by his contemporaries); and, although in a manner almost opposed to Strawinsky, he too was a chamber-orchestral specialist (in the song cycles and within the confines of his symphonies), an instrumentational virtuoso and a master of rhetoric. I have no wish to recapitulate what has already been written about Britten's relation to Mahler, but it is of prime importance to understand *the extra-chronological*[1] *relationship of Mahler to Strawinsky in so far as they stand in relation to a common unifying factor—Britten*, even if it is the attraction and common features of opposites. Given that Britten's personality, turning towards Europe, was seeking the culmination of an English tradition which had never been consummated, it was both historically and artistically inescapable that he should come to it via the Viennese school and the 'stateless' Strawinsky. This is not to neglect the important factor of the Verdi of *Otello* and *Falstaff* who must not be forgotten when considering *Grimes*, *Herring* or the children's opera. Nevertheless, it seems to me that Verdi's influence is more discernible in matters structural (compare *Herring* and *Falstaff*) than in concrete musical style[2]; although even here there is a far from negligible identity of spirit and method, a likeness in aesthetic approach, which make Verdi a figure of the first importance for Britten. This similarity in musical character leads to such affinities as exist between the openings of *Falstaff*'s Act I, Sc. 2 (Ex. 33)

Ex.33 *Allegro vivace brillante*

p   *molto staccato*   *etc.*

---

[1] Cf. *Keller*'s 'extra-historical', p. 319.

[2] *Billy Budd*, on the other hand, shows an increase in Verdi's influence on Britten. But while it is easy to catalogue certain Verdian mannerisms (very often as slight as the placing and instrumentation of an individual chord, sometimes more substantially as in the case of Vere's Act III, Sc. 2 aria "I accept their verdict"), it is more important to recognize Britten's new contextual use of them—as, for instance, in Billy's song "Billy Budd, king of the birds!" (Act I).

and *Herring*'s Act I (Ex. 34):

One is immediately aware of something rather more than a mere stylistic coincidence; two distinct musical personalities, to be sure, but their culture has much in common. Taking this into account, together with the Verdian contribution to European musical civilization which Britten has inherited, the juxtaposition of Britten and Verdi is as logical as it is inevitable.

VI. TRANSITION; THE EUROPEAN SYNTHESIS OF THE *SEVEN SONNETS OF MICHELANGELO*

Finished in 1940, the *Seven Sonnets of Michelangelo* were written during Britten's sojourn in America. They not only represent another completely achieved European stylization, as did the earlier *Les Illuminations,* but also (and perhaps more importantly) display in now developed form features of Britten's style which have become permanent, or at least as permanent as is safe to prophesy with a living and ferociously active composer. Once again Britten's extraordinary talent in handling a foreign language must be remarked upon—it is as effortless as the fluent, musical conversance with English to which we are now accustomed. The *Sonnets* are more important (deeper, too) than *Les Illuminations* in that they may be treated on two levels—their Italianism on the one hand and, on the other, their indisputable and quintessential Brittenish character. It is especially significant that Britten secured a settled, highly personal idiom in a work which at the same time was one of the most successful of his continental stylizations, a stylization absolutely purged of affectation or mannerism.

The Italianism of the *Sonnets* is not, as some might imagine, a mere illusion fostered by the hearing of Italian expertly set. The strong verbal rhythms of the language have a good deal to do with the excited rhetoric of *Sonetto XVI*'s opening (Ex. 35);

and the multiplicity of syllables in the *vivace Sonetto XXXII* find their equivalent in a hectic vocal line crammed with chattering semi-quavers (Ex. 36):

Britten's melodic inspiration is at its suavest, its most *cantabile* (see Exx. 27 and 28, pp. 32–33) in the largely placid *Sonetto XXX*.

Half operatic, yet extraordinarily intimate in its perfectly conceived rise and fall, it demands real *bel canto* from the singer. The Lydian fourth and the (un)common-chordal aspect of the accompaniment (whence derives the deceptively simple triadic nature of the vocal line) are immediately noticeable (see Ex. 37):

But the Sonnet's passionate conclusion (Ex. 38), partly created by the contrary motion of voice and accompaniment (a tension which invades the song's equilibrium) would seem to owe something to Mahler's *Kindertotenlieder* (No. 4, *Oft denk' ich, sie sind nur ausgegangen!*; see Ex. 39):

Ex. 89

If *Sonetto XXIV* is overtly southern in its sinuously drooping, quasi-recitativic, quasi-operatic vocal line (Ex. 40),

Ex. 40

Sonetto XXXVIII betrays its Italianism in the character of its tempo (*Allegretto quasi una serenata*); in the plucked sonorities of the accompaniment's left-hand tenths; and in the occasional whole-tone glide which suggests an improvisatory thumb slipping over the strings of a guitar. Contrastingly, *Sonetto XXXI* impresses its European styliza-

tion by virtue of its specifically classical proportions—above all in the
strict rhythm of its opening phrase and the symmetrical nature of its
(inverted) answer (Ex. 41):

Ex. 41 *Con moto appassionato*

The accompaniment's bass imitation of the vocal line, moreover,
which cunningly provides bridges between the singer's phrases, is
strangely reminiscent of Schubert: a parallel not at all at odds with
the predominantly Latin character of Britten's *Sonnets*, since German
Lieder themselves were not infrequent in their response to the *serenata*;
Schubert and Schumann come to mind, not to speak of Hugo Wolf's
Italienisches Liederbuch and his even more explicit (but instrumental)
Italian Serenade.

These European references accentuate the un-English nature of the
Michelangelo Sonnets; but it is in this work that we can see (if at a
distance) the full-fledged English parent of the *Serenade*, *Herring*, and
the *Spring Symphony*. It was via the compositional summit of the
Michelangelo cycle that Britten wrote himself out of his conscious
Europeanism and into the Englishry of his late pieces. The work was
both a terminus and a transition.

VII. THE ENGLISH SYNTHESIS; BRITTEN'S FOLK SONGS; HIS EXTERNAL ENGLISHRY; REGIONAL INFLUENCES; HIS INNOCENCE OF SPIRIT; HIS GIFT OF THE VERNACULAR

"Two times two equals four in every climate." ARNOLD SCHOENBERG[1]

Since the *Michelangelo Sonnets,* Britten has set no more foreign texts[2]; the way to the *Serenade* was paved by the *Hymn to St. Cecilia,* the Cantata *Rejoice in the Lamb,* and the *Ceremony of Carols.* The latter proclaims its English alliance by opening and closing the *Ceremony* with a plainchant[3] *Procession* and *Recession* (Ex. 42):

Ex. 42 Senza misura

Ho - di - e__ Chris - tus__ na - tus est:

Britten has not often made such direct references to an English tradition, and if I were asked to point to a single passage summing up in most characteristic form this new aspect of Britten's art which has developed since his return from the U.S.A. in 1942, I should choose Sid's song (*Lento con dignità*) from *Herring,* Act II, Sc. 1, and especially Exx. 43a and 43b,

Ex. 43a SID

and each choir - - - boy has got a new sur-plice.

---

[1] *Los Angeles Times,* 14th May, 1950.
[2] The volume of French folk songs excepted.
[3] The use of this particular antiphon was, I believe, Alec Robertson's suggestion.

Ex. 48b

Some of his listeners are so-lemn-faced, Some near to laugh-ter.

which, for all their Purcellian and pulpit parody are rooted in the deepest native soil. Absolute maturity of style allows Britten to smile occasionally at what matters most to him.

There are, of course, very many purely *external* signs of Britten's immersion in the English musical scene. The realizations of *The Beggar's Opera* and *Dido*; the Purcell realizations; the introduction of the 13th century *Soomer is icoomen in* into the *Spring Symphony*'s Finale (see Ex. 16 in *Redlich*, p. 100); and the very skilful folk song arrangements[1]. While the first and third volumes of the folk songs belong to the British Isles, the second, rather unexpectedly, is devoted to France, even in this sphere Britten has to remind us of his European outlook. The folk song settings are excellent enough to warrant a chapter to themselves if space permitted, but one or two random comments relevant to an examination of Britten's musical personality must suffice. It should be noted that his settings always *illumine* the folk song melodies; the melodies are never drowned beneath complicated accompanimental figuration or luxuriant harmony which diverts the listener's attention from the horizontal development to vertical machinations. Even where Britten does personally intervene, it is only modestly to focus attention on the folk song itself, and very discreetly to reflect the dramatic situation inherent in the text. Thus, in Ex. 44 (from *The Ash Grove*, Vol. I, No. 6), the obtrusive melody in the accompaniment—a slightly distorted imitation of the vocal line which faithfully records the nostalgia of the words—far from removing our attention from the theme itself, tends to rivet our ears on it all the more strongly:

[1] See also *The Light Music*, pp. 287f.—EDS.

Ex. 44

In addition, *The Ash Grove* shows an extreme psychological penetration of the text. Although the singer suggests that the environment is unchanged ("Still warbles the blackbird. . . . Still trembles the moonbeam . . ." etc.), the *reality* (to the poet) is quite different (i.e. ". . . what are the beauties of nature to me" when "she sleeps 'neath the green turf down by the Ash Grove"). The unaltered folk tune represents the observable certainties of nature, while the distortion in the accompaniment expresses the altered conception of the beholder. Britten's psychological and musical insight are displayed in matters both large and small.

It would, I think, be a mistake to imply that Britten has been much influenced by folk song; certainly not very literally, since he is far too complex a figure for so simple a musical constituent to be a determinant of his style, and his whole development has tended away from the folk song school. The *Michelangelo Sonnets* could hardly provide a starker contrast to folk art. Yet now and again it is possible that the melodic feel of folk lore is lurking somewhere at the back of Britten's melodic inspiration. For instance, *When will my May come* from the *Spring Symphony* (Part III, No. 1; see Ex. 45a)

Ex. 45a

recalls such pentatonic shapes as *Come you not from Newcastle?* from the folk songs (Vol. III, No. 7; Ex. 45b):

Ex. 45b

In fact, if one looks at these texts, one cannot exclude the possibility that this particular tune was actually active in Britten's mind.

In his preface to *Peter Grimes* [24], Britten has written:—

> One of my chief aims is to try and restore to the musical setting of the English language a brilliance, freedom, and vitality that have been curiously rare since the death of Purcell.

Inasmuch as folk song is astonishingly vital in its treatment of words, Britten may be said to have learnt something from it, above all in his always musical reactions to the potentialities of verbal phrases (which does not mean at all a strict equation with speech rhythms, or the music's subservience to the text).

Yet the impression of Britten's essential Englishry remains; and it is not merely because of the invigorating round *Old Joe has gone fishing* from *Peter Grimes* (Act I, Sc. 2), or the shanties in *Billy Budd* (Act II, Sc. 2 in particular), that the operas are recognizably English; nor do we speak of the Englishry of the *Spring Symphony* because it happens to set an anthology of English verse. It is, incidentally, interesting to speculate what would have been the result if Britten had proceeded with his original intention of employing Latin verses [27]. Would the *Spring Symphony* have been the less English?

Of what then does Britten's Englishry musically consist? For a start, it is easier to define what we do not mean by Englishry in Britten's case. Normally it implies a quite distinct musical style which has become identified with a national tradition—the modality of Vaughan Williams, for example; the occasionally rhapsodic folk song style of Holst[1] or Bax; the bluff geniality of Elgar; the pantheistic impressionism of Delius. Or it might indicate a sympathy with the English religious (and specifically choral) traditions (Vaughan Williams, Elgar, Howells, Rubbra, Walton even). At some time or other Britten might be said to have made use of all these traditional stylistic factors, but never as permanent, exclusive features; and it would be impossible to reduce his Englishry to any single element. This is not altogether surprising in view of the compound Europeanism he had attained in and through

---

[1] In the case of Holst I should like to emphasize my qualification "occasionally". I do not at all underestimate the value of Holst's highly original, and sometimes decisively un-English, stylistic experiments which prepared the more cosmopolitan path trodden today by many of the younger generation of English composers.

the *Michelangelo Sonnets,* an achieved style which he was then able to put at the service of his more ostensibly English tendencies. In passing, it is of value to note how Britten's Englishry can assimilate an in general un-English style, such as the barcarolle[1], without strain or conflict, e.g. *Canticle I*[2] (see Ex. 46):

Ex.46 *Andante alla barcarola*

It must not be forgotten that Britten's perfectly stable Europeanism resulted in a creative freedom which enabled him to make full and uninhibited use of all he had learned from 17th century English rhetoric. These twin lines of development have been evident in Britten's music up to the *Michelangelo Sonnets* and beyond, but it was after them, and after Britten's return to England, that they reached their final synthesis in the *Serenade, St. Nicolas,* the *Spring Symphony, Peter Grimes,* and the succeeding chamber operas[3]. The *Serenade's Dirge* is a magnificent example of Britten's fusion of both aspects of his development: the 'traditional', rhetorical character of the dirge itself combined with, and integrated into, the European and English inflections and implications (stylistic and formal) of the string fugato. It is, moreover, possible to detect the Europeanism latent in Britten's Elizabethanism (cf. *Pears,* p. 70, and *Stein,* p. 255). Compare, for instance, *O might those sighes and teares* from the *Donne Sonnets* (Ex. 47) with Mahler's 'sighes' from his *Kindertotenlieder* (No. 1, *Nun will die Sonn' so hell aufgeh'n!*; Ex. 48):

[1] Not to speak equally un-English of funeral marches and waltzes.

[2] The stylistic relation of this Canticle to the *Spring Symphony* (particularly *The Morning Star,* the closing number to Part I) should not be overlooked. Compare also Ex. 46 with Ex. 5 in *Del Mar (Albert Herring),* p. 153.

[3] Also, of course, in *Billy Budd,* where the synthesis is further refined upon (a purification which is intensified by the presentation of the action through the 'filter' of Vere's mind).

This may be no more than saying that Elizabethanism and 19th century Europeanism are not the poles apart that we might imagine them to be. Our historical inhibitions very often prevent us from seeing the very singular relationships which extend across widely separated centuries and cultures and emphasize the timelessness of certain musical symbols. Mellers's judgment that Britten brought "our seventeenth century rhetorical tradition to a belated consummation" [202] reminds us that we are much less conversant with the Englishry of the 17th century than with the Englishry of the 20th, and thus recognize it the less swiftly where it occurs in Britten's music. Inevitably so, since two hundred years elapsed before an English composer continued the tradition and vitally enlarged it; and Purcell was as much a European as he was an Englishman: he did not live in an age when an individual style depended on markedly national or local characteristics.

From these points of view alone, Britten sounds a new note in 20th century English music. None of his contemporaries has managed with such awesome brilliance to return English music to the main stream of European culture. Yet, in spite of this successful Anglo-European amalgam, it has always struck me as little short of miraculous that Britten could integrate two great English hymns into *St. Nicolas* without any stylistic or formal discrepancy and, more importantly and astonishingly, without causing any sort of psychological discomfort to the audience—a remarkable feat considering the very many emotional and associative links a hymn tune automatically accrues to itself throughout its career. Partly this integration is ensured by thematic anticipation—the listener is prepared for Ex. 49a (from *All people that on earth do dwell*)

by Ex. 49b

(from the preceding *Allegro maestoso*; No. V, *Nicolas comes to Myra and is chosen Bishop*).

Much has been made of Britten's love of East Anglia; and it is true that his intensely local, but hardly uncritical patriotism (cf. *Herring*), has proved to be a significant creative determinant in his music. The East Anglian *locale* of *Grimes*; the deliberate 'provincialism' of *Let's Make an Opera*; in a broader field the resuscitation of 18th century low-life in *The Beggar's Opera*; and the placing of *Billy Budd* on board an 18th century man-o'-war, are all evidence of Britten's English inclinations, and while not necessarily *musical* evidence, it nevertheless suggests that stylistically some indication of this character trend should be musically apparent and open to musical analysis. Britten, moreover, is well known not only as a composer with a social conscience, but also as an artist who feels himself as part of a community, with duties and responsibilities of his own. Hence the hymns in *St. Nicolas*, the audience songs in *The Little Sweep*, and the educationally purposeful *Young Person's Guide*. In fact Britten would seem to have an altogether excessively humble view of the rôle of the artist in the service of the community. He said on one occasion: "Today it is the community . . . that orders the artist about. And I do not think that is such a bad thing either. It is not a bad thing for an artist to try to serve all sorts of different people . . . it is not a bad thing for an artist to have to work to order" [345][1]. That Britten is very seriously and sincerely concerned with his communal function is not to be doubted, nor should his love for his home ground be underrated.

Thus Edward Sackville-West and Desmond Shawe-Taylor are partially right when they attribute to Grimes' *Four Sea Interludes* "the bleak and sinister beauty of the North Sea" [262].

The *Dawn* Interlude in *Grimes* (see Ex. 50) is characteristic:

Ex. 50

Likewise the early morning of *Lucretia's* Act II, Sc. 2 (see Ex. 51):

[1] Rather characteristically, Britten does not seem to have put to himself (or his audience) the question discussed by E. M. Forster in an essay revealingly entitled "The Duty of Society to the Artist" (*Two Cheers for Democracy*, London, 1951, p. 105).

In Ex. 51, however, basically the same technique as successfully serves quite a different climate—an instance which illustrates the unrestricted resourcefulness and adaptability of Britten's stylistic fingerprints, and conveys in some measure the futility of trying to attribute the consistency of his music to consistent regional, pictorial, dramatic, or poetic images.

As so often with Britten, and as always when in the presence of genius, we must seek for the explanation outside our usual terms of reference. For me Britten's Englishry may be ascribed to two creative tendencies, neither of which has been prominent before in English music, or perhaps in music anywhere. Firstly, the exploration and exploitation of a whole emotional territory which has otherwise remained undiscovered; and secondly, a gift for the musical *vernacular* —a term which is singularly inappropriate, but I can think of no better. The significance of this second point seems to me to be of far-reaching importance, and I am aware in advance of the severe inadequacy of my explanation.

The first is the more simply dealt with. Britten's childlike (not childish) quality—together with his capacity for penetrating the child in the child and the child in the adult—have often been remarked upon (see *Holst*, pp. 276ff.). It has been less frequently realized that here Britten has created a unique department of musical feeling which, in its turn, has created new textures and new musical ideas. For example in the *Spring Symphony*'s *The Driving Boy* (Part I, No. 4; see Ex. 15 in *Redlich*, p. 100) the newness of the *sound* alone is startling; and there are many other like examples, not only in the *Spring Symphony*, but in *A Boy was Born*, *St. Nicolas*, *Herring* and *The Little Sweep*—in fact in any work where Britten employs children as artistic collaborators.

Britten's childlike spirit, which almost defies analysis, is by no means dependent on verbal texts or dramatic situations; it can embrace the purely instrumental conception also—witness *The Young Person's Guide*. When this (internal) innocence of spirit (cf. *Berkeley*, p. 294) —"the very opposite of all that is mushy and inexact" [202]—is combined with the (external) facts of Britten's Englishry—the poetry, the opera libretti, the East Anglian *locale*—then his musical Englishry, in one aspect, is at its plainest. But while this exactness of technique may suggest, as it does to some critics, a link with the clarity of the East Anglian climate, it is misleading to suppose the geographical environment as a cause and the resultant technique as an effect. The reverse is surely nearer the truth: Britten's special 'innocence of spirit' finds a certain fulfilment in, or correspondence with, the climatic clarity of his native surroundings. Britten's clarity of technique[1] is of longer standing than his regular residence in Suffolk; all the musical evidence indicates that when he travelled to the U.S.A., it pursued him across the intervening Atlantic. It is by finding a musical outlet in a new and so far undeveloped emotional area that Britten has created something new in and for the English tradition; something which is distinctly and instinctively English for all its newness. In recognizing the essential Englishry of the *Spring Symphony* (*pace*

---

[1] I think that this very clarity—the precision—of Britten's technique possesses an extra-musical significance which is to be valued for its own sake. Leaving qualitative aesthetic judgments aside, it is to be admired as *an exact means of communication*. This fact, which has both a moral and a social side, was brought home to me by E. M. Forster in his essay on George Orwell (*op. cit.*, p. 74). Orwell, writes Forster,

"... was passionate over the purity of prose ... for if prose decays, thought decays and all the finer roads of communication are broken. Liberty, [Orwell] argues, is connected with prose, and bureaucrats who want to destroy liberty tend to write and speak badly, and to use pompous or woolly or portmanteau phrases in which their true meaning or any meaning disappears. ... He is unique in being immensely serious, and in connecting good prose with liberty. ... If we write and speak clearly, we are likelier to think clearly and to remain comparatively free."

I am not, of course, suggesting that there is a strict correspondence between prose and music, nor would I ascribe to 'freedom' a narrow political definition (perhaps as distinct from Orwell). Nevertheless, I see no reason why, in its widest application, Orwell's theory should not be relevant to music. Admittedly it is not (as yet) the language of bureaucrats, but it is interesting that in Eastern Europe, where the Western concept of cultural 'freedom' is either scorned or actively suppressed, the bureaucrats are busy doing their worst to make it so.

its European affiliations), I think we are recognizing something to date
unknown in the music of our country and of our time. *Britten has
created an Englishry of his own.*

The second tendency is the more difficult to account for; and it may
well be that the real significance of Exx. 52—(a) from *The Little Sweep*'s
third audience song; (b) from *Herring*, Act I, Sc. 2; (c) from the
Finale of the *Spring Symphony*; and, perhaps melodically and harmonically the extremest, (d) Billy's ballad from *Budd*, Act IV, Sc. 1—
may only be revealed at the very profoundest levels of musico-
psychological understanding:

Ex.52a

Ex. 52b

It may be countered that these examples are not more than evidence of a capacity for writing 'a good tune', a judgment which is partly relevant. But it was the critic who observed that the audience songs from *The Little Sweep* had almost established themselves as national folk songs who approached the heart of the matter. Not, I believe, *factually*—since all the instances from Ex. 52 seem to me to be fundamentally far removed from folk art—but *intuitively*: this critic was aware of the special nature of the attraction of these audience songs for the audience participant. Somehow it was sensed that Britten was making an assault on the deepest strata of our musical consciousness (as perhaps the best folk art does), tapping a creative source in himself, and finding a creative response in his audience which may have both been dormant for centuries, or perhaps never before utilized by a creative artist in this manner[1]. In these examples (52) Britten seems to have effected a real union (probably unconscious on all sides) between the artist, the public and the common heritage of our musical culture, however harassed or suppressed that culture may have become. I know of no other English composer who has re-introduced this truly elemental source into music; and as such it must stand as one of the most striking of Britten's many contributions to the English tradition. It seems likely that only a composer who had a whole European heritage behind him could have refreshed the more specifically national sources of his own art with such vitality. Hence the historical importance of Britten's European stylizations—a Europeanism which, as it appears in the new English synthesis of Britten's late music, inevitably makes his Englishry of European validity.

[1] An opinion echoed in *The Times*'s column on *Billy Budd* ("The Interval of the Second," *The Times*, 7th December, 1951): "For a maritime nation we have produced singularly little music of the sea. In this, as in his use of the shanties that belong to it, *Britten has turned his national heritage to account as no one before him*" [my italics]. [336].

The Vocal Music

IT would be strange if Benjamin Britten had never written for the voice. He was surrounded by singing as a child. He was not brought up on a gramophone or a wireless set. (Perhaps he will be the last composer of whom that can be said.) When music was wanted for parties or pleasure, he played the piano and his mother sang. She was a sweet singer, and like most musical amateurs in an English provincial town of the 1920's, she would sing some Schubert, Schumann and Brahms, Bach and Handel, some Gounod, Liddle's *Abide with me*, some opera arias (Puccini, Godard, Mozart, Wagner), early Frank Bridge and John Ireland, and for lighter fare, Edward German's and Arthur Sullivan's songs, and ballads by Eric Coates, Haydn Wood, Amy Woodforde-Finden, and the gifted Liza Lehmann. There were also a few folk songs such as *Oh no, John* and *The Keys of Heaven.*

Mrs. Britten was for some years Secretary of the Lowestoft Choral Society and used to entertain visiting singers in her house. They were still great days for provincial Choral Societies. Not only tremendous favourites such as *The Creation, Elijah* and *The Messiah* appeared on the programme, but works not so well known now, like Barnett's *The Ancient Mariner,* Parry's *Judith,* Coleridge-Taylor's *Tale of Old Japan* and Elgar's *King Olaf,* as well as *Hiawatha,* of course, and *The Dream of Gerontius* (Mrs. Britten's brother had conducted one of its earliest performances outside London). Agnes Nicholls was a household word: there is a tradition in the family that she once sang a duet with Mrs. Britten. Stiles-Allen made one everlasting admirer when she took her hostess's small son on to her knee and sang "O my sweet Hortense, she ain't good-looking, but she's got good sense."

The slump of 1930 put an end to a good deal of provincial music-making, but by then Benjamin Britten had already gone to a public school for two uneasy years, and thence, aged sixteen, to the Royal College of Music. It was farewell to the drawing-room parties, and the influences were no longer "Ho! there upon the heights" or "Peonies, peonies, crown the May."

The only piece of published music from these years is the setting of Hilaire Belloc's poem *The Birds,* of which Britten did several versions under Frank Bridge's watchful eye, until he found the right ending in the wrong key. But in fact, as might be expected, he had written a great many songs from an early age. He was nine years old when he chose to set *O that I'd ne'er been married* by Burns. This moving little tune is entirely convincing, though it owes a great deal to Schubert. Patient researchers will find in these early songs many premonitions of what was to come, and signs of influences which have since been absorbed. In Longfellow's *Beware,* the portamentos are deliberately written down —already an interest in vocal technique? At least one of the songs will be familiar to lovers of the *Simple Symphony* as the second subject of the first movement, and in another the young composer demands a range of voice greater than that in *Our Hunting Fathers.* Kipling's *Here's to you, Fuzzy Wuzzy* was an early choice, and the chorus is very stirring. There is a good deal of Tennyson and Longfellow, and an Elizabethan poem set "in the train to Lowestoft". From some years later there are three really excellent settings of de la Mare which should be published and performed, and a remarkable Blake song. Some settings of Verlaine, with orchestra, written when he was still at school, show great enterprise, though they are not so successful as the smaller songs. *The Birds* is by no means the only song of charm from Britten's schooldays.

It was presumably the fact that Britten's music was chosen for the I.S.C.M. Festival of 1934 as well as his East Anglian associations which made Norwich invite him to write a work for the 1936 Festival. It was a bold and enterprising step on the part of the Committee, and the young composer did his best. The encouragement of the very young composers by Festival Committees is not a feature of the present musical scene.

Our Hunting Fathers is described as a "Symphonic Cycle for High Voice and Orchestra". It consists of a *Prologue,* three songs and an *Epilogue.* The work was devised, and two of the poems written by W. H. Auden. Man's relations with the animals is the subject.

The outside movements are in the key of C minor, the three songs in D major, D minor, D major, which in a way reflects in great the motto theme used throughout, a major triad spread from the top, turning back to the minor third. Already each movement, typical in itself of the composer's later work, makes characteristic use of shapes and sounds. The *Prologue* is the first of those recitatives (inevitable precursors of later operas) in which Britten liberates the *parlante* style from stiffness and stuffiness: he gives it point, flexibility and attack. It is far from *secco*, though its accompaniment has a dry sound (so have the words indeed, almost parsonical). The composer extracts from the words their latent music, as he does seven years later with the same poet's *Hymn to St. Cecilia*. He can match the thorniest epigrams with an apt and memorable phrase. The musical motto (major to minor triad) well fits the poet's theme: "O pride so hostile to our charity". The music takes the words on its way, and the words respond freely.

The first song is of animals as pests. In the *Prologue*, a voice with a range of over two octaves was needed (not too excessive for a recitative). And in *Rats Away!*, after the very extended rodent upbeat, the voice has to start with a florid cadenza of great rapidity and agility. Britten's vocal writing always demands a comprehensive equipment. This cadenza, indeed the whole cycle, is no exception. It finishes with a long top A which needs power too. Thereafter comes the motto, punctuated by staccato interruptions and jerked this way and that, but one settles down into F for the loud *marcato* invocation against the rats. The vocal line suggests plainsong parodied, returning as it does continually to its reciting note of F. The motto is still the backbone of the music, in minim or in quaver, on tuba or flute. The rats cannot be expelled until, as it were, all the stops are pulled out; and the *In Nomine Patris* (cut in with cries of "Rats" at the top of the voice, literally), sung over sustained wind chords, confirms the sense of parody. Was it Wyndham Lewis who said that all art must be satirical today? Much of Britten's work has a satirical edge, though not immediately apparent[1].

Messalina (the song of animals as pets) is a lovely, touching and essentially simple lament, but one which uses the whole scale of colour in voice and orchestra. The motto, scored in characteristically 'solo' fashion, introduces a poignant cry three times repeated—increasingly

---

[1] "Pathos was one of the most admired merits of poetry about a hundred years ago; today it seems ridiculous, and it is used only for satirical purposes." Arnold Schoenberg, *Style and Idea*, New York, 1950; London, 1951.—EDS.

intense. Britten has always used the trick of accumulation by varied repetition most cunningly: only occasionally has it seemed overdone. The little tune for the dead monkey is a scale of five notes with a drop of a fifth in it from time to time. It reminds one of *There is no rose of such vertu* in the *Ceremony of Carols*: it has just the same sort of magic charm about it. Britten's melodic invention is one of his gifts to be most thankful for. This tune, suitably folky at first, breaks away into key after key, until back it comes to a great melisma on "Fie, fie, fie". Several of the characteristics of the composer are already clear in this song; the economy of material which creates a whole song from two phrases; the vocal line which makes use of the whole voice, in both simple and elaborate ways; the strongly pointed interludes between the phrases; the soloistic orchestration which turns right away from lush string tuttis; the rapid fan-like opening out in a *crescendo* modulation (cf. the Introduction to the *Spring Symphony*).

After *Messalina* comes the *Dance of Death*—the song of the killing of animals for pleasure. It is written *Prestissimo vivace* in 6/8, and the composer, alert to making new use of instruments, rattles the singer up the scale on a rolled -rr- like a whistle through the teeth, as the huntsman whistles to his dogs. It is a dance of death very near to the final rattle of the *Dies Irae* movement of the *Sinfonia da Requiem*. Apart from the rhythmic cries for and to the dogs which are fully worked out as material, the song itself, as opposed to the orchestral hunt, includes two tunes which savagely parody the traditional A-hunting-we-will-go type of melody. The vocal line lurches extravagantly through its compass. Melismas, such as that on "Mark" and the final cadenza were something new in English vocal writing, and though they may not have made much of an impact in this work, they were to do so some years later. Already it is clear that words must bow before the music. It is not each individual phrase which calls upon the notes to obey it; the poem suggests a certain overall musical shape and thereafter the words must obey the music. It is the method of the great classical English song-writers, Dowland, Purcell, Arne, Handel. To see, on the other hand, how far the words had dominated song by the first quarter of the twentieth century, it is enough to read Plunket Greene's book on *Interpretation in Song*. *Our Hunting Fathers* is a symphonic cycle, and therefore the shapes are drawn larger than voice-and-piano shapes. It is highly artificial vocal music. (The more realistic the setting of words becomes, the less interesting does its music tend to be). In any case, *Our Hunting Fathers* was all part of a brilliant twenty-two-year-old's revolt against the stuffy and sloppy. It was the first full orchestral piece of Britten's that he was to hear performed; in four years at the College nothing but the chamber *Sinfonietta* had been done. After the first performance only a small part of *Our Hunting Fathers* was changed. Britten re-orchestrated a little of the last movement—the *Epilogue and Funeral March*.

Of all these difficult songs, the last one is perhaps the most difficult. It needs first-class playing from every solo instrument, from xylophone and trombone to horn and violin. The words are scratchy and definitely un-*bel-canto*. But the composer is a match for them. Having decided on a Funeral March, he spaces the lines accordingly; the vocal line is a comment on the cryptic tune and rhythm. It takes some time to flower, and it is a sign of the times (1936) that the lines on which it chooses to flower are—

> That human company could so
> His southern gestures modify
> To make it his mature ambition
> To think no thought but ours,
> To hunger, work illegally,
> And be anonymous.

In another decade 'love' rather than 'anonymous' would have been chosen for such an expansive melisma.

Our Hunting Fathers is uncomfortable music. The English do not like brilliance, particularly in the young; satire disturbs them; so does parody, unless it is nice and gentle; obscurity bothers, unless the day-dream is induced. The vaguely pretentious and the jolly good fun are what we prefer, and *Our Hunting Fathers* is neither. It is spiky, exact and not at all cosy. That it had only two performances in England before 1951 is not surprising, though Sophie Wyss sang it with the utmost skill on both those occasions.

On This Island was written in 1937 (May–October). It consists of five songs to poems by W. H. Auden. The experience of hearing *Our Hunting Fathers* in the flesh has clearly been profitable. The vocal line, though just as instrumental and vivid, is rather less extravagant. In the first song, *Let the florid music praise!*, which is one of Britten's finest and a salutary challenge to a whole generation of English songs, the cadenza is brilliantly effective, yet perfectly manageable. It brings the opening fanfare[1] to a logical and admirable conclusion. At this time, Britten did not yet know very many of Purcell's songs. It is rather the influence of Strawinsky which lies behind these pages, and the score of *Apollon Musagète* in particular. But whereas Strawinsky was the great destroyer of the worn-out nineteenth century tradition, Britten belongs to the next generation, whose job it is to re-build. After revolution comes consolidation, and in re-building one takes one's choice from various materials to hand. The setting of the phrase "Time will bring their hour" could never have been made without Strawinsky, but already there has been discarded the rigidity which characterizes the vocal line of *Œdipus Rex* and *Persephone*. A close follower of Strawinsky did in fact reject the first four bars of the second song, because he found the third chord too full of associations. Strawinsky would certainly never have used it, but it remained for the next generation to do just that thing. Britten had to naturalize this artificial classicism. In *Œdipus Rex* the words are syllables to be juggled with—no more. In *Now the leaves are falling fast* the striking and essentially vocal pattern of running semiquaver duplets finds time to extend and pause on the keywords at the end of the phrase. Only the last two lines of the poem[2] are unconvincingly set. *Seascape* is nearer to the English traditional art song, though much more inventive and audacious. The melisma on "saunter" at the end is particularly happy, though the song as a whole is perhaps less well made and certainly less distinguished than its contemporary *Fish in the Unruffled Lakes*. Here the accompaniment is a characteristic Britten *trouvaille*, and the vocal line is nervous and subtle. As always, the voice is expected to be an instrument in its own right, as well as a mere projector of words, and the accompanist is supposed to be a pianist too. *Nocturne* makes different demands. Here there is no melisma, but nearly a note-to-a-word *bel canto* tune (suitable for a first-class Italian mezzo or even some heavenly torch-singer), into which "traction-engine, horse or bus" fits without discomfort. *As it is, plenty*[3] rounds off the volume amusingly enough; the false accents reflect the falseness of the sentiments, and the deliberately pert tune fits the cheapness of the story.

So far, Britten's poet for his adult songs had been Auden, and the

---

[1] See Ex. 4 in *The Musical Atmosphere*, p. 16.—EDS.
[2] See Ex. 14a in *The Musical Atmosphere*, p. 21.—EDS.
[3] See Ex. 9 in *The Musical Atmosphere*, p. 19.—EDS.

settings had been the first and only ones of new and strange words. This in itself was somewhat surprising in the thirties. Very few settings of contemporary poets will be found among the songs published in that decade. We are still lying on Bredon Hill, or rollicking it with Shakespeare's contemporaries. Britten's experience of setting Auden's words had confirmed his feeling that his own way was the right one for setting English—the deliberately musical, classical one. Still it would be nice to have a change—but the familiar poems were too full of associations. As a matter of fact, his vocal music for the next two years was to be settings of French and Italian poems, not English at all. Britten was obeying Nietzsche; he was feeling the urge to "*méditerraniser la musique.*" He had been classical up to now; but the sun begins to shine in *Les Illuminations* and with the *Sonnets of Michelangelo* we can feel the warmth in our bones.

The urge that sent Britten after Rimbaud and Michelangelo is not difficult to place. Apart from the natural fascination that such extraordinary geniuses must exercise, here was in Rimbaud the young sensitive innocent lost in great cities with whom it was easy for Britten to identify himself. The directness and clarity, the presentation of images by contrast rather than development (eighteenth century symphony rather than nineteenth century), the bright colours, economy and technique were all of a sort to make Britten the obvious composer for this poet. Also, *Les Illuminations* were in French, a language without close associations, and which could be treated objectively. At this time, too, Britten was fidgeting to be abroad, and abroad meant among other things, not setting English. It was not for three years that he was to realize that his roots (and his language) were English.

The music of *Les Illuminations* is much more controlled than *Our Hunting Fathers,* though not so fresh as some of *On This Island.* The opening is arrestingly suitable[1]; Britten can always set the stage with a few notes. *Villes* extracts all possible variety from the material used; its economy is exemplary; but the material used is somewhat ordinary for this very extraordinary poem, and the vocal line does not quite take flight. Though the persistent quaver movement is hectic enough, its almost mechanical changes become wearisome. *Phrase* is a very different affair. Here Rimbaud's fantasy is beautifully translated, and *Antique*[2] which follows is the song of which an older American composer said

[1] See Ex. 26 in *The Musical Atmosphere,* p. 32.—EDS.
[2] Cf. Ex. 27 in *The Musical Atmosphere,* p. 32.—EDS.

that he did not know how Britten dared to write the melody. The notes of the melody could not be simpler—the common chord of B flat. This is what Strawinsky had done in the "Alleluia" of the *Symphony of Psalms*, but Britten has gone farther. He has left the melody with its natural harmony—not a new procedure, only a forgotten one. In this clean and lovely song another of the composer's devices appears: two voices which imitate and follow each other in and out of the unison. *Antique* with *Parade* and *Being Beauteous* are the most remarkable songs of the cycle. In each case the modulations are fundamentally simple, but the timing of them is so perfect and the figurations so beautifully designed that one is only aware of a fascinating kaleidoscopic shifting, whether melodically as in *Antique*, harmonically as in *Being Beauteous*, or in rhythm and colour as in *Parade*. *Départ*[1] ends the cycle with the right amount of jaded nostalgia—not a note too many. The composer's sense of proportion has already grown. Indeed, if anything, his *Illuminations* are a trifle too pat. *Royauté* and *Marine* are almost mechanical.

The poems chosen for the next set of songs posed other problems. Rimbaud's were written in verse strict and free, of various metres, or in prose. Michelangelo's Sonnets are all in one form and in the same metre: they are highly concentrated and disciplined, and might not appear a suitable vehicle for varied lyricism. But in fact such a challenge always stimulates Britten, and the *Michelangelo Sonnets* are an extraordinary achievement. The first one sets a high Renaissance tone of tremendous athleticism and confidence[2]. The bare octave accompaniment might be thought to cancel the voice, but in fact it merely underlines the daring spacing of the line. The next four lines grow characteristically phrase by phrase. The composer's logic is again at work; each phrase leads to the next; there is no wandering. After the rhetoric of the first, the second Sonnet goes off at a passionate speed, the restless left hand never quite catching the voice until the return to the major key. The repetition of the last line is most apt and convincing, lengthening the Sonnet with a lovely modulation. The third Sonnet is a child of the Auden *Nocturne*, but how much finer. This sort of song had never been done by an Englishman before; it was this Sonnet and the last one of the set which, in the early performances of these songs, opened the eyes of his audience to what vocal writing could be. The eternal

---

[1] See Ex. 30 in *The Musical Atmosphere*, p. 34.—EDS.
[2] See Ex. 35 in *The Musical Atmosphere*, p. 42.—EDS.

feminine ending of the Italian lines must have been a problem throughout, but in Sonnet XXX, Britten uses it as part of his melodic line, balancing this softness with the same phrases echoed on the piano *without* the trochee; hence a strong sweetness.

As in all of Britten's cycles, the plan of the work is very carefully designed; key sequence, style of vocal writing, rhythmic contrast, the curve of speed and dynamics are all clear in his mind before a note goes on to paper. (This should not be so very exceptional, but it certainly is[1].) So the increasing speeds (or apparent speeds) of the inner Sonnets are carefully calculated, together with their rhythmic patterns, in order that the last noble Sonnet may appear to its best advantage. The vocal line of the whole cycle is full and rich, though there is not a melisma from start to finish. It is difficult to imagine Sonnets XXXVIII or XXIV existing in any other language than Italian, yet it was this excursion to Italy which liberated Britten, just as the Italians had helped Purcell two hundred and fifty years before. His next settings of English— Auden's *St. Cecilia*, *A Ceremony of Carols*, and *Rejoice in the Lamb*, all written within eighteen months or so—were full, sure and infused with Mediterranean confidence; they placed him as a master of English song.

For the *Serenade* the composer chose familiar poems; most of them are in all the anthologies. His method in this sequence of songs by different poets is the same as in single songs. His musical ideas are formulated, and the poems, once chosen for their suitability to the scheme, must fit in with his demands. Certain people seemed to expect that a twentieth century composer would want to set Tennyson like Balfe, a Ballad like a Folk Song, and Ben Jonson like Coprario or Lawes. In fact, rather obviously, he set them all in the same style—his own. A small anthology of poems had been used as early as *A Boy was Born* with perfect success. There was nothing to fear this time. The *Serenade* is very much a unity.

There are far fewer notes on the page than there were in *Les Illuminations*. It is sparer, cleaner. The economy is more complete and yet quite spontaneous. *Pastoral* makes use of little but a broken chord and a tiny repeated syncopation, yet the song is full of invention and atmosphere, a perfect twilight introduction to this night. The Tennyson is full of starry glitter and the last flashes of the sun. The accompaniment is characteristic. Spaced for the strings so that the utmost resonance is achieved, its darting rhythm looks at first disjointed, but

[1] Nowadays.—EDS.

an underlying logic reveals itself in the second and third verses. The cadenzas are Brittenish, simple but telling inventions which insist on a single pattern of thirds. Characteristic too is the plan which makes the string writing equally effective and well-placed in the first (*con forza*) and second (*pp*) verses, yet leaves out the lower strings in the second verse, to bring them back with full effect in the *esultante* third verse for their most important entry in the song. Such moments, it need hardly be pointed out, abound in Britten's music, where the skilled use of planned sound becomes the basis on which the imagination can build. So in the *Elegy* one notices the semitones in the basses at the end of the introduction, which, carried on by the voice's first phrase, are tremendously reinforced in the last two bars of the song— those strange squeezed slurs from open notes to stopped and back again. The *Dirge*[1] follows straight on, the voice high and difficult, an ostinato of six bars against a fugato with a subject of four bars, in some entries lengthened to five. The rhythm throughout is funeral march, but with downbeats anticipated or thrown away. The vocal ostinato outlines the common chord, the notes of which are important throughout the *Serenade*—and particularly in the *Hymn* which follows. No composer knows better how to use the varying timbres of the human voice. Just as G minor was as high a key as could be used for the *Dirge*, so B flat—no higher and no lower—sets the *fioriture* of the *Hymn*. The Ben Jonson poem which appears in so many anthologies is called a *Hymn to Diana*, and in a programme note this suggests solemnity. Britten saw at once, however, that all these sibilants and short vowels can only be delivered softly and quickly. It is the one gay piece in the *Serenade*—and the only quick movement in a sequence of eight. Light, silver and insubstantial, it cannot disturb the nocturnal mood, which continues in the *Sonnet* to gather more and more intensity. This last song is perhaps the loveliest of all. With minimal material magically spread over the strings, it seems to wander casually to the edge of silence. The melismas are cunningly spaced and the voice part leads the modulations; the song is a model of economy. The utmost is extracted from the midnight essence. The horn *Epilogue* (it *must* be played on the natural harmonics, like the *Prologue*; it is all part of the design) winds the *Serenade* to stillness.

After the *Serenade* (indeed after the *Hymn to St. Cecilia*), Britten's output becomes overwhelmingly concerned with the human voice.

---

[1] Cf. *The Incidental Music*, p. 307.—EDS.

Operas, songs and cantatas occupy ninety per cent of his composing time. With many of these, this chapter is not concerned, but between the *Serenade* (1943) and the *Holy Sonnets of John Donne* (1945) comes *Peter Grimes*, and in this work one side of his writing for the voice must be touched upon. *Peter Grimes* is in every way a remarkable work, but in no way more original and striking than in the setting of recitatives. In the pub scene, for instance, there is not a sentence of recitative which is not apt to the dramatic context, accelerating the action like *recitativo secco*, yet forcefully expressing the character of the utterer, as in accompanied recitative. Added to this fusion of classical procedures, Britten has produced a quality of inevitability of word-accent and cadence which is derived from traditional song. Witness Auntie's "That is the sort of weak politeness . . ." at the beginning of the scene. This revitalizing of the musical speech can already be foreseen in *Our Hunting Fathers*, even in *A Boy was Born* or *Friday Afternoons* (those enchanting fresh songs, a performance of which, given by well-trained boys and girls with their intelligent teacher at the piano, once heard is never forgotten). In the *Michelangelo Sonnets* the call was sounded to revaluation in vocal writing, but though the composer's recitative becomes more refined (in *Lucretia*) and more elaborated (in *Herring*), it was in *Peter Grimes* that the first impact was made. Not a note of the opera's *Prologue* is waste; it is full of musico-dramatic meat.

In the *Holy Sonnets of John Donne* Britten returns after five years to the tight restricted form of the sonnet. It is the kind of self-discipline which always fascinates him, to work in conditions which exact the quickest response in skill and concentration, whether in a medium deliberately chosen for aesthetic reasons (the operas between *Peter Grimes* and *Billy Budd*) or one caused by limited resources (*St. Nicolas*). In whatever form Britten chooses to work, the result will always appear to conform to its own category. He is not a composer whose every piece seems like a cut off the same roll of cloth; musically, he is not a Unitarian, he is a Greek, who worships all the gods. So his Sonnets will not sound like excerpts from operas, and his songs for voice and piano differ radically from his songs with string accompaniment. This helps to explain why piano transcriptions of his works present fierce difficulties and give the strangest idea of the sound of the music (except when they are played by the composer himself).

The *Michelangelo Sonnets* had discussed love; the theme of the *Holy Sonnets* is death. They were written in a week in August 1945, immediately after the composer's return from the German concentration camps whither he had gone as Yehudi Menuhin's accompanist, though during the tour he was continually referred to, by some official slip, as "Mr. Button, Mr. Menuhin's secretary". The *Sonnets* had been planned for some time before this, but it is hard to believe that the horrors of Belsen did not have some direct impact on the creative unconscious, already preparing itself to set John Donne. When Britten returned, he suffered a delayed reaction to an inoculation, and the *Holy Sonnets* were written on a bed of high fever.

The attack of the very first notes creates a tension which is not wholly relaxed for twenty-five minutes. Characteristically, in these Sonnets as in the others, Britten takes a rhythmic pattern or figuration or harmonic scheme, and works it out by logical balance and timed phrasing. In each one the tension is held by the persistent use of these patterns, unswervingly developed. The expression in these Sonnets is throughout extreme, and the line is much more jagged and nervous than it had been in the *Michelangelo* set. They had been Classical, these are Gothic. The prevailing 'affection' of each poem is strikingly presented; the semiquaver summons of the first, the battering figure of the second, the sobs and sighs[1] of the variation-form third (some echoes of Elizabethan vocal usage here), the inconstant, pattering semiquaver movement of the fourth, and the funeral march for the "world's last night". The sixth, "She whom I loved", is the centre of the cycle, the emphasis coming here more than on the last song. (In the *Michelangelo* set, it was the last song which received the greater thrust.) This is the one purely lyrical Sonnet, and a very beautiful one. Britten had not previously made such a highly impassioned utterance, which is yet so surely balanced and logical in structure. No one today but Britten could have covered such ground in those first twelve bars, no one but he could have used his material so fully without a suggestion of exhaustion. The return of the opening phrase, an octave up, comes with great force on the words "tender jealousy", the cadence chosen for the question "But why should I beg more love?" is an ordinary dominant-tonic one, but how beautifully placed, and the melody of the second section is all the more right for echoing the downward movement of the opening bass. In the seventh Sonnet, the trumpet summons is sounded, but the trumpet is not allowed to reach its top A until "God is beheld"; until then, frustrated, it must always hit the sharpened

[1] See Ex. 47 in *The Musical Atmosphere*, p. 51.—EDS.

fourth. Against it the clash of the vocal figure stands out, with the G natural prominent. The clanging of voice and trumpet continues until, in the last two lines, the voice is allowed to assert itself alone and to finish its cadence, fully revealing to us thereby the purpose of the first phrases: this last phrase reconciles the trumpet's sharp fourth with the voice's flat one. In all Britten's mature songs, such details can be considered (note how the G sharp lifts the voice up its final scale), and as he grows older and more experienced, his instinct becomes surer. In the eighth Sonnet, the key-phrase is "I run to death and death meets me as fast". The composer gives the piano an elaborate figure in broken octaves, the phrases always varying in length to set the mood, and against it the voice, after its first agonized cry, leaps up and down, trying as it were to escape. Almost the whole song is in strict two-part writing, but so figured that a much fuller impression is given. (Britten doesn't care for counterpoint that sounds like Counterpoint.) The last of the *Donne Sonnets* is not planned to make the same dramatic impact as the last of the *Michelangelo*. In "Death, Be not Proud" the first phrase modulates into B major for the ground bass, from the E flat minor of the previous chord; in "Spirto ben nato" the new attack in the fresh key of D challenges in quite a different way. The ground bass moves round the notes of the common chord of B major but never settles on the tonic, thus achieving great buoyancy. It starts regularly in 4/4, but moves into 3/4 against itself; as in the *Dirge* of the *Serenade* and the *Grimes* Passacaglia, Britten never allows his ostinatos to cling to the bar-line. The vocal line here breaks into Purcellian embellishment on the words "war" and "sickness". The voice at last is freed from the almost word-to-a-note movement and can flower in its own way. Death has been conquered, not by an old man who waits for it resigned and patient, but on the contrary by a still young one who defies the nightmare horror with a strong love, the instinctive answer to Buchenwald from East Anglia.

For two years after this, Britten was busy with opera—*Lucretia* in 1946 and *Herring* in 1947. (Notice how his fusion of lyricism and tension has expanded in tiny scenes like *Lucretia*'s "How quiet it is tonight" after the women's trio in Act I, Sc. 2, or the Sid-Nancy recitative in *Herring*, Act II, Sc. 2.) At the end of 1947 he did find time to write his *Canticle I* and the *Charm of Lullabies*.

During these years, Britten had been involved in many concerts in the programmes of which much Purcell had appeared, and he had realized several of the great *Divine Hymns* as well as some dramatic songs. Fascinated by the form of such pieces as *Lord, what is man?*, he found in it the ideal shape for an extended song, a sort of cantata.

The *Canticle*, a setting of a poem by Francis Quarles, is Britten's finest piece of vocal music to date. The hyper-tension of the *Donne Sonnets* has been relaxed, and with a classical shape has come repose and dignity. The voice is free, melismatic yet controlled, and independent throughout, whether as one of two or three parts in counterpoint or a melody with chordal accompaniment; the gentle barcarolle movement of the left hand with its rippling countertune grows convincingly up to the moment of the two brooks joining, and the melisma is rightly postponed to this climax. A less experienced writer might have given it away in the fourth line. The next section's recitative is more formal than some of Britten's, and is not allowed to break the sequence of the sections. The *Presto*, foreseen in the last phrases of the recitative, is a brilliant and tricky three-part invention, but it stops at the right moment with the right augmentation of the subject. This sort of coda has vastly improved since the days of *Les Illuminations*. The fine *lento* section never settles down on to the bar-lines or becomes four-square. Notice too how Britten's basses never remain solely harmonic; like Monteverdi's they assert themselves as voices, and Britten's figurative invention and melodic device are so plentiful that he can well afford to work over a pedal whenever he wants to. The *con moto* elaborates the movement and contrasts finely with the last ten major bars with its reminiscences of the opening barcarolle. Note the entirely characteristic structure of this last melody, four notes imitated in inversion, and the whole gradually diminished in its spacing. The form of this song is clearly one that suits the composer's gifts, and it is to be hoped that this *Canticle I* will not lie, like the piano Concerto No. 1, too long alone[1].

The *Charm of Lullabies* was written for Nancy Evans, and this cycle of five songs does indeed charm. It is simple lyric music, a world away from the *Donne* and very different from the *Canticle*. To find five contrasting lullabies is quite a feat, and to set them successfully is another. If this is not such an impressive cycle as the others, it is at least partly due to the subject-matter. Love and Death may easily be viewed from different angles, but a Lullaby is—a Lullaby, *sonst nichts* or almost *nichts*. The Blake song has the typical parallel

---

[1] Since the above was written, another Canticle has appeared, *Abraham and Isaac*, for contralto, tenor, and piano, a work which admirably matches the poem to the musical form. It appears simple yet is full of felicities, the most striking of which is the creation of, as it were, a third voice (the voice of God) out of the two voices singing together: a triumph of invention.

and close movement between the voice part and the right hand, with the latter following the former but never catching it. The *Highland Balou*, in 4/4, which makes good use of the Scotch snap, has three sudden fascinating bars of 3/4 in the middle, which syncopate and jolt deliciously for a moment. Sephestia is given a touching little tune to put her baby to sleep; one sees the poor rickety tot as clear as day. Britten's use of the grace notes—slow and quick—unite the *lento* and *allegretto* aptly. For Randolph's poem, the composer has written what must surely be the first *Prestissimo furioso* Lullaby[1], and in the last of the cycle, he finds a new way to surprise us with an old major-minor contrast, at the first entry of the piano. The vocal range of the *Charm of Lullabies* is less extended than those of Britten's other songs. They are more relaxed, quieter, inevitably so. They seem to show the composer writing for the first time for twenty years in a more conventional English way. Perhaps they are the forerunners of other songs of less intensity than the two sets of Sonnets, and less elaborate than the *Canticle*. We may be sure that there will be more cycles to come; for, to paraphrase Thurber, Britten has cycles the way most people have symphonies, and we can hope for more Canticles[2].

Britten has never claimed to be an innovator; the generation of revolutionaries was the previous one to his. He felt early that the academic tradition in this country was built on stale amateurishness and pretentious muddle. He learnt that as a result of the explosions in the musical world of the first decades of this century, the younger composer had to build his own tradition. In endeavouring to do this, Britten has gone to the purest stream of modern music. Monteverdi, Purcell, Bach, Haydn, Mozart, Schubert, Verdi and, of later figures, Mahler, Berg and Strawinsky—from all these he has learnt much in his search for the classic virtues of a controlled passion and the "bounding line". But if Britten is right, and he has made no actual innovations, there blows in his vocal music at least (and that is all that concerns us here) a strong revitalizing south-east wind which has rid English song of much accumulated dust and cobwebs, and has renewed the vigour of the sung word with Purcellian attack. If Britten is no innovator, he is most certainly a renovator, and having thus cleansed his house, he has a right to feel at home in it.

[1] There is a Da-daist poem consisting of repetitions of the word "Leise" which swell in a mighty crescendo until, at the concluding *fff* climax, the reciter smashes a plate on the floor.—EDS.

[2] See footnote ([1]) previous page.—EDS.

GEORGE MALCOLM

The Purcell Realizations

O F Benjamin Britten's realizations of the works of
Henry Purcell, the most recent and by far the most
extensive is that of *Dido and Aeneas*, to which a
separate chapter [1] is devoted. But in the course of the last ten or twelve
years, Britten has had occasion to complete the continuo-structure of
many other works by Purcell. Few of these realizations were originally
intended for publication, and many of them remain in fact unpublished;
but a certain number, chiefly extracts from the *Harmonia Sacra* and the
Orpheus Britannicus, have been issued by Boosey & Hawkes. Most of
them were originally devised for use at song recitals given by Peter
Pears and Benjamin Britten, the joint editors of the present series.
Their *Foreword*, which is printed at the beginning of each volume, not
only clarifies the artistic aims of their edition, but also successfully
disarms some of the criticism they have correctly foreseen. Controversy
has none the less continued to rage around the subject.

These realizations are meant to be played on a modern concert
grand pianoforte, not on a seventeenth century harpsichord. They
therefore make full use of the resources of pianoforte tone and technique
—a fact that has been forgotten by critics who have suggested that in
Dido and Aeneas Britten has apparently reverted to a more 'legitimate'
style of realization. It has escaped their notice that the *Dido* realization
was written for a small spinet. It should occur to them that the music
one writes for a little five-octave instrument, with an unvarying tone-
level and no sustaining pedal, *ought* to sound somewhat different from
music written for a Bechstein grand.

Now continuo-playing is, or should be, a highly individual affair.
The *Foreword* says: "It is clear that the figured basses in Purcell's day

[1] *Dido and Aeneas*, pp. 186—197.—EDS.

74

were realized in a manner personal to the player. In this edition the basses have also, inevitably, been realized in a personal way." In other words, a Purcell continuo as realized by Benjamin Britten is not even *meant* to provide a reproduction of what it sounded like when Purcell played it on the harpsichord in 1690; it merely records what it sounded like when Britten played it on the piano in 1940. Moreover, a good realization is intended to be *played*, not looked at, or studied in a library; and if it is devised for the pianoforte, or even the harpsichord, it is not meant to be sung by a church choir in four-part harmony. Composers no longer use a figured bass in their work; the device in modern times survives, for practical purposes, only as a means of teaching elementary harmony, and it is in this connection that most of us form our first acquaintance with it. The result is that many of us tend, unconsciously, to equate the figured basses of Bach or Handel or Purcell with those of Prout or Stainer. When we see the words "Continuo realized by So-&-So", we expect something like Ex. 1:

Ex. 1

And when instead we find ourselves looking at a live bit of pianoforte writing, we are shocked.

A continuo should be—and by Benjamin Britten always is—worked out at the keyboard, and in terms of keyboard technique. A good realization is primarily a piece of good effective *instrumentation*; it is not a harmony exercise. In its written form it is simply a record of one man's reactions to the composer's suggestions. "This edition", says the *Foreword*, ". . . is not intended to be a definitive edition or a work of reference". It makes no claim to finality; it is not produced in order to prove any musicological or historical thesis, nor to demonstrate any particular methods of procedure. "It is a performing edition for contemporary conditions." If this were kept in mind, much prejudice would evaporate. And it is common experience that when these realizations are played and listened to, instead of being merely looked at and talked about, prejudice tends to disappear altogether.

The *Harmonia Sacra* is a collection of Purcell's sacred music published by Henry Playford in 1688 (Part I) and 1693 (Part II). Four excerpts from this collection have been separately issued in the Boosey & Hawkes series: *The Blessed Virgin's Expostulation, Job's Curse, Three Divine Hymns,* and *Saul and the Witch at Endor.* The first three are for solo voice, the last is a trio for soprano, tenor and bass.

The Blessed Virgin's Expostulation carries an explanatory sub-title: *When our Saviour at twelve years of age had withdrawn himself,* etc. (*Luke* 2. *v.* 42). It takes the form of an extended dramatic recitative, relieved first by a short arietta ("Me Judah's Daughters once Caress'd") and later by a longer aria ("How shall my Soul its Motions guide?"). The prevailing mood of anguished agitation is wonderfully expressed by Purcell's vocal line, which in its turn is effectively and fearlessly supported by Britten's realization of the continuo (see Ex. 2):

Ex. 2

I call, I call,   I call, I call,   I call   Ga-briel!

Ga-briel!   Ga-briel!   Ga-briel!   He comes not: *etc.*

The first of the *Three Divine Hymns* (*Lord, what is man?*) is of a similar musical type, but on a somewhat less extensive scale: a dramatic recitative is followed by an arietta ("Oh! for a quill, drawn from your wing"), leading into a long, aria-like "Hallelujah". In the recitative there is a note of deep-felt wonder, and in the "Hallelujah" a fine sense of exultation, both of which are echoed and enhanced by a magnificently written piano part; in the arietta the contrasting atmosphere of quiet serenity is mirrored in the accompanying figures (see Ex. 3):

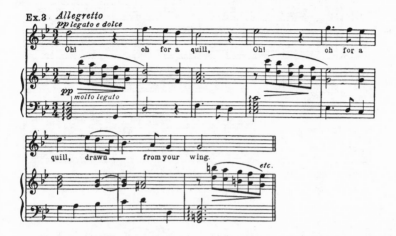

Ex.3 *Allegretto*

In the second Hymn (*We sing to him*) we have what may best be described as a metrical recitative, broad and declamatory in style, leading directly to a short concluding stanza ("And whilst we sing") which in Britten's realization is accompanied by a fluent and particularly felicitous counterpoint or descant in running quavers. Last comes the *Evening Hymn*, in which a quiet meditative cantilena is gradually transformed into a triumphant and repeated cry of "Hallelujah". A ground bass, five bars long, provides the musical framework of the whole, and stimulates Purcell to one of his most magnificent melodic inspirations. Britten in his accompaniment readily provides that variety of treatment which a ground bass inevitably demands, and—as in similar contexts in *Dido and Aeneas*[1]—he anticipates and supports every development of the vocal melody (see Exx. 4a, 4b and 4c):

Ex.4a *Andante non troppo lento*

Bar 1

(*il basso sempre distinto*)

[1] See Exx. 4—10 in *Dido and Aeneas*, pp. 192-194.—EDS.

Ex 4b

Ex. 4c

Job's Curse begins with a long recitative fraught with unhappiness and disquiet, now subdued, now impassioned; but, in the short aria which follows, the mood changes to one of tranquillity at the thought of death's release. The realization of the continuo is here devised in great detail and shows some really exquisite touches (see Ex. 5):

Ex. 5

the least kind beam of dawn-ing Light;   let un-born Babes

Saul and the Witch at Endor takes the form of a dramatic *scena* for soprano (The Witch), tenor (Saul) and bass (Samuel). The three voices sing together in trio only in the opening narrative ("In guilty night") and in the closing cry of "Oh! farewell", the rest of the scene consisting of extended utterances in dialogue. This piece permits, in fact demands, the widest freedom of treatment, and Britten is not the man to shy at the advanced harmonic implications of Purcell's own continuo. Those who feel uncomfortable about a passage such as Ex. 6

Ex. 6 *Lento* *pp sempre*

Fare - well,   Fare - well,   Fare - well,

Oh!__   Oh!__   Oh!__   Oh!__

pp sempre

Fare - well,   Fare - well,   Fare - well,

Lento

pp sempre

sost.

and who positively shudder at Ex. 7,

Ex. 7

A - - - - - las!

lamentoso

should remind themselves that in each case the vocal parts and the instrumental bass were written by Purcell, not by Britten.

The *Orpheus Britannicus* is a collection of Purcell's secular songs, published (1698–1702) after his death by the same Henry Playford who had previously issued the *Harmonia Sacra*. Two sets of songs taken from this collection have appeared in the present series, entitled simply *Six Songs* and *Seven Songs*. Along with one or two well-known favourites such as *Fairest Isle* and *Music for a while*, both sets contain songs which were previously almost unknown. The realizations are characterized by the same qualities as those of the *Harmonia Sacra*: each one shows the same musicianship, the same admirable piano writing, the same subordination of all effects and 'conceits' to the dramatic and musical character of the whole song.

The longest single item from the *Orpheus Britannicus* is the song *Mad Bess*, the first of the *Six Songs*, with a wonderful accompaniment full of such imaginative ideas as the characteristic figure, or 'grace', which repeatedly decorates the continuo (Ex. 8):

In *Sweeter than Roses*, No. 6 of the *Six Songs*, Britten employs a remarkable rhythmic and harmonic feature to introduce the second stanza ("What magic has victorious Love?"); the use of the 'upper dominant point' is particularly effective (Ex. 9):

In *Music for a while*, the realization has less personal appeal for me, partly because I am convinced (though all textual evidences may contradict me) that the sixth note of the ground bass should be an E natural, and mainly because I *feel* this song differently. But then, if and when you do not like a necessarily personal realization of a continuo, you are at liberty to play it your own way instead.

A set of five further songs from the *Orpheus Britannicus* is available in MS. from the Boosey & Hawkes Hire Library. Scored for strings, two flutes, two oboes, bassoon and trumpet, they are tremendously effective, perhaps especially *Sound, Fame, thy brazen trumpet*, in which the eight-note ground bass is allotted to a whole string orchestra playing in octaves, whilst a second string orchestra supplies the realization in support of the voice and of Purcell's own magnificent trumpet obbligato.

Under the serial heading *Odes and Elegies*, we so far have only *The Queen's Epicedium*[1], an Elegy on the death of Queen Mary in 1695. The Latin text is very poor—a pretentious, somewhat bombastic piece of pseudo-Arcadianism; but Purcell makes it the vehicle for some very lovely music, particularly in the aria *En nymphas! en pastores!*, to which Britten has set a beautiful and simple accompaniment (see Ex. 10):

Ex. 10 *Andante con moto*

---

[1] In the word *epicedium* (ἐπικήδειον, an elegy or dirge) the syllable *-di-*, representing the Greek *-δει-*, is long, and carries the stress-accent. This means that in English usage the word is to be pronounced as rhyming with 'buy 'em', not with 'tedium'. (Cf. *Iphigenia*, and other similar cases.)

The only instrumental work so far issued is the *Golden Sonata*[1] for two violins with a continuo-part arranged for 'cello and pianoforte—an excellent edition. The bowing indications are practical and effective, the expression marks apt and sympathetic. The pianoforte part is captivating, particularly in the *Canzone* and in the final *Presto* with its exhilarating passage-work. In the *Adagio*, the five-crotchet figure in the accompaniment supplies an exquisite background to the duet of the two violins.

The *Foreword* hopes—as will all true lovers of Purcell—that this series will eventually "include most of the songs from the *Orpheus Britannicus* and the *Harmonia Sacra*, as well as much of the chamber music, choral and orchestral music". Already the series has brought Purcell to life for many to whom his unique gifts were largely unknown. In Britten's words, "it has been the constant endeavour of the arranger to apply to these realizations something of that mixture of clarity, brilliance, tenderness and strangeness which shines out in all Purcell's music."

My own few comments can scarcely hope to have indicated how completely this endeavour has succeeded, but if they have so much as aroused the interest of a previously indifferent reader, it is enough.

[1] See also *The Chamber Music*, pp. 235f.—Eds.

H. F. REDLICH

The Choral Music

I. GENERAL ASPECT

EVEN the most cursory glance at Britten's catalogue of works conveys the impression that he belongs to the type of composer firmly rooted in the vocal element. If Britten is not as exclusively vocal as Palestrina, Monteverdi and Schütz (of whom not a single instrumental composition is recorded), he shares with his favourite Franz Schubert the numerical preponderance of vocal over instrumental works. With both Schubert and Monteverdi he further shares this basically important characteristic: that his music receives its specific shape and its general inspiration from the poetic word. Among the fifty-odd opus numbers Britten has so far published, there are hardly more than half a dozen making use of traditional sonata form, which seems uncongenial to him (cf. the two Concertos and two string Quartets)[1]. In vain, too, one looks for the traditional vocal patterns of motet, anthem, and oratorio, with their fugal episodes, their wealth of mock-polyphonic orchestral splendour. Neither the symphonic tradition of the Viennese classics nor the typically British growth of competitive music for choir, as composed from the days of Greene, Boyce, and Arne, down to Parry, Elgar, and the contemporary heirs of the "Three Choirs Festival" tradition, has found a supporter in Britten. These familiar types of music seem increasingly replaced by two forms, both representative of *vocal* processes in music: the chorale variation and the song cycle. Both belong to pre-classical periods. The principle of *chorale variation* (with folk tunes and plainchant motifs as favourite subjects) becomes manifest in William Byrd and his contemporaries, gathering momentum with the resourceful permutation technique displayed in Samuel Scheidt's Chorale Preludes for organ. The *cycle of madrigals*, taking

[1] See, however, *The Chamber Music*, pp. 211–233, and *The Musical Character*, pp. 344f.—Eds.

83

its cue from a fundamental poetic experience rather than from a preconceived musical structure, and reaching an early climax in cyclic creations such as Palestrina's *Vergini,* Monteverdi's *Sestina* and Lassus's *Lagrime di San Pietro,* paves the way for the *cycle of songs,* culminating in the famous works of Beethoven and Schubert. All three types have become determinants of Britten's creative genius.

Undoubtedly his best works (apart from his operas, where, however, similar variation processes may frequently be traced) are those composed under the stimulus of variation and song cycle. Among his instrumental works, both the early *Variations on a Theme of Frank Bridge* and the mature *Variations and Fugue on a Theme of Purcell*[1] seem to me to be superior to his string Quartets, displaying as they do the composer's inexhaustible resourcefulness in the subtle game of musical permutation. Britten's peculiar gift for that technique asserted itself very early in the masterly choral variations for mixed voices, *A Boy was Born.* The agglomerative process of piling up strands of proliferating melody around a central tune of ritual, or at least communal, significance is a feature of Britten's early work. It is only being contested by the increasing attraction of cyclic[2] vocal composition which discards the variational principle in favour of a selective process of tone-poetical associations. Among Britten's most original creations are soloistic song cycles based on a concentrated poetic experience of singular poignancy: Rimbaud's *Les Illuminations,* the *Serenade,* Michelangelo's and John Donne's *Sonnets.* They find their convincing corollaries in numerous cyclically[2] organized compositions for orchestra alone (*Sinfonia da Requiem, Soirées Musicales, Canadian Carnival* and others), in which the principle of the chorale variation is discarded, as well as in cyclic[2] choral compositions of wholly or partly un-variational character, such as the *Ceremony of Carols* and the *Spring Symphony.*

Within the bulk of Britten's vocal music, a special place must be reserved for his choral work. Numerically it easily exceeds the compositions for voice alone, despite the latters' intrinsic importance for the deeper understanding of Britten's style. But it also deserves special consideration for the sake of its sheer originality. Not one of these choral works of Britten's conforms to a traditional pattern. They ostensibly eschew well-trodden paths, and generally exchange the big

---

[1] i.e. *The Young Person's Guide to the Orchestra.*—EDS.
[2] Redlich does not, of course, use the word necessarily in its thematic sense, either here or later.—EDS.

orchestra of Elgar's day for the more flexible medium of intimate, consort-like combinations. They go even further, in that they often replace the traditional mixed chorus by unusual vocal combinations: trebles only in the *Ceremony of Carols*, mixed chorus, boys' chorus and soli in the *Spring Symphony*, men's, women's and boys' voices *a cappella* in *A Boy was Born*. Only the very greatest vocal composers (Palestrina in his Masses, Lassus in his *Psalmi Penitentiales*, Monteverdi in his *a cappella* Madrigals, and Schubert in his compositions for male chorus) have achieved infinite variety of tone colour and structural design within the narrow limits of unaccompanied choral singing. In works for unaccompanied mixed chorus like *A Hymn to the Virgin* and the *Hymn to St. Cecilia*, Britten shows a unique degree of resourcefulness and imagination.

Britten's choral music, in substance, frequently impinges on other sections of his *œuvre*. His greatest symphonic work—the *Spring Symphony*—is as much a choral composition as Mahler's Eighth. Even the operas occasionally take their cue from choral inspiration. It is almost a truism to state that the peculiar maritime flavour of *Peter Grimes* emanates from the tidal interstices of its choral sections; and even *The Little Sweep* culminates in the irresistible choral episodes of its community songs.

The handling of the severely limited and yet so flexible material of mixed voices with or without instrumental backing has stimulated Britten's creative imagination to a higher degree than other, more sophisticated, combinations of musical *valeurs*. This technique has called his most personal capacities into play: resourcefulness in the art of melodic variation; readiness to react to the most unusual stimulus emanating from the unusual poetic expression; facility in hunting up unused and unusual poetic sources and welding them together into organic cycles; and finally the ability to use single instruments rather than preconceived instrumental combinations and replace the post-romantic orchestral alfresco style by the spare but sharp contours of musical pen-and-ink drawing.

It is as a *choral* composer—apart from his probably even more popular achievements as a musical dramatist—that Britten seems to stand head and shoulders above his contemporaries (on both sides of the Channel). It is here more than in any other sphere of his work that the break with Edwardian conventions in particular, and with the 19th century in general, has become completest. It is here that he sets a shining example by creating a new musical style of idiomatic inevitability within a sonorous medium of very real limitations. The fact that among the Viennese classics Schubert alone comes readily to one's mind in this connection, and that one must hark back to the English Virginalists and Italian Madrigalists to find parallels to its intrinsic features, proves the absolute novelty of Britten's personal achievement. For this period of spiritual crisis and lack of direction, Britten's choral style may (in the eyes of posterity) have the same significance as did Schubert's cyclically conceived *Lied* for the dawn of the Romantic movement.

II. THE CHORAL MUSIC: A SURVEY

(a) *Works for Unaccompanied Chorus*[1]

A Boy was Born (broadcast by the B.B.C. late in the spring of 1933) was the first vocal composition of Britten's to reach British audiences, and the second of his works to be publicly presented. Like the earlier *Sinfonietta*, *A Boy was Born* immediately established its creator as a new force in contemporary music, and it has remained one of his indisputable masterpieces. Making a most ingenious use of old Carol melodies and texts (mostly stemming from the 15th century), it succeeds triumphantly in welding a motley crop of poems (ranging from an ancient German Christmas Carol to a Christmas poem by the Jacobean poet Francis Quarles) into a superb musical organism by way of chorale variation technique, which the eighteen-year-old composer uses with Mozartian self-assurance. The theme (Ex. 1),

x : principal motif

given out *choraliter* in four-part setting, is subjected to six variations in which the limitations of the chosen medium are miraculously overcome by virtue of subtle changes in the respective mixture of vocal

[1] Within each group the works are discussed in their chronological order.

sonorities. In Variations I and IV some voices deliberately imitate the peculiarities of instruments (horns, flutes, oboes), thereby providing the parts which carry the theme with a quasi-instrumental mosaic of motifs, proceeding in bare fifths or in pentatonic scale progressions (see Exx. 2a and 2b):

With astonishing effect, the boys' choir is occasionally introduced as an additional colour. Variation V is a special case in point, where the boys' voices intrude with a gay tune in 6/8 time upon the melancholy landscape painted by the sopranos and altos who sing of "the bleak midwinter" in mournful accents and dissonant suspensions. The masterly combination of two different melodies, texts and rhythms reminds one of the 13th century motet, the *Duplum*, with its two Latin texts and rhythmical schemes. This ancient contrapuntal practice has been splendidly revived in Britten's fifth Variation (Ex. 3):

The finale (Variation VI), using four widely differing poems from the 15th and 16th centuries, is an early specimen of Britten's facility for setting a prodigious number of often intractable words to music of most compelling rhythmical impetus. The forty closely printed pages of this movement operate almost exclusively with the few motivic particles of Ex. 4:

At the end, the young composer has one more effect of transformed sonorities up his sleeve (comparable to his success with the vocal guying of instruments earlier on): an effect as of rolling bells, remaining on level pitch and yet creating the impression of shifting colours—a device which could be classified as an offshoot of Schoenberg's famous opalescent, ever-changing and yet immobile chord in the third of his

Five Orchestral Pieces, op. 16[1]. Here is the beginning of Britten's passage in open score (Ex. 5):

A Boy was Born has so far remained Britten's most ambitious excursion into the magic realm of *a cappella* music. Neither the gentle choral dialogue of *A Hymn to the Virgin*, nor even the beautiful *Hymn to St. Cecilia*, can compete with its freshness of harmonic and thematic invention and its irresistible rhythmic drive. The *Hymn to the Virgin*, with its regular four-bar periods and antiphonal echo effects, comes nearest to the conventional conception of English devotional music;

[1] Originally entitled, in fact, *The Changing Chord*, Schoenberg's third *Orchestral Piece* can in its turn be considered an offshoot of his early idea of writing a melody on a single note played successively by different instruments. Schoenberg had argued about this possibility with Mahler (who had vehemently denied it), and he returned to it two years after composing the *Five Orchestral Pieces*, at the end of his harmony textbook *Harmonielehre* (1911), where he suggested that "pitch is nothing but timbre measured in one direction", that colour is the great realm of which pitch is but a province. The *Harmonielehre* ends with these words:

"Tone-colour-melodies! How sharp the senses which here discriminate! What a highly developed mind which may enjoy such subtleties! Who dares here to demand theory!"

EDS. (trans. H. K.)

whereas the *Hymn to St. Cecilia*, intended for a small choir of about fifty voices and based on a moving poem by W. H. Auden, develops the idea of vocal imitation of instruments (first introduced in *A Boy was Born*) by passages marked *quasi Violino*, *quasi Flauto*, *quasi Timpani*, and *quasi Tromba* which occur at the final section's cadential halts. Throughout this inspired composition, tenors and basses are singing in long notes, thus reviving the old practice of the medieval 'Tenor', the customary medium for plainchant quotations. These long notes offset the frothy effervescence of light-hearted motifs in treble and alto, and so provide great variety of tone colour (see Ex. 6):

Britten has only recently, and after a long interval, returned to the *a cappella* medium. The cycle *Five Flower Songs*, for mixed chorus, based on exquisite poetry by Robert Herrick, George Crabbe, and John Clare, is the work of a consummate virtuoso of composition, less genuinely inspired than *A Boy was Born*, but of unsurpassed mastery in the use of every possible formal device towards the greatest variety of structure and colour within narrow madrigalian limits. No. 1 with its bare two-part counterpoint and its deliberate parallel octaves is easily put in the shade by the delightful fugato of No. 2 ("The Succession of the Four Sweet Months"), as well as by No. 3's pungent harmonies. No. 4, with its immaculate four-part harmonies in the blandest B major, conjures up a sonorous *fata morgana* of tonal beauty such as is almost extinct in contemporary music, whereas No. 5's romping ballad revives the fun and bustle of the earlier *Ballad of Little Musgrave*, this time, moreover, providing the desirable happy ending.

(b) *Choral Compositions with Instrumental Accompaniment*

Already in the earliest of Britten's choral compositions, the *Three Two-Part Songs* for boys' or female voices, certain principal features of his future style are evident: his fastidious choice of unusual poetry, an uncommon dexterity in the declamatory treatment of recalcitrant elements in the text, and his imaginative use of the piano either in percussive glissando effects (obviously influenced by contemporary jazz practice), or in spare contrapuntal contours. Ex. 7, for instance, taken from No. 2, proves that the eighteen-year-old composer had a remarkably clear conception of a new piano style in that it avoids cloying post-romantic clusters of harmonies and excels in the athletic simultaneity of a motif of piled-up fifths and its augmentation:

The work also abounds in canonic devices (vocal two-part canon *all' unisono* in No. 1, canon *all' ottava* in the piano accompaniment of No. 2), and reveals one of Britten's most significant fingerprints in No. 2's final cadence (Ex. 8) which is distributed over several storeys of octaves:

The titles of these three songs are in the manner of programmatic introduction to the music: *The Ride-by-nights* (No. 1) is a grotesque broomstick ride of witches from Goethe's 'Walpurgisnacht'; *The Rainbow* (No. 2) a pensive landscape; and *The Ship of Rio* (No. 3) a romping sea-shanty with humming effects in the voices, wide skips in the piano part, and a marvellous capacity for bringing the ship's cargo of "ninety-nine monkeys" miraculously to life. The poems are by Walter de la Mare, and nobody but Britten could have discovered their musical potentialities.

The kind of grotesque realism championed by German and French composers in the 1920's can be felt in *Lift Boy* (a part song for mixed voices on a slightly surrealistic poem by Robert Graves). Most of the time the voices are treated in declamatory unison against a musical backdrop of prickly staccato passages on the piano. But when the boy suddenly cuts the cords of the lift to put a stop to Old Eagle's nauseating preachings (which sound like a parody of a negro spiritual) the collapsing voices fall into the abyss over four octaves.

I Lov'd a Lass (on words by George Wither, 1588–1677) remains even today one of Britten's most characteristic creations. It has become a determinant of his style, especially when he handles folk-like melodies and sets a poem of definitely popular features. His approach to Wither's Guarini-inspired pastoral poetry with its traditional 'Falero' refrain is utterly different from Vaughan Williams's or Peter Warlock's to similar texts. Romanticism has been exorcised and with it the rule of the folky four-bar period. Subtle irregularities of metre and periodization are utilized toward a haunting breathlessness, a mood of tragic inevitability and pre-ordained doom. Ex. 9a shows how a composer of Stanford's school might have scanned Britten's tune, while Ex. 9b indicates how Britten himself has contrived to avoid Ex. 9a's hidebound stodginess by eliminating the bar accents of the four-bar period:

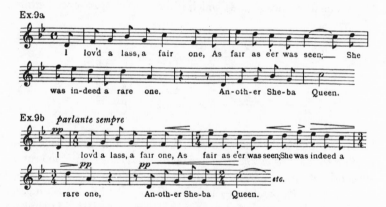

Devotional, if not strictly liturgical music soon begins to play a part in Britten's choral output. Surely one of the greatest assets of his music is his new approach to religious subjects, which differs widely from the traditional cathedral music of the 18th and 19th centuries. The words of the 'Te Deum laudamus' (no less than its Gregorian chant) have inspired many celebrated composers of the past (among them Berlioz, Bruckner, Verdi, Dvořák and others) to symphonic settings of the *Latin* text. But compositions of the 'Te Deum' text in German and

English vernacular translations were already becoming frequent during the 16th century. Britten composes the customary English translation of this so-called 'Ambrosian Hymn' in a more sober and modest mood than his more orchestrally-minded forerunners of the late 19th century. Hitherto he has given us two different musical settings of the Hymn, both dedicated to great English churches and their choirs, and both set plainly for four-part mixed choir with organ accompaniment. Yet the musical treatment of the ancient chant is utterly different. The two settings were published in 1935 (*Te Deum* in C major) and 1945 (*Festival Te Deum* in E) respectively, and a comparison of both scores drives home, even to the uninitiated, the tremendous atmospheric change that has come over Britten's music within that decade. Both compositions are strictly, almost fanatically, tonal, ignoring the traditional arts of counterpoint and fugue, and reaching a dynamic climax in each instance by sole means of motivic development. The beginning of the C major *Te Deum* is a marvel of thematic simplicity and tonal economy with Ex. 10's motifs (a) and (b) as the principal material of the whole composition:

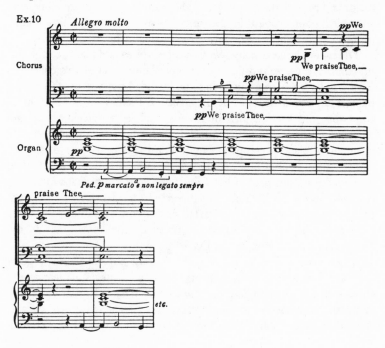

The *Festival Te Deum* in E proves how loosened the joints of Britten's musical texture have meanwhile become. The angular 4/4 metre is here replaced by constantly changing time-signatures and the chordal polyphony of the previous setting has to give way to an almost complete unison treatment of the choir. The irregular scansion of the reciting chorus against the organ's perpetually reiterated E major chord results in a curiously primitive alfresco design which is only occasionally offset by imitatory episodes and a liturgically chanting treble solo. The harmonic scheme of the composition is Spartan. The work begins and ends in a kind of Lydian E major which easily enables the composer to touch upon F sharp major, with occasional enharmonic asides to A flat (G sharp). The middle section ("Thou art the King of Glory")—which in the setting of 1935 had led to a contrasting episode in the lower mediant of A and had been conducted in a kind of dramatic dialogue between the exclamations of the treble solo and the solemn responses of a chordally conceived chorus—is here kept in an expressly marked E minor (with diminished fifth) and backed by skipping intervals in the organ pedal. The recapitulation simply returns to E major and repeats the first pages of the composition, but this time with an added counterpoint in the organ pedal—the only contrapuntal element in an otherwise purely chordal treatment.

The two volumes *Friday Afternoons* for voices and piano, to delightful children's verses mostly taken from Walter de la Mare's collection *Tom Tiddler's Ground*, might here be included by way of sheer contrast. They are a triumph of the realist Britten, who is never more admirable and lovable than in his wonderfully modelled, spare and muscular music for children (and adults, who must delight in the highly imaginative piano accompaniments). The tragi-comedy of the pigtail which "hung behind him" could not be more vividly expressed than in the monotonous bare fifths of the piano, and the brilliant catch *Old Abram Brown* is nothing else but the youngest offspring of an ancient British singing tradition that started once upon a time with "Soomer is icoomen in" (itself gloriously revived by the boys' choir in the *Spring Symphony's* Finale; see Ex. 16 below).

A Ceremony of Carols, one of Britten's most popular works, repeats with a differently organized chorus the earlier stupendous feat of the chorale variations on *A Boy was Born.* In both cases Britten succeeded in welding together an exquisite selection of ancient Carol texts and creating a cyclic unit. What the structural principle of the chorale variation was for the earlier work, the peculiar sonorities of the accompanying harp become for the quasi-dramatic *Ceremony* which proceeds within the liturgical framework of a *Procession* and *Recession* inspired by plainchant. The quaint medieval atmosphere is most convincingly expressed by the bass ostinato and the harmonic excrescences of the harp which offset the mysterious liturgy of chanting boys' voices, as in the magical passage of Ex. 11:

The cycle consists of ten carols for trebles, mainly on medieval anonymous texts. Often canonically intertwined in three-part settings, they are very effectively interrupted by an *Interlude* for the harp (No. 7), wherein harmonics and chordal progressions are piled up over an ostinato which tolls its four-note motif in sweet imperturbability.

Britten's penchant for freak poets and experimental poetic design (he has literally reclaimed 17th century poets such as George Wither, George Herrick and Francis Quarles for musical purposes) may be responsible for the strange choice of Christopher Smart's *Rejoice in the Lamb*. This poem was written while Smart was inmate of an asylum, and it is replete with a cloudy and mystical religiosity, sometimes reminiscent of Blake's visionary poetry. Britten's Festival Cantata for mixed chorus and organ is based on Smart's poem and consists of ten short sections, of which the quaintest is the fourth, dealing with the poet's cat Jeoffry. The section's feline nature is reflected in a sinuous motif in the right-hand stave of the organ. In the ninth section the chorus endeavours once again (as in the earlier choral cycles) to characterize the sonorous properties of instruments ("For the instruments are by their rhimes . . ."). In addition there are several sections for four soloists and even a *quasi recitativo* for the whole chorus, one of the most original passages in this Cantata which—though abounding in delightful detail and excelling in unusual rhythmic combinations, especially in the 'Biblical' second section—seems to me to suffer somewhat from the text's lack of coherence.

A brilliant *pièce d'occasion* is *The Ballad of Little Musgrave and Lady Barnard* for male chorus and piano accompaniment. This little choral *tour de force* was written and performed in 1944; the place of its first performance was a British prisoner-of-war camp in Eichstaett, Germany. It was the highlight of a music festival there, organized by Richard Wood, the well-known singer, who relates most amusingly in E. W. White's study of Britten[1] the circumstances of its war-time production. The music very successfully parodies the style of the traditional narrative ballad, and the treatment of male voices in staccato-parlando or highly declamatory style is as imaginative and stimulating as the piano part.

A *pièce d'occasion* of a very different nature is the *Wedding Anthem*, composed for the wedding of the Earl of Harewood and Miss Marion Stein on 29th September, 1949. The composition is a setting of a poem by Ronald Duncan (the librettist of *The Rape of Lucretia*) in which Latin phrases alternate with English poetry of a hymnic character. The *Anthem* employs a four-part mixed choir, two soli and organ. The music establishes the tonic of B major by the unusual detour of an initial D major. The choral sections—mainly gentle canonic exclamations, supported by toccata-like passages in the accompanying organ—are interrupted by lyrical interludes by the two soloists, who reach an ecstatic climax in a two-part canon to a tintinnabulous figure in the organ (Ex. 12):

The concluding Latin hymn "Per vitam Domini" finally unites soli and chorus in a recapitulatory reminiscence of the B major opening. In the highest register of the organ and in the chorus's blissfully reiterated, exclamatory "Amen", this piece of musical gossamer fades gently away.

(c) Works for Chorus, Soli and Orchestra

The only choral work among Britten's early compositions conceived on a more ambitious scale is the *Ballad of Heroes* for tenor (or soprano) solo, chorus and orchestra. Based on a political poem by W. H. Auden and Randall Swingler, it celebrates the fortitude of those men of the International Brigade's British Battalion who fell in action during the Spanish Civil War. It is almost the only composition in which Britten has been inspired by a distinctly political text. But it has a lightweight companion which experiments on a smaller scale with the musical possibilities of political harangue: the little known *a cappella* chorus *Advance Democracy*[1] for eight-part mixed chorus, also to words by Randall Swingler. Some of the poetry has an ominous ring:

> There's a roar of war in the factories,
> And idle hands on the street,
> And Europe held in nightmare
> By the thud of marching feet. . . .

Words of such inflammatory character inspired the young Britten to a stirring march tune. I am not so sure that the composer would find today—as easily as in 1939—the blatant C major conclusion to match the poet's final dictum:

> Life shall be for the people
> That's by the people made.

That Britten was profoundly affected by the moral issues at stake in the Spanish Civil War, nobody can doubt; and his temporary identification with continental politics resulted musically in a stronger affinity with continental models of style. Both these works from 1939 remind one of Hanns Eisler's rousing choral pronunciamentos of the late 'twenties, and both reveal the influence of Mahler's march rhythms and military fanfares. The titles of the *Ballad of Heroes'* movements— *Funeral March, Scherzo (Dance of Death), Recitative and Choral, Epilogue (Funeral March)*—read as if taken bodily from one of Mahler's

[1] See also *The Incidental Music*, p. 299.—EDS.

own apocalyptic symphonies. Sinister trumpet fanfares 'off stage', a prodigious use of percussion, and a Phrygian C minor tonality, only serve to confirm that impression. Yet, in the florid *recitativo* for tenor solo, expanding over sustained orchestral discords, something very typical of the future operatic dramatist comes surprisingly to the surface.

A perfect work of art, representing the mature artist at his unassuming best, is the Cantata *St. Nicolas*, composed in 1948 for the centenary celebrations of Lancing College, Sussex. Like his delightful opera for children, *The Little Sweep*, his *Simple Symphony* for strings, and some of his smaller choral works, it is deliberately planned to suit the talents of musical amateurs; and notwithstanding its high originality, the work never oversteps the limits of non-professional executants. To conjure up the motley pageant of the Saint's biography (in Eric Crozier's tasteful versification) Britten asks for a tenor solo (containing the only difficult music of his score), mixed chorus, and an orchestra consisting of strings, percussion, piano duet and organ. To the breathtaking adventure of *Nicolas and the Pickled Boys*, boys' voices provide the climax in the angelic "Alleluia" section. The tempestuous journey to Palestine proceeds on the waves of a romping sea-shanty which is accompanied by a colourful combination of pianoforte and percussion (see Ex. 13):

Two traditional hymn tunes are included at the end of Sections 5 and 9 respectively: *All people that on earth do dwell*, to the tune of *Old Hundredth* (Psalms, 1563), and *God moves in a mysterious way*, to the

tune of *London New* (Psalms, Edinburgh, 1635); sung together by
performers *and* audience, they provide a novel kind of community
song with roots in the traditional past. Musical peaks of this happily
conceived work are *The Birth of Nicolas*, inspired by a veritable waltz
tune, and the masterly fugato in Section 5, celebrating St. Nicolas'
election as Bishop of Myra. Perhaps the most moving episode is Section
9, *The Death of Nicolas*, in which the "Nunc dimittis", chanted by the
chorus, creates a mysterious backdrop to the dying Saint's ecstatic
outpourings, whose dissonant melodic meanderings are offset by
the immobile Dorian mode of the chorus and the liturgical jingling
of the piano (Ex. 14):

Britten's most ambitious choral work, his *Spring Symphony*, should at
least be mentioned; its twelve movements are based on fourteen
English poems of various epochs, thus again creating a cyclic musical
organism closely related to choral works like *A Boy was Born*. Including
in its artistic orbit poetic contrasts as marked as W. H. Auden's *Out on
the lawn I lie in bed* and the 13th century round "Soomer is icoomen in",
the work is certainly as much a genuine choral composition *sui generis* as
Mahler's Eighth, which accommodates the ancient hymn *Veni creator
Spiritus* and the final scene of Goethe's *Faust*. Erwin Stein[1] has made a
strong case for the relevance of the *Spring Symphony*'s title, tracing the
traditional symphonic scheme of Allegro, Adagio, Scherzo, and Finale
in its multitude of lyrical movements. Similarly, earlier analysts rediscovered the pattern of classical symphony even in the tremendous
dualism of Mahler's Eighth. Seven out of the twelve movements of

[1][291].—EDS.

Britten's work are mainly choral, even if intersticed by longer orchestral
bridge passages. The use of the chorus is, as always, unorthodox and
imaginative; witness the opening dissonant *a cappella* setting of the
anonymous 16th century poem *Shine out, fair sun*; or, later on in *The
Driving Boy*, the boys' choir (in evidently very high spirits) alternately singing and whistling with startling effect (Ex. 15):

To Auden's sophisticated ruminations (in Part II), a seated chorus
singing with closed lips acts as a distant organ stop. In Part IV, i.e. the
Finale, a waltz tune, sung by the mixed chorus, is ultimately combined
with the "Soomer" round chanted by the boys' choir in unconventional
counterpoint (Ex. 16): the majestic climax to a development of cyclic
choral compositions initiated so brilliantly by *A Boy was Born*.

ARTHUR OLDHAM

Peter Grimes

I. THE MUSIC; THE STORY NOT EXCLUDED

THE impact on the musical world of the first performance of *Peter Grimes* on 7th June, 1945, at Sadler's Wells Theatre, was immense. At first the reaction was astonishment. Later it changed to delight mingled with apprehension. The explanations followed.

The majority of people before that night would not have believed it possible that an English composer was about to make a contribution to operatic literature which would not only be on a level equal to the highest contemporary musical standards, but become a major box-office attraction in the repertory of theatres throughout the world. Since the death of Purcell, many English composers had attempted to do the same thing; all, to a greater or lesser degree, had failed. We had suffered the discomfort of seeing our literary classics become operatic masterpieces in the hands of an Italian genius and had been powerless to compete. By 1945, the failure of English opera had become axiomatic. It seemed too good to be true that, after more than two hundred years of disillusionment, England was again to lead the world in this most complicated sphere of musical achievement.

There can be no doubt whatever that the composer of *Peter Grimes* was as fully aware of these existing prejudices as of the enormity of the problems involved in the composition of an opera. Nor can there be any doubt that he approached his task with much more confidence than most of his predecessors. He was already equipped with a formidable technique and had achieved outstanding success in many branches of musical composition relevant to opera. His fertility of invention was apparently limitless and could be so little disputed that his critics used it as a rod with which to beat him, labelling him "clever", "facile", and "superficial". But nobody ever called him dull.

Peter Grimes was more than another manifestation of Britten's powers as we already knew them from the songs, the chamber music, and the orchestral pieces. I cannot recall any previous examples in his work of the ability to delineate a character clearly and unmistakably— often with the simplest phrase or figure of accompaniment. Yet it is in evidence continually throughout the opera. The pomposity of the lawyer Swallow's advice to Grimes in the *Prologue* to Act I (Ex. 1)

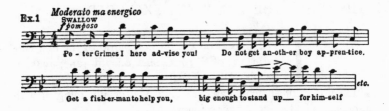

is the very essence of municipal dignity and at the same time smacks of the provincial courtroom. It is astonishing how macabre this short phrase becomes in Grimes's mouth when it breaks across the delirium of his scena in the last act[1]. It is more than a mockery of Swallow; it is a bitter condemnation of complacent self-righteousness. Grimes's own first phrase, his repetition of the oath (Ex. 2),

[1] See *Peter Grimes*—II, p. 123, Ex. 3.—EDS.

at once establishes him as Swallow's manifold opposite. He is a character
of depth, a dreamer, a man "at odds with the society in which he finds
himself", in contrast to whom Swallow is little more than a puppet
whose actions depend on the strings jerked by public opinion. The
composer has succeeded in communicating all this with one change of
chord and an accompanying change of orchestral colour. Later, melody
adds poetry to these facets of Grimes's character (see Ex. 3):

In the hut scene, where some of Grimes's most beautiful music is to be
found, his character is revealed in its entirety. From the moment of his
tempestuous entry, with his shouted orders to the apprentice (Ex. 4),

through his excitement at the prospects of a good catch, his feeling that
at last he has the chance to become rich and attain respect in the eyes
of The Borough (see Ex. 5),

and his dreams of marrying Ellen, of "some kindlier home" (see Ex. 6),

our sympathy for this strange and lonely man is constantly maintained, so that the succeeding tragedy is all the more poignant. Even at the moment of his death he is denied any comfort from his tormentors; the report of his sinking boat is dismissed as "one of these rumours" (Ex. 7):

Although no other character emerges from the drama so complete as Grimes's, all have been as carefully considered and each makes a distinct impression. Ellen Orford continually takes Grimes's side against the Swallows and Hobsons of The Borough (see Ex. 8),

while the simplicity and beauty of her 'Embroidery' aria invite our complete sympathy for all she is trying to do. Auntie, with her loud mouth and hearty manner, lets us know very early her attitude to this or any other business (see Ex. 9),

and such minor characters as Ned Keene, Mrs. Sedley, and the Rector are all immediately recognizable from the musical shape of their interjections.

But the music itself, quite apart from stage personalities, always has a clearly defined character; and perhaps it is in this respect that Britten differs most of all from the majority of his contemporaries. When he portrays a dance band, not only is his orchestra reduced to dance band proportions, but the tunes he gives it to play are correspondingly square and sentimental: one at once associates them with any village hop on a Saturday night. Yet such music, deliberately banal as it is, always remains part of the opera's broader musical structure, as does the music for the pub piano in *Wozzeck*. In fact one tune (Ex. 10)

is later lifted bodily to become one of the work's most superb dramatic choruses.

From first to last the chorus is used with the maximum of effect, with eloquence and grandeur. Employed as an entity, it is perhaps the most powerful dramatic element in the opera. Just as the character of Grimes is step by step revealed, so does the attitude of the village likewise emerge. We see it at the inquest, inquisitive and gossiping; and subsequently, when the fishermen are busy mending their nets, the village looks much as it might to a passer-by who is unaware that anything out of the ordinary could happen in this peaceful backwater (see Ex. 11):

In the pub the villagers enjoy themselves and don't care for trouble-some folk interfering with their pleasure (see Ex. 12):

But Grimes's nature is so alien to anything they know that, when he enters to collect his new apprentice, they conclude he must be either "mad or drunk". The first open manifestation of the vicious lengths to which the villagers are capable of being driven occurs at the very end of this act when, as a derisive comment on Ellen's few words to the boy, "Peter will take you home", they shriek Ex. 13:

Here is no longer any consideration for the apprentice, only a malicious delight in persecuting Grimes. Fresh from the Sunday morn-ing church service, the villagers resume their baiting, consciousness of their own hypocrisy being farthest from their minds (see Ex. 14):

Frustrated in their desire to annoy Grimes—perhaps encouraged by his absence—they turn against Ellen Orford and virtually put her on trial, accusing and taunting, never letting her finish a sentence (see Ex. 15):

Finally, inflamed by Boles, they depart to hunt out Grimes—the Rector himself among them.

That the whole of this development of the villagers' attitude is felt as inevitable is due to the composer's careful planning. One never feels that he himself is holding anything back, and yet excitement accumulates with the unfolding of the drama—testimony to the astonishing skill and variety of means which he has employed to achieve his object, and proof of the soundness of the overall dramatic structure of the opera.

There is abundant evidence in *Peter Grimes* of Britten's gift for creating dramatic situations which depend upon the music for their exposition. While the collaboration between librettist and composer must always be complete, it must finally be the composer who knows where, and to what extent, he can transcend the action and effect that aural apotheosis which is the essence of greatness in opera. He alone is capable of hearing the work before it is written and he alone can direct the dramatic structure into channels of musical potentiality.

In spite of careful preliminary work, however, many problems still remained for Britten to solve. The strange aria which Grimes sings in

Peter Pears as Peter Grimes

The Beggar's Opera
Catherine Lawson as
Mrs. Coaxer

—

Nancy Evans as Polly

—

Ottokar Kraus as Lockit

—

Nancy Evans as Polly

1948

Rose Hill as Lucy in *The Beggar's Opera*

The Beggar's Opera

Gentlemen of The Road

—

Peter Pears as Captain Macheath

the pub, "Now the Great Bear and Pleiades . . ."[1], is completely effective in performance. But it was written by the librettist in the form of three equal stanzas and apparently was meant to be set accordingly. Unfortunately the intense underlying activity in the words of the last stanza made this treatment impossible. The composer overcame the problem by making the last line do the work of a fourth stanza and by treating the remainder of the verse as an *animato* interlude[2]. With comparable success he overcame the banality of the words which close the first scene of Act II; and a rather conventional exhibition of self-pity on the part of the four women left behind by the crowd, became an episode of outstanding beauty, convincing, and deeply moving.

The musical structure of *Peter Grimes* offers further evidence that the Wagnerian method of through-composition is not essential to the success of a continuous, mounting tragedy. Britten has preferred to follow the later examples of Verdi; and, as in *Otello*, the music is formalized into set numbers, introduced and relinquished by related accompanied recitative. But in addition the orchestral interludes play a significant part. They either prepare for the music which is to follow or relate retrospectively to preceding material. Thus the substance of the first Interlude becomes the background accompaniment to the villagers' chorus when the curtain rises; while the *Storm* Interlude is compounded of elements heard sung during this scene. The melody for violas and 'cellos in the *Sunday Morning* Interlude becomes Ellen's first song at the beginning of the next scene. Perhaps the most conspicuous example of such organic construction is to be found in the Passacaglia, the fourth Interlude, of which the ground (Ex. 16b) is a derivative of Grimes's intensely dramatic acceptance of his failure to live up to Ellen's ideals (Ex. 16a):

---

[1] See *Peter Grimes*—III, p. 126, Ex. 1, and Ex. 17 in *The Musical Atmosphere*, p. 23. —Eds.

[2] See also *Peter Grimes*—II, pp. 116ff.—Eds.

Thus each Interlude is both integrated and functional.

In *Peter Grimes* Britten set out to do more than write a successful opera. He made an extremely bold attempt to found an English operatic tradition. This is apparent not only from the fact that he followed it with four more operatic works in as many years, but from the inherent characteristics and texture of the music contained in *Peter Grimes*. He had previously worked industriously to perfect a musical language which, while being capable of the widest range of emotional and intellectual expression, would be simple enough to be universally accepted in spite of many prejudices against its contemporary idiom. With the completion, and consequent success, of the *Serenade* he can no longer have had any doubts that he had achieved his object. By drawing extensively, but always with the utmost personal discrimination, upon musical developments without regard to age or nationality, he had succeeded in equipping himself with the means to succeed where, for two centuries, all others had failed. The reasoning was entirely logical; but to put such a theory into practice required little short of genius. As the inevitable result of this intensive study of the work of other composers—a practice employed, surely, by every creative artist of note from time immemorial—Britten was accused of being derivative instead of being commended for it. All sorts of minor and major critics gleefully observed in *Peter Grimes* the influences of Verdi, Berg, Strawinsky and even, rather mistakenly I feel, of Puccini. "Had Schoenberg never lived, the last Interlude in *Peter Grimes* could never have been written", asserted one rather more perceptive detective. I am sure the composer would agree with him.

But after more than six years of vigorous life, *Peter Grimes* must be relieved to feel that he has graduated from the phase in which his own ancestry is so industriously traced. Now he has become the parent. Inevitably, I suppose, the whole tedious and slightly malicious search will begin all over again in somebody else's opera.

HANS KELLER

Peter Grimes

II. THE STORY; THE MUSIC NOT EXCLUDED

Originally written to accompany a recording of excerpts from *Grimes* which never materialized, this chapter gives the complete narrative, while including musical comments on those parts of the opera which were to be recorded—thus forming, by accident, a complement to the contributions of Arthur Oldham and Erwin Stein.—Eds.

ERIVED from George Crabbe's poem, *The Borough*, the scenario of *Peter Grimes* was sketched by Benjamin Britten and Peter Pears; Montagu Slater undertook the libretto. "In writing *Peter Grimes*", says the composer, "I wanted to express my awareness of the perpetual struggle of men and women whose livelihood depends on the sea. . . ."[24] This, together with the light thrown by the story on the early 19th century practice of buying apprentices from the workhouse, pertains to the sociological aspect of the work. Psychologically, however, the significance of the story transcends its time and place. Peter Pears once wrote: "There are plenty of Grimeses around still, I think!" [243]

Peter Grimes is the living conflict. His pride, ambition, and urge for independence fight with his need for love; his self-love battles against his self-hate. Others too, he can (sometimes) love as intensely as he can despise them, but he cannot show, let alone prove his tenderness as easily as his wrath—except through the music which, alas, the people on the stage don't hear. Thus he is destined to seem worse than he is, and not to be as good as he feels. *Peter Grimes* is the story of the man who couldn't fit in.

I should indeed go further than Pears and say that in each of us there is something of a Grimes, though most of us have outgrown or at least outwitted him sufficiently not to recognize him too consciously. But we do identify him, and ourselves with him, unconsciously, which is one reason for the universal appeal of this work.

Another reason is the composer's ability to satisfy both the "connoisseurs" and the "less learned"—I put these words in inverted commas because Mozart used them with reference to his first three Vienna piano Concertos. It is in fact the outer perfection of Britten's music that prevents some listeners from realizing its depths.

Prologue

The time is 1830, the place a court-room in the Moot Hall of The Borough, a small Suffolk fishing town. An inquest is held on Peter's first boy apprentice who died of thirst at sea when Peter made the imprudent attempt to sail to the London market with "a huge catch—too big to sell here". Though the verdict is accidental death, the coroner-lawyer Swallow is nowise convinced of Peter's innocence. He advises Peter not to get another boy apprentice[1], or else to "get a woman help you look after him." Peter: "That's what I want, but not yet!" "Why not?" "Not till I've stopp'd people's mouths!" Indeed the townspeople are just as unconvinced of Peter's innocence as Swallow. But he has a friend among them, Ellen Orford, the widowed school-mistress, who had helped him to carry the dead boy home. Now, after the court has been cleared, she comforts him. The inquest has, incidentally, shown that he has another friend: the music (including the orchestration).

The music of the *Dawn* Interlude which follows now continues during the first part of, and later reappears in,

Act I, Scene I,

which opens, a few days later, on a cold grey morning on the Borough beach and street. The fisherfolk work and sing quietly to themselves[2]; here and at the end of the opera the librettist quotes directly from Crabbe. This first episode comes to a sudden end as Peter is heard off stage: "Hi! Give us a hand!" There is silence. Again he shouts: "Haul the boat!", and again nobody moves; Bob Boles, fisherman and Methodist preacher, shouts back: "Haul it yourself, Grimes!" It is

---

[1] See *Peter Grimes*—I, p. 102, Ex. 1.—Eds.
[2] See *Peter Grimes*—I, p. 106, Ex. 11.—Eds.

certainly no easy matter for Peter to work without an apprentice. But at last the local apothecary and quack, and Captain Balstrode, a retired merchant skipper, come forward to help him. Balstrode's attitude towards Peter is in fact benevolent. As for the quack—

> Grimes, you won't need help from now,
> I've got a prentice for you . . .
> I called at the workhouse yesterday.
> All you do now is fetch the boy.
> We'll send the carter with a note.
> He'll bring your bargain on his cart!

The quack's bargain, rather.

Carter Hobson, however, who is also the town constable, wants to keep out of this business. He is supported by the townspeople: "He's right! Dirty jobs!" But at this point Ellen Orford steps in: "Carter! I'll mind your passenger." The people: "What! and be Grimes' messenger?" Ellen: "Whatever you say, I'm not ashamed. Somebody must do the job." She offers to accompany the carter to the workhouse at Ipswich and to welcome and comfort the boy on the way back.

The crowd protests: "Ellen, you're leading us a dance, fetching boys for Peter Grimes . . ." The bass here develops from the tune of the carter's refusal to fetch the boy, a tune that has also been used in the crowd's "Dirty jobs!" as well as in Ellen's subsequent intervention. Ellen now again interrupts the people, first with her previous words: "Whatever you say . . ." But she leaves the sentence unfinished, using the phrase as introduction to her D minor aria, "Let her among you without fault cast the first stone."[1] The two musical phrases of these words are the thematic material of the piece, an arioso that is overpowering in its simultaneous ardour and dignity. The listener may like to observe how Britten turns toward his characteristic C major at the end of the last-quoted words and at the corresponding place in the restatement ("Will have no trouble to find out how a poor teacher . . ."), as well as at the end of the number: "Mr. Hobson, where's your cart?"

Small wonder, after this music, that Hobson is willing to fetch the boy with Ellen's assistance.

Earlier in the scene Balstrode has forecast a storm; he now announces its approach by way of the subject of a stormy fugue in which every-

---

[1] See *Peter Grimes*—I, p. 105, Ex. 8.—EDS.

body below and on the stage participates, except of course Peter. We find him still working at his boat after the approaching storm has driven the crowd into the local pub, "The Boar". Balstrode stays with him: "Grimes, since you're a lonely soul . . . why not try the wider sea, with merchant-man, or privateer?" "I am native, rooted here." They talk about the inquest and the hostility of the townspeople. "Your boy was workhouse starved," says Balstrode, "maybe you're not to blame he died." This rouses Peter to "picture what that day was like, that evil day" when the boy died. (Here follows a minor version[1] of Ex. 1a [p. 115].) Involuntarily, he also pictures his own character:

> They listen to money
> These Borough gossips.
> I have my visions, ...
> I'll win them over . . . .
>
> I'll fish the sea dry,
> Sell the good catches . . . .
> I'll marry Ellen!

Marry her now, without your booty, says Balstrode. "No, not for pity!" "Then," Balstrode warns him,

> the old tragedy
> Is in store.
> New start with new 'prentice
> Just as before!

Inevitably, Peter abuses even Balstrode—"Take your advice, put it where your money is!"—who finally leaves him for the more pleasant atmosphere of "The Boar". Alone, gazing intently into the sea and the approaching storm, Peter shows what lies beneath the storm in his own mind (see Ex. 1a [p. 115]):

> What harbour shelters peace,
> Away from tidal waves, away from storm.
> What harbour can embrace
> Terrors and tragedies?
> With her there'll be no quarrels,
> With her the mood will stay,
> Her breast is harbour too,
> Where night is turned to day.

---

[1] *Peter Grimes*—I, p. 103, Ex. 3.—EDS.

The turbulent and the yearning aspect (Ex. 1a) of Peter's mind are further contrasted in the following *Storm* Interlude in which the gale breaks out in all its strength. This music develops out of the latter part of the above scene and breaks into

SCENE 2

(inside "The Boar", the same evening) whenever somebody opens and struggles with the door. In fact the storm music plays here the paradoxical and therefore fascinating role of intruding into the scene which, structurally, it unifies. (Britten employs the same device in the last act of *Albert Herring*, where the rhythm from the preceding 'Manhunt' Interlude is the unifying intruder.)

The first part of the present scene offers not so much essential story as characterization and a strained atmosphere which is never really relieved, not even by Balstrode's number, "We live and let live, and look—we keep our hands to ourselves", in which refrain everybody joins[1].

Suddenly the door opens and Peter enters, accompanied by a wild version of Ex. 1a.   Indeed, by recurring at vital junctures, this theme contributes a great deal to the cyclic structure of the opera. At the same time its characteristic ninth, associated with loneliness and yearning, has also 'super-cyclic' significance in Britten's work. That is to say, we have met it before in the *Michelangelo Sonnets* (Ex. 1b)[2] and we shall meet it again in *The Rape of Lucretia* (Ex. 1c):

Ex.1a GRIMES *largamente*
         espress.
What   har - bour shel - ters peace,

See *Peter Grimes*—III, p. 126, Ex. 5, and I, p. 107, Ex. 12.—EDS.

[2] Beyond which the theme derives from the 2nd movement (or the 2nd part of the 1st movement) of Mahler's Fifth; see, for instance, this quotation from the coda:

Bn.

Britten, one gathers, had heard the Symphony only once.—EDS.

Ex.1b

il so - - le

Ex.1c LUCRETIA

Both wait - ing,

The theme recedes, though not the tension it has created. Peter's E major arioso[1], however, poises above the excited atmosphere. He looks to heaven—

> Now the great Bear and Pleiades
>   where earth moves
> Are drawing up the clouds
>   of human grief
> Breathing solemnity in the deep night

—and so does the music. But in the last stanza—

> But if the horoscope's
>   bewildering
> Like a flashing turmoil
>   of a shoal of herring
> Who can turn skies back and begin again?

—he seems to divine the inescapable tragedy of his character.

This sublime piece of music falls into four parts, though the verse consists of three stanzas. The first two musical strophes, that is, coincide with the first two stanzas, while the third (last-quoted) stanza is at first taken up by a contrasting *molto animato* middle section, and then returns, in the last line, to the music of the first two strophes. These are constructed (with the help of the strings) as a repeated canon which proceeds from the double basses upwards. But when the canon returns in the last line, it starts upstairs and proceeds downwards, and the entries are drawn closely together. The uncanny, expressive stillness of the canon is in part due to the fact that the melody proceeds in conjunct motion. The vocal line, moreover, is motionless for more than four lines of the first and second stanzas respectively, and again for more than two bars at the end.

[1] See *Peter Grimes*—III, p. 126, Ex. 1, and Ex. 17 in *The Musical Atmosphere*, p. 23.— Eds.

It remains to be added that at the end of the second stanza we observe again a turn into Britten's own C major.

Peter's arioso creates understandable bewilderment—"He's mad or drunk!"—and when in the course of events Boles is about to throw a bottle at him, Balstrode knocks it out of his hand and shouts: "For peace sake, someone start a song!" An elaborate round is now sung by all (except, at first, Peter) which is thematically connected with Exx. 1a and 2 as well as with the above-mentioned storm fugue (Sc. 1). When Peter enters the piece he disturbs it by distorting each of its three tunes, but eventually the round overwhelms him.

A dramatic return of the storm music accompanies the entry into "The Boar" of Ellen, Hobson, and Peter's new boy apprentice. "Peter takes the boy out of the door into the howling storm" whose music ends the act with more than one bang.

ACT II

Again the Interlude (*Sunday Morning*) is the basis of what follows it. In point of fact, the Interlude and the first part of Scene 1 are really one and the same piece of music and, as such, go to form the concert version of the Interlude.

The curtain rises again on the village street and beach. It is a Sunday morning, weeks after Act I. While the townspeople are going to church —we hear the church bell—Ellen and the boy (who doesn't speak or sing a word throughout the opera) enter, and Ellen sings what we know already from the Interlude: "Glitter of waves and glitter of sunlight . . ." As the organ sounds from the church they sit down on a breakwater and Ellen tries, still by way of the Interlude music, to make the boy talk. But the only reply she gets is her own previous tune, given by the strings in (fairly) canonic imitation.

"Nothing to tell me, nothing to say?" she asks as a new section begins with the church chorus singing off stage; here her notes are no longer those of the Interlude, yet derive from it.

The listener will easily note how impressively the successive phases of the church service (including the organ) on the one hand, and Ellen's and the orchestra's (and later Peter's) part on the other hand, are integrated and together build up what is to become a dramatic and musical climax.

As the boy does not want to talk, Ellen tries to guess what his life at the workhouse was like, and also tells him about her own experiences with children. Then—

> John, you may have heard the story
> Of the 'prentice Peter had before;
> But when you came I
> Said, Now this is where we
> Make a new start. Ev'ry day
> I pray it may be so.

Here the Hymn in church ends. So does, of course, this section as a whole, though Ellen uses the notes of her last-quoted words in the following *recitativo agitato*: "There's a tear in your coat. Was that done before you came? Badly torn."

This recitative proceeds together with the responses in church: ". . . and we have done those things we ought not to have done. . . ." Here Ellen sings: "That was done recently. Take your hand away. Your neck, is it?" The recitative closes with her cry, "A bruise—well, it's begun!"

Then follows, after the Gloria has started in church, her moving piece—"Child you're not too young to know where roots of sorrow are". The accompaniment, and later also her own part, take over from the Gloria. When, after she has finished, she rises and fastens the boy's shirt, the oboe reminds us of her discovery of the bruise.

At the beginning of the Benedicite, Peter enters excitedly: "Come boy!" He has seen a shoal. Ellen objects: "This is a Sunday, his day of rest." Peter: "This is whatever day I say it is! Come boy!" Ellen reproaches him:

> This unrelenting work,
> This grey unresting industry,
> What aim, what future,
> What peace will your hard profits buy?

Peter's reply derives, musically and otherwise, from his excited vision near the end of Act I, Sc. 1 ("They listen to money. . . . I'll marry Ellen!"):

> Buy us a home, buy us respect,
> And buy us freedom from pain
> Of grinning at gossip's tales
> Believe in me, we shall be free!

The Credo starts in church, and Ellen asks Peter to tell her "one thing, where the youngster got that ugly bruise?" "Out of the hurly burly!" (A minor ninth here which does not readily betray its kinship with the minor version of Ex. 1a, though it also goes on to the octave.) "Take away your hand!" (same minor ninth) he shouts when she asks him whether they were right in what they planned to do. Suddenly he grows tender: "My only hope depends on you, if you take it away—what's left?" But when Ellen suggests again, "Were we mistaken when we schemed to solve your life by lonely toil?" he bursts out: "Wrong to plan! Wrong to try! Wrong to live! Right to die!"[1] This forceful passage is again based on the previous minor ninth motif (which interval is now inverted) and shows a striking rhythm which has gone unrecognized in the last Interlude [264].

Peter repeats this angry shout to other words, and into Ellen's insistent "Were we mistaken . . ." And when at last she says, "Peter! We've failed, we've failed!" he cries out in despair and strikes her, the orchestra accompanying him with his own previous shouts. From the church we hear an "Amen", and from Peter Ex. 2[2], which is four times

imitated in the orchestra while he "drives the boy fiercely out in front of him".

Here we have reached the turning point of the opera. As far as the action is concerned, Peter has now shown that he is even unable to keep peace with, indeed capable of hurting, the woman he loves, his only friend. There is only one future for him, namely, none. And musically, Ex. 2 is the last chief theme to be stated for the first time. In fact it, together with the other Grimes-theme whose first phrase is quoted in Ex. 1a (and to which it is related), are the two most important tunes of the work.

Via Ex. 2, the now following part of the scene looks forward[3] into the next Interlude, i.e. a Passacaglia on Ex. 2[4].

[1] *Peter Grimes*—III, p. 126, Ex. 2.—Eds.
[2] See also *Peter Grimes*—I, p. 109, Ex. 16a.—Eds.
[3] See *Peter Grimes*—I, p. 107, Ex. 14, and III, p. 128, Exx. 9b and 9c.—Eds.
[4] For the actual ground, see *Peter Grimes*—I, p. 110, Ex. 16b.—Eds.

The tragic scene between Ellen, the boy and Peter has not gone un-observed, and the rumour that "Grimes is at his exercise"[1] (cf. Ex. 2) spreads among the departing churchgoers who collect outside the church door. They develop a savage hatred against Peter—surely the man is going to murder the boy. Eventually the Rector and Swallow, with a crowd of men behind them, go to see Peter in his hut.

The Passacaglia follows, and once again this Interlude anticipates the subsequent

SCENE 2

which takes place inside Peter's hut (an upturned boat). Peter arrives with the boy to prepare for the fishing. He blames the child for the quarrel with Ellen. His mood alternates between fury, tenderness—"There's the jersey that she knitted, with the anchor that she pat-terned"—and ambition (a quotation here from Act I: "They listen to money"[2]).

With deep and tender passion he dreams aloud of an illusory happiness with Ellen: "In dreams I've built myself some kindlier home . . ." (Here we get yet another moving turn to C major.) A lyrical *Adagio* of great beauty develops its accompaniment out of the preceding vocal line. "But dreaming builds what dreaming can disown. Dead fingers stretch themselves to tear it down." With these words the music reverts to the beginning (complete with C major turn), despite its opposite emotional content. We observe that even the last-quoted sentence is sung to the same notes and note-values as the initial phrase, ". . . warm in my heart and in a golden calm", though the character of this passage is, of course, altered in the restatement in order to reveal the contrast in mood and meaning. Britten shows him-self often able, in fact, to express contrary feelings by similar means, and we always find a point in this procedure. Psychoanalysis has taught us that in the unconscious mind opposite emotions are intimately connected; in the case of a man like Peter, whose mind is really swayed by his unconscious, the togetherness of contradicting impulses will inevitably show on the surface.

From afar Hobson's drum is heard: the Borough procession approaches, unnoticed, for the moment, by Peter, who is overcome by a hallucination of "that evil day" when his first apprentice died. This section is still based, in voice and orchestra, on the preceding

[1] See *Peter Grimes*—I, p. 107, Ex. 14, and *Peter Grimes*—III, p. 128, Ex. 9b.—Eds.
[2] See *Peter Grimes*—I, p. 104, Ex. 5.—Eds.

Adagio, whose music is, however, distorted, and alternates with Hobson's drum. This is heard coming nearer and nearer, until Peter finally hears it. He turns on the boy: "You've been talking! You and that bitch were gossiping! . . . The Borough's climbing up the hill. To get me. . . ." He "isn't scared", but all the same it seems best to go fishing before they arrive. The boy goes out of the door that opens to the cliff. "Careful or you'll break your neck! Down the cliff side to the deck. . . . Now shut your eyes and down you go!" We hear a scream—the boy has fallen to his death.

The Rector and Swallow enter, but all they find "is a neat and empty hut". The act ends with Ex. 2.

Act III

The searching, yet simple *Moonlight* Interlude prepares us for

Scene 1,

once again the village street and beach, three nights later. There is a dance in the Moot Hall, and people pass to and fro between the Hall and "The Boar". Thus we gather that Peter has not been seen since Sunday, nor has his boat. Mrs. Sedley, a widow who is Peter's chief antagonist besides Boles, suspects, for a change, murder.

The street empties for a while, and Ellen and Balstrode appear from the beach. They believe themselves alone, but Mrs. Sedley eavesdrops.

Balstrode has discovered that Peter's boat has been in for more than an hour. Peter himself, however, seems to have disappeared. Ellen has found, down by the tide-mark, the boy's jersey (which, as we remember from the last act, she had knitted and embroidered). Upon identifying it with the help of Balstrode's lantern, she sings two verses of meditation, and full of restrained sorrow. Here is the first:

> Embroidery in childhood was
> A luxury of idleness,
> A coil of silked thread giving
> Dreams of a silk and satin life.
> [Refrain] Now my broidery affords
> The clue whose meaning we avoid!

Before the second strophe there is a short *parlando* middle section of

1½ bars: "My hand remembered its old skill. These stitches tell a curious tale." This beautiful B minor aria is the most independent number of the opera.

Balstrode reminds Ellen that "in the black moment when your friend suffers unearthly torment, we cannot turn our backs ..." They walk out together, with the pledge: "We shall be there with him" (Ex. 2 in counterpoint, straight and inverted).

Mrs. Sedley informs Swallow that Peter's boat is back. Swallow summons Hobson, and soon a Ländler[1] from the previous dance music is uncannily transformed to serve a brutal manhunt after poor Peter, who by now is more dead than alive, anyway.

For about his condition the Interlude which follows here does not leave us in any doubt. Mental pain and physical stress have driven Peter all but insane. His madness and Britten's method combine to make this short piece an immensely gripping fantasy, which integrates Peter's disintegrated mind with the help and against the background of a constant dominant seventh on D, sustained by three muted horns. Throughout, too, we hear disjointed, fragmentary reminiscences of Peter's own music. First the flute recalls his "They listen to money.... I'll marry Ellen!" from the latter part of Act I, Sc. 1. Next the harp introduces, downstairs, a reminiscence of his dream in the hut (Act II, Sc. 2). This is the only quotation of a theme that has made its first appearance later than Ex. 2. Now Ex. 1a is heard on three solo violins; it is, however, disturbed by the oboe's excerpt from Peter's E major arioso in Act I, Sc. 2, which in its turn is followed by two clarinets' version of what was once his outburst, "Wrong to plan! Wrong to try! . . ." (Act II, Sc. 1). Into this, double basses and double bassoon enter with another distortion of Ex. 1a which is imitated by the clarinets. This theme then renders its hidden help to the building up of a climax, where it leads into its brother theme, Ex. 2 (inverted and straight). The latter finally disrupts and ends on a repeated minor second which comes both from Ex. 2's minor second and from the minor version of Ex. 1a.

Every second Interlude in the opera, we realize now, is a Grimes Interlude. Or to put it another way, those Interludes which are really Preludes to the three acts are Sea Interludes, while the Interludes between the scenes are Grimes Interludes. The *Storm* Interlude, however, is both.

[1] Cf. *Peter Grimes*—I, p. 106, Ex. 10.—EDS.

SCENE 2

The same scene, a few hours later. Fog. We hear the distant fog-
horn (tuba) continuing the minor second with which the previous
Interlude has ended. But it has not really ended; its dominant seventh,
too, is now continued in the far-off cries of the townspeople: "Grimes!
Grimes!"

Peter stumbles in, demented. "Steady! There you are! Nearly home!"
This again to the same minor second. In fact this fateful interval will
be heard to remain faithful to Peter right to the end.

The preceding Interlude has of course once again foreshadowed
the scene: Peter's mad recitative consists of reminiscences (Britten's
title figures—Lucretia, Albert Herring, Billy Budd—are always given
reminiscences in the end). But now we do not hear solely his own
music. Thus, in Ex. 3, he quotes Swallow's verdict from the *Prologue*,

though Swallow sang other (if rhythmically related) notes to these
words. At the same time the tune of Ex. 3 (with which the opera
actually opened) is not only Swallow's own characteristic theme, but
was sung by him in his initial warning: "Peter Grimes, I here advise
you! Do not get another boy apprentice. . . ."[1]

A quotation easily recognized is "Turn the skies back and begin
again!" from Peter's arioso in Act I, Sc. 2. "There now my hope is
held by you" will also be well remembered (Act II, Sc. 1: "My only
hope depends on you . . ."). But Peter interrupts his own tenderness:
"Take away your hand!" These words and this motif previously
(Act II, Sc. 1) preceded the tender passage which they now interrupt;
it is as if we were given a concrete example of Peter's mental retrogression.

"The argument's finished, friendship lost . . ."—again the "I'll
marry Ellen!" tune from the latter part of Act I, Sc. 1, whose derivatives
we have previously heard at "Buy us a home, buy us respect" (Act II,
Sc. 1) and at the beginning of the last Interlude. Here, incidentally, we

[1] *Peter Grimes*—I, p. 102, Ex. 1.—EDS.

are offered a further instance of the expression of opposite emotions by similar means.

"To hell with all your mercy! To hell with your revenge, and God have mercy upon you!" This, of course, is Ex. 2.

The voices of the townspeople have now come very near, and Peter roars back at them. Just as he calms down, Ellen and Balstrode appear. Ellen sings, "Peter, we've come to take you home. O come home out of this dreadful night!" She, too, uses her previous music, i.e. "Peter, tell me one thing, where the youngster got that ugly bruise?" from Act II, Sc. 1.

Peter, however, does not hear her. Nor is he now disturbed by the shouters who seem to have lost the track and are again heard from far away. He sings his last notes—Ex. 1a. The words, too, are the same as in Act I, Sc. 1 (see their quotation above), though two lines are omitted, namely: "With her there'll be no quarrels, with her the mood will stay. . . ." And the end of the theme, once so yearningly insistent, now dies down in pairs of semitones. An unworldly desire for death and rebirth has taken the place of his worldly (though unrealistic) struggle for a new life.

The fog-horn has the last word, or rather the last minor second.

Balstrode tells Peter to sail out and sink the boat. Peter does so.

Dawn begins and the music reverts, slowly but unperturbedly, to the first Interlude and the opening chorus of Act I. Crabbe's own words, too, appear once more:

> To those who pass the Boro' sounds betray
> The cold beginning of another day . . .

Peter's was a lonely tragedy.

ERWIN STEIN

Peter Grimes

III. OPERA AND *PETER GRIMES*[1]

IN opera, the action proceeds at a slower pace than in a
play; song needs more time than speech to state its
case. The French term *drame lyrique* is very appropriate,
because in opera the emotional, meditative and descriptive qualities
of music come into their own. There is not much scope for events.
They may occur at the culmination of a musical climax, like the boy's
death in the second act of *Peter Grimes*, or the advent of Lohengrin
after Elsa's prayer. But actual events avail less in musical drama
than the situations which arise from the action. Dramatic situations
provide the proper occasions for music to grow and to develop
its lyrical qualities. The emotional, pictorial or other implications
of the scene are the immediate source of the composer's inspiration.
They present the opportunities for arias, ensembles, choruses, and
all those vocal high-lights which constitute the essential feature
of opera. For the singing human voice is the vehicle of music; it is
indeed the substance itself of which the musical drama chiefly
consists.

The ability to portray any character or mood with a few touches
has always been one of Britten's happiest gifts. The principal persons
of the opera are each characterized by some peculiarities of
their melodies. Peter Grimes himself sings dreamily on recurrent

[1] Part of an article from *Tempo*, September, 1945.

notes (see Ex. 1), or excitedly in ragged intervals (see Ex. 2). His human feeling becomes manifest only in connection with Ellen (see Ex. 3).

Ellen Orford is distinguished by the warmth of her melodic lines, and her humbleness shines in frequent descending passages (see Ex. 4):

Balstrode's *bonhomie* is expressed in clear-cut cadential phrases (see Ex. 5):

"Square" Auntie makes square statements (see Ex. 6):

Ex.6

That is the sort of weak po-lite-ness makes a pub-li-can lose her cli-ents.

Pompous Swallow sings boisterous intervals (see Exx. 7 and 8):

In this way the music invests the singers with appropriate features and becomes part and parcel of their acting.

Opera consists of dramatic situations. Their specific atmosphere gives music its head. There is no need, and rarely an opportunity, for action as speedy as in a film. The dramatic situation may well remain stationary while its implications are resolved by the music. Arias or other set pieces often seemingly retard the story while actually revealing the internal drama. Ellen's aria[1] in the last act, on finding the dead boy's embroidered jersey, is extremely moving because it mirrors the drama of her emotions, expressing utter sadness and despair, yet still pervaded by the warmth of her humanity. Similarly, when in the second act the revengeful crowd has marched off, the music exposes the inner conflicts of the four dejected women left on the stage. The situation yields apposite music. When Peter stays in the storm and Balstrode approaches him sympathetically, there is occasion for a duet, which discloses much of Peter's temperament. The entrance of Auntie, Keene and Boles, after they have watched Peter's and Ellen's quarrel, starts a gossiping scherzando terzetto. Again, Ellen's profession that she will stand by Peter begins an expanding ensemble, showing the reactions of the individuals and leading to the climax of the scene. The interplay of dramatic situation and music is inevitable. Where the action relaxes, the musical form becomes looser; where speech prevails, as in the *Prologue* to the first act, there is the right place for the old-

[1] See *Peter Grimes*—I, pp. 121f.—EDS.

established form of recitative, sharply pointing the sense of the words. Yet the most striking dramatic functions of operatic music are built-up climaxes and lyrical relaxations. *Peter Grimes* contains many perfect examples of both.

There are six orchestral interludes or preludes. Here music emerges in its own right, though still contributing indirectly to the drama. Some of these interludes are descriptive; the first, depicting dawn on the shore, sets the stage for the grey morning of the first act; the second evokes in rondo form the turbulence of a sea storm—a protagonist who does not appear on the stage; the third heralds the bright Sunday morning of the church scene; and the prelude to the last act suggests the play of moonlight on the waves of the sea. The remaining two interludes clearly pertain to Peter[1]. One, short and rhapsodic, forms a prelude to the last act's mad scene and refers to phrases of Peter's earlier songs, only to disintegrate them. The other, a full-size and elaborate Passacaglia, stands between the two scenes of the second act in the centre of the opera. Its theme is derived from Peter's fateful cadence (Ex. 9a) which, in various transformations (Exx. 9b and 9c), dominates the music of the ensuing scene until it becomes the bass of the Passacaglia (Ex. 9d):

Ex.9a
GRIMES *largamente*
God have mer - cy u-pon me!

Ex.9b *Allegretto*
AUNTIE
Grimes_____ is at his ex-er-cise!

Ex.9c *Presto*
BASSES *pp*

Ex.9d *Andante moderato*
pp deliberato

---

[1] Cf., however, *Peter Grimes*—I, p. 122, last paragraph.—EDS.

The theme is stubbornly repeated by the bass instruments and its irregular rhythm is frequently at cross purposes with the common time of the music built upon it. This music is a set of variations on a new theme, introduced by the solo viola. Fragments of the variations appear in the following scene between Peter and the boy, forming, as it were, the only utterances of the unhappy child. The viola theme is repeated in its entirety, but with inverted intervals, at the end of the act after the boy's death.

While the Passacaglia is musically the most integrated section, there is one moment in the opera where the music completely fades out. After the Interlude of the third act the orchestra pauses; Peter's delirious song is accompanied only by the distant chorus and fog-horn which, as they vanish, sound like beckoning voices from the sea itself. Then, during a prolonged silent *fermata,* Balstrode's subdued speech bids Peter to do the inevitable. The tension of this extraordinary scene is still felt when the violins enter to prepare the stage for the recurrence of ordinary life in the closing scene.

We have seen how dramatic situations create musical set pieces. There remains the bigger task—the biggest for the composer—to co-ordinate them, so that they fit together into the larger unity of scenes, acts and finally the whole opera, and in a manner which is not only dramatically but musically satisfactory. In old operas the single numbers had proper endings and the space between them was filled with dialogues or *secco* recitatives. Composers seem not to have bothered too much about their formal relation, but to have relied on the solid construction of their libretti. Still, there were instances where the pieces followed each other without interruption, and I know no better example than the second finale of *The Marriage of Figaro*, in which a series of very contrasted pieces (by the way, each born out of some new surprising situation) is perfectly balanced and built up to a brilliant climax. In 'through-composed' operas of later times, two different methods have been employed, represented by the two greatest opera composers of the nineteenth century, Wagner and Verdi. I should like to call Wagner's treatment epical and Verdi's lyrical, because these terms express fundamentally different approaches to the problem of musical drama. It must be said at once that Britten follows Verdi's rather than Wagner's example. While with Verdi self-contained numbers prevail, Wagner abolishes them almost entirely. He builds his acts as units, which consist of a series of quasi-symphonic movements.

Wagner's dramatic action proceeds at a very slow pace. He has a broad way of exposing and repeating his story which well suits the epic character and solemn subjects of his dramas, but which would be less appropriate to humbler topics. The imitation of Wagner's style has spoilt generations of opera composers who have applied his methods to unsuitable subjects and without his ingenuity.

In Verdi's operas almost the entire musical substance emanates from the singers. After all, they are the *dramatis personæ* and have to present the play. The demands of the voice also determine the musical form. The succession of dramatic situations is resolved in a series of lyrical numbers, of varying length and character, as the occasion demands, and they are co-ordinated and linked according to the requirements of both music and drama.

Britten's opera is built on principles similar to those of Verdi's last works, *Otello* and *Falstaff*. One can easily distinguish between, and follow the course of, recitatives and closed numbers. The way these are balanced and joined, and then integrated and built up to terrific climaxes, shows a skill and mastery of form almost unbelievable in a composer's first opera. The details are treated with no less care. Among the recitatives are some with elaborate accompaniment; others, particularly in the pub scene, have only a pianissimo background of sustained orchestral colours or repeated figurations.

The chorus, representing Peter Grimes's main adversary, has a big share in the music with such memorable pieces as the opening chorus, the storm ensemble, the round and the ensembles of the second and third acts. These ensembles contain some of the most impressive moments of the opera. Yet the main characters are even more lavishly provided with a variety of solos and ensembles. On three occasions what the Italians call a *scena* occurs: the stage is left to a singer's monologue, including *recitativo, arioso,* and *aria*. Peter's scenes in the hut and when he is demented, and Ellen's scene before the church, are all fine examples of this operatic device. The orchestra is handled with wise economy. It produces many new and surprising colours but, except for the interludes, its force is more restrained than in any modern opera I know. The human voice always dominates.

If there is a national character in music, *Peter Grimes* is surely very English. Not only because of its Suffolk background or the seascapes of the interludes. The round in the pub and the whole of the church scene are, to my mind, feasts of Englishness. There is also a modal tendency, one still very much alive in English music, and a particular predilection for the Lydian augmented fourth. The beginning of the second act is definitely in the Lydian mode with D as tonic, although the key signature indicates A major. Even more significant are the rhythmic and melodic peculiarities that result directly from the intonation of English speech. I am referring to the frequent syncopations, asymmetric patterns and surprising inflexions of the melody in Britten's music. The indigenous rhythm and intonation of a nation's language inevitably bears on the character of its music. At some time it would be worth while studying this connection in detail.

NORMAN DEL MAR

The Chamber Operas

I. THE RAPE OF LUCRETIA

AFTER the immediate and overwhelming success of *Peter Grimes*, many observers felt some anxiety about the possible effect of such universal admiration on Britten himself. It was suggested that international recognition so rapidly attained might lead to complacency in the form of an over-ready acceptance of the superficial (often the companion of great facility). Alternatively, the composer might become increasingly self-conscious, thus damaging his confidence and halting his flow of ideas.

It was not long before Britten dispelled these premature forebodings, although the line he proceeded to take proved utterly different from any that could have been anticipated. The production of *Grimes* had not been without its birth-pangs, and these, together with other post-war artistic problems, caused the composer to think deeply about the future of opera in this country. He resolved finally to experiment with what was, for all intents and purposes, a virtually unexploited form—Chamber Opera.

In an attempt to widen the scope of opera beyond a few national institutions by reducing as far as possible the normally vast financial liability, the number of performers both on the stage and in the orchestra was to be severely limited. Where the stage is concerned, such limitations of personnel are by no means without precedent. Mozart's *Così fan tutte* and Ravel's *L'Heure espagnole* are obvious examples, not to mention such experimental pieces as Schoenberg's *Erwartung*[1] and the two miniature operas of Holst.

In the case of the orchestra, however, there are far fewer examples,

---

[1] We do not consider *Erwartung* experimental since for Schoenberg there was no alternative.—EDS.

and those which exist are set for such widely varying combinations as to hamper rather than improve their chances of performance. For his part, Britten decided to experiment with an orchestra of twelve musicians; a string quintet (each player representing one of the five normal departments of the customary string orchestra), a wind quintet (one of each wind department, including a horn), a harp, and a single player to handle the percussion. With his inexhaustible knowledge and understanding of instrumental capabilities, Britten was bound to be attracted by the inherently wide contrasts and variations of colour provided by this combination, in addition to such possibilities as the exploitation of its individuals as chamber players, or even soloists[1].

Since the initial problems attending the composition of a new kind of opera were inevitably those of pure form, Britten chose as his subject one which was of particular interest from a structural angle. This was the recent treatment of the Lucretia legend by André Obey. One of the most remarkable features of this unusual play is the introduction of two Narrators who not only comment on the situations but in many places take over the actual presentation of the plot, the characters meanwhile miming the actions in dumb show.

Ronald Duncan, who adapted the work for Britten's purpose, saw in Obey's Narrators a link with Greek classical drama, and he accordingly retitled them the 'Male and Female Choruses', each of the classical groups being represented, as with the orchestra, by a single performer. And Duncan discovered in these figures a further link with formal art, this time in the realm of painting. He made them into observers standing at right angles to Time (as it were in J. W. Dunne's "Time 2") and thus able to view the action in the light of events taking place at a totally different epoch. In this way he was able to present the pagan drama from a contemporary religious standpoint, and interpret the action, which occurs in ancient Rome at the time of the Tarquins, as reflected against the Passion of Christ and the Immaculate Conception. This apparently irrelevant framing of the main drama finds its precedent in the device used so frequently by the classical Italian school of painting which depicted Biblical scenes, or representations of the Madonna and Child, against a contemporary and local background.[2]

[1] See, at the same time, *The Symphonies*, p. 256, and *Billy Budd*, pp. 199 and 209f.—EDS.

[2] Britten's tendency towards re-interpretation can, intra-musically, be observed in his realization of *The Beggar's Opera*.—EDS.

Duncan next compressed Obey's list of characters into small representative groups which correspond to the formalized orchestra. On the one hand stands Lucretia herself with two attendants; on the other, Tarquinius with two Generals. As the opera unfolds, each group is first presented by itself, before the interplay between them takes effect; and since the Male and Female Choruses act as an all-encircling frame, they appear first, and on either side of a closed curtain.

Act I

Recitative

Framing Hymn
(see Ex. 3)

The Male Chorus gives an historical account of the political state of Rome leading to the rise of the Tarquins. The thread is picked up by the Female Chorus who explains the state of war between Rome and Greece and establishes the lapse of time between these events and the coming of Christ. Together the two figures announce their identity as Christian observers and commentators. The inner curtain rises; the Male Chorus describes the scene of action.

Scene i

Atmospheric music [see music example in editorial footnote[2], p. 137] surrounding:
1. Drinking Song
2. Recitative

3. Junius's aria "Lucretia!"

N.B. 1st appearance of motto melody (Ex. 4)
4. Collatinus's aria
5. Duet "Why does the Nubian"

The three foremost Roman Generals, Tarquinius the Prince, Junius (later to become the leader of the successful revolt against the Tarquins), and Collatinus, husband of Lucretia, are drinking together. They discuss the recent wager among the Roman officers which proved that only Lucretia was virtuous among Roman wives. Junius, driven partly by the faithlessness of his own wife, and partly through shrewd political ambition, indirectly incenses Tarquinius to besiege Lucretia's virtue. The Male Chorus comments on the psychological battle within the two men.

INTERLUDE

N.B. 2nd appearance of motto melody (Ex. 4)

Tarquinius calls for his horse, the curtain falls, and the Male Chorus graphically describes the Prince's ride to Rome.

SCENE 2

Spinning chorus

Recitative and arietta (Lucretia) "How cruel men are"
"Linen" ensemble
(cf. Ex. 16)

Scena and pantomime

leading to
"Good night" ensemble

Lucretia is spinning with her nurse and maid, Bianca and Lucia. Between the philosophical comments of the Female Chorus, the three express their inner thoughts. Lucretia halts the spinning and reveals her anxiety and love for Collatinus. Her fears temporarily at rest, Lucretia directs the folding of linen while the Female Chorus soliloquizes on the homely functions of women. As Lucretia prepares for bed, the two Choruses describe the Prince's wild approach through sleeping Rome. From this point until the end of the act Obey's device is used directly; that is to say, the action is mimed by the characters, but described in detail by the two Choruses. Tarquinius arrives at the house and demands admission. The women receive him with varying degrees of courtesy and uneasiness, and wish him "Good night"[1] as the curtain falls.

ACT II

Recitative

As in the first act, the two Choruses begin by discussing the historical setting of the action, this time, however, concentrating on the growing discontent among the Roman people. Cries of revolt are heard off-stage, available members of the cast representing the turbulent voices of the crowd.

[1] The unfailing appearance of a "Good night" and/or "Good morning" ensemble in each of Britten's operas has been the source of much amused comment in recent years.

Framing Hymn (see Ex. 3)

Once more the observations of the two figures turn towards Christianity and after they reaffirm their function as Christian observers the curtain rises. This time the Female Chorus begins the description of the scene.

Scene 1

Sleeping music surrounding:
(a) Female Chorus's lullaby "Thus sleeps Lucretia" (cf. Ex. 14)
(b) Aria (Tarquinius) "Within this frail crucible"
Scena, duet and ensemble
N.B. 3rd appearance of motto melody (Ex. 4)

Lucretia is asleep. The Male Chorus announces the approach of Tarquinius. He wakens Lucretia with a kiss. A passionate ensemble ensues in which the two Choruses take part.

INTERLUDE (Chorale Prelude)

At the climax[1] the curtain falls and the Choruses sing a prayer to the Virgin Mary as the music gradually subsides.

Scene 2

Duet "O what a lovely day" (see Ex. 8)

Recitative and arietta (Lucia) "I often wonder"
Scena and aria (Lucretia) "O hideous Flower"

"Flowers bring to every year" (see Exx. 6, 7)
Arietta (Bianca) "I remember"

Recitative

Lucia and Bianca greet the bright morning. They gather flowers and arrange them, but leave the orchids for Lucretia. To the Romans, however, orchids were symbolic and, when Lucretia enters, the sight of them sends her into a paroxysm of rage and grief. She sends Lucia with a wild message for Collatinus, and then sings a lament before wandering off. The nurse indulges in brief, solitary reminiscences until Lucia suddenly returns with the news that Collatinus is already at the house accompanied by Junius.

[1] An important feature of the original Obey, entirely omitted by Duncan, explains the comparative ease with which Tarquinius quenches his desire. Shortly before the end of the scene appear the following lines for Tarquinius: "Listen! If you refuse me— I shall slay you in your bed. Then I shall cut the throat of one of your meanest, lowest slaves. I shall throw his body into your dead arms, and I shall swear before the immortal gods that it was in his embrace I slew you."

Funeral march and scena (see Exx. 12 and 13)

N.B. *4th appearance of motto melody* (Ex. 4)
Passacaglia[1] (see Ex. 5)

The events of the previous night are disclosed and Lucretia re-enters in funereal manner. She tells of her shame and, despite Collatinus's attempts at consolation and forgiveness, kills herself.

In the succeeding ensemble each of the parts commences in character (Junius, especially, calls upon the crowd to rise against the Tarquins in his favour) but merges into a united outcry against the transitory nature of beauty and the finality of death.

As the curtain falls, the two Choruses, who have been participating in the ensemble, continue the argument alone; they protest against this irrevocable view of mortality and reaffirm their belief in Christ as a perpetual and all-embracing consoler.

Epilogue and final return of Framing Hymn (see Ex. 3)

Lucretia was the first work in which Britten employed an elaborate scheme of musical motifs. These recur sometimes in connection with actual characters of the drama, sometimes to emphasize the formal structure of the work. Much as one would expect, it is Lucretia and

[1] The passacaglia, too, is a funeral march. See editorial footnotes on p. 142.—EDS.
[2] The parent cell of the Lucretia and Tarquinius motifs, the two principal thematic units of the work, is the (in every sense) pregnant harp figure

which depicts the persistent and somewhat oppressive noise of crickets in the heavy atmosphere of the opening scene, and to which the Tarquinius motif adds one note, the Lucretia motif two [131].—EDS.

Tarquinius who, as principal protagonists, are graced by individual
motifs: Lucretia by Ex. 1[1],

Tarquinius by Ex. 2[1],

while the Christian frame is represented by a chorale-like theme
(see Ex. 3; referred to in the above synopsis as the Framing Hymn)
which always appears in its entirety:

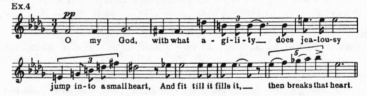

Of particular importance in the unification of the entire musical
form, though perhaps less direct in its philosophical implications, is
Ex. 4, described in the synopsis as the 'motto melody'. It is here
quoted as it first appears in Act I, Sc. 1:

This melodic line occurs four times during the course of the opera,
always at some important juncture of the dramatic action.

Besides such direct thematic references, Britten achieves a subtle
unity within the work by constructing many of the apparently independent sections out of material the germs of which can be found in
the basic motifs. For example, the rising phrase (bracketed in Ex. 5)
from the great passacaglia in Act II

[1] See footnote ([2]) on preceding page.—EDS.

follows both rhythmically and melodically the bracketed phrase from
Ex. 3, while the slight variant which occurs a few bars later at the
words "So brief is beauty" is naturally anticipated (Ex. 6) in Lucretia's
lament, as dictated by the libretto:

This lament provides a further example in its accompanying
figure (Ex. 7),

which is obviously related to the duet "O what a lovely day" (see
Ex. 8) from the beginning of the scene,

while the origin of both can be traced back to the bracketed figure
of Ex. 4. It might be considered fortuitous to point out such resemblances if research did not reveal so many within the pages of the
work. As always in cases of this sort, the mistake is to over-stress the
extra-musical significance of such stylistic devices.

There is, however, not the slightest obscurity in the application
of the two principal motifs Exx. 1 and 2. Indeed, the way in which
they are varied in order to create fresh figures for sections of widely
contrasted character is exceedingly skilful—as can be seen in the case

of Ex. 1 by comparing Junius' aria from Act I ("Lucretia! Lucretia!") with the ariettas of Lucia[1] and Bianca from Act II, Sc. 2[2].

This elaborate motivic integration is, of course, entirely in keeping with a work in which formal elements play so large a part. It is interesting, on the other hand, to find it employed simultaneously with the revival of a device belonging to a very different operatic tradition and until now largely obsolete—the use of recitative, both *accompagnato* and, above all, *secco*. Taking his model from classical tradition, Britten specifically directs the 'dry' recitative to be accompanied by the conductor, though naturally, for a contemporary work, on the piano. Nor is it used merely as a convenient method of linking the groups of short sections which form the bulk of the work. It is full of intrinsic merit; indeed, as a glance at the above synopsis will show, both acts start with substantial recitative. That this should be the case with Act II is relatively less unusual, but that the entire opera should commence with no less than seventy bars of recitative is of exceptional interest.

A notable feature of the recitatives in *Lucretia* is their natural adoption of an earlier device of Britten's: the use of long stretches of music punctuated by repetitions of a single chord, examples of which can be found not only in *Grimes*, but as far back in Britten's development as *Our Hunting Fathers* of 1936. In *Herring*, as will be seen, the apparent simplicity of this device is handled with captivating ingenuity.

Another stylistic device particularly in evidence in *Lucretia* is the repeated use of thematic inversion, so frequently employed that it might be thought to contain some special significance. Examples such as the following (Exx. 9, 10, 11)

[1] Shortly after the vocal score had been published, Britten became dissatisfied with certain features of the libretto, including the characterization of Lucia. He accordingly had a number of radical revisions made to the text which involved many alterations in the score. Collatinus's aria in Act I, Sc. 1, was completely rewritten, while the new and exquisite arietta for Lucia was inserted into the first recitative in Act II, Sc. 2. Moreover, many of the recitatives themselves were considerably improved. An entirely fresh edition of the score was thus necessitated, and a careful comparison of the two versions is extremely rewarding.

[2] The last-named, major-key application of the Lucretia motif contrasts strongly not only with the tragic character of previous forms of the motif, but also with the tragic character of the present dramatic situation itself, the 'innocent', scherzo-like accompaniment of Bianca's arietta representing both Lucretia's innocent youth and perhaps her moral innocence at the present dramatic juncture: a case of what one might call 'dramatic counterpoint' between stage and music (Mozart, Verdi!) where, just as in real counterpoint, the antithesis enhances the simultaneous thesis. Incidentally, this scherzoid version of the Lucretia motif seems to be Britten's only thought so far which shows the influence of Mendelssohn [131].—EDS.

The Rape of Lucretia: Act I Scene I
(from the Salzburg 1950 production)

Elisabeth Höngen as Lucretia

Richard Lewis as Albert Herring

Margaret Ritchie as Miss Wordsworth

Joan Cross as Lady Billows — *Albert Herring*

Peter Pears as Captain Vere

—

Theodor Uppman as Billy Budd

Billy Budd aboard the "Indomitable" before his execution

suffice to show the ease with which Britten handles the device, without ever allowing it to become a cramping influence on his inventive powers by a too rigid observance of the letter rather than the spirit.

One of the most important ways in which Britten's work matured during the years preceding the composition of *Lucretia* was in an increasing desire to achieve the maximum effect by the simplest possible means. *Lucretia* marks a great stride in this direction, as is shown in such passages as Lucretia's funereal[1] entrance (see Ex. 12) towards the end of Act II:

The broken phrases of the cor anglais gradually coalesce until, at the climax, a continuous melodic line is reached in a passage of un-accompanied two-part counterpoint with the voice (Ex. 13). This is a masterstroke:

(Note also the five-beat phrases of the voice part which fall across the bar-lines.)

---

[1] It is noteworthy that Lucretia's death is framed by two threnodic pieces both of which bear characteristics of the funeral march. The music to Lucretia's funereal entrance (see Ex. 12)—the anticipatory, spiritual funeral, so to say—is more of a dirge than of a march, though on the stage its march element is confirmed by Lucretia's protracted and stylized entry. In the case of the passacaglia (see Ex. 5) after Lucretia's death—the actual funeral music—nobody marches on the stage, but the character of the funeral march is quite outspoken, including even the typical funeral-march figure[2] which pro-duces the cadential emphasis of the ostinato's consequent. Either piece shows Britten's art of essentially operatic complementation: the music never states the dramatically obvious, and always explains the dramatically implied. The 'song' of the first dirge is orchestral (cor anglais): Lucretia has not really—as distinct from spiritually—died yet. The actual (normally instrumental) funeral march, on the other hand, is vocal: now is the time, not to have a quasi-realistic and hence tautologizing funeral march,

In discussing Britten's handling of the orchestra, emphasis must be laid on the discrimination with which small groups of the already diminutive ensemble are selected for the shorter sections of the work. Most obviously striking is the trio for bass flute, bass clarinet and muted horn which accompanies the aria (lullaby) for Female Chorus in Act II, "Thus sleeps Lucretia" (see Ex. 14):

Britten's predilection for bass flute and bass clarinet appears again in *Herring*, and has continued to manifest itself in later works, such as the *Spring Symphony* and *Billy Budd*.

but to proceed to the meaning and towards the interpretation of the drama. Thus the (in both senses) 'instrumental' rhythmic figure (funeral drum) emerges as the most vocal and verbal and conceptual—the most *eloquent* element. The basic, falling third that opens the 'Framing Hymn' (Ex. 3) wherefrom the whole ostinato derives, has grown, by way of Lucretia's last words ("See, how my wanton blood washes my shame away!"), into the funeral-march figure with its crucial refrain ("Is this all? It is all! It is all!") and thence leads to the Female Chorus's question in the Epilogue, "Is it all? Is all this suffering and pain, Is this in vain?" and finally—now in the orchestra because all has been *said*—to, and indeed beyond, the resolution of the tragedy.—ED. (H.K.)

[2] As a falling fifth (cf. *Lucretia*'s funereal falling third in Ex. 5), this "typical funeral-march figure" made its first appearance in Britten's music in the second of his funeral marches—the *Funeral March* from the *Frank Bridge Variations*, op. 10:

The first of Britten's funeral marches was the *Alla marcia funebre* which closed the symphonic song cycle *Our Hunting Fathers*, op. 8; the last—to date—is the execution 'march' in Act IV, Sc. 2 of *Billy Budd*, op. 50.—ED. (D.M.)

Another passage of exceptional imagination (Ex. 15) occurs shortly after the section just quoted:

It will be observed that the notation employed is that of Schoenberg's *Sprechstimme*[1]. The effect, however, is not intended to reproduce that of *Pierrot lunaire*, but is closer to those parts of Berg's *Wozzeck* which are directed, as here, to be spoken. The effect is even more radical than Berg's, since in neither orchestra nor voice are there any sounds of definite pitch. Broadly speaking, the passage owes greater allegiance to Milhaud's precedents of the kind in such works as *Christophe Colomb* and *Les Choëphores*.

Finally, no survey of this remarkable work would be complete without a quotation (Ex. 16) from the instrumental score of the 'Linen' ensemble, which shows outstandingly the supremely transparent orchestration in which Britten was at that time acquiring complete mastery:

[1] In America, Schoenberg adopted a different notation, writing the *Sprechstimme* on, above, and below a single line: see the *Ode to Napoleon*, *A Survivor from Warsaw* and, last, the unfinished and as yet unpublished Psalm "O du mein Gott: alle Völker preisen Dich und versichern Dich ihrer Ergebenheit", op. 50c, for reciter, mixed chorus and orchestra.—EDS.

The Chamber Operas

II. *ALBERT HERRING*[1]

*A*LBERT HERRING was composed immediately
after the production of *Lucretia*, to which it
stands as the *Meistersinger* does to *Tristan*[2]; and
indeed, despite *Herring*'s broadly jovial nature, there is a profound
touch of pathos underlying its situations.

The opera is based on *Le Rosier de Madame Husson*, one of the more
savagely bitter of Guy de Maupassant's short stories. Britten's librettist,
however, who was none other than Eric Crozier, the original producer
of both *Grimes* and *Lucretia*, smoothed over much of the irony in the
story, and used the framework to present instead a number of vivid
character studies typifying English rural life at the turn of the last
century.

This enabled Britten to continue the process of deepening insight
which, together with rapid sureness of touch, was becoming a feature
of his output. At the same time the unrestricted use of colloquialisms in
Crozier's libretto exploited Britten's penchant for constructing his vocal
lines by following the most natural inflexions of the voice.

The resultant local character of *Herring* was at one time considered
detrimental to its appeal outside Great Britain. This has proved to be by
no means the case, with the possible exception of the U.S.A., where
the similarity between the languages of the two countries is obviously
an impediment rather than the reverse. Such quips as "Sorry, Miss

---

[1] See also *The Light Music*, pp. 289ff.—EDS.
[2] Bearing in mind the quotation from *Tristan* in *Meistersinger*, Act III, the quotation
from *Lucretia* in *Herring*, Act III, strengthens this parallel in an amusing way.

Pike! Punctured my bike!", or "Felo de what?" "Done himself in!", or "Well, you've gone and done it now!", though a continual source of delight to audiences in this country, are, strange to say, virtually unintelligible to the average American and require translation into the local patois as if for a continental production.

In its essentials *Herring* follows the Maupassant story very closely.

The village termagant, whom Crozier calls Lady Billows, has determined to improve the morals of local girls by reviving the ancient custom of crowning a May Queen. The prize, however, will be awarded not for beauty, but for chastity, and with this in view she has invited applications on behalf of suitable candidates from the most important representatives of the village community (the vicar, the schoolmistress, the mayor and the superintendent of police) whilst commanding her housekeeper to assemble all the available gossip.

Act I

Scene 1: Not one of the suggested candidates has escaped the breath of scandal and Lady Billows is outraged. The situation is saved by Superintendent Budd, who proposes that a May King be substituted in the form of Albert Herring, a backward young man utterly dominated by his mother who keeps a greengrocer's shop. The vicar, asked for his opinion, sings the delicious aria "Is Albert virtuous, yes or no ? " in praise of virtue for its own sake[1], and Budd's proposal is unanimously accepted during a fugal ensemble.

Scene 2 establishes the gauche figure of Albert, an object of scorn to the village children, and of amused pity to Sid and Nancy, two amorous young people of about Albert's age. They flirt in front of Albert's eyes and arouse unknown desires and wistful dreams which, on his being left alone in the shop, he strives to express. His visions of emancipation are interrupted firstly by the matter-of-fact necessity of serving a customer, and secondly by the deputation of the committee from Scene 1, which announces the honour Albert has had bestowed upon him as a result of his virtue and simplicity. A keen sense of the ridiculous position into which he has been forced by his shyness stirs Albert to show the first signs of initiative, and no sooner has the deputation departed than he opposes his mother, whose gratification has known no bounds. In the ensuing struggle he naturally loses, much to the delight of the village children who renew their taunts; but the seeds of rebellion have been sown.

[1] Cf. Maupassant: "What do you wish to reward, Madame Husson? Virtue, I take it, virtue pure and simple. In that case, what does it matter to you whether its exponent be male or female? Virtue is eternal, and knows neither country nor sex. Virtue is simply virtue."

[This is the beginning of the main deviation from the Maupassant story, in which Isidore, the equivalent figure to Herring, remains entirely acquiescent at this juncture: "When Isidore received the intimation, he blushed deeply, and seemed pleased."]

ACT II

Scene 1 of Act II needs no elaboration, being entirely concerned with last-minute preparations and the May Day feast itself, complete with speeches. Each character is given an opportunity to shine (with the possible exception of Albert himself, whose turn is yet to come) and is depicted to the point of caricature by librettist and composer alike. As essential to the plot, it is only necessary to record that Lady Billows presents Albert with a prize of twenty-five sovereigns, and that Sid and Nancy lace his lemonade with rum when no one is about.

Scene 2 contains the kernel of the opera. Albert has returned home alone and in a long solo *scena* suffers a gradual psychological change, which is accelerated by his accidentally overhearing Sid and Nancy discuss his problems in the street outside. Here the deviation from the original becomes more important. Maupassant covers the scene as follows: "Who knows, who can tell, what grim struggle raged in the Rose King's soul between the powers of good and evil; with what headlong attacks, stratagems, and temptations Satan beset that timid and virgin heart; what suggestions, images and desires the Evil One conjured up, to compass the ruin of that elect soul?" Compare with the irony of this, Herring's devastatingly bitter soliloquy: "Nancy pities me! Sid laughs! Others snigger at my simplicity—offer me buns to stay in my cage; parade me around as their white-headed boy! 'Albert the Good!' Albert who Should! Who Hasn't and Wouldn't if he Could! Albert the Meek! Albert the Sheep! Missus Herring's Guinea-pig! . . . But when shall I dare and dare again? How shall I screw my courage up to do what must be done by everyone?"

Whatever the differences in the psychological approach, the consequences are the same. Albert discovers his prize money which he has forgotten in the excitement, hesitates for a few moments, and then making up his mind slips out into the night. His mother, all unsuspecting, returns to an empty house.

ACT III

It is the afternoon of the following day and the entire neighbourhood is searching for Albert, while Nancy tries to comfort Mrs. Herring who, however, is indulging her grief to the full. After false alarms the discovery of the battered remains of the orange-blossom wreath from Albert's coronation hat is accepted as sufficient evidence of his decease and the serious and deeply moving *Threnody* is sung.

At this point Crozier's departure from Maupassant takes full effect. A dishevelled Herring returns home to find a scene of mourning on his behalf, which rapidly changes into a concerted attack upon his character.

Though bedraggled, he is not, however, blind drunk "and utterly degraded by a whole week of debauchery" as in the story, and before long he retaliates with more self-confidence than he has hitherto been able to show. His emancipation in fact proves to be so complete that Crozier's conversion of Maupassant's week into a single night 'on the booze' seems too radical to have accomplished so much! But this, no doubt, is operatic licence, and as the curtain falls Albert is seen as a kind, jolly, extrovert young man, beloved of the children and respected by Sid and Nancy.

A hint of Maupassant's end to the story (in which Isidore, a confirmed drunkard, dies of *delirium tremens*) is contained in Lady Billows' final words as she sweeps out of the shop accompanied by her retinue: "You will pay for your night's holiday! You will pay for your sins of the flesh. You will creep to the shade of a profligate's grave, a disgrace to your name and your sex."

Technically *Herring* marks an advance on *Lucretia* from various angles. The melodic invention is more spontaneous and inevitable, and such tunes as the children's catch (Ex. 1) at the beginning of Act I, Sc. 2

contain within them the seeds of a new and living folk music. This more recently developed power of Britten's to create first-class and yet truly simple melodies represents one of the surest indications that he will occupy a leading position in the future of music. Other examples of the kind exist not only in *Herring* itself, such as the hymn of praise to Albert in Act II, Sc. 1 (Ex. 2),

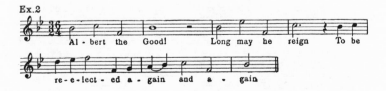

but in subsequent works, like *St. Nicolas*, *The Little Sweep*, and the *Spring Symphony*.

An interesting feature of Ex. 1 is its repetitive treatment above a shifting harmonic base. This invaluable device can already be found in the *Dirge* from the *Serenade*, and stood Britten in very good stead later, when, in the audience songs from *The Little Sweep*, he was bound to preserve the strophic nature of the songs, and yet was enabled to imbue the accompaniments with continuously fresh harmonic interest.

In *Lucretia* Britten tackled the problems of his medium from the standpoint of formal balance and the interplay between small contrasted groups. This is also largely true of *Herring*, but the number of such groups is bigger and far more stress is laid on the relationship between their individual members. Never has an opera been written in which it is more important for the artists, both instrumental and vocal, to work as a team rather than as a collection of potential soloists. This shows itself in two ways: in the first place in the ensemble recitatives where the ball, so to speak, is thrown from one to the other with lightning rapidity, as in the committee scene (Act I, Sc. 1), in the hiccupping episode (end of Act II, Sc. 1), and, above all, in the questioning of Albert (Ex. 3) in Act III:

On the other hand, one of the most striking characteristics of the
work is the use of such contrapuntal forms as fugue, where a similar
collaboration is necessary between the individual performers, and yet
each has a consistently interesting path to pursue. There are, in all,
three extended fugal passages (excluding the prelude to Act III, which
is more imitative than fugal), two of which occur in Act I, Sc. 1:
"We've made our own investigations", in which, moreover, many of
the entries are presented canonically (see Ex. 4),

and "May King! May King! Remarkable position", the finale to the scene, of which more is said below.

The third example is the tremendous instrumental fugue, based on a variation of Ex. 2, which describes Albert's experiences during the feast while under the influence of Sid's rum. This forms the first part of the Interlude between the two scenes of Act II, while the second part displays another aspect of Britten's contrapuntal skill. It consists of a most remarkable two-part invention, set unaccompanied for those favourite instruments of Britten's, the bass flute and bass clarinet. After the rough and tumble of the preceding fugue, such peaceful simplicity is magical (see Ex. 5):

Ex.5

Yet another passage remarkable for its use of strict counterpoint applied with the utmost imagination is Sid and Nancy's duet, "We'll walk to the spinney" (Ex. 6),

which is accompanied not only by a freely moving bass, but, in addition, by an elaborately conceived canon 'two-in-one' on the woodwind.

But easily the most remarkable section, both from the point of view of contrapuntal virtuosity and emotional intensity, is the *Threnody*. It is said that this was originally intended to be no more than tragi-comedy, but it is palpable that Britten's inspiration soon took him far beyond the realms of satire (see Ex. 7):

Ex. 7 becomes a constantly recurring *canto firmo* from which each of the nine voices departs in turn, in order to superimpose a solo counter-melody. At first these counter-melodies differ widely in character, but as the piece progresses they gradually lead into one another, thus supplying shape and continuity to the whole. Finally the ground is abandoned and, over a pedal B♭, the individual melodies are sung together in a gigantic outburst of nine-part counterpoint.

The recitatives in *Herring* deserve special consideration. They show an advance on *Lucretia* not only in the complex interplay between a large number of participants as described above, but also in the technical mastery with which the accompanying skeletal harmony is devised. A particularly fine instance is Ex. 8, drawn from the moment in Act II, Sc. 2, when Albert, home from the party, overhears Sid and Nancy in the street outside:

Note in Ex. 8 the introduction of *Tristan*'s famous chord at the word "rum". This is in fact one of the many references to that significant chord which is here associated with a very different *Trank* from Wagner's! Initially introduced in the form of a more substantial quotation, this humorous stroke is later isolated and treated in the 'repetitive chord' manner already discussed in connection with *Lucretia* (*vide* the hiccupping episode referred to above). Jocular touches of this kind abound in the score of *Herring*, such as the gong-stroke of mock solemnity for *Foxe's Book of Martyrs*, the miniature tragedy of Cissie's aria, the glissando kiss-music, Sid's whistle motif and Albert's imitation of it[1], and so on. Somewhat more elaborate, but no less riotous, is Miss Wordsworth's pitchpipe and her discomfiture at the children's in-attention while she is trying to brush up their little hymn of welcome to Albert in Act II, Sc. 1. No praise is too high for the way Britten has converted into a perfectly contrived and delicious scherzo this example of what critics who like their opera made of sterner stuff describe as 'charade-like' passages.

The use of musical motifs also shows a certain technical advance on *Lucretia*, particularly in the felicitous ways in which they undergo metamorphosis. It represents, moreover, the furthest point towards which Britten has gone up to the present time in the development of this kind of thematic treatment[2]. The motifs are of two kinds: basic motto-themes and themes of special application. The basic themes vary in importance according to the position of their first mention; for example, the most important of all (Ex. 9)

Ex.9

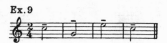

occurs early in Act I, Sc. 1, while the following (Ex. 10), which also acquires very great functional significance, does not appear until late in Scene 2.

Ex.10

---

[1] For a further example in Britten of this unexploited medium, see Ex. 15 in *The Choral Music*, p. 100.—EDS.

[2] This chapter was written before the first performance of *Billy Budd*.—EDS.

It might have been expected that one of the most important of the basic motifs would supply a direct characterization of the figure of Albert himself. This, however, is not the case; and when in Act II, Sc. 1, all the characters make their several entrances, Albert, the most important, is the one figure who is not greeted in the orchestra by some salient phrase associated with his earlier music. The subtlety behind the apparent omission lies in the fact that both Exx. 9 and 10 refer indirectly to a phase in Albert's development, the progress of which is observed through the impinging of these and certain other themes (as, for instance, Ex.2) upon him. For Ex. 10 depicts the bustling tyranny which Albert's Mum exercises over her wretched son, while the fanfare-like Ex. 2 stands for the May Day celebrations through which his emancipation comes about.

Ex. 9 is first heard when, in the first scene of the opera, Lady Billows expounds her plans for the crowning of a May Queen (see Ex. 11):

It is important to observe that the theme is delivered against a background consisting of a variation of the fugal subject, Ex. 4. At the end of the scene, Ex. 9 is itself worked fugally (this being the finale "May King! May King!" already referred to above), while it dominates Act II throughout. In the first scene of this act it rings forth majestically either as a horn solo (Ex. 12),

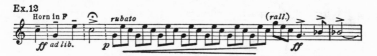

or as a resounding carillon, while overt references to it can often be heard in the texture of the music.

In the second scene it is again predominant, but in a very different guise (Ex. 13):

Ex.13

This outstandingly beautiful transformation is closely associated with the music of the two-part invention (Ex. 5), as the continued use of the bass woodwind instruments suggests.

Ex. 10 is rather more direct in its application, and is accordingly developed with considerable thoroughness on the occasion of its first appearance. This naturally coincides with the initial arrival of Mum immediately before what has come to be known as the 'annunciation', the passage in which the Festival Committee bring the news of his impending glory to a dumbfounded Albert. True to its characterization of a woman who will never allow anyone to get a word in edgeways, Ex. 10 has a positive genius for combining with any other theme which might be around. The first victim is Ex. 9 (*vide* Miss Pike's "We shall get on much quicker if you will be silent . . ."), the next, not unnaturally, Albert himself. Albert's gripping battle with his Mum at the end of Act I (see Ex. 14) works up by developing Ex. 10 together with the theme[1] of Albert's first soliloquy

Ex.14

and culminates in the mocking return of the children's catch (Ex. 1). As can be seen from the shape of the musical figure, Ex. 10 is less

[1] See Ex. 16 in *The Musical Atmosphere*, p. 22.—EDS.

adaptable than Ex. 9 for far-reaching transformation, but it proves itself capable of much colourful variation, especially by the use of augmentation and diminution, as Albert's harangue (Ex. 15), shortly before the end of the opera, shows very clearly:

A lesser kind of basic theme, but vitally important from a formal standpoint, is that which holds together the overall structure of one of the scenes or major sections of an act. The children's catch (Ex. 1) fulfils this purpose for Act I, Sc. 2, by providing a thematic frame, and extends its unifying function by reappearing at the very end of the entire opera, where its development is carried a stage further.

Exx. 5 and 13 together perform a similar duty for Act II, Sc. 2, while for Act III Britten invented a simple rhythmic figure (Ex. 16) typifying the turbulent search of the whole village for the missing Albert. Dominating the prelude to the act, it recurs at intervals over a wide period, and connects all the sections of which the music is made up until the reappearance of the delinquent is established.

Little description need be given of the long list of themes of special application. These correspond for the greater part to the different characters, generally being built out of some striking phrase from their vocal line or its accompaniment. The references to these themes at later stages of the opera are self-evident.

But recognition of this considerable motivic interplay throughout the opera should not blind one to the very large number of wholly independent sections which, consisting equally of arias and ensembles, constitute a substantial portion of the score. The most moving of these are Albert's second soliloquy from Act II, Sc. 2, "Why did she stare, each time I looked up at her?" and Nancy's constantly interrupted aria from Act III, "What would Missus Herring say?" which has great pathos, and to which further intensity is given by the beautiful cadenza-like clarinet obbligato[1].

This freely contrived accompaniment is wholly typical of the instrumentation of *Herring*, in which one continually finds that emphasis is laid on the soloistic treatment of the instruments. For example, the double bass solo which accompanies Budd's speech in Act II, Sc. 1 ("I'm no great shakes as a speechifier") requires a performer of quite unusual skill; indeed Britten seems to have taken exceptional trouble to ensure that each player has passages in which he or she can shine. Moreover, a further unconventional feature of *Herring* is the intrusion of various members of the orchestra upon certain passages of *recitativo secco*, and it might even be said that the part for the conductor is itself of a virtuoso nature[2], for there is no doubt that very quick thinking is required if all is to go well during the Festival Committee's suggestions in Act I, Sc. 1.

This is not to say that the treatment of the orchestra as a whole is less than remarkable. On the contrary, in *Herring* Britten profited by the less stern subject to make some astonishing and most original colouristic experiments with his splendidly selected ensemble. In this connection the Interlude in Act I springs to mind, or the following passage (Ex. 17) from Act III, which, for delicacy and imagination, has

[1] See *The Musical Atmosphere*, pp. 35f., Ex. 31.—EDS.
[2] It will be remembered that, like *Lucretia*, *Herring* is conducted from the piano.

yet to be surpassed even by Britten himself. (Note, by the way, the amusingly prosaic words to which this highly sophisticated web of sound is set!)

Ex. 17

NORMAN DEL MAR

The Chamber Operas

III. *THE BEGGAR'S OPERA*

BRITTEN composed his realization of *The Beggar's Opera* in 1948, one year after the production of *Herring*.

Controversial as is much that Britten writes, nothing that he has produced so far has received such varied criticism as the 'Beggar'. This is doubtless a result of the additionally controversial nature of the subject itself since it is, paradoxically, one of his very finest works. This must not be taken to imply that there are no problems contained within it. Indeed, as will be seen in due course, Britten himself has indicated that he considers some of the fundamental problems not yet fully solved to his satisfaction.

Although Gay's libretto is so well known that it is unnecessary to dwell on the action of the piece, there are a number of features and variations of the text which arise in connection with this new version and which require discussion. In the preparation of the work both for production and publication, Britten collaborated with Tyrone Guthrie, who had much to contribute of interest and value. The basis on which the two men worked is described in a prefatory note to the vocal score:

> The original edition of John Gay's ballad-opera included sixty-nine songs, or bits of songs, and much more dialogue than is printed here. Only three of his songs are omitted from this version. . . . The production of this new version sprang from a hint given in the original Prologue to the play, which stated that the opera had previously been performed in the beggar's "great room at Saint Giles", to celebrate the marriage of two ballad-

singers. Accordingly the producer and the composer planned to stage the opera in this 'great room', which they imagined as a laundry frequented by beggars, who worked there in return for food and warmth.

A permanent setting of this laundry was the scene of the performance: all changes of scene were made by the swift adjustment of screens and furniture in full view of the audience. This was done by the beggars for whose entertainment the opera was being given, and who took part in the action as stage-audience, as chorus and as small part performers.

This way of presenting the opera demanded the rewriting of some parts of the text, and the insertion of a few extra speeches. The additional dialogue was written by the producer, Mr. Tyrone Guthrie, and is distinguished from the original text in this edition by being printed in italics.

It will be seen from this that some liberties were taken with the original. These are less radical than might be anticipated, amounting to a few minor omissions, two direct revisions, and some interpolations of rarely more than a line or so.

The omissions resolve themselves primarily into the excision of seven short scenes—two from the original Act II[1], the remainder from Act III—as follows:

(1) Gay's Act II, Sc. 6, thus giving far greater effect to the curtain after Macheath's arrest.

(2) Act II, Sc. 5, which again provides a more dramatic curtain to the end of the act. This, by the way, was the only cut which involved the loss of an air ("The Lass of Patie's Mill"), but the excision was amply justified by the opportunities it presented for Britten's exciting finale, into the action of which Guthrie incorporated the chorus and showed Lucy releasing Macheath from prison; in Gay's version this accomplishment was presumed to take place between Acts II and III.

(3) Act III, Scenes 3 and 4. Scene 3, though highly entertaining, is invariably omitted in performance for reasons which the most superficial examination will make clear. Filch's métier in life only goes to prove that one can have too much of a good thing.

---

[1] It is necessary to refer to the original Act II since Guthrie and Britten juxtaposed the divisions between the acts, making Scenes 1 to 7 of Act II into a second section of Act I, while Act II now starts with the scene in Newgate Prison. In view of the large number of scene changes in Act II, this was a wise decision, but threw some new problems into the lap of Act I (see p. 167).

The following scene contains the Lilliburlero which was so dear to the heart of Uncle Toby[1]. The amount of original dialogue retained in this scene has never ceased to vary; indeed at one time Britten's setting of the air was in two sections and encompassed a major portion, if not the whole, of the text. In view of the great length of the act and the number of scene changes, this proved too cumbersome in performance, and one of the first somewhat radical stages of the revision is shown in the printed score. The entire dialogue of the scene is now cut, leaving only the air (to which Britten has attached a new and most sensitive ending), while the *mise en scène* is partially rescued from its otherwise isolated and inexplicable state by a short but ranting tirade from the Beggar ("Our scene doth represent a Gaming House. Lords and fine gentlemen at play—and women, too—lewd sluts"). A further solution, recently applied, consisted of resubstituting no more than Macheath's opening lines, since these have the dual advantage of explaining concisely not only the presence of Ben and Mat, but also the song's reference to "the Modes of the Court". This is one of the main instances where the published version does not represent the composer's final word on the subject.

(4) Act III, Sc. 12. This short scene, which stands between Macheath's arrest and his *scena* in the condemned cell, contributes nothing to the situation and, moreover, seriously holds up the action at a crucial moment. Its original purpose may have been to facilitate the change of scene, but in the present circumstances this is no longer necessary and the excision enables the music to run continuously at this point. As will be seen, Britten does not allow this opportunity to slip past him.

(5) Act III, Scenes 16 and 17. This cut, which also comes under the heading of a revision, was a positive inspiration that never fails to come off in performance. The original text supplies a somewhat mannered device (although not without its bitter shafts of irony), while Macheath's choice between his wives and his affirmation of the validity of his marriage with Polly are terribly lame. The splendidly virile scene which Guthrie substituted—many lines of which are, in fact, drawn from the original—keeps up a superb tension until the final curtain.

The remaining omissions consist of isolated lines, or short dialogues, such as are cut in any normal production of a play.

The majority of Guthrie's interpolations consist of brief lines given

[1] In Sterne's *Tristram Shandy*.

to the Beggar in order to cover the public scene-changing within the single basic set demanded by this conception of the original scheme. None impinge on the musical sections; they can thus be omitted at will. The particular importance of the interpolations lies in the indication they give of the underlying attitude to the whole work. They are, as has already been suggested in connection with the Lilliburlero, predominantly aggressive and in the unmannered slang of the 18th-century lower classes (viz. "Lend a hand, you trapesing, trolloping maypole you!" or: "Away! Screech owl! Away and hang yourself in your own garters!") In other words, the version is based fundamentally on realism, an approach consistently adopted by Britten in his realization.

Since the opera was in no way to be a stylized 18th-century 'period piece', the Handelian Overture of Dr. Pepusch was abandoned and in its place Britten composed a pot-pourri in which the principal melodies are developed, sometimes separately, often in combination, as the various characters with which they are connected appear on the stage and set the scenery.[1] (This involves the only other important revision, since Guthrie now abridged and rewrote the prologue, adding a short speech for the Beggar to link the new Overture and the opening number.)

As stated in the preface quoted above, Britten realized no fewer than sixty-six of the original sixty-nine airs, and his was the first version to employ anywhere near so many of the songs. One might be inclined to regret the absence of the last three once the goal of absolute completion had been so closely achieved. "The Lass of Patie's Mill" was, as has already been pointed out, sacrificed to the far greater dramatic effect of Guthrie's curtain to Act II, for which the "Irish Howl" ("Horay in Amborah") was extended into a most thrilling finale. But the reason for the omission of the other two airs is less clear, except possibly on the grounds of overall length and continuity (particularly applicable in the case of "Now Roger, I'll tell thee" from Act III). In the course of time perhaps Britten might be persuaded to make settings of these last airs which could appear as an appendix to later editions, together with Nos. 5, 10 and 11 from Act I. These latter, although contained in the published score, were jettisoned at an early stage in the

---

[1] In subsequent productions this device was actually abandoned, though Britten's highly ingenious Overture was retained. The fact that this continued to be entirely satisfactory after its *raison d'être* had been abolished is of the utmost significance in assessing the value of Britten's score.

work's life—a result of the redistribution of the acts referred to earlier, which threw too great a weight on the first act if it was to be played uncut. This is a further important place where the printed edition cannot be taken as the definitive version.

Britten's realizations range from the supplying of original accompaniments, to elaborate operatic forms such as melodramas, scenas and finales based on one or more of the tunes. In view of the complexity of the work, a briefly descriptive table of the airs may be of value:

ACT I

NO. IN ORIGINAL	NO. IN BRITTEN	TITLE	CHARACTERS	KEY	SETTING	GROUP
1	1	Through all the employments	Peachum	Transposed	Straight (canons, etc.)	I
2	2	'Tis woman that seduces	Filch	Original	Straight	I
3	3	If any wench Venus' girdle wear	Mrs. Peachum	Original	Straight	I
4	4	If love the virgin's heart invade	Mrs. Peachum	Original	Straight	I
5	5	A maid is like the golden ore	Mrs. Peachum	Original	Straight	I
6	6	Virgins are like the fair flower	Polly	Original	Introductory Melodrama and link Coda. Tune straight	V
7	7	Our Polly is a sad slut!	Mrs. Peachum and Chorus	Transposed	Straight tune in elaborate setting	IV
8	8	Can love be control'd	Polly	Original	Straight	I
9	9	O Polly, you might have toy'd	Mrs. Peachum, Polly and Chorus	Original	Straight in elaborate setting	IV
10	10	I, like a ship in storms	Polly	Transposed	Straight	I
11	11	A fox may steal your hens	Peachum and Mrs. Peachum	Original	Straight canon	I
12	12	O, ponder well!	Polly	Original	Straight	I
13	13	The turtle thus with plaintive crying	Polly	Original	Straight with separated phrases	II
14	14	Pretty Polly, say	Polly, Macheath and Chorus	Original	Introductory Melodrama and elaborate setting	V
15	15	My heart was so free	Macheath	Original	Straight with separated phrases	II
16	16	Were I laid (Over the hills and far away)	Polly, Macheath and Chorus	Original	Straight in elaborate setting	IV

NO. IN ORIGINAL	NO. IN BRITTEN	TITLE	CHARACTERS	KEY	SETTING	GROUP
17	17	*O what pain it is to part!*	Polly	Transposed	Straight	I
18	18	*The miser thus a shilling sees*	Polly and Macheath	Original	Free in elaborate setting (extra verse)	IV

ACT I, SCENE 2 (ORIGINAL ACT II)

NO. IN ORIGINAL	NO. IN BRITTEN	TITLE	CHARACTERS	KEY	SETTING	GROUP
19	19	*Fill ev'ry glass*	Chorus (men)	Original	Elaborate setting	IV
20	20	*Let us take the road*	Chorus (men)	Original	Elaborate setting with separated phrases	IV
21	21	*If the heart of a man*	Macheath	Original	Straight	I
22	22	*Youth's the season made for joys*	Macheath and Chorus (ladies)	Original	Introductory Melodrama and elaborate setting	V
23	23	*Before the barn-door crowing*	Chorus (ladies)	Original	Straight with elaborate Coda	IV
24	24	*The gamesters and lawyers*	Chorus (ladies)	Original	Elaborate setting with separated phrases and Coda	IV
25	25	*At the tree I shall suffer*	Macheath	Transposed	Straight	I

ACT II (BRITTEN)

NO. IN ORIGINAL	NO. IN BRITTEN	TITLE	CHARACTERS	KEY	SETTING	GROUP
26	26	*Man may escape from rope and gun*	Macheath	Original	Tune elaborated in straight setting	III
27	27	*Thus when a good housewife*	Lucy	Transposed	Straight with free Coda	III
28	28	*How cruel are the traytors*	Lucy	Transposed	Straight with Introduction and free Coda	III
29	29	*The first time at the looking-glass*	Macheath	Original	Straight with free Coda	III
30	30	*When you censure the age*	Lockit	Original	Straight with free Coda	III
31 } 32 }	31 {	*Is then his fate* *You'll think e'er*	} Lucy and } Lockit	{ Transposed } { Transposed }	Free combination } setting	} VI
33	—	*If you at an office*	NOT IN BRITTEN			
34	32	*Thus when the swallow*	Polly	Transposed	Straight	I
35 } 36 }	33 {	*How happy could I be* *I'm bubbled*	{ Lucy, Polly and Macheath	{ Original { Transposed	{ Free combination } setting	} VI

NO. IN ORIGINAL	NO. IN BRITTEN	TITLE	CHARACTERS	KEY	SETTING	GROUP
37	34	*Cease your funning*	Polly and Chorus	Transposed	Straight in elaborate setting	IV
38	35	*Why how now, Madam Flirt!*	Lucy and Polly	Original and Transposed	Straight with elaborate Coda	IV
39	36	*No power on earth (Horay in Amborah)*	Ensemble and Chorus	Transposed and Modulating	Elaborate setting with extended Coda	V
40	—	*I like the fox*	NOT IN BRITTEN			

ACT III

NO. IN ORIGINAL	NO. IN BRITTEN	TITLE	CHARACTERS	KEY	SETTING	GROUP
41	37	*When young at the bar*	Lucy	Transposed	Straight with separated phrases	II
42	38	*My love is all madness*	Lucy	Transposed	Tune elaborated in straight setting. Introduction and Coda	III
43	39	*Thus gamesters united*	Lockit	Transposed	Straight with few separated phrases	II
44	40	*The modes of the court (Lilliburlero)*	Macheath and Chorus	Original	Introductory Melodrama, eleborate setting and Coda	V
45	41	*What gudgeons are we men!*	Lockit and Peachum	Original	Tune elaborated with free Coda	III
46	42	*In the days of my youth*	Mrs. Trapes	Transposed	Straight in elaborate setting with separate Coda leading to 43	V
47	43	*I'm like a skiff*	Lucy	Transposed	Straight with Melodrama, Introduction and Coda	III
48	—	*When a wife's in her pout*	NOT IN BRITTEN			
49	44	*A curse attends a woman's love*	Lucy and Polly	Transposed	Straight setting with free Coda	III
50	45	*Among the men, coquets we find*	Polly	Transposed	Straight with separated phrases	II
51	46	*Come, sweet lass*	Lucy	Transposed	Straight with separated phrases	II
52	47	*Hither, dear husband*	Lucy and Polly	Original	Straight	I
53	48	*Which way shall I turn me?*	Macheath	Original	Straight	I
54	49	*When my hero in court appears*	Polly	Original	Straight with separated phrases	II
55	50	*When he holds up his hand*	Lucy	Transposed	Straight with separated phrases	II
56	51	*Ourselves like the great*	Lockit and Peachum	Transposed	Free canonic treatment of tune in simple setting	IV

NO. IN ORIGI- NAL	NO. IN BRITTEN	TITLE	CHARACTERS	KEY	SETTING	GROUP
57	52	The charge is pre- prepared	Ensemble and Chorus	Transposed	Elaborate setting with big Coda from No. 3	V
58		O cruel, cruel case!	Macheath	Original		
59		Of all the friends	,,	Transposed		
60		Since I must swing	,,	Original		
61		But now again my spirits	,,	Transposed		
62	53	But valour the stronger	,,	Original	Nos. 58-66 are all worked as a con- tinuous Scena connected by the Ground of No. 67	VI
63		If thus a man can die	,,	Transposed		
64		So I drink off this bumper	,,	Transposed		
65		But can I leave	,,	Transposed		
66		Their eyes, their lips	,,	Original		
67		Since laws were made (Greensleeves)	,,	Transposed	Straight Chaconne (closing move- ment of Scena)	
68	54	Would I might be hanged	Lucy, Polly and Macheath	Original	Elaborate setting	IV
69	55	Thus I stand like the Turk	Ensemble and Chorus	Original	Virtually straight with free Coda	V

It is clear from the above chart that the variety and resourcefulness of Britten's settings are very great, and that every degree of strictness and freedom of treatment is represented. Nevertheless, allowing for a few borderline cases, it is possible to classify the airs into some six groups of ascending complexity:

I. Straight settings

There are no less than fifteen of these, including, for simplicity's sake, four in which the air itself is very slightly amended[1]. The accompaniments are, as might be expected, similar in style and taste to Britten's already famous folk song settings. Even within this simplest category there is an astonishing variety, ranging from the suave

---

[1] Since the airs are largely traditional, this probably comes about as a result of the choice of some alternative source other than was available to Gay or Dr. Pepusch.

harmonizations of " 'Tis woman"[1] (No. 2), and "If love the virgin's heart" (No. 4), to freely imaginative numbers such as Macheath's tirade "At the tree I shall suffer" (No. 25; see Ex. 1):

The gradations in between these extremes include settings which feature contrapuntal ingenuities, whether elaborate as in "Through all the employments of life" (No. 1), or fully executed canon as in the duet "A fox may steal your hens" (No. 11); settings in which the background consists exclusively of the development of some entirely original figure calculated to provide the necessary histrionic effect (the best example of this is Lockit's "Thus gamesters united" (No. 39[2]), where the savage cruelty of the Prison-keeper is caught superbly), and lastly, settings which are rendered utterly moving in their simplicity by some strikingly original touch of harmonic, or instrumental, character (see Ex. 2).

[1] The alternative version of Filch's air, in which the vocal line is split up between the Ladies of the Town, should not have appeared so prominently in the vocal score. It was a mere expediency to meet the problem arising from the fact that the part of Filch was taken by a baritone when this version was first performed.

[2] Since it is Britten's version which is under discussion, his numbering is used throughout in this section of the chapter.

II. Straight settings, but with the phrases of the air spaced apart

These are not far removed from the first group, especially in the case of the simpler examples of the kind, such as Polly's and Lucy's adjacent ariettas "When my hero in court appears" and "When he holds up his hand" (Nos. 49 and 50), but the effect of the device is to emphasize the poignancy of the accompaniments (see Ex. 3):

At the same time, the opportunities afforded for irregular bar-lengths are of immense value in supplying interest to the often too consistently square designs of the airs themselves. Ex. 4 is particularly imaginative:

III. Straight settings, but with the melody itself treated freely

The most obvious instance of this category is Macheath's gloomy prison air "Man may escape " (No. 26), in which the phrase-lengths of the air itself are varied, either by the elongation of functional notes as suggested by the harmonic implications of the accompaniment, or by the repetition of some important word or idea.

This group also includes a number of borderline cases, such as those which are predominantly simple, but have a free and interesting ending, and those which are so free in treatment that they would come into the scope of one of the later categories, were the settings more elaborate.

A perfect instance of the first borderline type is Lucy's "Thus when a good housewife" (No. 27), with its virtuoso cor anglais part (see Ex. 5):

Ex. 5

Comparable is Lockit's "When you censure the age" (No. 30)[1], with its delicious coda.

Another of Lucy's airs, "My love is all madness" (No. 38), provides the best example of the free variety of these borderline cases. With its phrases separated by the extra beats of the frequent 9/8 bars, the air is very similar in treatment to Lucy's later "Come, sweet lass" (No. 46) quoted in the previous group. It has, however, an additional point of interest in the incorporation of "Ungrateful Macheath!", a remark which originally formed part of the spoken dialogue immediately preceding the number, but now frames the air at beginning and end; the splendidly furious cross-accent in which it is set contributes enormously to the effect of the piece.

IV. Settings in which the air is worked into an elaborate, but formally concise, musical scheme

This again is a large and varied category which for clarity requires subdivision into numbers with chorus, and those without chorus but of especial and individual interest.

The use of the chorus (or *Omnes* as it is designated) is perhaps a little unusual, and for that reason its function is described in the

[1] Reference must be made to an important misprint in the vocal score. No doubt the metronome mark ♩=88 was intended to read ♩=88. The composer now asserts that the correct tempo is ♩=108.

prefatory note quoted above. The intrusion of *Omnes* is chosen primarily according to a number's musical requirements and therefore occurs far more often than is dictated by the dramatic situation. This fact is explained by the Preface's suggestion that the chorus of Beggars should be presupposed to be omnipresent even when its members are not officially on the stage in some minor capacity; and in such hauntingly beautiful movements as "O Polly, you might have toy'd and kissed" (No. 9), the famous duet "Over the hills and far away" (No. 16), and above all "Cease your funning" (No. 34)[1], the sound is enhanced immeasurably when, for purely musical reasons, the chorus is sung from the very back of the stage.

In all these numbers the first part, the 'air simple' so to speak, is sung by one of the principals. In Act I, Sc. 2, however, where *Omnes* divide into the Men and Women of the Town, there are two numbers, one for each sex, in which the solo is taken by one of their group. The men's number of this kind, an air taken from Handel's opera *Rinaldo*, has given rise to especial comment on account of the poly-tonality[2] provided by the horn part. It is without doubt one of the most daringly brilliant of the settings (see Ex. 6):

Ex.6

[Ex. 6 cont'd overleaf.]

[1] It is interesting to note that in the 2nd Edition (1728) of the original text (the first in which the airs are printed within the body of the play), this is the only air the source of which, if only the character of the tune or its first words, is not given. It has even been hazarded that in this isolated instance the tune may well have been original, perhaps even by Gay himself. On the other hand, the recent Austin version supplies the title "Constant Billy", which seems to indicate that the omission is mere accident. Such a slip in the printing would be by no means unique since, for one thing, the tune of Air XXVIII is set upside down.

[2] See footnote (3) overleaf.—EDS.

The preceding number "Fill ev'ry glass" (No. 19) is similar in conception to the 'Bell' trio "Would I might be hanged" (No. 54), though the former is choral while the latter is for the three principal soloists. It is fascinating in both numbers to follow the weaving of the original air in and out of the various parts; and the instrumentation of the bell effect in the latter piece should not be overlooked.

An additional feature of not only the two numbers just discussed, but the other choral movements in this category, is the frequent use of free canon; this is an important characteristic, moreover, of some of the numbers referred to above as belonging to the subsidiary group— "without chorus but of especial and individual interest"[1]. For example, the fury of the duet "Why how now, Madam Flirt!" (No. 35) is re-doubled by the brilliant idea of adding a third verse in which the two earlier verses are combined in strict canon at the third above and at the distance of half a bar. Excitement is further increased by a step by step rise in pitch from verse to verse[2].

Another amusingly canonic example, though somewhat freer, is afforded by the delightful duet "Ourselves like the great" (No. 51);

[1] p. 174.

[2] This raises the question of the faithfulness of the version to the keys in which the airs were quoted in the original edition. The table on pp. 167-170 sets out the facts of the matter, from which it will be seen that the original pitch is retained in no less than thirty-five of the airs.

[3] There is an exact, if germinal precedent to this bitonal number in *Herring*, Act II, Sc. 1, where the *D major* accompaniment of Sid's "I'd like to see him go for good" is (likewise bi-rhythmically) contrasted with a later version, again in *F major*, of p. 157's Ex. 12: a scenic parallel (off-stage effect of muted horn) as well as an harmonic, thematic, and instrumental one.—ED. (H.K.).

in this, one of the most startlingly original of the settings, the accompaniment consists of little more than a few flips and gurgles (see Ex. 7):

Ex.7

But the most interesting and profoundly moving of the pieces in this subdivision (if not, indeed, in the whole work) is the duet "The miser thus a shilling sees" (No. 18), one of the many airs omitted from the Playfair-Austin version. Here Britten altered both text and melody to his own purpose. Although the Scotch snap was already implied (but not more than that) by the air's character, Britten not only introduced it into the melody but proceeded to make a feature of it in the accompaniment. As for the text, he decided that a third and new section was needed in order to bring the two voices together for the air's climax and subsequent fading away. In other settings where a similar need arose he had been satisfied with a combination of the two existing verses, but for this occasion Britten felt that such a solution would be inadequate and he prevailed on Eric Crozier to supply the extra lines. These were a conspicuous success and now appear on pp. 58-59 of the vocal score ("The sailor climbs the swaying mast", etc.).

V. Settings embodied in larger musical designs

This section is devoted to those numbers which have extensive introductions and codas built on original matter, though often on motifs derived from the airs forming the main body of the movement[1]. These, too, vary greatly in complexity, the simplest being Polly's "Virgins are like the fair flower" (No. 6), one of the two Purcell airs[2], which is supplied with an Introduction incorporating by way of Melodrama all the preceding words of Gay's Scene 7, and a similarly melodramatic coda which acts as a bridge to the music of the following number. Within these extremities the setting of the air itself is absolutely straight, thus making this number almost a borderline case. On the other hand, in overall outline of form it is not far removed from the intricately worked and large-scale "Pretty Polly, say" (No. 14), the Melodrama of which actually derives its material from Mrs. Peachum's air "If any wench" (No. 3).

The rôle of Mrs. Peachum is, of course, one of the main problems of the work—although of outstanding importance in the first scene, she is never again referred to in the original text. This repetition of her first air's theme is thus well contrived, and anticipates the even more skilful use of it towards the latter part of Act III. By transposing the great chorus "The charge is prepared"[3] (No. 52) to E minor, the original key of No. 3, the similarity of style and rhythm between the two becomes so close that the switch from one to the other is simplicity itself. Britten was quick to realize that from the point of view of formal design the advantage to be derived from the reintroduction of the sinister figure of Mrs. Peachum at the moment of Macheath's downfall would be considerable, while the dramatic effect would be overwhelming. His solution (Ex. 8) was no less than a stroke of genius.

---

[1] A striking exception lies in the cadenzas which precede the Cotillon (No. 22). These are, of course, entirely original, and indulge Britten's penchant for giving the members of the orchestra an opportunity to shine as individuals.

[2] The other is Lucy's "When young at the bar" (No. 37).

[3] Originally a solo air for Macheath.

Ex.8

VI. *Settings in which two or more airs are used in combination*

This category represents the height of Britten's understanding of the requirements of dramatic form necessary for the conversion of a folk piece into an operatic work on the highest artistic level. Twice he fused two of the airs into a single number though, be it noted, for opposite reasons. In one instance he accentuated the bitter contrast between the moods of the two airs, while in the other he profited by the similarity between them. The first example is Lucy's "Is then his fate decreed, Sir?" (No. 31) which merges into Lockit's "You'll think e'er many days ensue". Lucy persistently reiterates her opening phrase at each gap in Lockit's melody, ultimately breaking into a continuous and freely expanded outburst on this same figure; then, giving way entirely, she leaves her cruel father to finish his malicious refrain alone.

The second of these fusions is a *tour de force* of rhythmic subtlety. The first tune "How happy could I be with either" (No. 33; one of the best known, incidentally, in the whole work) is reduced to 21/8 in a pulse of 3+2+2, the other to 27/8=2+2+3+2 (Ex. 9):

Ex. 9

It remains only to discuss the most elaborate setting in the entire work—Macheath's great *scena* towards the end of Act III. This presents problems which, for all intents and purposes, have long been regarded as insoluble. Of the ten airs which constitute it, most are quoted by Gay in so fragmentary a state that this was considered reason enough for their omission—not to speak of the inherent difficulty of satisfactorily stringing them together. As before, Britten overcame all the dilemmas with the assurance of genius. He set the concluding air, an unusual form of "Greensleeves", as a chaconne, and then used his newly invented ground bass as a motif to link the preceding nine songs ("or bits of songs" as he himself put it in the preface), none of which he now needed to omit. By varying the routine he avoided the mechanical alternation of air with ground bass motif; twice the airs fit perfectly over the ground, while towards the end he twice moves directly from one air to the next (Ex. 10), thus keeping the now familiar motif fresh for a climactic reappearance in connection with its parent air:

Ex. 10

If one important aspect of Britten's work has so far been insufficiently surveyed, it is the key relationship between the different numbers. The table on pp. 167ff. shows in detail the extent to which the keys of the airs as quoted in the original editions of Gay's text have been retained. Certain features of importance and interest arise therefrom. Firstly, the device must be mentioned which Britten used in order to soften the transition between speech and song, always a problem in 'opéra comique', a genus of which this realization of *The Beggar's Opera* is a true example. For this transitional purpose a very large proportion of the numbers have dialogue superimposed above some suitably constructed opening and closing instrumental passages. Many of these introductions and codas, moreover, are so conceived as to lead to one another despite the intervening dialogue, the listener's musical awareness being maintained, as it were, by some distinctive

harmony or melodic figure. An outstanding instance is the bridge
(Ex. 11) between the settings of Polly's two ariettas "O, ponder well!"
and "The turtle thus" (Nos. 12 and 13):

Ex. 11

De-pends poor Pol-ly's   life

MRS PEACHUM
But your duty to your Parents, hussy, obliges you to hang him.
What would many a wife give for such an opportunity!
POLLY
What is a jointure, what is widowhood to me? I know my heart.
I cannot survive him.

In Ex. 11 the matter was simplified by the original proximity of key
between the two airs. On the other hand, each of the three airs (Nos.
44 to 46) "A curse attends", "Among the men, coquets", and "Come,
sweet lass" has been transposed into keys widely opposed, and yet so
arranged that a single note could form a connecting link between them.
The way in which the note performs a wholly different function in

each of the three keys is another example of the mastery with which Britten executes his ingenious devices[1].

Naturally, however, Britten's choice of keys was also profoundly affected by their suitability for the particular ranges of voice which he envisaged for the different rôles—the most controversial of which was Macheath's. Originally set for a tenor, in recent years it had been sung exclusively by a baritone; Britten then restored the part to a tenor, and since no fewer than ten of the airs in which Macheath takes part involve either ensembles or choruses, this restoration had a considerable influence on the design of the work. Nevertheless, in a recent production Britten himself sanctioned the employment of a baritone and authorized the extensive transpositions and adaptations which thus became necessary. The revisions of the score, which also included some variations of instrumentation, were skilfully effected by Julius Harrison (including, for example, an extended bridge passage between "The charge is prepared" and the great *scena* "O cruel, cruel case" which, of course, required in itself a lion's share of the alterations). However, the resultant preponderance of low voices in the score, together with the increased sombreness of instrumental colour, persuaded Britten that the change had not been altogether successful and he has since expressed the desire that a reversion be made to his original scheme.

It will have become apparent that the differences between Britten's work and earlier versions of *The Beggar's Opera* can scarcely be over-emphasized. As a result, when the Britten first appeared, some em-

---

[1] This point is elaborated by Keller [150]:
"With the entry of Polly, three numbers follow which between them make up the episode between the two girls that leads up to Lucy's poisoning attempt. The airs are therefore linked with one another by means of an interesting diatonic suspense. That is to say, at the end of the duet 'A curse attends a woman's love' in B♭ (No. 44), an ascending chromatic motion leads logically to a D♭ which, however, assumes a mysterious significance in that it is left alone by the harmony, sustained, and not resolved: it ends the duet melodramatically. Our expectancy as to the meaning of this D♭ is roused and, sure enough, it reappears, again singly and melodramatically, at the beginning of Polly's 'Among the men, coquets we find' (No. 45; fl. and str. only). Indeed, at first it seems as if we had already arrived at a (re)solution, for the accompaniment of this song starts off A-flatishly, with the D♭ in apparent dominant seventh function. Anon, however, we find ourselves in E♭, and the D♭, which runs through the air's flute figure, ending up once more as unaccompanied accompaniment to the dialogue, still awaits diatonic elucidation. At last, when we reach Lucy's 'Come, sweet lass' (No. 46, F♯) we find it as (enharmonically changed) dominant in the clarinet figure which again starts and runs through the number. We have arrived—an impression which is reinforced by this tune's having opened the Overture."
Many of the transitional links between the *Spring Symphony's* otherwise (thematically) unrelated movements are based upon a similar procedure: see Stein, *The Symphonies*, pp. 252–256.—ED. (D.M.).

barassment and even antagonism was inevitable, especially in view of the fabulous and long-standing popularity of the Playfair-Austin version dating from the early 1920's. For this, stylized as it was, had become both musically and theatrically the standard by which Gay's masterpiece was judged by a very wide public. Prejudices born of affection die hard, but there can be no doubt whatsoever that the sensitivity, tasteful style, and mastery of Britten's achievement will ultimately establish it as the definitive version of *The Beggar's Opera*, as in fact it is already becoming in the many countries where traditional obstacles have not blunted its impact.[1]

[1] cf. also [157a].—EDS.

GEORGE MALCOLM

Dido and Aeneas

WHEN in the early part of 1951 the English Opera Group announced its forthcoming production of Purcell's *Dido and Aeneas* "in a new realization by Benjamin Britten", there was an immediate sensation and a certain amount of alarm. "What has he *done* to it?" "Does it all sound very modern now?" "Is it true that he's added *whole scenes* of his own?" "Is it *entirely* re-written, or would Purcell still recognize parts of it?" Those who were already familiar with Benjamin Britten's many published realizations of Purcell were, of course, quite undismayed; others, who later saw and heard the actual production, came away reassured. It is to those who are still in doubt that this essay is addressed. The faithful, however, may profitably read on; for, while they already know how little there was to fear, they may yet not realize just how much there was to *do* in preparing this opera for the stage.

The first essential was to establish a workable text, and this in itself was a task of considerable difficulty. Purcell's autograph score is lost and there is no contemporary witness to the composer's original intentions. (The only contemporary document now surviving is a printed libretto, a copy of which is held in the library of the Royal College of Music; it is reproduced in facsimile in the Purcell Society's edition of the opera.) Several eighteenth century manuscript copies exist, of which all save one present an abridged 'concert version' of the work; the remaining manuscript (which appears to be the earliest in date, and is now in the library of St. Michael's College, Tenbury) is the only one to contain the complete opera. These manuscripts bear the usual crop of copyists' errors and omissions, and are widely divergent in detail.

There are already three printed editions. The earliest of these was issued by the Musical Antiquarian Society in 1841 and gives no more than the concert version current in the eighteenth century. Next came the score published in 1889 by Novello for the Purcell Society and edited by Dr. W. H. Cummings, who had previously discovered the Tenbury manuscript and was thus able to produce a version incomparably better and more complete than that of 1841. But, as Professor Dent remarks[1], "he seems to have overrated the value of the concert version, perhaps because at the time . . . there was little or no idea of its ever being put on the stage again." The third and most recent edition, published by the Oxford University Press, is by Professor Dent himself, and in this the Tenbury manuscript is accepted as the chief, indeed, the overriding authority in nearly all the many instances of textual ambiguity.

Benjamin Britten collated and compared all this available material, and, true scholar, personally examined and transcribed the whole of the Tenbury manuscript for himself. His conclusions agreed with those of Professor Dent as to the superiority of the Tenbury readings over all other manuscript traditions. Even the Tenbury MS., however, is often far from satisfactory, containing as it does many obvious errors and inaccuracies. Occasionally these can be corrected by comparison with other versions; but for some passages of the opera there *is* no other textual authority, and the editor must rely on his own taste and knowledge in deciding what were Purcell's original intentions. Whilst it is, therefore, obvious that no definitive text is attainable with such defective manuscript sources, Britten's version represents a scrupulously faithful adherence to every extant indication of the composer's intentions.

There is, however, one element in Britten's treatment of *Dido and Aeneas* which has, perhaps quite reasonably, caused a certain amount of discussion; and this is the so-called 'interpolation' at the end of Act II. The situation is as follows: According to all the manuscripts, and to the editions of Cummings and Dent, Act II ends with Aeneas's soliloquy ("But ah! what language can I try", etc.). But in the abovementioned printed libretto this is followed by the reappearance of the witches, and by a concluding chorus and dance. No music by Purcell is extant for this scene. The original libretto reads as follows (from after the last words of the soliloquy):—

[1] *Dido & Aeneas*, O.U.P., p. iv.

The Sorceress and her Inchanteress

Cho. Then since our Charmes have Sped,
A Merry Dance be Led
By the Nymphs of *Carthage* to please us.
They shall all Dance to ease us.
A Dance that shall make the Spheres to wonder,
Rending those fair Groves asunder.

The Groves Dance

It has so far been taken for granted that Purcell omitted this scene, for reasons of his own. But the only such reason which it is possible to assume is that the scene would constitute a dramatic anti-climax to the wonderful and moving recitative which precedes it. Now to use this kind of argument is to try to interpret the formalized stage-craft of the seventeenth century in terms of the more realistic technique of a modern drama; it is, in fact, an historical blunder. In the seventeenth century, the 'lowering of the curtain' on a recitative, however significant, without the customary chorus and dance to round off the act, would have been unthinkable—quite as unthinkable as *we* should find Wagner's *Tristan* if the opposite procedure were adopted and the *Liebestod* were to be rounded off by a Grand Chorus and Funeral Dance. It is quite true that Purcell was not the man to let a mere convention interfere with his dramatic inspiration, but we must not make the mistake of transporting him right out of his artistic climate. (It is significant that, as late as the middle of the nineteenth century, it was still considered so difficult to end this scene with the soliloquy that, in the Musical Antiquarian Society's edition of 1841, the *Sailors' Chorus* and *Dance* from Act III are pressed into service as the concluding items of Act II!)

For Benjamin Britten, there was another and even more cogent reason to believe that this scene did form part of the original score: Purcell is a rigorous formalist in one respect—that of key-relationship and key-sequence. In an act or dramatic scene by Purcell, the movements are quite as closely related in key as those of any classical suite or sonata. In *Dido and Aeneas* itself, the first scene of Act I begins in C minor and ends in C major; the second scene opens in F minor and finishes in F major. The third act, commencing in B flat major, retains the key-signature of two flats throughout, and ends in G minor. But Act II, as it stands without the final scene, starts in D minor; it continues in that key for some one hundred and forty bars until, at the entry of Aeneas, the minor gives place to the tonic major for a further thirty bars. With the appearance of the Spirit the key suddenly changes to A minor, and it is in this key that Aeneas, less than thirty-five bars later, finishes his soliloquy. To Benjamin Britten it was unimaginable that Purcell should have *intended* the act to finish here, with the whole tonality screaming for a return to the original tonic of D.

The scale, thus heavily weighted, was finally turned by the evidence of the libretto, in which the additional scene does in fact appear. Britten therefore decided to restore it, and adapt it to music composed by Purcell for other purposes.

In the final version, the first four lines of the scene have been allotted to the Sorceress and her two attendant Witches or 'Inchanteresses'. The two remaining lines are sung by the chorus, and the act concludes with the *Dance of the Groves*. (It will be noted that in the libretto itself, the whole six lines are indicated as being sung by the chorus. This, however, is of little significance: the stage-directions of the libretto are in general quite incomplete and throughout the opera Purcell frequently redistributes the lines of the text in accordance with his own requirements, ignoring the marginal rubrics. And if *The Sorceress and her Inchanteress* are not to take a vocal part in the scene, it is, moreover, difficult to see why they are mentioned at all at this point.) Thus the additional scene now consists of three numbers:

1. TRIO (Sorceress and the two Witches):
   > *Then since our charms have sped,*
   > *A merry dance be led*
   > *By the nymphs of Carthage, to please us;*
   > *They shall all dance to ease us.*

2. CHORUS: *A dance that shall make the spheres to wonder,*
   > *Rending those fair groves asunder.*

3. DANCE OF THE GROVES.

For the first of these, Britten has used the trio sung by Envy and his two Followers in Act II of *The Indian Queen* (c. 1690). This in its original form is a trio for alto, tenor and bass, in C minor. In its new setting it is transposed into D minor, and the vocal parts are allotted to two sopranos (the two Witches) and contralto or mezzo-soprano (the Sorceress)—see Ex. 1:

Original text: "What flatt'ring noise is this At which my snakes all hiss?"

The chorus which follows is again a simple transposition, from C major to D major, of the final chorus from the last of the nine *Welcome Odes* (1687)—see Ex. 2:

Original text: "To Urania and Caesar delights without measure."

The Dance has been set to a movement from the Overture to *Sir Anthony Love,* a play for which Purcell wrote incidental music in 1690. This remains in its original key (see Ex. 3):

I maintain that, in the theatre, no member of an audience previously unacquainted with the standard editions of *Dido and Aeneas* can possibly guess that this scene, as it now stands, was not part of Purcell's original score. The adaptations are musically perfect, and the dramatic coherence and balance of the act, far from being destroyed or even disturbed, are immeasurably improved and strengthened.

The text being completed and established, the realization could at last be proceeded with. And here it may not be out of place to correct a popular misconception as to the meaning of this word. Used in a musical context, the word 'realization' carries no merely general meaning, such as 'interpretation' or 'rendering'; it is a technical term indicating the process by which a thorough-bass (or *basso continuo*) is built up, on the keyboard, into a complete and fully harmonized accompaniment. In the seventeenth and early eighteenth centuries, it was not customary to make use of a fully-scored orchestral accompaniment throughout an extended work such as an opera; and in this respect *Dido and Aeneas* is typical of its period. The orchestra as a whole was only intermittently employed, and the remainder of the work was accompanied, in accordance with contemporary usage, by the *basso continuo* alone (usually referred to briefly as the 'continuo' and consisting, on paper, of a single-line bass part). This was to be played by a stringed instrument (in modern practice by a 'cello, with or without the support of a double bass), and at the same time by the harpsichord. But no harmonies were written out, and it was the duty of the harpsichordist to supply them. In this he was often assisted by figures under the bass notes, which indicated appropriate chords. Within the limits imposed by such harmonic directions, the player was free to use his own taste and invention in improvising a suitable accompaniment.

The harpsichordist thus had a truly creative part to play in the performance of a seventeenth or eighteenth century work. It is well known that musicians of the calibre of Bach and Handel (and—no doubt—Purcell) were extremely free in their realizations, both in their own works and those of other composers; indeed, a musician was often judged by the originality and artistic interest displayed in his treatment of a continuo.

Britten's realization of *Dido and Aeneas* is the result of over ten years' intimate and practical acquaintance with Purcell's continuo parts. He maintains, rightly, that the art is essentially one to be learnt and perfected at the keyboard, and in terms of keyboard idiom and technique. If a realization is subsequently committed to paper, it is merely as the record of an individual 'slant', not as a pattern for future imitation by others. Nevertheless, where knowledge, experience and technique are combined with a rare creative talent, it would be surprising if the results were not indirectly instructive—even though we are to eschew direct imitation. I therefore offer no apology for quoting, in conclusion, one or two passages from this new (and as yet unpublished) realization of *Dido and Aeneas*.

Dido's aria in Act I ("Ah, Belinda, I am prest with torment") is written over a ground bass of four bars (Ex. 4)—

—which is repeated twenty-one times: eleven times in C minor as quoted in Ex. 4, then twice in G minor, and finally eight times more in C minor. This was the kind of thing which gave real scope to a good harpsichord player—to superimpose upon the studied monotony of a repeated bass a wealth of harmonic and contrapuntal variations, devised both to support the vocal *cantilena* and to emphasize, sometimes even to anticipate, its dramatic and musical unfolding.

Britten's realization sets the atmosphere at once (Ex. 5):

At bar 17, the gradually mounting tension of the song is echoed by an increased movement in the upper parts (Ex. 6):

In anticipation of the words "Peace and I are strangers grown", a restless dotted rhythm appears at bar 33 (Ex. 7):

At the words "I languish till my grief is known", the sudden and immensely moving transition to G minor produces Ex. 8:

Now comes one of Purcell's greatest dramatic inspirations: Dido's heart-rending cry "Yet would not have it guessed"; and Ex. 9 shows how Britten rises to the occasion:

The emotion subsides, and, as Dido once more laments that "Peace and I are strangers grown", the accompaniment resumes the figure already associated with these words. The whole dies quickly away to that wonderful and characteristic moment where Purcell suddenly, but very gently, lifts the accompaniment from the keyboard, and himself scores for the strings a final exquisite meditation on Dido's grief (see Ex. 10):

Britten's treatment of this aria is an epitome of his style throughout the opera; space forbids more than a few further quotations.

The realization is simple where simplicity is called for, as at the beginning of Act II (see Ex. 11)—

—and passionate as well as adventurous where the dramatic situation demands such treatment, as in the introduction (Ex. 12) to Dido's tragic protest against her fate ("Your counsel all is urged in vain"):

All the devices inherent in the technique of the harpsichord are exploited to their best advantage, as in the typical and appropriate arpeggiandi at the end of Aeneas's soliloquy in Act II (Ex. 13):

Ex. 13

Colourful and characteristic touches abound, such as the trumpet-like figure (see Ex. 14) that suggests the panoply of the departing fleet in Act III:

Ex. 14

Quotations could be multiplied indefinitely, but these few may serve to illustrate the general style of the whole. The harmonic vocabulary is everywhere strictly within the historical terms of reference; and those who shudder at an occasional 'false relation' or unprepared discord had best avoid Purcell altogether. Every bar is dramatically appropriate, and not once in the whole three acts are the composer's expressed or implied intentions ignored. For Benjamin Britten, *Dido and Aeneas* is too great a work to be treated otherwise than with complete fidelity and humility.

This was apparent to all who were privileged to be associated with him in the actual production. In an age of narrowing specialization, it was indeed exhilarating to watch a man who could successfully grapple with the *whole* of a musical job-of-work—as in the great days of Purcell himself, before it became customary to parcel everything out among a committee of 'experts'. In preparing this opera, Britten undertook (not to say 'usurped') the functions of research scholar, textual critic, musical interpreter, dramatic adviser, singing coach, orchestral trainer, and, finally (at the performances themselves) conductor and harpsi-chord-player-in-chief. In all these varied capacities he displayed not only the true inspiration of a great artist, but the minute technical *expertise* of a trained craftsman. In an artistic world that is drifting unchecked towards the final stages of the specialist heresy—which holds the critical, the creative and the interpretative faculties to be separate and incompatible—we should do well to applaud so notable a challenge.

ERWIN STEIN

Billy Budd

HERMAN MELVILLE'S story tells of the handsome sailor Billy Budd, blessed with all virtues of body and mind, who was impressed from the merchantman *Rights o' Man* to be foretopman on H.M.S. *Indomitable*, and who is beloved by the ship's whole company. Wrongly accused of mutiny by the evil Master-at-Arms, John Claggart, he is overcome by his only weakness—a stammer that chokes him. Desperate efforts to speak make his fist shoot out, and inadvertently he kills the accuser. Captain Vere and the officers of the court-martial sympathize with Billy's innocence and youth, but it is war, the mutinies of Spithead and the Nore have only recently occurred, and they pronounce the death sentence which the articles of war prescribe. Though Billy is the central figure, the opera is framed by Captain Vere. It is his eyes through which the events are seen, and his mind that reflects on them. In the *Prologue*, as an old man, he recalls Billy's tragedy and he is pained by the part that he had to play. His memory's vision becomes the reality of the stage and unfolds before us: the scene is on board the *Indomitable*; the harsh discipline and routine of 1797 provide the setting.

Clearly this austere subject demanded austere treatment. Though conceived as a large-scale drama of general human significance, it had to be expressed with limited means. There is no place for women on a man-of-war. The libretto presents the grim story in the terse speech of men on duty. The words are simple, direct and apt, yet the lines contain poetry of a high order. There are also quotations from Melville's own dialogue and in particular from the ballad "Billy in the Darbies". Otherwise the libretto is, of necessity, mainly in prose.

198

To Britten, the restrictions imposed by the subject became a source of inspiration. Faced with an all-male cast, he coped with the limitations of range and timbre by carefully selecting the voices he needed. Beside the principals, Vere, Billy and Claggart (tenor, baritone and bass), there are eight parts of importance in the opera each given to a well-defined type of voice: a trio of sailors, Red Whiskers (buffo tenor), Donald (light baritone) and Dansker (dark bass)—joined by Billy to form a quartet; a trio of officers (heavy baritone, bass baritone and lyrical bass), occasionally joined by Vere; and two more tenors, the Novice (lyrical) and Squeak (buffo). The chorus, of course, also contributes to the diversity of colours and texture, as do a number of small parts. By grouping the voices in a variety of ways, Britten has exploited their contrasting characters. Claggart, the heavy bass, for example, has important scenes with each of the tenors. The ensemble of officers, on the other hand, serves Vere's voice as background.

The unusual vocal apparatus of Billy Budd required a new method of scoring. Tenors and basses have less penetrating power than sopranos. Therefore the texture of the orchestra had to be kept sufficiently transparent. Now Britten's scores have always been distinguished by their transparency. He has always preferred the clean sound of solos, or of groups of similar instruments, to mixed orchestral colours. The *Spring Symphony*, in particular, with its selected ensembles, can be regarded as a forerunner of the *Budd* score. In the opera there was the additional task of blending the wide range of the orchestra with the narrow range of male voices; their sonorities had to be kept in proportion. On the other hand, the warlike surroundings of the drama obviously demanded powerful sonorities. Britten, in fact, employs a very large orchestra, but he uses it sparingly. Woodwind and brass predominate over the strings; their colours seem to fit the character of the opera well. Also, strings are more likely to 'cover' the voices than wind instruments. The crystal-clear tone and the rhythmic precision of the wind allow the singer still to dominate when masses of strings would have drowned the voice. The fiddles do not play first fiddle in *Billy Budd*. Actually, the orchestral part of the first trumpet covers as many pages as that of the first violins, and the parts of the first woodwind players are still bulkier.

Restrictions of a different kind have been imposed on the music by the fact that the libretto is in prose—it was of far-reaching consequence for the musical form. Opera libretti are usually in verse, though paragraphs of prose are often interspersed. Roughly speaking, verse serves for the arias and ensembles, and prose for the recitatives. Lacking metrical symmetry, prose does not, like verse, present the composer with a rhythmic scheme as the nucleus for musical shapes; he cannot rely on the flow of the metre to carry his imagination. On the contrary, the diction of the prose is easily a burden on the growth of melodies, and therefore on the structure of set pieces. Only in the shanties, in the ballads of the last act, and in a few instances of near-verse prose, did Britten derive the musical form directly from the word-rhythms. Otherwise he secured the structure of his set pieces by solid frames of orchestral patterns. In *Billy Budd* the accompaniment is more exposed and dramatically more important than is Britten's wont; yet the pre-dominance of the singers is preserved, and not only by the trans-parency of the texture. Though rarely mere background, the orchestra always serves as foil to the voices. Many set pieces are conceived and shaped so ingeniously that the voice, when it enters, forms the comple-ment to the orchestral pattern. When at the beginning of the first scene the stage is set by the rhythms of the wind instruments, the calls of the First Mate appear as the music's inevitable continuation.

The prose of the libretto might have caused recitatives to abound. The opposite has happened; there is but little recitative in the whole of the opera. Even the calls, commands and reports during the ship's routine are built into the musical context. On the other hand, some of the set pieces are but loosely knit. There is no rigid alternation of compact numbers and free recitatives. Instead we have a sequence of more or less firmly or loosely shaped pieces which are more or less closely joined to each other. To be sure, there are arias and ensembles of compact form whenever the dramatic situation warrants it, but in general Britten has established even in the set pieces a degree of flexibility which allows him immediately to tighten or loosen the form according to the action on the stage. At any moment a suitable line of the libretto may flower into an arioso without impairing the music's consistency.

The music of *Billy Budd* is highly integrated. Certain themes, motifs, chords and rhythms recur as part and parcel of the opera's musical idiom. They are characteristic of certain persons or situations, principles or ideas, and are at the same time the material for the opera's archi-tecture. Similar instances can be found in Britten's earlier operas, as in *Peter Grimes*, where variations on the cadence "God have mercy upon me"[1] dominate some of the subsequent scenes. Yet in *Billy Budd* the integration of the thematic material goes much further and is more than a means of dramatic expression. In a sense, the unusually close coherence of the music makes up for the prose of the libretto. Much of the opera's material is derived from the very first page of the score, though Britten was not even aware of some of the derivations—an interesting example of how a composer's mind works.

An atmosphere of doubt prevails in the *Prologue* (see Ex. 1); Vere's meditation is expressed in an orchestral texture suggestive of his scruples:

The initial thirds B♭–D and B♮–D, and the chord (c) on the same notes in Ex. 1, bar 5, are ambiguous—is the key to be B♭ major or B minor? The *Prologue* closes in B♭, but the first scene begins in B minor; the ambiguity remains unsolved until at the end of the opera B♭ is definitely established. Keys, it may here be said, their individual colour and their tonal relations, are often used both for dramatic and formal purposes.

The groups of notes (a) and (b) of Ex. 1 recur in many guises, in fact, patterns of three notes consisting of intervals of a third and a second, or vice versa, are to be found on almost every page of the score. If we closely inspect Ex. 1's chord (c) we see that it contains in a nut-shell all possible combinations (Ex. 2) of the two intervals:

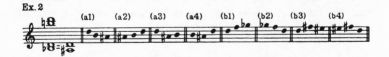

To make the point clearer, B♭ is written as A♯; the patterns under (b) are the inversions of (a), the note D serving as pivot. These patterns are not motifs in the technical sense, because their rhythm is not

[1] *Peter Grimes*—I, p. 109, Ex. 16a.—EDS.

defined, but they belong to the opera's idiom. They may gain any
rhythmic shape, become a real motif or part of it and be varied in many
ways. To quote one single example out of hundreds, the motif (Ex. 3(a))
announced in the first act on the muted brass during Vere's speech
"The French are bold enemies" is taken up in the second act and
appears as Ex. 3(b), and, varied, as Ex. 3(c):

The group (d) of Ex. 1 is another melodic pattern of idiomatic significance. Combined with (a) it yields the motif of Billy's stammer
(Ex. 4):

The first act, less compact than the others, gives the exposition of
the drama and of its characters. The texture of the strings shown in
Ex. 1 alternates at first with rhythms of the brass which, in bar 14,
anticipate the characteristic fourths of Claggart's motif; later the strings
join in the tenor's big melodic phrases. When Vere sings of "the good"
that "has never been perfect", Billy's stammer (Ex. 4) is quoted. At
the end of the *Prologue*, the arioso treatment of the voice drops into
recitative. Then, when the ship's deck becomes visible, we hear the
bustling rhythms of naval routine (Ex. 5):

The many incidents that pass on the stage are held together musically by relentless rhythms and by the working song of the crew (Ex. 6) which recurs refrain-like and, in extended form, closes the scene:

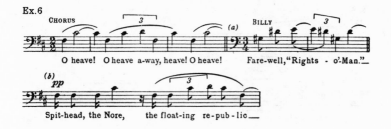

Ex.6

O heave! O heave a-way, heave! O heave!   Fare-well, "Rights - o'-Man."

Spit-head, the Nore,   the float-ing re-pub-lic__

Variations of the working song become important in the course of the opera; they refer to mutiny, suspected or real, and the first occurs when Billy's farewell to his old comrades of the *Rights o' Man* (Ex. 6(a)) arouses the suspicion of the officers.

After a moment of stillness on the B major chord, a play of soft fanfares on the common chord begins to alternate with distant calls. Is it Billy Budd who is heralded? Fanfares and arpeggio figures in various rhythms are to become one of his musical attributes. Here the fanfares, gradually growing more powerful, are the frame for a transitory scene during which Billy and two other impressed men are brought on board. Vocally, there are short recitatives, an arioso for the Sailing Master, and Claggart's smooth phrase (Ex. 7) with his motif (a):

Ex.7

I am   at your dis-po-sal__   Brass

Jem-my-Legs is   down on you!

Harmonic progressions over a pedal B, in sharply marked rhythms on the strings, provide the structure of Claggart's questioning of the men. Their individual replies—Red Whiskers' buffo ariosos, Arthur Jones's dull ostinato and Billy's self-assured singing, though once interrupted by his stammer—form apt divisions of a loosely knit set piece. An important motif arises when Claggart, consulted by the officers, gives his opinion on the new recruit (Ex. 8a):

He is accompanied, as in many later instances, by common chords on the trombone.

Billy exultantly greets his appointment as foretopman in an E major aria and bids farewell to his old life. Here the famous passage from Melville occurs (Ex. 6(a)). The officers advise Claggart to keep an eye on Billy.

Claggart is left alone and his music expands (Ex. 7(b)). E major turns to F minor—it is Claggart's own key, and related to E major as B minor is to B♭ major. There is one particular colour combination representing Claggart: the tonic chord of F minor without the fifth, *pp*, spread over the whole range of the orchestra and tinged by a soft cymbal stroke. Claggart's motif, its inversion, and variations on both, dominate his arioso and the succeeding *presto* duet with Squeak.

The key of F minor is maintained during the lament of the flogged Novice. It is the first extended lyrical piece of the opera, beautiful music, beautifully placed in the centre of the act as the first respite, if a grievous one, after the bustle of the previous scenes. The voices, a trio of tenor, baritone and small unison chorus, are preceded by a ritornello (Ex. 9) on the saxophone, of a strange rhythmic pattern.

A scherzando quartet for Red Whiskers, Billy, Donald and Dansker follows immediately. They are interrupted by the signal "Captain's

Ex. 9
Slow and deliberate

Muster". Vere's motif (Ex. 10), representing the beloved head of the company, is introduced. It is the exact inversion of the motif of the lament (Ex. 9):

Ex. 10

While the men assemble, Claggart tries to irritate Billy and to trap him, but is disarmed by the latter's compliance; his stern recitative turns into the arioso phrase of Ex. 8(a) to the words: "Look after your dress. Take a pride in yourself, Beauty! And you'll come to no harm." During a choral transition the scherzando rhythm of the quartet is taken up, and leads to the finale.

Accompanied by the rhythms of Ex. 5, now dignified and in C major, Vere addresses the crew. His speech is shaped into five sections by entries of the chorus, enthusiastically singing Vere's motif (Ex. 10). Then Billy, with Ex. 8(b), takes the lead of the cheering crowd.

I have tried to outline the expository first act in some detail because the form is very complex. There are eight major sections which may be described as *Prologue*—Working Scene—Transition (arrival of the impressed men)—Questioning Scene—Claggart's Arioso and Duet with Squeak—the Novice's Lament—Scherzando Quartet—Transition (gathering of the crew) and Finale. No more than a few hints could be given of the permanent cross-references between music and drama and of the countless combinations and variations of the motifs.

If the first act gives a picture of the ship's company on their daily duty, the second shows them coming into their own, the officers over a glass of wine, the men singing and dancing. The act is a nocturne, or rather a sequence of nocturnes, ranging from happiness to terror.

The scene of the officers in the Captain's cabin, in conversational tone and amazingly flexible form, comprises three set pieces, a scherzando duet (see Ex. 3(c)) and two substantial ariosos. They are surrounded by recitatives and short arioso phrases during which Ex. 6(b) occurs.

Shanties are heard from below; their tunes form an orchestral interlude at the climax of which the curtain rises on the berth-deck revealing the singing sailors: it is one of the most fascinating moments of the opera. The soloists in turn begin a new gay tune, the chorus joins in and spirits grow high. Suddenly Billy is heard stammering. He has found Squeak meddling with his kit; they fight and Billy floors him at the moment when Claggart appears on the scene. Billy's poise again disarms Claggart and to the melody of Ex. 8(a) he sings Melville's words "Handsomely done, my lad. And handsome is as handsome did it, too." While the men sling hammocks and the tune of a nostalgic shanty continues from the distance, Claggart remains deep in thought. His repeated "Handsomely done" leads to his great aria: Billy's goodness and beauty, to which Claggart himself had for moments succumbed, are shaking his evil mind. He determines to annihilate him.

Two uncanny night pieces follow; they are scenes for the Novice, with Claggart and with Billy. Whispered recitative and arioso phrases, accompanied by loose textures of the softest orchestral colours, are here combined into forms of amazing consistency. The music of Billy's later ballad is the frame of his duet with the Novice and comes in like a lullaby when he slowly awakes. Two new versions (Exx. 11(a) and 11(b)) of the mutiny motif (see Ex. 6) arise:

The act concludes with another duet, for Billy and Dansker. It forms a passacaglia whose theme (Ex. 7(c)), sung by Dansker, is a variation of Claggart's motif (Ex. 7(a)); Billy enters with the melody of Ex. 8(c).

The third act anticipates, during the first few bars, the song and the ostinato rhythm (Ex. 12) which become the backbone of the battle ensemble:

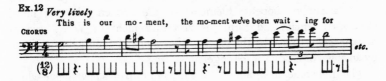

This great, gay and daring scene is in three sections: the growing expectation of the crew; the choral prayer for the wind to fill the sails; and the shot, with the subsequent anticlimax of frustration. The motif of the interfering mist (Ex. 13) is important:

All notes remain sustained so that a blurred, dissonant sound results.

Even before the battle, Claggart has begun to denounce Billy to the Captain. As soon as he continues after the battle, the real drama is brought to the forefront again.

The dramatic reason for placing the battle in the midst of Claggart's calumnious attempt is, I believe, that in Vere's mind the fog and Claggart mean the same evil thing; for let us not forget that we see everything through the eyes of Vere's memory. When Vere has dismissed Claggart and turns to the officers, exclaiming, "O this cursed mist!" they have the enemy in their minds, but he thinks of deeper problems. They are, we may assume, expressed in the subsequent orchestral interlude: the music of the mist surrounds a chorale-like melody, until the blurred chords give way to Billy's clear fanfares in D major.

The curtain rises on the Captain's cabin. Vere's confident arioso and his duet with Billy are followed by Claggart's entry. The melody of the accusation (Ex. 14) is based on the mutiny motif (see Ex. 6):

Ex. 14

Billy, urged to defend himself, is choked by his stammer (Ex. 4) and the catastrophe happens. Elements of the broken Claggart motif (Ex. 7(a)) remain and form the accompaniment to Vere's aria of despair. He is joined by the officers. Vere sings Melville's line " Struck by an angel of God. Yet the angel must hang."

The trial scene, in F minor, is mainly built up on a new theme which opens as a broad and dignified melody of the strings; it is derived from Claggart's accusation (Ex. 14) and from his motif (Ex. 7(a)). When Billy is led back, the theme is inverted—the dramatic effect of the device is telling. An immensely moving trio of the officers follows. Though each voice has its individual phrases they are dovetailed so as to form a single melody. The officers would like to save Billy, but they have no choice; the verdict is (Ex. 15):

Ex. 15

While the officers leave, the theme of the trial is heard on the harp with the dominant chord of F softly held on the strings.

At this moment, Vere's aria in F minor comes in with the inevitability of Fate. To me, the whole tragedy of the opera is crystallized in the poise of his melody, accompanied by the subdued power of four unmuted trumpets, and in the sudden outbreaks of his emotions. He goes to Billy to tell him the verdict. The stage remains empty and a sequence of sustained chords, in fact a huge cadence in F major, is heard. The changing colours seem to convey rapid changes of emotions, ranging, one might conjecture, from surprise to fright—from terror to resignation and composure; and an even higher state of mind is perhaps suggested by the last chords of the divided strings and of the muted brass.

When in the last act, after his slumber song on Melville's "Billy in the Darbies", and after his scene with Dansker and his ecstatic ballad, the cadence recurs, Billy is contented and strong. An orchestral interlude, loosely built from the motifs of the verdict (Ex. 15) and the ship's routine (see Ex. 5), leads to the last scene. The crew assembles during a funereal fugue on a rhythm of timpani and drums. Distinctive themes accompany the entry of various groups of men and officers; when Billy is led in his fanfares are heard; at the climax the motif of the verdict is sounded (Ex. 15(a)). Billy sings "Starry Vere, God bless you!" and is led off to execution. Then, during the climax of a wild fugal chorus based on the mutiny motif (see Ex. 6) the men rise in rebellion, but are quickly subdued. The music recedes and the scene is blotted out.

In the *Epilogue* the music of the *Prologue* is recapitulated against a background of the funereal drum rhythm. Vere, again an old man, concludes the story. He finds contentment in the thought of Billy's fortitude when he blessed him, and he sings quietly the ecstatic ballad tune which had been Billy's farewell to life. Here the tune is combined with the cadence of comfort and ends on the sustained B♭ major chord of the full orchestra. The rhythm of the timpani dies away and Vere alone sings the last few words of an opera rich with beautiful and striking music.

Though limited by cast and setting, the operatic scope of *Billy Budd* is amazingly wide. It includes features that are usually to be found only in the spoken drama. The intimacy of the conversation in the Captain's cabin, or the restrained dignity of the court-martial, with everybody's mind at cross purposes with his duty, is, I believe, new in opera. Here the subtlety and simplicity, the suppleness and directness specific to either of the two mediums, are combined. That music and words do not trespass upon each other's domain is ensured by the soberness of Britten's music and by his realistic attitude towards the words. They are always composed so as to be to the point, and always audible when they need to be understood. The musical diction even compels the singer to deliver them with a nicety of which, in speech, only very good actors are capable. This would not be possible, of course, without the utmost transparency of a flexible texture. In the Novice's night scenes the accompaniment is given to two flutes, solo viola and harp, and later to a trio of two oboes and English horn; there are many other instances in which the instruments are treated in chamber-music fashion. It was indeed Britten's small-scale operas that had prepared the ground; the intimate stage needed flexible forms and transparent textures. When he applied similar principles to certain scenes of *Billy Budd,* the large-scale opera also gained in subtlety. None of its more spectacular features has been abandoned, but operatic expression has been given wider scope.

PAUL HAMBURGER

The Chamber Music

WITHIN Britten's wide scope of musical forms,
the chamber-musical works are relatively few
and far between. They are the *Phantasy* Quartet
of 1932, the Suite for violin and piano of 1934, the two string Quartets
of 1941 and 1945, and the *Lachrymae* ('Reflections on a Song of
John Dowland') for viola and piano of 1950[1]. Yet with the exception
of the light *Suite*, they are all conceived and planned with a seriousness
that earns them the name of major works. The reason for their infre-
quency may be found in the fact that modern many-movement form,
and particularly sonata form, allows of no patent solutions for the

[1] Britten's latest piece of chamber music is the *Six Metamorphoses after Ovid* for oboe
solo, op. 49, the music of which was not available to Hamburger in time for him to
include the work in his chapter. Composed for the 1951 Aldeburgh Festival, it was first
performed by Joy Boughton on the nearby Meare at Thorpeness, player and audience
sitting in punts. It is a real open-air piece written by way of relaxation during the creation of *Billy Budd*. The titles of the movements refer to well-known stories in Greek
mythology:

 I. *Pan*, "who played upon the reed pipe which was Syrinx, his beloved."
 II. *Phaeton*, "who rode upon the chariot of the sun for one day and was hurled
   into the river Padus by a thunderbolt."
 III. *Niobe*, "who, lamenting the death of her fourteen children, was turned into
   a mountain."
 IV. *Bacchus*, "at whose feasts is heard the noise of gaggling women's tattling
   tongues and shouting out of boys."
 V. *Narcissus*, "who fell in love with his own image and became a flower."
 VI. *Arethusa*, "who, flying from the love of Alpheus, the river god, was turned
   into a fountain."

Like Ovid's poems, the movements present dramatic scenes in lyrical form, for which
purpose the expressive tone, as well as the limited range of the oboe, seemed most
suitable. The pieces are short. Left without the support of an accompaniment, the form
of each rests solely on the development of its melody, which is throughout imaginative
and strictly logical. For example, when Narcissus sees his image in the brook, snatches
of the melody are imitated in inversion in the high range of the instrument. The variety
of moods and contrasts of character which Britten obtains in these limiting circumstances is amazing.—EDS.

conscientious composer. To the classical demand for strict *integration*[1] in this form has been added a demand for formal, tonal, if not indeed motivic *progression*[2] in the course of a work, of such refined, and quite unprogrammatic, sensitivity that the composer must needs consider each new 'sonata' a special case whose form has to be re-created according to the requirements of the material. Sonata form, therefore, forces the modern composer who is aware of its risks, to bide his time in a way no other form does.

The *Phantasy* for oboe, violin, viola and 'cello, first performed in London by Leon Goossens and the International String Quartet and given successfully in 1934 at the I.S.C.M. festival at Florence, was the first work to spread abroad the name of the nineteen-year-old composer. Written at a time when Britten's compositions were by no means flawless, this work's invention and form are yet completely mature; with the proviso that about its invention there exists a quality which, as with Schubert and Mendelssohn, can be called 'youthful maturity'. A theme such as Ex. 1b or the oboe cadenzas (fig. 28)[3] would not have been written by an older composer although they youthfully fit the context. The form, on the other hand, would do credit to a composer of any age if, indeed, an older man could bring off this combination of sonata form and phantasy with so unconsciously secure a grasp. This is the lay-out of the long single movement:

Introduction (*Andante alla marcia*) with basic intervals (sixth, third) and with principal theme of work.	Sonata exposition (*Allegro*) with three themes.	Development of sonata (fig. 14).
Development of introduction (*Andante* after fig. 18).	Central section for strings only (fig. 20) on new theme evolved from principal theme.	Return of oboe (fig. 27) in free recapitulation of introduction.
Shortened sonata recapitulation (fig. 30) with new counterpoint derived from principal theme.		Coda: recapitulation of introduction (*Tempo I* before fig. 27) restating principal theme and, at the end, the basic intervals.

[1] Hamburger does not, of course, use the term in Stein's sense (see p. 249) of *thematic integration*.—EDS.

[2] Hamburger does not, of course, identify the term *tonal progression* with Dika Newlin's recent, extremely useful concept of *progressive tonality* (see, *inter alia*, *Bruckner, Mahler, Schoenberg*, New York, 1947).—EDS.

[3] All figures according to Boosey and Hawkes' pocket score.

What Britten has done here is to combine two cyclic structures, one of them a ternary variation form, the other a full-blown sonata cycle. If A^1–[A]–A^2 stands for the first, B^1–[B]–B^2 for the second cycle, and C for the central section—which is, though derived from A, formally a resting-point—we arrive at the following scheme:

$$A^1-B^1-[B]-[A]-C-A^2-B^2-A^1 \text{ (coda).}$$

This scheme severely restricts the composer in his choice of material if unity is to be maintained between A, B and C, but leaves him considerable freedom as to the actual, 'local', relations and bridgings of A, B and C. As with all good phantasies, the description "Phantasy" turns out to be ambiguous: with reference to form, it is an understatement, in the absence of a better word, for a scheme whose inception may be fanciful, but whose realization must, of necessity, be stricter than a single sonata cycle; with reference to detail and texture, it is a challenge to the composer to disguise the rigours of this scheme by the most free and easy manner of realizing it.

The formal problems inherent in the scheme are the following:

(I) Since two developmental derivations are to be drawn from sections A^1 and B^1 ([A] and A^2, and [B] and B^2), the rondo principle of strict contrast between the A's and B's is ruled out, and some motivic link (principle of similarity) must be instituted. On the other hand, monothematicism is out of the question. How far dare one travel in the direction of polythematicism without upsetting the peculiar balance of this double cycle?

(II) If C (which, of course, must also be derived from a germinal theme) is to take the rôle of a resting-place after two developments, the question arises how afterwards to re-enter the cycle progressively, enhancing, that is, not only the stature of A^2 (which has to happen in a single cycle) but also, climactically, of B^2.

(III) How is one to differentiate between the function of A (here always called 'introduction' for convenience's sake) as a main section, giving rise to [A] and A^2, and as an introduction proper and coda to the sonata form B's?

(IV) What is the key-scheme to be? (Part (IV) is, strictly speaking, inseparable from (I) and (II), but is here treated by itself.)

These are Britten's solutions:—

(I) In the course of A^1, the principal subject, a very adaptable tune, is established in four versions of which the second (Ex. 1a) is the most germinal:

The sonata subject of B is Ex. 1b:

The second subject of the sonata is Ex. 1c:

and the subject of section C is Ex. 1d:

A glance at the above formal scheme will show that these are the
main subjects of the work. The differences between them prevent
monothematicism; their inter-relations create formal unity.

The table of Ex. 2 will make their relationship clear; Exx. 1a,
b, c, and d are hereafter referred to simply as (a), (b), (c), and (d):

In this combined example—

(a) is printed in its original form, as a *cantus firmus*;

(b) is transposed a fifth up and has its note-values quartered;

(c) is transposed a sixth up, and the values are halved;

(d) is transposed an eleventh up and fitted into 4/4 time;

(x) refers to the end of (d), being the sequential alteration of the
end of (a) whose possibility is implied by (d);

(y) whose two parts should be read *successively*, derives, in addition,
the intervals of the first part of (d) from a diminution of (a).

It will be seen that these are not the relationships usually existing between theme and variation, but those obtaining—mainly in the classics, and since then largely neglected—between the first and second subjects of a movement, and between the different movements of a quartet or symphony.

(II) At $C \rightarrow A^2$, the little ritornello which served as interlude between the appearances of C proper (in this section, rondo procedures are, of course, permissible) is contrapuntally combined (fig. 23) with C, out of which springs a new form of it very near to (b) (fig. 25). These processes raise our expectations for an early sonata recapitulation, and when, instead, the music calms down and the oboe enters (fig. 27) with a highly embellished version of (a), we understand that now the theme is not to be taken as principal subject, but functions as melodic introduction to the recapitulation of B. As so often with Britten (and Schubert), melodic variation, unexpectedly introduced, partly replaces a formal node and partly postpones its re-modelled appearance. Thus, at the crucial stage $A^2 \rightarrow B^2$, ample space is gained for the entry of B^2 which can now rise from a sufficiently low level of tension. And when the entry occurs, Britten offers another surprise: (b) creeps into the embellished version of (a) (fig. 30), soon gains momentum over the lingering oboe and, sweeping over a mere reminder of (c), pushes right into the coda with its clear restatement of (a) which now definitely resumes its rôle of 'principal subject'. The second part of this work therefore affords an interesting example of progressive formal movement through devolution of motifs: while (a) is devolved from the oboe version to, at the very end, a dry repetition of its basic cell, the form unfolds to the climactic first part of the coda (fig. 32), thereafter only to dissolve:

$$C \; < \; A^2 \; < \; B^2 \; < \; \text{coda (1st part)} \; > \; \text{coda (2nd part)}$$
$$(a) \; > \; (a) \; > \; (a) \; > \; (a) \; \longrightarrow \; (a)$$

$<$ being an increase, and $>$ a decrease, of formal, and again of melodic tension.

(III) Part of the answer is evident from the preceding paragraph. But there is more to it: starting from, and ending on, a repeated minor third in the 'cello, the introduction proper gradually compiles, and the coda proper gradually dissolves, the intervals (major second, minor third, major and minor sixth, major tenth) that go to the making of the principal subject, and therefore of all the themes. The complete (a) in section A¹ and in the coda is a clearing-station between the almost impersonal motivic molecules of the work and the themes that are derived from (a) itself. This clears section A of any duplicity: all later developments of it can be definitely, though perhaps unconsciously, heard as either pre- or post-principal subject.

(IV) Many subtleties aside, this is a sketch of the basic sectional tonalities in a work with many subsidiary modulations:

A¹:	G major with a strong implication of C major.	
B¹:	C minor (Aeolian) [theme (a)], A major [theme (b)];	via C minor
[B]:	Modulatory, viz. D minor, F♯ minor, B♭ minor, D minor; all Aeolian.	
	Roots form complete augmented triad;	via C minor
[A]:	G major with a strong implication of B minor.	
C:	G major and C minor (in interlude); digression into sharp keys;	via C minor
A²:	G major with strong implication of B minor; C minor continues to appear.	
B²:	B minor [theme (a)], C♯ minor [theme (b)], and C minor (ostinato) form tritonality;	via C minor and Gv
Coda:	G major.	

A few reflections on the above scheme:

(1) Britten's flattened (Aeolian) seventh is already in evidence.

(2) The solo F♯ that begins and ends the work can be understood not only as leading-note to G but also as dominant to the prominent third-related[1] B minor.

(3) According to the nature of its form, the variation cycle (A) progresses moderately:

G major . . . G major + B minor . . . G major + B minor + C minor

whereas the sonata cycle (B) progresses rapidly:

C minor . . . modulatory . . . C♯ minor + C minor + B minor → Gv.

(4) The sonata cycle, apart from the motivic influences discussed above, exerts a certain tonal pull on the variation cycle in that the local sequential modulations of A² are modelled on those of [B].

[1] Hamburger here translates, adjectivally, the German term 'Terzverwandtschaft' (i.e. relationship between keys a third apart), for which there is no English or American equivalent.—EDS.

The variation cycle, apart from the motivic influences discussed above, exerts a great tonal pull on the sonata cycle in that the recapitulation of (b) occurs on the minor Neapolitan sixth of section B^1 (C♯ minor), and thus accommodates the B minor which the variation cycle (A) has reached at this point. B's own C minor is still present in B^2, acting as ligament between its own Neapolitan sixth and the key (B minor) of which it is the Neapolitan sixth itself. The two tonal paths and their inter-relations can therefore be outlined thus:

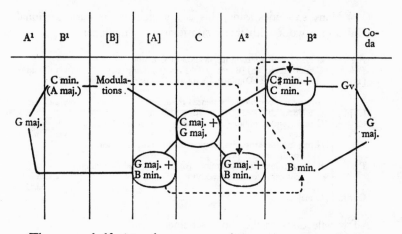

The upper half gives the progress of the sonata cycle, the lower half the progress of the variation cycle; the dotted arrows show their chief tonal inter-relations. At section C and at the coda the cycles naturally unite.

(5) The greater dynamic of the sonata cycle is clear from the fact that its tonic, C minor, is called into action at almost every formal juncture (see the diagram above). It is heard in all these cases as the tonic of section B, and only at the link of the coda (before fig. 31) as the subdominant of the work's basic G major.

It was not until the *Spring Symphony* that Britten employed again, on a larger scale, these subtle procedures of linking up the several movements, and even cycles of a work. Having satisfied himself, at the outset of his career, that he could successfully manage a novel form, he could subsequently devote himself, in his chamber music, to the ordinary four movement work with the certainty that he would not take the classical pattern for granted but could modify it to suit his needs. Since we have now discussed some of his technical methods in our analysis of the *Phantasy* Quartet, we are at liberty to pick and choose points of particular interest in our discussion of the better-known two string quartets.

But before these, there was a diversion. The Suite for violin and piano, written in Vienna and London in 1934–35, and first performed by Antonio Brosa and the composer at the Barcelona I.S.C.M. Festival in 1936, shows the other Britten: the brilliant miniaturist, the sparkling technician, the writer of French and middle-European pastiches which are as loving as they are witty. There is a quasi-Strawinskian *March* (No. 1) that tumbles into and out of angular dotted rhythms with the skilled gaucherie of a first-rate clown, and a *Moto Perpetuo* (No. 2) that puts to shame all the virtuoso pieces of that name and, by the way, vitalizes harmonically a form of *étude* that suffers constitutionally from a surplus of commotion over a paucity of action. In the *Waltz* (No. 4), Britten gleefully points out to us what strange bedfellows are the Viennese *Walzer*, with its lilt and sinuous lines, and the French *Valse*, with its clipped accents and neat tunes: under the common blanket of 3/4 time, they come to blows immediately—an altercation especially amusing when both try to get a word in at the same time, the Viennese waltz in the violin, the French waltz in the piano. But despite all these brilliancies, the Suite falls short even of Britten's other pastiches. Trying to say too much that is really important, he makes us experience here a sense of loss at the serious, or serene, work that has somehow gone overboard. Lennox Berkeley, in his occasional continental pastiches, always avoids this fault: he says little enough, but his mordant irony hits the mark. Thus, the best piece of this Suite is the directly written *Lullaby* (No. 3)—the first of a distinguished series of nocturnes to come.

The first string Quartet was written for the Coolidge Quartet during Britten's stay in America, and first performed at Los Angeles in September, 1941. If the second Quartet of five years later was to be reflective and dramatic, the first is lyrical and exuberant. The work of a nature poet, it yet owes little to the pastoral tradition of the modern English school. For, with all its atmosphere, this music is too near the great tradition of quartet writing to allow folkloristic influences. On the contrary, one is reminded rather of the early, 'northern' Brahms. Britten had at this time an impressionable, romantic mind which, eager to plumb its own depth, subjects itself to form, discipline and tradition, thus gaining validity for its products.

In the first movement, Britten is able to combine lyrical and energetic elements at close quarters thanks to an ingenious handling of sonata form. A slow introduction (see Ex. 3) of soft, bright chords high up in the strings, with *pizzicati* on the 'cello, leads to a sonata exposition whose energetic theme is subtly related to the introduction:

(Compare the numbered notes with those in Ex. 4.)

After such a beginning of complements which follow each other like antecedent and consequent, it is natural that the form should proceed by alternating sections of very nearly the same length:

| Lyrical introduction | — | energetic, worked exposition (bar 25) | — | introduction (82) | — |

| simple, leisurely development (96) | — | energetic, worked recapitulation (144) | — | introduction (coda) (179). |

This is a very original and successful attempt to plane off the top-heavy development and coda of late romantic sonata form by introducing binary elements. Given suitable material, it is perhaps the only way of placing the thematic working out into the exposition and recapitulation. The first subject readily lends itself to imitation and is stated thrice, the last time (Ex. 4) in triple canon:

The second subject (bars 62 ff.) is—brilliantly so—no more than an ornamented ascending scale, capable of inversion and close imitation. Its statement here, and its reappearance in the development, are the only places where flat keys shade off the radiance of the work's basic D major. Otherwise, dominants are piled upon dominants. The introduction is a treatise on how to combine tonic, dominant, and enhanced dominant for long stretches, and the recapitulation starts on the dominant. Even the Neapolitan sixth of the introduction's momentary third-related[1] F major is used, enharmonically, to become D's dominant, thrice enhanced, and thus leading home to D at the structural juncture before the coda (see the extremely daring passage of bars 166–175).

The second movement is a scherzo (*Allegro con slancio*) of the impish-to-boisterous variety; i.e. the four-note snippet that is tossed *ppp* between the instruments, develops into a second subject (*con*

[1] See editorial footnote on p. 217.—EDS.

esagerazione, bars 38 ff.) which carries most of the movement. The phrasing of a good deal of this scherzo is genuinely asymmetric, the modulations wilfully jerky; fast four-instrument unisons alternate with brisk triplet counterpoint criss-crossing the score; trills and drones abound in all the instruments. In short, this is a contemporary application of the scherzo devices of late Beethoven quartets.

The third movement (*Andante calmo*) is a nocturnal sea-piece, foreshadowing the *Moonlight* Interlude of *Grimes*. Its form A^1–A^2–B–A^1–A^2, where A^2 is a long-drawn melody of ravishing beauty (bars 367 ff.) based on the simple ebb and flow of A^2 (viola, bars 325 ff.), does not insist on strict demarcation-lines between its component sections and themes. The middle part B is, on the one hand, a development of A^1 and A^2; on the other hand, it states the major triad from A^1's accompaniment, linking the beginning to the first movement's introduction, as an independent motif of touching simplicity (bar 390). (The strangely plain solo cadenzas of the second Quartet's *Chacony* seem to be modelled on the second, arpeggio-like version of this motif.) There are other, subtler and perhaps more potent, connections with the preceding movements. The ravishing tune of A^2 is the beautiful *alter ego* of the first movement's quizzical second subject; inversion (see Ex. 5) works the wonder:

(The first movement's second subject is here transposed a semitone down.)

The asymmetrical phrasing of the scherzo and the multi-rhythmic scansion of the first movement's first theme (see Ex. 4's two alternative rhythms sketched in under the viola part) are consolidated into the quiet lilt of the slow movement's thoroughgoing 5/4 time. Also, A^1, imperceptibly as it merges into A^2, has throughout the movement the preparatory, and at the same time complementary, function of the introduction in the first movement.

The last movement is a sonata-rondo (*molto vivace*, 3/4) whose wittily abbreviated form sweeps its tunes along, among laughter and shrieks, in ever faster circles—a well-oiled merry-go-round:

| Introduction (fugato) | — | 1st subject (bar 498*) | — | bridge (524) | — | 2nd subject (related to introduction, 532) | — |

| 3rd subject (552) | — | Development on 3rd subject (572) | — | on 2nd subject (588) | — |

| Recapitulation of introduction combined with repeat of 1st subject ('cello) (609) | — | full recapitulation of 1st subject (627) | — | recapitulation of 3rd subject (643) | — |

| bridge (651) | — | repeat of 2nd subject in form of coda (658) |

* of entire work.

As in the first movement, the working-out sections are unconventionally placed. The introduction refreshingly anticipates the laboured fugato that is nowadays being inserted in all rondo recapitulations with such pat regularity. Thus, when the first theme with its triumphant major sevenths and Purcellian cross-rhythms (Ex. 6 (A)) arrives over the continued theme of the introduction in the 'cello, complexity of texture is already yielding to pregnant statement—a thing that ought to happen frequently in a good last movement:

Ex.6

In this finale it happens again, when the second subject group gives way to the plain, yet somehow tenser third subject and when, in the coda, this third subject, extended and played *ff*, epigramatically indicates its relationship to the "beautiful tune" of the slow movement (see Ex. 7):

Ex. 7

As in the first movement (and in the corresponding passage of the second Quartet's first movement) the climactic moment is the beginning of the recapitulation: the first subject ('cello) is pitted against the full force of the opening fugato in the other instruments. Since, again corresponding to the first movement, the development has (sequentially and canonically!) treated the third subject, and then the second, the recapitulation omits the latter which, however, turns up, strikingly enough, to form the coda of this exhilarating piece. It will also be observed that (A) in Ex. 6, is melodically a near-relation of the first movement's first subject (*Allegro*), but that its sprung rhythm derives from the scherzo. This is but another of the formal, melodic and rhythmic links that connect this finale to all the foregoing movements. Another, harmonic one, is that the flattened seventh in (A) is the (Mixolydian) seventh, here rendered melodic, that underlies the first subject of the first movement as an ostinato. Again, as was the case with the thematic material of the other movements, these cross-references, whose associative value naturally increases towards the finale, are by no means programmatic and romantic, but architectural and classical.

The second string Quartet, written to commemorate the 250th anniversary of Purcell's death, was finished on 14th October, 1945, and first performed on 21st November of that year by the Zorian Quartet. It is the best-known of Britten's chamber works. Though admirers of Britten's earlier chamber music will not find it superior to the first Quartet, it cannot be denied that it will make a more lasting impression on the general public. Youthful exuberance, such as is manifested in the earlier works, is often mistaken by the public for an experimental style if it appears in a modern idiom. A reflective utterance, as in the second Quartet, on the other hand, impresses an audience by its authority though the style may be essentially the same and the idiom in itself just as modern. This 'authority' of the second Quartet with its quiet insistence on the validity of classical proportions from Purcell through the classics to the moderns, is best epitomized in the final cadence (Ex. 8) of the first movement,

—an unforgettable moment of reticent conclusiveness[1].

There exists a very comprehensive analysis of this work by Erwin Stein which is attached to the Boosey and Hawkes pocket score, and furthermore an excellent article by Hans Keller in *Tempo* of March, 1947. The latter piece cannot in my opinion be improved upon, and as the issue in question is out of print, I feel it best in every way to quote it in its entirety.

BENJAMIN BRITTEN'S SECOND QUARTET
BY HANS KELLER

The entire thematic material of the first movement is announced at the outset, within less than one third of the exposition. We are thus confronted with an exposition *within* the exposition, and accordingly the structure of the movement reveals the following five main sections:

(1) The (short) first part of the exposition.

(2) The (considerably extended) second part of the exposition.

(3) The development section.

(4) The (considerably compressed) recapitulation.

(5) The (extended) coda.

In the first part of the exposition, the three subjects are announced in immediate succession (see Exx. 9–11). They are given at octave intervals by three instruments while the fourth supplies the pedal of a tenth, which interval is the *fons et origo* (not the *Leitmotiv*) of the whole movement. The tenth forms the root motif of each subject and is subsequently used at the beginning of each of the above-named five sections. At the same time, it assumes a dominant rôle in the

---

[1] Britten's tendency towards understatement is of course particularly active in his codas, whether they themselves are shortened (e.g. in the *Spring Symphony*'s Finale) or extended, as in the present case, where a formally (harmonically) necessary enlargement is counterpoised by an eventual condensation. (In fact, while the extension of the coda and the ultimate compression of Ex. 8 enhance each other, it may be suggested that without this final cadence, the coda could be accused of lacking content.) Mozart's, as opposed to Beethoven's attitude towards conclusions springs to mind, but at the same time it seems to me that this particular ending is the only sign of Beethoven's direct influence on Britten: hear the end of the Eighth's first movement. (See, however, Hamburger on p. 232.) Perhaps it was the very fact that this ending was exceptional among Beethoven's conclusions which impressed itself fruitfully upon Britten's mind. —ED. (H. K.).

coda, thus making an end out of the beginning and completing the movement's ternary circle (see Ex. 8).

Of the three subjects, the third, which is constructed as a cadence, roots most strongly in the tenth interval (see Ex. 11); and similarly as the tenth is used at the beginning of each section, the third subject is used at the end of each section. Throughout the coda, the tenth and the third subject re-unite in C major (see Ex. 8).

From the first part of the exposition, a bridge passage leads, as of old, to the establishment of the second subject in the dominant. Indeed the first part of the exposition corresponds to the classical first subject, and the second part to the classical second subject. Nevertheless, the whole of the thematic material having already been stated at the outset, the second part of the exposition (including the bridge) also decidedly assumes *developmental* character, as will be seen from the treatment of the subjects in canon, sequential repetition, inversion, etc.

Two terms occasionally employed instead of 'development' are 'working-out section' and 'free fantasia'. The latter rather than the former applies to the present movement's development section, which is more loosely organized than the exposition and which thus affords contrast within the continued utilization of the thematic material. Having left the more formal aspects of 'development' to the second part of the exposition, the development proper is free to phantasize.

Pianissimo chords and scattered, misty entries of the tenth bring about the transition to the phantasy. The progress of the development is variational, with two *agitato* outbreaks, or rather in-breaks, into its later part.

It is noteworthy that this informal development does not concern itself with what is formally the most developed subject, i.e. the first. Nor are the other two subjects knit together. As distinct from both the exposition's second part and the recapitulation, the development virtually handles only one subject at a time[1].

The recapitulation, highly condensed, brings all three subjects simultaneously (Ex. 12)[2], a climactic event unprecedented (though

---

[1] If we put 'A' for each section in which we get only one subject at a time, and 'B' for each section which offers more than one subject at a time, the five sections of the movement form themselves into the pattern A–B–A–B–A: a simple scheme of variety within unity, yet executed with such refinement that nobody notices it.—ED. (H. K.).

[2] See also *The Symphonies*, p. 248, and *The Concertos*, p. 258.—EDS.

not unprepared) in the course of the movement. This section is exactly as long (and short) as section (1).

In proportion to the recapitulation's intense compression, the coda itself is not compressed, but lingers for quite a while in C major. The continued stress on the home key is needed for complete tonal appeasement.

It has been said[1] that "English composers have never taken naturally to sonata form, which is for all its universal validity an essentially Austrian way of thinking in music." My knowledge of English music is not yet nearly wide enough to allow my discussing this interesting suggestion,[2] but as one who has grown up in Austria and in Austrian chamber music, I may say that Britten seems to solve the modern sonata problem—the achievement of symmetry and unity within an extended ternary circle based on more than one subject—with perfect ease.

The scherzo, in C minor, is one in structure and rhythm rather than in mood. As I write, Charles Stuart describes it as "uncanny"[3].

Its three ternary features, i.e. (1) the scherzo's ternary form; (2) the trio's ternary form; (3) the whole movement's ternary form (scherzo-trio-scherzo), are clearly recognizable, though we get varied recapitulations. In fact, in the final recapitulation of the scherzo, the theme itself is not recapitulated; the effect of the recapitulation (and coda) is achieved by the repetition of the ostinato which dominates the scherzo's main section (see Ex. 14), and by quaver beats indicating the main rhythm.

The ostinato, a *saltando* arpeggio figure, is foreshadowed in the first movement (Ex. 13), while the scherzo theme in its turn foretells later events in the *Chacony* (e.g. Ex. 15).

Whereas the first and second movements have their themes announced in partial unison, i.e. by three and two instruments respectively (see Exx. 9, 10, 11, 14), all four instruments join in unison in the third movement to give out the powerful theme of the *Chacony* (Ex. 16).

This theme retains the chaconne rhythm, but not the chaconne's rhythmic structure: it extends over nine instead of the usual eight

---

[1] *English Chamber Music*, by the Music Critic of *The Times*, 17th January, 1947.

[2] Meanwhile it has become so, and I have discussed some historical and psychological aspects of Austrian sonata form and English sonata troubles in [159].—ED. (H. K.).

[3] *The Observer*, 9th February, 1947.

bars. The whole idea grows out of the first bar, not only (as a matter of course) rhythmically, but also melodically.

There are twenty-one variations of the theme, grouped into four sections which are divided by solo cadenzas. "The sections", says Britten[1], "may be said to review the theme from (a) harmonic, (b) rhythmic, (c) melodic, and (d) formal aspects."

The first three groups each contain six variations, leaving three variations to form the coda. The third section occupies an exceptional position, for here a melody, accompanied by the theme, is in its turn subjected to variations, thus furnishing a set of variations within the variations[2]. In this section, which contains four polytonal variations, the movement reaches lyrical heights of the greatest beauty.

The *Chacony* ends, as do the preceding movements, with a reiterated figure, i.e. C major chords linked with, and obtruding themselves upon, the theme. But while the preceding movements die away (*pp*), the last drives itself away (*ff*).

Considered in its entirety, the Quartet innovates in many respects, but it innovates smoothly—as smoothly as, for instance, *mutatis mutandis*, the Walton viola Concerto.

Not even the slow and massive last movement breaks forcibly away from convention and tradition. The idea of ending with a passacaglia (or freer-type variations, or an old dance form) has its counterparts in the present and its roots in the past.

Ex.9   First subject

[1] In his short programme note for the first performance [353].—Eds.

[2] The principle of what might be called 'structural involution' is characteristic of Britten: see the first movement's exposition within the exposition, or the Finale of the *Spring Symphony*, where a ternary theme, itself variationally constructed, forms the basis of a free, ternary set of variations which in its turn emerges as the central section of the entire ternary movement with its variational outer (waltz) sections and their tenor recitatives.—Ed. (H. K.).

Ex.10   Second subject

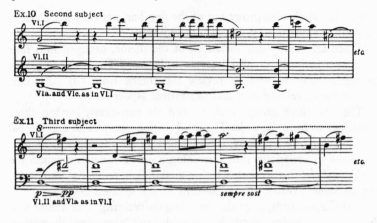

Ex.11   Third subject

Ex.12   Recapitulation of 1st movement

2nd subject,
augmented

1st subject

3rd subject

Ex.13   From 1st movement, exposition

Ex.14   Scherzo, bar 6

Ex.15 CHACONY, 19th variation

Ex.16 Theme of CHACONY
Sostenuto (♩ = 88)

*   *   *

A few additional remarks of my own may help to place Keller's analysis within the wider context of Britten's chamber music.

(1) Classical sonata form is more closely approached here than in any other former sonata movement, yet the ideas of having an "exposition *within* the exposition" and the shifting of the working-out sections away from their usual places are essentially modern.

(2) The loosely organized development section of the first movement ("free fantasia") is a feature of most of Britten's developments. Equally, the simultaneous restatement of all three themes at the beginning of the recapitulation has its counterparts in the oboe Quartet and the first Quartet.

(3) In most chaconnes, the melodic variations occur in the middle, as a quiet interlude. Brahms, in his fourth Symphony, makes a point of forcefully breaking into them with his original theme, sweeping on from there to the coda, in ever-contracting circles of variations. In other chaconnes, such as Bach's C minor organ *Passacaglia*, or Beethoven's passacaglia-like C minor variations, the series of related variations that form the first part are followed, after some lyrical variations, by mosaic-like contrasting variations. It must have required considerable courage on Britten's part to discard these well-proven forms of construction by placing his lyrical section last before the coda; but his daring is justified by the result. Variations 14–19 (the "set of variations within the variations") attain to towering spiritual heights through simplification of style. Here again is apparent Britten's

tendency to intensify his meaning by a devolution of idiom when approaching the end of a work: a cyclicism of proportions, classical in the exactest sense, that gradually admits the listener within the precincts of a work, and releases him when its meaning has been revealed to him in its clearest form. Seen from this angle, the real forebear of this chaconne may be the last movement of the *Eroica*.

(4) Once a composer can intensify his meaning through simplification, his harmonic range, and particularly the available range between consonances and dissonances permissible to him, widen considerably: all the doors between concords and discords become swing-doors. Thus it is not surprising to find that the acutest conglomerations of discords (as in variations 12 and 13, or in the quasi-early-Bartók harmony of the trio) accommodate themselves with the greatest of ease to the crystal-clear C major of the first movement's beginning or the last movement's end.

(5) The three solo cadenzas ('cello, viola, and first violin) of the *Chacony* are a successful attempt to incorporate in the chaconne some elements of the free fantasia that would have preceded it in old times. Their purpose is not so much the formal one of separating cleanly one section from the other, but rather the dynamic one of preparing, as every good recitative does, the ensuing ensemble, by musical meanderings that more and more approach their sequel as they progress.

(6) A special word of praise is due to the lucid string writing. The tenth which underlies so much of the first movement is a very grateful interval for the strings, both horizontally and vertically. Its contrast to the legato conjunct motion which characterizes the remaining thematic material expresses itself to particular advantage in the string quartet, for this medium is much more sensitive to the alternation of small and large intervals than the piano or orchestra. The second movement is a showpiece for a good quartet. Its *martellé* theme against the flying arpeggio of the accompaniment and, in the trio, the syncopations of second violin and viola against the 'cello, need careful rehearsing, while the high-lying passages and octaves of the first violin part ask for a very good player. The last movement, as is to be expected in an extended variation movement, is a microcosm of quartet technique. There is hardly a kind of bowing, a rhythm, a texture, a problem of intonation that does not occur, and all of them for good musical reasons. Played well, this movement conjures up

the impression, peculiar to great quartet writing, that the string quartet is a much richer and more variegated medium than the full orchestra : a compliment to the composer's skill in giving a polished surface to the most spiritual form of music.

Lachrymae—'Reflections on a Song of John Dowland'—for viola and piano—was written in the spring of 1950 for William Primrose, who gave the first performance with Britten on 20th June, 1950, at the Aldeburgh Festival. The word "reflections" in the subtitle is by no means an arty paraphrase of the more usual 'variations' but is, in the absence of a technical term, the only right denomer for Britten's procedures. These keep half-way between variation form proper and symphonic development; a precarious position that attracts many modern composers intent on revitalizing the old variation form. But it needs a Britten to steer a safe course between the, at bottom, irreconcilable demands of the monothematic chaconne and the poly-thematic sonata. In spite of all the Introductions, Minores, '*Charakter-variationen*' and fugues of the time between Mozart and Brahms, and all the internal extensions and contractions of single variations, after Brahms, variation form stands or falls with the preservation of formal and structural identity between variation and theme. Not only when the variations keep too close to the theme, but also when they move too far away in the direction of symphonic motif-development, we become conscious of the lack of a second subject. Therefore, the simple 16- or 24-bar ternary form whose middle-part could be con-sidered, short of a second subject, as an alternative (*alternativo*) to the tune, was preferred by the classics for their variation works. But while the inherent playfulness of an A–B–A theme could still legiti-mately attract the Brahms of the *Haydn Variations*, this same scheme would, under the calculated and concentrated technique of a respon-sible modern composer, turn too bi-thematic, and thus too symphonic. Hence the modern avoidance of A–B–A variation themes, and the preference for either chaconne, or sectional, or partial variation.

Britten, faced with this dilemma, does not make it easy for him-self. He chooses a fully developed theme, an entire song, in fact: Dowland's *If my complaints could passion move*. Its thirty-two bars consist of an 8-bar 'A'-group in C minor, which is repeated, and an 8 + 8 bars' 'B'-group which, starting in E♭ major in both its halves, returns each time to C minor. This is, strictly speaking, a binary subject but presents in view of its modulations, the same difficulties to a modern composer as the above-mentioned ternary themes. Naturally, it is out of the question to vary this theme bar by bar, even for the first two variations. On the other hand, it would be desirable, in order to counter the pull of any sonata development, to show different figurative and instrumental aspects of the theme in sections approximating in length to normal variations. So Britten detaches the 'A'-section (C minor) of the theme and writes ten variations exclusively on these eight (or sixteen) bars. There are no breaks between the variations, but their beginnings and ends impress themselves quite clearly on the listener. Thus, the actual variation work can be as concentrated as in a chaconne. It is by this inspired device of writing partial variations on eight bars in the guise of full variation movements of twenty to fifty bars that the balance between our incompatibles is struck.

The other all-important problem is how to present the theme and how to construct the coda. Obviously, these peculiar partial variations cannot be preceded by the entire theme but at the same time must be preceded by something of the *length* of the entire theme. Britten solves this problem by writing a twenty-eight-bar *lento* introduction that begins with a sequence on the theme's first bar, a first inversion of the rising A♭ major chord which is to play the rôle of a motto throughout. To this is added entire, at the ninth bar, the original 'A'-section of Dowland's song in the bass of the piano, against the continued motto in the viola. After a further bridge-passage based on the motto, the first variation enters. The beginning of this work is unique in that it combines the functions of an introduction with those of the statement of a variation theme.

Throughout the ten partial variations, Britten refuses to tell us whether he feels the 'B'-section of his well-known theme (which so far we have not heard either straight or varied) as a second subject or as a variation on 'A'. But he gives us an ambiguous hint in his sixth variation. Over an accompaniment of mixed C minor and E♭ major chords, with some D♭ major triads that can be heard, according to taste, as Mixolydian E♭, or as C minor Neapolitan sixths, he introduces in the viola another Dowland song (*Flow, O my tears*) in E♭ major which melodically is fairly closely related to our 'B'-section. It is clear that he has objections to introducing the E♭ major 'B'-section as a second subject here, in the middle of the ten partial variations; the question is whether he wants us to hear this new song as a second subject proper of a hypothetical sonata exposition or as a *'majore alternativo'* to the preceding five variations on 'A'. The artistic purpose of this ambiguity, however, reveals itself eventually to those whose ears are long enough to span the remaining four variations, including the ninth with its side-tracking inversion of 'A', and the tenth with its diminution of the motto. At the end of this tenth variation, the first half of 'A' appears, in augmentation in the viola, on the tonic major's relative minor (A minor), and descends sequentially over several keys to become the starting point in E♭, of the theme's entire 'B'-section in Dowland's original version and with his original bass. This is heard immediately as the real, inspiredly delayed second subject of that hypothetical sonata exposition which was implied by the dualistic methods of the preceding partial variations; at the same time the turn to the relative major announces the beginning of the coda, as the later turn to the Picardy third defines its end. At the same time, the E♭ entry of section 'B' is an unprecedented homage to Dowland's famed modulations to the relative major; in a sense, this whole variation work was wrought as a mount for this single pearl. At the end, Britten is once more able to enhance his meaning through simplification, and the quiet Elizabethan conclusion is one of the most touching passages in the literature of music.

A diagram of the form may clinch our argument:

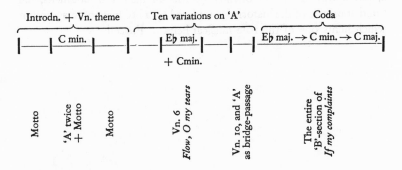

Finally, there is Britten's realization of Purcell's *Golden Sonata*, for two violins, 'cello and piano. This completely escapes its previous editors' inexhaustible supply of stodgy block harmony—the result of years of bad writing for the organ. Restoring this masterpiece to its original status of a trio sonata by adding a 'cello which plays the bass-line throughout, Britten gives the keyboard player an opportunity to deal freely with the figured bass, in the manner of an inspired improvisation. This freedom is not abused, for Britten realizes that in many passages it would be pointless to separate the 'cello from the left hand of the piano. (Yet even in these passages he often contrives amazing effects, as in the *Adagio*, where the whole chord is given to the left hand, in close position arpeggio.) When, in the course of the fast movements, he splits 'cello and piano bass, this is done to provide florid middle parts or sustained chords, as of an accompanying orchestra. As in all his realizations of Baroque music, Britten is refreshingly unafraid of clashes between the melodic and the harmonic seventh, and of appogiaturas sounding against their resolutions—the bogies of those editors whose conservatism reaches back a mere hundred years instead of the required two hundred and fifty. The plaintive harmony of the slow movements benefits most from such open-mindedness. In the fast movements, Britten also has the rare knack of introducing sham imitations of the theme in the piano's right hand which last just long enough to sound improvisatory. The keyboard part with its wide spacing, frequent skips and large arpeggios is emphatically a piano part although, apart from its range, it contains nothing in harmony or figuration which a gifted virginalist might not have attempted. But Britten's realization is not only practical; it is inspired: while he never offends against our historical judgment, the timid approach of the historian is replaced by a boldness of imagination which befits one of the true musical heirs of Purcell.

BOYD NEEL

The String Orchestra

IF we except *Les Illuminations* and the *Serenade* for tenor, horn, and strings, Britten's works for string orchestra consist of the *Simple Symphony*—a youthful *jeu d'esprit*, the *Variations on a Theme of Frank Bridge* of 1937, and the *Prelude and Fugue* of 1943.

The *Simple Symphony*[1] is described on the score as "by E. B. Britten (arranged B. B.)"—an indication, this, of the composer's attitude towards a work which he has never taken very seriously. I always feel that he has somewhat underestimated this composition: wherever I play it, I find that it makes a profound effect on audiences of all kinds, especially the moving simplicity of the *Saraband*. In many ways it is as characteristic of the composer as some of his later works.

A note in the score states that the Symphony ". . . is entirely based on material from works which the composer wrote between the ages of nine and twelve. Although the development of these themes is in many places quite new, there are large stretches of the work which are taken bodily from the early pieces, save for the re-scoring for strings." The re-scoring apparently took place between December 1933 and the following February, when the work was published in its present form. The alliterative titles of the movements give a clue to the nature of the music. The first movement, *Boisterous Bourrée*, is taken from the first *Suite* for piano dating from 1926. Most original in design, the *Bourrée* is founded on three main themes, two of which are always heard simultaneously. After four bars of *forte* introductory chords, the first group (see Ex. 1) is announced by 'cello and second violin:

[1] Cf. *The Symphonies*, pp. 246f., and *Britten and the Young*, p. 279.—EDS.

Ex.1

The second tune (Ex. 2), in the relative major, is taken from a song of 1923 and is well contrasted with Ex. 1:

Ex.2

We might think that we are set for a sonata movement, and there certainly follows a development of Ex. 1 against a descending phrase of four notes occurring in all parts in turn, which leads to a restatement of Ex. 2, this time in D major, accompanied by the loud opening chords. The movement ends with a short coda. While the *Bourrée* is only a short movement, much is compressed into a few bars, and there is not a superfluous note.

The second movement, *Playful Pizzicato*, is *pizzicato* throughout for all the strings, and is a brilliant example of its use. The marking is *Presto possibile* and, for proper execution, demands finished playing. It consists of a principal section taken from a *Scherzo* for piano of 1924 and a trio based on a song of the same year. The movement shows a great deal of sly humour and never fails to bring down the house.

The *Sentimental Saraband* is the most extended of the four movements, and by far the best. The main tune, taken from the *Suite No. 3* for piano of 1925, is sung by the first violins over a bass pedal on G which holds the tonality firmly down until the forty-second bar, where the basses jump up to a *sforzando* D with thrilling effect. The second tune in this A-B-A movement with coda is taken from a *Waltz* for piano dating from 1923, and has a rather wistful charm. The *Saraband* is really an astonishing achievement when we consider the composer's age at the time of its composition.

The *Frolicsome Finale* is a concise little piece built on much the same lines as the *Boisterous Bourrée*—two main subjects and a development of the first. The first subject is taken from the piano Sonata No. 9 of 1926 and the second from a song of 1925. The *Simple Symphony* is dedicated to Audrey Alston, who used to teach Britten the viola in Norwich, and who introduced him to Frank Bridge.

It is interesting to compare this work with Britten's next composition for string orchestra, the *Variations on a Theme of Frank Bridge*, written three years later. The extraordinary acquisition of mastery in the medium during those three years is apparent in every bar of the later work which to date represents Britten's greatest achievement in string writing.

As I was personally concerned, a word about the birth of this work might perhaps be of interest. In 1937 I was invited to take my orchestra to the Salzburg Festival of the same year and give a concert of English music, one of the conditions being that the programme should include the first performance of a new English work. As it was then May and the concert was to take place on August 27th, the prospect seemed well-nigh hopeless; but suddenly I thought of Britten (till then hardly known outside inner musical circles) because I had noticed his extraordinary speed of composition during some film work in which we had been associated. I immediately asked him whether he would take on the Salzburg commission, and in ten days' time he appeared at my house with the complete work sketched out. In another four weeks it was fully scored for strings as it stands today, but for the addition of one bar. This was one of the most astonishing feats of composition in my experience. I saw at once that we had here, not just another string piece, but a work in which the resources of the string orchestra were exploited with a daring and invention never before known; indeed, it remains one of the landmarks of string orchestral writing in musical history. Here are unprecedented sounds, as astonishing today as they were to that first Festival audience in 1937 when the work caused a major sensation, and was soon to be played all over the world.

The *Variations* are of great difficulty, yet written with the inside knowledge of the fine string player. There is no doubt that Britten's study of the viola in his student days has been of inestimable value to him in his writing for string orchestra. Frank Bridge, with whom Britten studied composition, was also a fine viola player, and I well remember them both attending the first run-through of the work and discussing at length a certain passage in harmonics for the solo viola in the *Wiener Walzer* variation, with which my principal viola had encountered some difficulty. First Britten, then Bridge, picked up the instrument and played the passage quite perfectly.

The theme Britten used for the *Variations* was taken from Frank Bridge's *Idyll No. 2* for string quartet dating from 1911. Of a nebulous waltz-like nature, it is first heard on a solo violin after an eleven bars' *Introduction* (Ex. 3)

and immediately afterwards on the violins *tutti* in a more elaborate version, a kind of variation within the theme (Ex. 3a):

One has to go no further than the *Introduction* to realize that this work is something out of the ordinary, the chromatic rushes in the sixth bar holding the attention immediately. The double basses throughout are used in a soloistic manner; their part is often of extreme difficulty. For instance, the transition passage from the theme to the first variation (*Adagio*) depends entirely for its perfect execution on the intonation of the double basses, who have the chief moving part.

Variation I consists of chorale-like chords for the lower strings interspersed with references to the theme on the violins (Ex. 4):

Variation II, March. The *March* is of the 'patrol' type with the theme transformed into the march tune, first heard softly in the lower intruments, and working up to a climax through these highly characteristic harmonies (Ex. 5):

The *March* gradually dies away in the distance with the first violins playing interjections of this nature (Ex. 6):

As Ex. 6 suggests, the paths of the executants are not strewn with roses.

Variation III, Romance. An ingratiating tune sung by all the violins accompanied by the theme in the bass, *pizzicato*.

Variation IV, Aria Italiana. A superb burlesque in the style of Rossini. After a preliminary cadenza, the first violins sing a florid aria ending on an A in alt. The accompanying instruments are directed to lay down the bows and to play *quasi chitarra*. The manners and mannerisms of the florid Italian style are splendidly parodied, not the least amusing being the *pianissimo* at the descent into the minor key halfway through.

Variation V, Bourrée Classique. A vigorous piece built on a quaver figure derived from the falling fifth of the theme, an interval which permeates the whole of the *Variations*. The *Bourrée* has a brilliant part for solo violin.

Variation VI, Wiener Walzer. No doubt included by Britten as a leg-pull for the first performance's Austrian audience. All the tricks of the Viennese waltz composer's trade are mercilessly guyed.[1] In the opening bar we again find the falling fifth which, later on, is hammered home in this passage (Ex. 7):

Variation VII, Moto Perpetuo. This was one of the variations which caused a stir at the first performance. The whole orchestra, in unison tremolos, plays rapid figures passing from the highest register of the violins to the lowest of the basses. It is hard to find the connection with the theme, but as a brilliant *tour de force* it stands alone in string-orchestral writing. The third bar from the end was inserted after the first few performances, as the composer felt that the original ending

[1] Cf. *The Musical Atmosphere*, p. 11.—EDS.

had been too abrupt. This, incidentally, was the only alteration he made in the entire work.

Variation VIII, Funeral March. Again an employment of the string orchestra which for sheer originality it would be hard to beat. This moving tone picture of a funeral *cortège* is a unique example of what can be done with strings alone. The illusion is of a large orchestra of wind and string instruments with an unmistakable battery of muffled drums continuing throughout. The use of glissandos in the middle section, to give an effect of wailing, is wonderfully effective.

Variation IX, Chant. Yet another exploration of the possibilities of string sound. Sustained harmonics with high *pizzicatos* form a background to the chant of muted violas in three parts: again a very typical example of Britten's harmonic idiom (see Ex. 8):

Ex. 8

Variation X, Fugue and Finale. The fugue subject, based once more on the fall of the fifth, forms the basis of a complex movement whose parts eventually divide into as many as eleven distinct lines. When the music has reached its greatest complexity, the theme enters on the solo string quartet in octave unison, and then is sung in a nobly transfigured version on all violins, against rich harmonies for the lower strings. A short coda ends the work.[1]

The *Prelude and Fugue* of 1943 "for eighteen part string orchestra" is dedicated "to Boyd Neel and his Orchestra on the occasion of their tenth birthday, June 23rd, 1943." Thus, once again, I have a very personal interest in this composition. The tenth anniversary of my orchestra's formation occurred in the dark days of 1943, when most of the players were scattered in the forces and I myself was involved in war work of a medical nature. Somebody suggested a concert to celebrate the event, and I began trying to collect members who might be available to play. By some means which I shall never be able to understand, more than half the orchestra managed to gather together in London on that day—I myself having obtained special leave—and,

---

[1] A slight anticlimax, to my mind. I have always felt that the full statement of the theme should form the actual ending of this brilliant and, at appointed times, extremely moving composition.

with the aid of some deputies, we succeeded in giving a concert in the Wigmore Hall. A few weeks previously I had mentioned to Britten that we were going to make the attempt. Imagine my delight when, a few days before the concert, I received the score and parts of the *Prelude and Fugue* which thus received its first performance at this tenth anniversary. As each member of the orchestra had his own solo to play, the work was indeed a charming, multi-personal birthday gift.

Originally forty-two bars long, the Prelude has been extensively revised by the composer since the first performance. It now numbers thirty-six bars; nor has the revision proved merely excisive: certain passages have actually been rewritten.

After eight bars of violent introduction, in which high sustained chords alternate with left hand *pizzicati*, the solo violin plays a long sustained melody in a high register over an octave-unison *pianissimo* ostinato derived from some of the introductory material. The music gradually softens until the Fugue, which commences in the second double bass, each instrument entering in order, from lowest to highest. The subject (Ex. 9) is about as uncompromising as any fugue subject I know:

Ex.9

Ex. 9 is the subject as played by all the instruments except the double basses, who play Ex. 10 instead of the triplet figure:

Ex.10

When each part has entered, the triplet figure is tossed from one to another like a ping-pong ball on a fountain. Each episode consists of a solo instrument playing the subject over sustained harmonies in the other voices. Later an impressive stretto occurs which, in score, looks like one side of the Great Pyramid. The Fugue ends with the descending quaver figure of the subject pealing out on the violins like cathedral bells. The slow tempo of the Prelude returns, and this time the violins and violas in unison sing the solo violin tune *fortissimo,* while the 'cellos and basses play the ostinato figure *pizzicato*. This ending was also revised by the composer, and its complexity slightly reduced. After twenty-four bars of the slow *tempo primo*, the work concludes with eleven bars of *allegro* based on the fugue subject.

I sincerely hope that it will not be long before Britten gives us some even finer compositions in this medium, in which he seems to excel.

A page from the autograph score of the *Spring Symphony*

[Boosey & Hawke

ERWIN STEIN

The Symphonies

THE fact that Haydn wrote not a single symphony
during the last fourteen years of his life, that he
suddenly abandoned what had been his greatest
achievement, has often been commented upon. Legend has it that
stirring performances of *The Messiah* and *Joshua* turned his interest
to the oratorio. To me this explanation seems quite plausible. It is
fascinating to study in a composer's life work his changing inclinations
to write for instruments or for voices. Even after the most successful
excursions into the fields of pure music, where notes alone constitute
form and meaning, he may return to what is supposed to be music's
source, the singing human voice.

No doubt the symphony, when it emerged, was a revelation. Here
was a scheme that enabled the composer to expand his ideas at will. The
pliant form allowed for contrasts of character, for diversity of shapes,
for easy changes of texture, and for an infinite variety of colours; yet
everything was so pre-arranged as to preserve the unity of the whole.
And the cycle of different movements, from the simple minuet to the
complex sonata, gave the symphony so wide a scope that it seemed the
perfect form for delivering almost anything the composer wanted to
convey—except when, for the purpose of direct and unequivocal
expression, the human voice was needed. Mozart, in whose output
instrumental and vocal works are evenly balanced, may not have felt
the choice between the two media as so great a dilemma as did Beethoven, who cut the Gordian knot by introducing the human voice into
the symphony at a point where it was about to disintegrate. The case
was too singular to be easily imitated. Schubert's lyricism is direct even
in his symphonies; the song remained for his intimate utterances.
Mahler, on the other hand, felt the problem keenly. In his 1st Symphony

he derived the themes of the opening movement from melodies of an early song—a dangerous procedure, though highly successful in this special case. In other symphonies he introduced vocal movements; and two, the 8th and *Das Lied von der Erde*, are vocal from beginning to end. Particularly in the 8th Symphony, voices and orchestra share equally in the symphonic texture: the integration of vocal and instrumental elements is carried as far as the different media permit.

The vocal symphony and Haydn's late oratorios would seem to spring from similar sources: from the composer's desire for more direct and unequivocal expression than the orchestra alone can yield. Symphonic form has grown to considerable complexity and disclosed its limitations. The convenience of the scheme is such that there is a temptation to test how much it can carry, and, in particular, how reliable the formula of the sonata is for preserving the unity of an extended piece. Yet integration driven too far will defeat its own ends and produce monotony. Also, the arrangement of keys and modulations, the traditional cornerstones of the symphony, have come to play a lesser part because our sense of tonality has become both wider and less strictly defined. The symphony, once the standard type of great music, has become problematic.

Significantly enough, none of Britten's works is straightforwardly called 'symphony'. The few which so far bear the name have warning qualifications added. They have little in common; each approaches the symphonic idea from a different angle. Seen as a whole, Britten's output rather illustrates a tendency away from what constitutes symphonic form, and towards the essentials of vocal music. This tendency, however, would be less apparent if symphonic thinking were alien to the composer. It is easy to declare him a writer of operas and song cycles; in the present context it is more interesting to realize that his musical thinking is on a large scale. And he has always been aware of the wide scope the symphony offers.

We see this even in his *Simple Symphony* for strings, an arrangement made when he was twenty of tunes composed between the ages of nine and twelve[1]. The titles of the movements, such as *Boisterous Bourrée* or *Sentimental Saraband*, would indicate a suite, yet the arrangement of the tunes of the *Bourrée* is symphonic; and in the finale we have a well-built theme which stands the strain of development

[1] Cf. *The Vocal Music*, p. 60　*The String Orchestra*, pp. 237ff., and *Britten and the Young*, p. 279.—EDS.

and augmentation. The work may be slight but the tunes are fresh and the setting is brilliant. It will hold its place as the first of Britten's works written for the young.

In the *Sinfonietta*, a chamber symphony for ten instruments, written when he was eighteen, Britten employs symphonic devices with great cunning. During the first few bars already no less than five motifs are exposed (Ex. 1) which yield the material of the ensuing three movements:

The motifs are inter-related; the motif of a second (a) is the nucleus of every succeeding thing; in (b) the motif is varied; in (c) the interval and the rhythm are broadened; in (d) the motif is inverted; and in (e) the inversion varied. In (c) we have intervals of the fifth and seventh which are to become important. The exposition of the motifs proceeds over a pedal B♭–A, another interval which is to play a constructive part in both harmony and melody. When the main theme gains shape it appears in three parts in triple counterpoint (Ex. 2):

The horn call heralding the theme, the working out of the motifs, and the way in which elements of the 'horizontal' melody are reflected in the 'vertical' harmony, and vice versa, are reminiscent of Schoenberg's 1st Chamber Symphony. The *Sinfonietta*, I believe, is the only work of Britten's in which Schoenberg's influence is directly apparent.

The movement continues in sonata fashion with a bridge passage and a second theme which grows to full stature before, dying away, it closes the exposition. What follows is the development section, if only in the technical sense: fragments of the themes are set in short sequences. It is the quietest part of the movement, and the form remains loose, until an ostinato, derived from the first motif, prepares the return of the beginning. Successive *pizzicato* entries of the ostinato figure gradually pile up to six-part harmonies—the chords as consequence of the melodic growth—while motifs on the wind and finally the call of the horn lead to the recapitulation. This, however, is very much abridged, in the character, in fact, of a coda. The themes, principal and subsidiary, appear simultaneously, the latter in the broad rhythm of the strings. Thirteen years later, in his 2nd string Quartet, Britten used a similar device·when he combined three themes in the recapitulation of the first movement[1]. The tendency is the same. The return of the beginning is felt as the rounding up, the conclusion: at this stage there is hardly room left for the explicitness which prevailed in the exposition. Obviously the old masters felt otherwise. Is our changed attitude due to a less firmly anchored sense of tonality? Or to a desire for terser expression?

The *Andante* of the *Sinfonietta* is headed *Variations,* but these are not of the usual type. At first, motifs from the preceding movement are exposed. Their character has changed; the horn call has become an ascending arpeggio figure from which the theme (Ex. 3) arises:

The variations begin loosely, almost like a transition or bridge passage, but later they grow to a climax, in modulatory sequences like a sonata development. Another transitory variation leads to the original key and the recapitulation of the theme. The finale is a brilliant tarantella, mainly built from previous motifs. The pedal A–Bb reappears and the six-part harmonies, again arising from successive entries of the first motif, are now in the shape of five intervals of the seventh towering above each other.

The mastery of form in the early work is astounding. Britten has obviously taken pains to fulfil symphonic requirements, with the result

[1] See Ex. 12 in *The Chamber Music,* p. 230. Cf. also *The Concertos,* p. 258.—EDS.

that the *Sinfonietta* has become the least unorthodox of his symphonies. Nowhere else has he so thoroughly carried through the integration of the thematic material; in the 2nd string Quartet, whose first movement represents his most important essay in sonata form, the single movements are highly integrated but there is no obvious thematic connection between them. The composer's language may not be as personal in the *Sinfonietta* as in later works, yet there is more than one hint of what is to come. One instance of special significance (Ex. 4) occurs in the first movement:

The sound of the alternating ninths and sevenths derived from the main motif is most typical of Britten. One is immediately reminded of such passages as the ritornello of the women's ensemble in *Peter Grimes*, or the opening of the 1st string Quartet. In the later works, the ninths or sevenths are often inverted, that is, narrowed down to intervals of the second. They frequently occur as the result of close melodic strands, as in the theme of the variations (see Ex. 3). I should like to call this discovery of Britten's "the sonority of the second". Composers before him have indulged in the exploitation of the interval, but Bartók and others used it mostly for its stridency. In Britten's music the second has become beautiful and tender—"a new sound symbolizing a new personality", as Schoenberg, in his *Harmonielehre*, defined similar events of the past.

Eight years after the *Sinfonietta*, Britten wrote what is so far his only large-scale orchestral work, the *Sinfonia da Requiem*. Three movements—*Lacrymosa* (*Andante ben misurato*), *Dies Irae* (*Allegro con fuoco*) and *Requiem Aeternam* (*Andante molto tranquillo*)—follow each other without a pause. To describe them as sonata, scherzo and finale would hardly suffice. The title, and still more the sub-titles with their references to the words of the Requiem Mass, show that the composer was not aiming at an abstract symphony, but at finding the adequate form for the expression of defined sentiments and reflections. One cannot speak of how the themes are integrated when the whole of the first movement is already conceived as an integral unit, and analysis only confirms the homogeneity of the substance. One rhythm prevails (Ex. 5(a)), the dragging syncopations with which—after the heavy opening beats have receded—the principal theme (Ex. 5) begins:

Both shape and character of the other themes are related to the first; even the motif of a seventh, entering on the saxophone, is an augmentation of Ex. 5(b). What one may call exposition and development are built as a single climax reaching beyond the recapitulation, and culminating in the midst of the main theme, at its own natural climax, on the tonic chord of D. Mourning and desolation pervade the persistent 6/8-time syncopations. When they cease it is only to give way to the nightmare of the *Dies Irae*. Against the uniformity of the *Lacrymosa*, the chaotic turmoil of doomsday calls for a diversity of contrasting motifs; it is chaos painted somewhat differently from the opening of Haydn's *Creation*.

Fright and panic are the prevailing sentiments. They are felt throughout the movement, from the *pianissimo* opening with the rhythmic motif on the flutes (Ex. 6a) and the scampering figure of the strings (Ex. 6b); during interjections of the percussion, threatening scales on the muted brass, screaming runs on the woodwind and the alarm of the trumpet signals; up to the final catastrophe. As a central section there is a march or dance of death in which the saxophone intones a distorted,

rhythmically amorphous version (Ex. 7) of the mourning theme
(Ex. 5) from the *Lacrymosa*:

The recapitulation leads to a shattering climax: the main rhythm is
announced by the full orchestra on the D minor chord with added
dissonant E; then the music seems to disintegrate during bizarre suc-
cessions of unison notes, zigzagging up and down the orchestra's whole
compass, intermingled with shrieking *glissandi*, yet, intermittently,
resting upon the tonic D. I do not think that disorder has ever before
been conveyed in so convincing a musical form.

The ragged unison line[1], decreasing in violence and with its compass
narrowed down, slowly gains definite shape and finally emerges as the
accompaniment (see Ex. 8) of the last movement, *Requiem Aeternam*:

With the rocking crochets of the harp, the theme (see Ex. 8(x)) is like
a slumber song. Remarkable are the 'sonorous seconds' resulting from
the close strands of the flutes. This movement is in smoothly balanced
ternary form, with the middle section developing yet another variation
of the mourning theme (Ex. 5), which now appears in the major and
straight rhythm (see Ex. 9):

[1] Cf. *The Vocal Music*, p. 62.—EDS.

Consolingly the melody grows to a climax at which the slumber song returns, forming both recapitulation and coda of the movement. Now the rocking accompaniment, on the strings and harps, encompasses the whole range of the instruments. It stays to the end, once more gliding up and, to close the work, down.

Notwithstanding the contrasts of its three sections, the *Sinfonia* is conceived very much as one piece, with a fast movement between two slow ones. Their characters are complementary. There are several formal links. All three are in the key of D and mainly in triple time; variations of the first theme (Ex. 5) appear in each movement (see Exx. 7 and 9); and, less obviously, the motif (c) of the first theme (Ex. 5) which concludes the first movement turns round in the second to become in retrograde and speedier motion the "scampering" motif of the strings (Ex. 6b); also, the burlesque variation of the same motif in the middle section of the second movement (Ex. 7(c)) emerges in the last, in the major and 3/4-time, as the slumber song (Ex. 8).

Shortly after the *Sinfonia da Requiem*, Britten began to concentrate on vocal music. There is perhaps no direct analogy with Haydn's case, but it is obvious that Britten became increasingly concerned with subjects within the orbit of human life and feeling, and less wit' abstract musical form. Musically, it was the specific problem of the extended vocal form which occupied him during the following years. In his song cycles, choral works and operas he did not so much aim at integrating the pieces, movements or acts thematically, as at achieving unity of the whole by skilfully co-ordinating the parts. And when he wrote a vocal symphony, nine years after the *Sinfonia da Requiem,* he did not follow the method of Mahler's 8th. Rather, the *Spring Symphony* formally resembles *Das Lied von der Erde,* though Britten grouped his movements in more symphonic fashion.

The *Spring Symphony*[1] is written for soprano, contralto and tenor soli, mixed chorus, boys' choir and large orchestra. There are twelve movements, all settings of English poems which range from the 13th century

[1] See also *The Choral Music,* pp. 99f.—Eds.

"Soomer is icoomen in" to our own time. Each movement presents a different aspect of man's relation to spring, and is conceived for a different vocal and instrumental combination; they are arranged in groups and so organized as to form four 'Parts' which correspond to the traditional four movements of the symphony, Allegro, Adagio, Scherzo and Finale.

There is a *lento* introduction to the first Part: a prayer for spring to rise, on the anonymous 16th century poem *Shine out, fair sun*. Four movements of the Allegro type follow: *Vivace* (*The Merry Cuckoo* by Spenser), *Allegro con brio* (*Spring, the Sweet Spring* by Nashe), *Allegro molto* (*When-as the rye reach to the chin* by George Peele, together with *The Driving Boy* by John Clare), and *Molto moderato ma giocoso* (*The Morning Star* by Milton).

The stanzas of the wintry introduction are sung by the chorus *a cappella* and alternate, after an opening by percussion and harps, with fugal interludes of the muted strings, the woodwind, the muted brass, and finally of the full orchestra, when the instrumental groups recapitulate their individual passages simultaneously. But the choral prayer prevails; the motif on the repeated words "shine out" eventually becomes the minor third A–F♯. The same notes are immediately taken up as the call of the "merry cuckoo" in the following *Vivace*. The bright sound of the tenor solo, duetting with a trio of trumpets, changes the scene. Built almost as loosely as a *recitativo accompagnato*, the piece is like yet another introduction. In the last bar the cuckoo calls telescope into the tremolo that recurs when, in the course of the third movement, more birds join in the singing. For now spring is in bloom: the music gains full shape. The solo voices, supported by a solo string quartet, share a soaring melody between them, the chorus continues to repeat the opening phrase "Spring, the sweet spring", and the orchestra, like a gigantic harp, accompanies with a chordal ostinato. In the subsequent stanzas the melody is widely varied, but the scheme of the accompaniment remains the same. At the end of each verse, the soloists sing their bird calls to the tremolo chord anticipated in the previous movement. A short coda repeats the opening phrase; and again the last notes (the falling fifth on the word "spring") link up with the woodwind accompaniment of the next song. Boys' voices, entering for the first time, add with an enchanting tune a new and vigorous colour to the vernal picture. A soprano solo forms the middle section, accompanied by the violins only, which are divided into four parts in their highest register.

While the soprano sings, the boys whistle bits of their own tune until they resume the song.

The first Part of the symphony ends with a movement for chorus, brass and percussion on Milton's *Morning Star*. It is in evenly balanced, strict ternary form, so as to round up surely and conclusively the Part's variety of movements. After the introduction, they all describe spring in its prime; but there is no musical connection apparent between them other than the transitional links. The formal consistency of the Part as a whole is based on the ingenious co-ordination of seemingly heterogeneous elements. They are so fitted as to complement each other. And it is similar with the second and third Parts.

Three movements of contemplative character represent the slow Part of the symphony: *Allegretto rubato* (*Welcome, Maids of Honour* by Herrick), *Molto moderato e tranquillo* (*Waters Above* by Vaughan) and *Adagio molto tranquillo* (*Out on the lawn I lie in bed* by W. H. Auden). In the first, four stanzas are composed in the form of a theme with three variations for contralto and a delicate ensemble of woodwind, harps and lower strings. The tenor solo of the second movement is in a unique mood of subdued happiness. Only the violins accompany, in steady semiquaver triplets within quaver figurations which meander, now in narrow, now in wide bends, round the note A♯.

The last movement of Part II is highly developed. It is placed like a pillar in the centre of the symphony to balance the architecture. Four stanzas from W. H. Auden's poem, each framed by the wordless *a cappella* ritornello of the chorus, are sung by the contralto and accompanied by woodwind and muted brass which, to begin with, contribute only occasional *pianissimo* chords, heavy and suggestive of a sultry night in spring's maturity. In each of the verses the music develops a different character with changing orchestral colours. Duets of alto flute and bass clarinet, and of two oboes and bassoons (*a 2*) form the background to the first two stanzas; in the third, the atmosphere becomes more oppressive when flute figurations, high above the voice, alternate with heavy wind chords. A sudden outburst of warlike fanfares on trumpets and trombones accompanies the fourth stanza. The coda recapitulates the beginning and the movement ends with fragments from earlier phrases and hummed cadences of the chorus. The music is largely built up from the opening ritornello's (Ex. 10's) motif (b) and its inversions. Links with the preceding song are provided by the first note B♭ which, as A♯, had been its pedal and final note, and by the rising interval (a) which in various forms was prominent in the tenor's melody.

If the second Part was in a reflective vein, Part III is as direct as Britten can be. There are again three movements: *Allegro impetuoso* (*When will my May come* by Barnefield), *Allegretto grazioso* (*Fair and Fair* by George Peele) and *Allegretto molto mosso* (*Sound the Flute* by Blake). The first, a tenor solo accompanied by passionate arpeggios of the strings and harps, is a strophic song. Its form sounds simple enough, yet the melody is ingeniously devised by ever new variations of the opening recitative phrase. The tenor closes on the notes C–A and the arpeggios turn to the simultaneous keys of F and A; here again an immediate connection with the following movement is apparent, for the singer's last notes are taken up by the oboe solo in the key of F, while *pizzicato* strings accompany in A. The key of A returns when soprano and tenor sing their gay and tender duet, at first in succession; later when they follow each other in close canon at a quaver's distance, the voices sound like the twittering of birds. The easy grace of the tune is immediately appealing, yet the rhythm sounds intricate to ears accustomed to the squareness of 19th century symmetry. There is little doubt that Elizabethan music has inspired its rhythmic freedom.

In the last movement tenors and basses, sopranos and contraltos, and trebles and boys' altos sing in turn little duets, accompanied by light staccato rhythms of brass, woodwind and strings; again, the narrow strands of two parts move in consecutive seconds. After the third verse the groups of chorus and orchestra combine into a sprightly coda.

Part IV is in one movement and in large ternary form. The words are from Beaumont and Fletcher's *The Knight of the Burning Pestle*, "London, to thee I do present the merry month of May", and the music is in rollicking spirits. A jaunty waltz is heard, softly, as from the distance, when the rough call of the cow horn and the tenor's recitative summon the people. All join in a boisterous *Allegro* which forms the middle and main section of the movement. It develops into a series of free variations on two themes, one sung by the voices, the other played by the orchestra. Even in the many guises they assume in the course of the movement their distinctive vocal and instrumental characters are maintained. After brilliant brass solos answered no less brilliantly by the chorus, the *Allegro* ends abruptly and makes way for the return of the opening. The cow horn calls again; the soloists resume their recitatives; while chorus and orchestra tentatively begin with the waltz which, however, soon gathers momentum. The soloists join in the tune; and at the culmination the boys, reinforced by four horns, chant their "Soomer is icoomen in" across the whole ensemble[1]. The music recedes and dies away during the last words of the tenor. One sudden *fortissimo* chord ends Britten's most exhilarating work.

Quite apart from the work's own merits, the style which Britten has adopted in the *Spring Symphony* holds good promise for the future. In the first place, it is a brilliant example of how to achieve unity in a large form by the greatest diversity of its component parts. Secondly, the scoring for selected ensembles, while using the full orchestra for specific purposes, is a method of artistic economy which, to my knowledge, has never been applied so consistently. To my mind, it even queries the propriety of the orchestra's traditional composition. I confess that for many years I have found the thick sound of the masses of strings, as against the slender tone of the individual wind players, disturbing even with the best orchestras, and not only in classical works. It is by no means a question of balancing only the dynamics. I believe that with the score of the *Spring Symphony*, Britten is continuing what he began when he chose the instruments for his operatic chamber orchestra: to employ only such instruments as he really needs.

---

[1] See *The Choral Music*, p. 100, Ex. 16.—Eds.

JOAN CHISSELL

The Concertos

BRITTEN was a questing young composer in his twenty-fifth year when he wrote the first of his four concertos, that for piano and orchestra, and in his twenty-sixth, when he followed it up from America with a second for violin and orchestra. Both were 'full dress' concertos, in four and three movements respectively. When he returned to this *genre* during the next two years to write two further works for Wittgenstein's left hand, and Ethel Bartlett and Rae Robertson's four hands, he abandoned the traditional concerto pattern (incorporating one or more movements in sonata form—never particularly congenial to him[1]) for a theme and variations in the former case and a ballad in the latter. Since then he has made no more experiments of any kind in the field of the concerto, which cannot be said to have helped to stabilize his style or to touch his heart to the same extent as did words at approximately the same time.

The piano Concerto, written at Snape during the spring of 1938 and dedicated to Lennox Berkeley, had its first performance with the composer as soloist, with the B.B.C. Symphony Orchestra under Sir Henry Wood at a Promenade Concert on 18th August, 1938; in 1945, however, a new slow movement was substituted in place of the original *Recitative and Aria,* winning the revised concerto a warm reception at 1946's Cheltenham Festival.

Britten's own Prom programme note provides the main clue to the work: "It was conceived with the idea of exploiting various important characteristics of the pianoforte, such as its enormous compass, its percussive quality, and its suitability for figuration; so that it is not by any means a Symphony with pianoforte, but rather a bravura Concerto with orchestral accompaniment"[2]. He did not add that the thematic material is of a direct and almost popular kind, such as would win the

---

[1] See, however, *The Chamber Music,* pp. 211ff., and *The Musical Character,* pp. 344f.—EDS.

[2] [22].—EDS.

work immense favour in the U.S.S.R. Its harmonic piquancy results less
from new chords than from familiar chords in unfamiliar sequences,
frequently providing arresting false relations—in fact the unifying
factor in the Concerto is a recurrent motif (introduced between first
and second subjects in the first movement) of two alternating, unrelated chords (Ex. 1):

Ex.1

The form of each movement is unproblematical, the scoring (for full
orchestra, including substantial percussion) brightly coloured, and the
piano writing has the inestimable advantage of having been conceived
through the hands of a pianist.

The opening *Toccata* in D (*Allegro molto e con brio*) is concerned with
two main topics, a flamboyant fanfare-like first subject introduced by
and closely identified with the piano (but subsequently extended by the
orchestra) and a much more lyrical and winsome second subject introduced by the orchestra; between them comes the alternating chordal
motif (Ex. 1) which is of greater significance in the work as a whole
than in any one movement. Throughout this movement the piano
adopts the anti-romantic manner fashionable in the 1920's and constantly mocks the orchestra's attempted sentimentality, but in the *molto
più lento e tranquillo* coda immediately following the cadenza (a brilliant
embellishment of Ex. 1's alternating chords) it is finally melted into
submission by the orchestra's persuasive wooing. The only departure
from convention is the simultaneous recapitulation[1] of first and second
subjects (the latter in augmentation) after a demonstrative development
section, but the student of composition can learn a lot from the
composer's masterly cunning in making a little go a long way—notably
in his treatment of the opening fanfare.

The *Waltz* in D (*Allegretto*), striking in its clarity of texture and
subtlety of orchestration, is in simple ternary form. A laconic melody
tinged with a sophistication again typical of the naughty 1920's, is

[1] Cf. also *The Symphonies*, p. 248, and *The Chamber Music*, pp. 227f. (and Ex. 12 on
p. 230).—Eds.

introduced by the orchestra and taken up by the piano after the latter's
deceptively solemn entry with the alternating chordal motif (Ex. 1)
from the previous movement. A stealthy *poco a poco più mosso* trio
leads to a big moment of recapitulation when, to borrow the composer's
own phraseology, it is as if "the door has been slightly opened" and the
music is no longer "overheard from the next room" as at the start.

In the original *Recitative and Aria* the piano was once more the
enfant terrible, burlesquing, in the recitative, the successive attempts of a
solo oboe, clarinet, bassoon, flute and horn to introduce a warm tune,
with its frivolous interpolations in polka, 'blues' and waltz rhythms,
among others. Finally it is cowed into the subsidiary rôle of accompanist by a romantic orchestral tune of sufficient succulence ultimately to
bring a blush to the composer's cheeks and decide him to suppress the
movement. The new *Impromptu* (*Andante lento*) only salvages one
fragment of delicate pianistic figuration from the original movement
(Ex. 2):

Cast in that passacaglia form which invariably stimulates Britten to
his best, it is music of simple, grave beauty which shows up the composer's remarkable maturing and mellowing during the war years
rather too acutely for the comfort of the remaining movements in
present-day performance. After introducing the nine-bar theme (whose
harmonic piquancy again results from false relations: Ex. 3),

the piano merely decorates each of the seven subsequent orchestral
statements of it with various distinctive figurations calculated to

heighten the predominant orchestral tone-colour and throw new harmonic light on the melody. The last, halting statement of the theme, culminating in the profound tranquillity of a C major harmonization of the final E, is supremely beautiful.

The final *March* (*Allegro moderato*) allows its stirring rhythms (including a reference to the alternating chordal motif of Ex. 1) to be interrupted by a plangent, second-subject-like chant, which makes an impassioned contribution to the development, but not to the recapitulation. The main tune (Ex. 4), like a popular marching song, is not one of Britten's most subtle inspirations,

Ex.4

but its *ff largamente* recapitulation after the long *crescendo* of the cadenza (with rigid accompaniment for bass drum and cymbals) is invariably an exciting moment.

Britten's second Concerto, that for violin and orchestra, dedicated to Henry Boys, was his first undertaking after crossing the Atlantic; written during the summer of 1939 at St. Jorite, Quebec, and Amityville, Long Island, it had its first performance at Carnegie Hall, New York, with Brosa and the New York Philharmonic Symphony Orchestra under Barbirolli on 27th March, 1940, and eventually reached London on 6th April, 1941, when Thomas Matthews played it with the London Philharmonic Orchestra, under Cameron. The slightly revised version of 1950 was first introduced by Gimpel and the Royal Philharmonic Orchestra under Beecham at the Festival Hall on 12th December, 1951.

Though the soloist's virtuosity is taxed just as much as in the piano Concerto, the violin Concerto is a work of much more searching idiom, solid substance and serious intent. Even so, the first two of the three continuous movements are completely dispassionate and extrovert in kind; not till the final passacaglia (the first instance of this subsequently much favoured form) does the composer make any heart-felt appeal to the listener's emotions.

The sparingly scored *Moderato con moto* is an urbane discourse on
two clearly defined topics, both introduced by the solo violin: the first
(Ex. 5) a suave but short-breathed melody indicative of the composer's
liking for unexpected turnings,

the second (Ex. 6) a more determined, masculine outburst:

Of no less importance than the melody in both cases is the strikingly
individual scrap of rhythmic figuration which each subject has for its
accompaniment; it is the persistence of these rhythms throughout that
enhances the orderliness of the movement. As the development section
(which hangs fire rather badly at the start) is almost entirely concerned
with the second subject, the recapitulation is monopolized by the first,
save that the lengthening of the bars from four to six crotchet beats
enables the soloist to work in, as a thrummed accompaniment, the
second subject's attendant rhythm alongside that of the first subject
(Ex. 7):

Ex.7

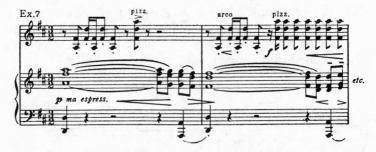

The deep diatonic warmth of D major at this point is particularly welcome after the preceding restless surface chromaticism.

The *Vivace,* a brilliant scherzo with contrasting trio, puts the work out of bounds for all but the virtuoso player: glissandi, harmonics and breath-taking scale-passages in thirds, sixths, octaves and tenths abound in the pungently chromatic opening and closing sections, where the interest lies not so much in the quality of the material itself as in the music's rhythmic drive and the brittle and sometimes freakish scoring (such as the duet for piccolo and tuba with additional tremolo harmonics from the violin at the start of the recapitulation). The lyrical trio in an appealing A minor is like a penitent child after a bout of bad temper; its melody recurs after a free recapitulation to herald the Concerto's sole cadenza, which serves not only to link second and third movements, but also to unify the work as a whole by harking back to first movement rhythms and, eventually, themes.

The solo violin's last *andante lento* reference to the first subject of the first movement at the start of the finale is no less eloquent than the gravely beautiful, shapely main passacaglia theme itself which trombones introduce simultaneously in the bass (Ex. 8):

Ex.8

This last movement has an easy, continuous flow in spite of the sharply defined character and colouring of each of the nine substantial variations which follow the fugal opening section; the soloist occasionally merely comments on the theme, but at other times takes an active part in its development, as when inverting it in the sixth (*comodo molto*) section.

The gradual abandonment of chromaticism for lucid diatonic harmony in the last two variations enables the Concerto to end in a mood of confident serenity; the beautiful last *lento e solenne* section, in particular, allows a remarkable fore-glimpse of the mature Britten with his very clear sense of harmonic direction.

The several 1950 revisions do not add up to anything as substantial as the new movement in the piano Concerto, and mainly serve to tighten the argument by omitting odd bars here and there which could be regarded, in the case of this most unrhetorical composer, as rhetorical[1] or redundant. Notable instances occur in the cadenza and the lead into it. Two phrase endings in the scherzo are given sharper heads, the violin is given longer comments in the third (*pesante*) section of the passacaglia, and there are slight but desirable adjustments to the rhythmic figurations in the first and last movements. The only instances of rescoring are the lightened orchestral doubling of the violin's second subject tune in the first movement, and the excision of four triangle strokes from the scherzo.

The *Diversions on a Theme* for piano (left hand) and orchestra[2] which followed from Maine in the summer of 1940 were commissioned (like Ravel's left hand Concerto) by the one-armed Austrian pianist, Paul Wittgenstein, who held sole performing rights until 1951, and was unable to bring the work to England until 14th October, 1950, when he played it with the Bournemouth Municipal Orchestra under Trevor Harvey. Britten's foreword[3] to the score explains his approach: "I was attracted from the start by the problems involved in writing a work for this particular medium, especially as I was well acquainted with and extremely enthusiastic about Mr. Wittgenstein's skill in overcoming what appear to be insuperable difficulties. In no place in the work did I attempt to imitate a two-handed piano technique, but concentrated on exploiting and emphasizing the single line approach. I have tried to treat the problem in every aspect, as a glance at the list of movements will show: special features are, trills and scales in the *Recitative*; widespread arpeggios in the *Nocturne*; agility over the keyboard in the *Badinerie* and *Toccata*; and repeated notes in the final *Tarantella*."

The form of the work is that of a theme and eleven succinct variations entitled *Recitative* (for piano alone), *Romance, March, Rubato, Chorale, Nocturne, Badinerie, Ritmico* (omitted from the revised version

---

[1] See footnote (¹), *The Musical Atmosphere*, p. 14.—EDS.
[2] See also *The Incidental Music*, p. 300.—EDS.   [3] [23].—EDS.

of 1951, throughout which the solo part is slightly simplified and the orchestration modified in the finale), *Toccatas I* and *II*, *Adagio*, and *Tarantella*. The theme is not so much a self-significant melody as a pregnant note-series built out of the stark intervals of the fifth and its inversion; not till the ensuing variations is this 'raw material' moulded into meaningful patterns and rhythms. The composer's uncanny skill and economy of effort in devising these patterns and rhythms is equally in evidence when it comes to "exploiting and emphasizing the single line approach"; given a player of Wittgenstein's muscular strength, the soloist can hold his own against the orchestra throughout in spite of somewhat heavy percussion. Yet, while challenging Britten's mind, the work as a whole does not give the impression of ever having warmed his heart. The uningratiating character of the two basic intervals of the fifth and fourth may in part account for its frigidity—certainly it lacks the charm of the earlier *Frank Bridge Variations* as well as the humanity of the composer's more recent works.

From one hand Britten turned to four hands for his last essay (to date) in the concerto medium, writing his *Scottish Ballad* in California, shortly before returning to England in 1941, expressly for the two-piano duo of Ethel Bartlett and Rae Robertson, who gave the first performance with the Cincinatti Symphony Orchestra under Eugene Goosens on 28th November, 1941. At its first English performance at a Prom under Cameron on 10th July, 1943, Clifford Curzon was partnered by Britten himself.

Though in one continuous movement, the *Ballad* divides into two distinct sections, the one slow and dour, the other fast and gay, in both of which the composer draws on Scottish traditional tunes for his thematic material. After *Dundee*, a grand old hymn tune, first appearing in the Scottish Psalter of 1615, there comes a funeral-march-like Strathspey melody in C minor which combines with the oboe's *Turn Ye to Me*, and is followed by *Flowers of the Forest* in a brighter F major, before a recapitulation of the first three tunes concludes the slow section. The fun then begins in *allegro molto* tempo with three familiar reels before a still faster final fling in the coda. But though the work is a brilliant *tour de force*, audaciously clever and frequently witty, some listeners who love folk song may wince at the sophistication at variance with the intrinsically simple character of each tune in the slow section—the dissonances that acidify *Dundee*, for example, and the tremolo-cum-glissando clatter of the pianos' comments on *Flowers of the Forest.* Still more they may deplore the element of parody in the quick section. But that was in 1941, and on the other side of the Atlantic. Homesickness was soon to bring Britten back to England, and to awaken in him a new sympathy for the great legacy of national tunes inherited from Great Britain's past.

GEORGES AURIC
(*translated by Tony Mayer*)

The Piano Music

I. ITS PLACE IN BRITTEN'S DEVELOPMENT

ONE of the surest proofs of the importance we attach to an artist's work, and of our lively interest in him, is our sudden wish to discover all we can of the way in which he reached his mastery. Together with the vast and anonymous crowd of his admirers, we acknowledge and salute his present stature. At the same time we feel an acute curiosity about his first and his lesser known works.

We inquire into his first essays, his minor pieces. Already arresting in many ways, they are still incompletely expressed. In them we detect various—sometimes conflicting—styles, not, as yet, definitely blended.

As we all know by now, the personality of the composer is unquestionable—brilliant even. We know, too, that we should be able to recognize this personality in his earliest and least accomplished works, and that, if only we took the trouble, its discovery would prove to be one of the most rewarding tasks imaginable.

Do they not make most exciting reading, these early works of Benjamin Britten? His genius is now an undisputed fact, but it is precisely the 'mixture' of styles that they sometimes show, their ingenuity and unconcern, which it is so fascinating to compare with the perfection of form he later achieved. They are more valuable, no doubt, than any of the composer's personal recollections; they tell us what, around his twentieth year, were his tastes, his feelings, his worries. And the road he has followed since gives us an example of a technique as, step by step, it becomes more certain, more solid, and finally reaches complete fulfilment.

It would of course be absurdly paradoxical to spend too long a time in seeking this great musician elsewhere than in his most perfect works. It is clear that henceforth he represents a 'tone', a 'manner', a 'style', all of which are definite and definable, which only he possesses and with which none else can contend. But, once again, this 'tone', this 'manner', this 'style', did not appear suddenly, abruptly, in a work representing a break with all its forerunners. On the contrary, patient study of his earlier works will show us, like an echo, the composer's slow and fascinating development. We shall notice then, as they fall upon the ear, those harmonic combinations and rhythmical discoveries which we joyfully recognize later, elaborated by a composer who has learnt, and learnt magnificently, the secret of using and moulding his technique, and finally of submitting it to the boldest and most unexpected impulses of his inspiration.

I know that there are all sorts of methods of presenting a very important composer to an audience, of throwing some illuminating light on his name. I also know that it is useful and helpful to linger awhile on his years of apprenticeship, before one attempts the study of his major works. Let us not however—for it would be both unnecessary and, at the present juncture, tiresome—require the machine which explores the past to take us back too far. Let us not recall the successive 'manners' of a Mozart, a Beethoven, or a Wagner: let us not attempt to compare *Rienzi* and *Parsifal*.

These thoughts come to me as I read the works of Benjamin Britten. With him we find ourselves at one of the most advanced positions in contemporary music. To do justice to the masters who preceded him in our admiration, let us only remember the lesson taught to us by the first works of Debussy, Ravel, Strawinsky, and Schoenberg.

While playing the *Holiday Diary,* this book of youthful recollections, I marvelled at finding there—and with a kind of really delightful freshness—the very *accent* which, little by little, was to claim and later to compel recognition of that strong, remarkable (and now so rich) personality of Benjamin Britten.

Let us underline this most interesting case. The flexibility and intelligence of his piano playing impressed me unforgettably when, some time ago, I heard him accompany several of Peter Pears's recitals. And in fact his accompaniments are always most cleverly and skilfully written. But when we peruse the impressive list of his compositions, how can we fail to be astonished by the small number inspired by an instrument which does not, in fact, seem to mean very much to him.

The art of Britten is evidently not of the kind which develops in long-drawn hours spent in the solitary company of the piano. His mind is attracted above all by the sort of writing which, whether for orchestra or for choir, deliberately uses the tightest and most complicated combinations. What is admirable is the ease with which it is all done, such ease that the less experienced listener can, in his turn, follow him easily and closely along ways where so many others would find themselves in difficulties. Here one should draw a picture of Britten the writer of music for the stage—the stage where, from *Peter Grimes* onwards, he has won the first place in composition, with the disconcerting ease to which I must now pay the tribute it deserves.

The *Introduction and Rondo alla Burlesca* and the *Maȝurka Elegiaca* for two pianos are, with the *Holiday Diary*, the only works wherein he has agreed to limit himself to his own instrument. And, of course, his musicianship is there too! The *Rondo alla Burlesca* in particular is both so witty and so compactly written that one cannot but admire it whole-heartedly. Not one bar is without a purpose; not one suggests improvisation. A trifle indeed, but also an excellent lesson in style. A piece where quality is so evident that we cannot help being struck. And yet these two works are decidedly not amongst Britten's *magna opera*. Nor are the four short pieces of the *Holiday Diary* Suite; but for the reasons I mentioned at the outset it seems quite indispensable to study the composer's second *opus* very thoroughly. The slow movements of the book, in particular, have already a resonance and a poetic quality which are genuinely personal. Play again *Sailing* and *Night* and think of the evolution of the composer who, eighteen years ago, wrote those charming early pieces.

One of the last signs, one of the surest proofs of his true mastery, is certainly the trend of thought to which this little Suite has led us. After the admirable Britten of today let us give a friendly greeting to the delightful beginner of 1934 and let us thank him—the opportunity should not be missed—for what he has done for us since, in so unforgettable a way.

A. E. F. DICKINSON

The Piano Music

II. CRITICAL SURVEY

FOR a composer who has appeared from time to time as a concert pianist, Britten has published surprisingly little for piano. There are an early Suite for piano solo and two pieces, of somewhat later date, for two pianos. It is safe to assume that Britten has composed, or partly composed, considerably more than these three works, and has extemporized many more pieces, without bothering to heat them up, or cool them down, to coherent compositions. One cannot talk *pianoforte* in a day. The published works betray no fumbling about the keyboard, nor, again, a mere cosmopolitan technique; and structurally the earliest errs, if anything, on the side of an excess of thematic impulses and textual formulae. Such as it is, this group affords a glimpse of the composer at work on purely musical ideas and in the comparatively inflexible medium (as regards tone-quality) of the commonest of mechanical instruments, as opposed to the art which is linked with the stage and with the natural inflections of the human voice. These pieces may also be regarded as more or less early adventures into the glittering surfaces and bitter, unfathomable depths of sound-relationship, of which the piano is a particularly candid and penetrating explorer. So far they form an index of the kind of phraseology and assertions by which the composer steered between the shoals of domestic convention and the insidious undertow of modish chromaticism.

The Suite, originally entitled *Holiday Tales* and since re-published as *Holiday Diary*, was written in 1934 and published in the following year. It might be described as Prelude, Andante, Rondo-Scherzo, and Epilogue; the official titles being, *Early morning bathe*, *Sailing*, *Fun-*

fair, and *Night.* The sequence is not quite that of the normal suite, descriptive or imaginative, but it is clearly discernible, and the key-scheme of C-D-A-C major, somewhat 'bumpy' but decisive at the finish, encloses the various displays of mood. The first movement places a clear, swinging tune (Ex. 1) in mainly 8-bar phrases, in C and later E,

Ex.1
Vivace ma non troppo presto   cf. folk song *The Lawyer*

in a flow of arpeggio which runs diatonic and clear after a preliminary sally in the salt sprays of pantonality[1]. A dominant pedal, and an equivocal chord of fourth and fifth above it, avoid triteness of texture, and the music returns to the careless (but not formless) sprays at the end. Definitely a salt *and* fresh water bathe, it may be said. The slow movement, in D, pursues a short melodic curve (Ex. 2) resourcefully:

Ex.2 *Andante comodo*

Its interludes of fresh tonality (F, A, E) which stand in clear relation to a persistently affirmed central point, and a supple rhythm, both in respect of phrase-lengths and of stimulating variants of note-values, lend conviction to the re-establishment of the prevailing tranquillity. This is sailing for pleasure and contemplation, not racing.

The next movement (*Fun-fair*) is restless in mood and idea. There is a toccata-like opening, bitonal (A-F sharp) and conveniently collapsible in content for purposes of interim entries, by means of a sequential ending which summarizes the whole. It is contrasted, in rondo fashion, with no less than four separate episodes. The first of these is pert and capricious, the second resolved to be definite in phrase and key but dismissed after nineteen bars, the third in pursuit of biplanar sonorities in a cosy diatonic style, and the last more mischievous than amusing. A full restatement of the main theme, which avoids a too easy anticipation by its subtle pattern of $4+5+2/2+6$

[1] Originally Schoenberg's term: see his forthcoming *Structural Functions of Harmony.*—EDS.

(bars) and is readily extended for a coda, seeks to absorb all these distractions and incidentally comes down in favour of A major; but the total impression is rather confusing, and almost needs the title to explain its heterogeneous quality. The last movement (*Night*) lets a recurring phrase (Ex. 3), soaring remotely above the treble clef, and mainly of three bars with an occasional two, wander steadily into chromatic keys and keylessness, on a firm basis of tonic and related pedals, with a rhapsodic 'alto' counterpoint derived from the tune of the first movement.

Ex.3 *Molto lento e tranquillo, sempre rubato*

If one is on the prowl for anticipations of later events, the plain but colourful persistence of this nocturne might be singled out for a more microscopic examination of harmonic properties; but I find it somewhat monotonous. This Suite appeared under the banner, so to speak, of Frank Bridge, Delius, Ireland, Arthur Benjamin, and others in the same series. As its title truly declares, it is not an overpowering or even a challenging work, but it betrays a firm hand, especially in the second movement.

The two-piano pieces were written in 1941. It might be added that this creative activity marked the composer's recovery from a streptococcal infection in California, and was followed or concluded by his decision to return to England and not to become an American citizen [309]. It was a time of headaches for all, both great and small. Whether any awareness of that period of strain and devastation necessarily found its way into these particular works is very doubtful. At the right time, music may grace or invigorate man's struggles against his declared enemies, or his efforts for the establishment of a new order. But in a tragically sundered world mere music can only assert its own logic for what it may be worth, as a series of universal conclusions in an atmosphere of social suspense, and an image of order, refreshing but distant from common needs.

The *Introduction and Rondo alla Burlesca* for two pianos (published in 1945, three years after the companion duet), introduces a grave contrapuntal framework (Ex. 4a), which soon thickens harmonically (Ex. 4b), as the setting for the main motive (Ex. 5),

the second presentation of which is quoted. Two short but highly distinct episodes provide contrasts, the second just narcotic enough to justify the elaborate and excitable process of recovery. For this purpose a contentious and continuous canon, at the octave at one bar's distance, is carried out in a series of interlinking stages (8+4/8/5+6 bars in measure, on my estimate—beginning at the *third* bar of p. 14), until the conflict of accent resolves in a statement of the main theme in melodic unison. This still leaves the ascent of the third bar (Ex. 5) good for a considerable extension, by challenging, in the name of the

second pianist, intrusive modulations and sonorities under the signature of the first pianist. As the *Allegro* sinks to a point of exhaustion,
the *Grave*, quiet but stiffened with fresh harmonic tension, steps in for
a moment, leaving the *Allegro* its cue (cadenza) for returning for a
quick, forcible finish, in which the second piano's direct inversion of
the first piano's figures seems to find consummation in the painful and
almost ominous E flat which both pianists hurl at the final chord of
D minor. The 'burlesque' is so far grim enough to be a sign of the
times.

The *Mazurka Elegiaca*, a tribute to Paderewski, strikes a deeper
note. A test of detail is that when the sum of the various strands made
available has determined the urge (Ex. 6a)

from which the main movement is derived, the effect later (p. 5) of the
first bar duplicating itself, so that the descending and sequential octave
figure falls now on the third and other more accented bars, is impressive
and not corrective. It is heard in relation to the inner impulse of
the music. The pronounced escape from this otherwise unbearable
threnody (no title is seriously needed to point the evocative and
obsessional fixations of pitch-centre) is strengthened by a plain but
riveting counterpoint to the repeated chordal rhythm, in a manner
almost as unrelenting as in one of the Species beloved of the
schoolmen (Ex. 6b).

The melodic integration of the two figures in a qualified contrapuntal
inversion of the original (Ex. 7),

inverted and uninverted in alternate phrases, leads to an emphatic
climax of tone in a remote key, in the reiterated rhythm. This lends
weight to the more elaborate recovery of the basic counterpoint, with
interesting revisions of the interval between the component lines and
other ingenuities. In the returning elegiac sequences, the expected
repetition of the first six bars (p. 13) is enhanced by melodic inversion
in the three main strands, a novel application of an old fugal device to a
fundamentally melodic situation. By way of a kind of compensation,
the counterpoint of the next stage (p. 14) is ironed out into a sonorous
and indeed solemn rhythmic unison. In a faltering resumption, the
descending figure is placed again in the third and stronger bar, and
this time it does not drop pitch in repetition. Instead, it lingers on as it
is, while the rhythm twice attempts to recover itself after breaking
down. The figure persists, in essential, as the 'extraneous' seventh in the
final chord. Thus one type of sequence eloquently replaces another
at this concluding point. Throughout, the need for two pianists
and pianos is paramount. In many works for this combination, the
ponderous and pompously inefficient duplication of rhythms often

sounds futile and misplaced, and the antiphony and polyphony seem so trifling a part for one player or the other as hardly to justify carrying the disadvantage of two interpreters, each on the same type of independent instrument. (One accepts the jolting ensemble of two on piano and strings[1], or of a group of soloists in one genre of tone, complementary and contrasted in detail; but two on two pianos, each of which is self-sufficient by boundless historical example, are another matter.) Here, however, the duality is apposite to the imagery.

At the *Mazurka Elegiaca* the strictly pianistic record breaks off. So far the contrapuntal call has not come again in the necessary percussive or kaleidoscopic terms for two pianos or one, and the mere dynamic and otherwise vivid varieties of assertion within the scope of two hands on one piano have seemed less appealing than the dramatic interplay of voice and voice and accompanying instruments as such. Failing which, another piano concerto is a more likely proposition than a Prelude, Aria and Finale of sonata proportions. Britten is not alone in this rejection of the piano[2]. Amongst English supporters Elgar, Holst, Vaughan Williams and Walton might be cited. It must be admitted that the piano excels as an accomplished mimic or substitute, or accompanist, for voices and other instruments, or for dancing, rather than as a singer *per se*[3]; and that the exploration of texture by Bach, Scarlatti, Chopin, Liszt, Debussy, Ireland and Bax, for example, has narrowed the orbit of the explorer of today. Not being a protagonist of texture, except as an unfailing 'contingent matter' and technical problem, Britten has not aspired to be counsel for the piano's fresh release from its common confinement in ancillary posts.

---

[1] Unfortunately, often.—EDS.

[2] Cf. *The Pianist*, p. 314.—EDS.

[3] Significantly, Alan Rawsthorne, exceptional amongst English composers in the exclusively instrumental inspiration of his instrumental music, is equally exceptional in his resuscitation of the piano.—EDS.

IMOGEN HOLST

Britten and the Young

WHEN Britten writes music for young people to sing or listen to, he is fortunately unaware of the school-teacher's habit of classifying human beings into separate age-groups. He has obviously never thought of youth as a 'problem' demanding special measures in education: the Young Person for whom he wrote his Guide to the Orchestra might just as well have been eight or eighteen or eighty. Originally written for the film *Instruments of the Orchestra*[1], the work consists of variations and a fugue on a dance tune from Purcell's *Abdelazar, or The Moor's Revenge* (Ex. 1):

Ex. 1

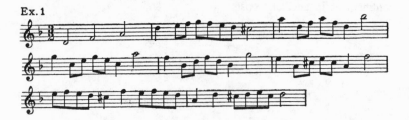

Even those who have never heard an orchestra before are able to recognize its main sections when each in turn is given this theme. The woodwind's sustained minims and *staccato* quavers suggest some of the

[1] See also *The Incidental Music*, p. 295 —EDS.

many possibilities of contrasting mood; the held semibreves of the brass, played *fp* with a *crescendo,* convey a welcome impression of flexibility; while the strings manage to combine *arco* and *pizzicato* in their eight short bars (the double basses wasting no time in asserting their right to be treated as soloists). During the variations for each instrument, from flute and piccolo to xylophone and whip, the listener becomes acquainted with the many-sided and frequently conflicting characteristics of each individual voice in the orchestra; the fluttering grace-notes of the two flutes chase each other up to the sudden piercing trill of the piccolo, the oboes' expressive *pp* alternates with a passionate *ff*, and the clarinets' agile arpeggios blossom into a mellow *rallentando*. The two distinct sides of the bassoon's nature are heard in a duet (see Ex. 2), where the deliberate tonguing of the dotted quavers is answered by a high-held *rubato* that is plaintive without being peevish:

The *Polacca*, in characteristic polonaise rhythm, gives the violins an opportunity to clamber from the depths to the heights and to enjoy the full resonance of their energetically repeated double stopping. No one listening to the warm legato of the violas' variation could ever make the mistake of regarding this instrument as an inferior version of the violin. The *pianissimo* accompaniment to the 'cellos' cantabile tune shows Britten's use of the seventeenth century manner of achieving a *piano*: he transforms his full symphony orchestra into a temporary chamber orchestra without interfering with the balance of his texture (see Ex. 3):

Ex. 3

The double basses add their characteristic comment in rising staccato quavers, but they also become expressive in their highest register, and their rapid four-octave flourish serves as a reminder of their virtuosity. In the following variation one is aware of the beauty of their resonant *pizzicato* octaves as they move through the hushed tremolo which surrounds the harp's majestic solo. This continuity in the accompanying instruments helps to prevent the filmed close-up of the soloists from turning the music into a mere catalogue of events: the strings' tremolo is still audible, and the harp still quoting from its own solo, when the four horns fling their challenge to each other, allowing their sforzandos to fade into a *dolcissimo* distance that is reminiscent of those dying echoes in the *Serenade* for tenor, horn and strings. The lively staccato of the trumpets brings back the cheerful mood of the dance, while the trombones extract every ounce of enjoyment from the flavour of parody in the sustained marcato of their pompous progress. As was to be expected, the timpani are given a real tune to play, accompanied by a dry, parchment-like mutter from the *saltando* strings: one by one the percussion instruments add their appropriate gestures to the dance. The xylophone's chromatic contribution encourages the strings to play *col legno* and the chattering excitement mounts higher and higher until the whip, one of Britten's favourite instruments, is given the privilege of silencing everyone else while it makes its solo appearance. The work ends with a fugue in which all the instruments come in one after the other, in the order of their solo variations. At the climax, when horns and trumpets and trombones bring in Purcell's *maestoso* dance tune to join the *Allegro molto* of the fugal subject, the music is characteristically labelled *con slancio*. It is this unfailing enthusiasm which prevents the noise from becoming oppressive and saves the ingenuity of the cross-rhythms from becoming over-intellectual.

Such exuberance is surely one of the ingredients that makes Britten's music immediately acceptable to so many inexperienced listeners, whatever their ages may be. The same exuberance can be recognized in his *Simple Symphony* for strings, transcribed from piano pieces written as a child. The four movements are in no danger of being set aside as interesting period pieces, for they sound thoroughly convincing. The mature Britten has never abandoned the warmth and enthusiasm of his youthful *Sentimental Saraband*.

Not having lost touch with this early warmth, he has never fallen into the error of writing for children as if their language were different from his own. In the songs *Friday Afternoons*, which he wrote for small boys to sing at school[1], the frequent use of repetition is the result not just of the practical need for simplicity and economy, but also of knowing that children have an insatiable appetite for repetition and that they will seize hold of it, as in *Old Abram Brown*, with a dramatic seriousness of purpose that would put most opera choruses to shame. As always in Britten's music, there is an imaginative awareness that knows no barrier of age or environment: it reaches out to the old woman in *Lucretia* who realizes that she is "shorn of beauty", and it reaches back to the helpless infant in the *Charm of Lullabies* who is unable to protest against the violent shakings and the harsh threats of a *Prestissimo furioso*.

This imaginative sympathy for the defencelessness of the very young has brought about some of the most beautiful passages in Britten's music, such as the verse about the children in the *Hymn to St. Cecilia*, where the vocal writing demands a simplicity that is rarely achieved by

---

[1] The earliest published work in which Britten made use of children's voices was the *Three Two-Part Songs* (1932) for boys', or women's, voices and piano (see *The Choral Music*, pp. 90f.). Children's voices also appeared in Britten's score to the G.P.O. film *H.P.O., or 6d. Telegram* (1939): see *The Incidental Music*, p. 299.—EDS.

adult singers. He had already discovered, in *Friday Afternoons*, that the quality of children's voices was indispensable for the unselfconscious grace of the song about the cuckoo and for the tranquil assurance of "Sing levy dew, sing levy dew, the water and the wine, The seven bright gold wires, and the bugles that do shine". It is a quality that is very nearly indispensable in the *Ceremony of Carols*, for the music loses some of its grace when sung by women instead of children. The loss is particularly noticeable in the solos. If a small boy sings the line about the nightingale whose "song is hoarse and nought thereto" he makes no fuss about it and the meaning looks after itself. But an adult, however intelligent, is likely to feel burdened by the implications of the words and will strive to 'interpret' the phrase, in spite of the relentless repetition of the harp's falling semitone which is already saying everything that needs to be said. The treble solo in *Rejoice in the Lamb* is also apt to lose some of its simplicity unless it is sung by a child: when the poet considers his cat Jeoffry, who "worships God in his way . . . by wreathing his body seven times round with elegant quickness", no sensible child is likely to think that there is anything improbable in the words.

In *A Boy was Born*, Britten makes use of the contrast between the direct simplicity of the boys' chorus and the controlled technique of the S.A.T.B. choir. The contrast is particularly effective in the variation where the sopranos and altos sing a sustained four-part setting of "In the bleak midwinter" while the boys sing a 12/8 version of the "Corpus Christi" carol, their voices lending a suggestion of the impersonal dignity of a traditional folk singer to their repetition of " Lulley, lulley, lulley, lulley, The falcon hath borne my mate away".

These contrasts in tone-colour have their dramatic possibilities. In *St. Nicolas* there is an overwhelmingly dramatic moment when the boy Nicolas leaves his childhood behind him and the piping treble voice of the smallest choir-boy, singing Ex. 4

Ex. 4
ad lib.
God be glo - ri - fied!

is transformed into the full, ringing voice of the tenor soloist, in all its power and confidence. The storm in *St. Nicolas* also has its moments of drama. When the distant choir of schoolgirls describes how the lightning hisses through the night, there is a slight breathlessness in the white tone of their untrained voices: this breathlessness, which can often be such a disadvantage in singing, is here turned to advantage, conveying exactly the right atmosphere of anxiety and endeavour.

By accepting the limitations of children's voices and giving them what he knows they will enjoy, Britten gets what he wants from them. There is raucous glee in the tone of all those schoolboys' voices in the *Spring Symphony* as they let themselves go in the line about "strawberries swimming in the cream": it is the one tone of voice that can hold its own at that level of pitch against the energetic scurrying of the *fortissimo* woodwind and the *pesante* determination of the solo tuba. And the undisguised enjoyment of those youthful singers is the only possible mood that can provide the necessary link between the swiftly-fluctuating changes of thought and feeling in the Symphony's various sections. The children's enjoyment turns to sheer ecstasy when the composer invites them to whistle[1]: that sudden streak of sound that whisks its way up to the roof must surely offer its performers more delight than any other half-bar of music that has yet been written.

In the Finale of the Symphony there is a wonderful blend of tone-colour when the boys sing of the swollen river (see Ex. 5):

Ex.5

The rum-bling ri-vers now do warm,___ for lit-tle boys to pad-dle

Their low-lying voices have a peculiarly hollow resonance when heard through the sustained *pianissimo* of the brass and the quivering trickle of the two harps whose waves of sound lap against each other in gently conflicting semitones. The boys keep up a muttered repetition of the word "paddle", their voices laden with the absorbed, unhurried seriousness of those who are intent on exploring a river-bed. This passage sounded particularly effective in the first performance in Amsterdam, for the Dutch boys have an astonishing resonance in their low register and need no encouragment to exaggerate all their consonants. There was tremendous conviction in their tone at the climax of the movement, where they are given the tune of "Soomer is icoomen

[1] Ex. 15 in *The Choral Music*, p. 100.—EDS.

in"[1]. Unfortunately our English boys have not yet been able to make themselves heard here through the *fortissimo* entry of the four horns' *cuivré* unison. We must hope that before long they will have learnt how to produce the necessary tone, for the whole structure of the movement is built round the secure inevitability of this entry.

The structure of *Albert Herring* also depends, to a certain extent, on children's singing. When Emmie, Cis and Harry bounce their ball against the door of Mrs. Herring's greengrocery shop at the beginning of Act I, Scene 2, their singing-game, with its inevitable insistence, becomes the frame-work surrounding the tragi-comic drama that is to be unfolded within the three walls of the shop. At the very moment when Albert is beginning to wonder whether he is missing everything that makes life worth living, his bewilderment is made all the more poignant by the entry of Emmie, who dashes into the shop in tearing high spirits, telling him she's got "extra holidays", and waving him a cheerful farewell after having paid him in farthings for her two-pennorth of herbs. When the scene changes to the vicarage garden on May Day, it seems almost a pity that the opera should have been intended for grown-ups, since there must be whole audiences of schoolchildren who would enjoy to the full the delicious absurdity of the flutteringly over-anxious Miss Wordsworth as she gives out a well-meaning but incongruous "doh" on her pitch-pipe and beats out a determined but unhelpful "One-and-two-and" to her inattentive pupils whose gaze keeps wandering to the trestle-tables covered with pink blancmange and sausage-rolls and trifle.

However, there is no need to complain. For Britten has given whole audiences of children an opera of their own in *The Little Sweep* (from *Let's Make an Opera*).[2] As with the *Young Person's Guide to the Orchestra*, this "Entertainment for Young People" is rapturously enjoyed by the young of all ages, who insist on going to see and hear it over and over again. He has given the seven children in the cast just the right songs to sing and just the right story to act. And he has given the hundreds of children in the audience a chance of joining in the singing. Instead of feeling frustrated and cut off by a dark, impenetrable barrier from the excitement of the lights and the colours and the sounds, they find themselves caught up into the very centre of things. It is the members of the audience who provide the overture which sets the scene for the drama: it is they who send Black Bob and his son Clem and the little sweep-boy Sammy riding through the Suffolk lanes one morning in 1810, to sweep the chimneys at Iken Hall. By the time the curtain goes up there is no longer any dividing-line between audience and performer or between amateur and professional, so there need be no fear of any self-consciousness, either on or off the stage. And as soon as the story begins to unfold, one realizes that there is no dividing-line in Britten, whether he writes a tragic opera for grown-ups or a light-hearted entertainment for children. When Black Bob and Clem threaten the eight-year-old Sammy, the moment is as fraught with tragedy as the bullying scene in *Peter Grimes*. Five bars (Ex. 6), are enough to convey the sense of desolation as Sammy is left alone in the narrow chimney, with his rope dangling in the fireplace of the empty nursery:

The children's voices are first heard in a game of hide-and-seek off-stage: their distant cries of "Where are you?" bridge the narrow gap between speech and song. The rescue of Sammy who is stuck in the chimney bridges the still narrower gap between singing and dancing, for the children's 12/8 tune, to the words "Pull the rope gently until he is free, Pull O! Heave O!" brings its own action with it. When Sammy has been rescued, the falling semitones of his pathetic appeal, "Please don't send me up again!" follow the dateless tradition of all operatic laments. The children plan to hide him in their toy-cupboard; in an excited *Vivace* (Ex. 7), they lead him across the room, deliberately planting his sooty feet down on the clean dust-sheets in order to make false tracks between the fireplace and the window:

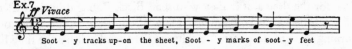

Soot - y tracks up-on the sheet, Soot - y marks of soot-y feet

There is a dramatic moment when they hear someone coming and have to hide under the dust-sheets that are shrouding the chairs. Black Bob and Clem are hustled back into the room by the irate housekeeper, Miss Baggott, whose entry has a paralysing effect on the *vivace* tune; it staggers into an astonished augmentation (Ex. 8):

Soot - y   tracks up - on the   sheet

But Sammy is safe, and as soon as they get a chance to emerge from their hiding places, the children prepare to give him a bath. The audience sings a rapid, syncopated description of this transformation scene, undeterred by the noisy splashings and the chromatic showers of soapsuds provided by the strings' accompaniment to the third verse. When the curtain rises again, a gleaming white Sammy is thanking the children for their help. They are distressed to think that he has to work for such a cruel master; the almost unbearable pathos of "home is a hundred miles away" is saved from any suggestion of sentimentality by the extreme dignity of the children as they stand patiently waiting for their solo lines in the ensemble. Their unruffled resignation, as they watch the conductor for their lead, is unconsciously appropriate and deeply moving.

Comedy returns with the indignant approach of Miss Baggott (Ex. 9):

Sammy is once more hidden in the toy-cupboard and the other children gleefully stick their tongues in their cheeks as they drape themselves into a sedate imitation of a Kate Greenaway *tableau*, the eldest boy leaning nonchalantly against the mantelpiece as he reads from a leather-bound volume, and the smallest girl sitting demurely on the floor as she inspects her toys. When the intolerable Miss Baggott threatens to open the cupboard door, a panic-stricken gasp of dismay can be heard throughout the theatre. But one of the children on the stage saves the situation by pretending to faint. "Help! help! she's collapsed!" exclaims Miss Baggott, in a ridiculously fussy sequence of *marcato* crotchets. The children, in the approved style of many an operatic ensemble, take no notice whatsoever of the violent commotion going on all round them, but chant "Poor Juliet! Can she be dying?" in a wickedly lugubrious legato, kneeling in an early-nineteenth-century row, and lengthening their faces to an expression of mock piety. Miss Baggott retires, defeated, and the scene ends with the children's boisterous dance of triumph. It is left to the members of the audience to convey the passing of the hours with the haunting 6/8 of their *Night Song* (Ex. 10):

At the end of the song, as the last "Tu-whoo!" fades away, the silence that receives it has a quality that is seldom to be found in a theatre.

It is morning. The coach is coming to take three of the children home, and Sammy is to be smuggled into their trunk and taken back to his own family. The children run in, one after another, to wish him good-morning, the rapid entries in their *allegro* ensemble being free from all peril of anxiety owing to the pianist's *sforzando* octave leap which gives the new note to each soloist exactly two bars before it is wanted. Sammy's mood of courageous, but somewhat embarrassed, gratitude is enhanced by the fact that he has to count his silent first beats before coming in (Ex. 11):

The children manage to conceal him in the trunk before the comic arrival of Tom the coachman and Alfred the gardener who have been sent to carry the luggage downstairs. But at the very last moment there is a dramatic set-back to their adventure, for the two men complain that the trunk is too heavy: either it must be unpacked, or it must stay where it is. "Oh no!" the children exclaim, with a hint of genuine tragedy in the sudden darkness of their C minor chord. But all is well: they offer to help carry the trunk, and Sammy escapes. There is a blaze of light on the stage as the audience sings the chorus of the last song (Ex. 12):

The children have improvised a coach with the nursery rocking-horse and a couple of chairs: the eight-year-old twins are twirling brightly-coloured parasols round and round to the rhythm of the wheels, while the whole theatre is filled with the trotting and the cantering of the percussion. The *con slancio* in this final *Allegro* is unmistakable, and not even the weariest of middle-aged observers could hold aloof from its spell.

Of all Britten's achievements, none is more miraculous than this certainty of effortless happiness. It is to be found in all the music he has written for the young.

LENNOX BERKELEY

The Light Music

LIGHT music being a somewhat vague term, it is necessary to attempt a definition. One would not, I think, go far wrong in saying that music may be called light which does not require, on the part of the listener, any previous education in taste or knowledge, but that can be immediately enjoyed even by those who do not regard themselves as musical in the usual sense of the word. Light music, thus defined, would oblige us to include certain types that are not normally so designated, for instance, most of the more popular kinds of church music. In however pious a garb it may appear, such music is essentially light from the aesthetic point of view. Most light music is written by composers who do not attempt music of any other kind; we are here concerned with the light music of one of the most outstanding craftsmen of our time. It is, for that reason, a long way removed from ordinary light music, and yet it falls within the scope of my definition.

One of the most remarkable things about all Britten's music is that it is far more accessible to the ordinary musical listener than is the work of most contemporary composers. Accordingly light music comes more easily to Britten than to most, because, even in his most serious moments, he is not obscure. He is profoundly traditional, and his music, though intensely individual, is easily connected with what has gone before. His arrangements of folk tunes, for example, show this very strikingly. He provides the tunes with a background into which they merge, so that when one of his settings becomes familiar, it seems inseparable from the tune. I am thinking particularly of *The Sally Gardens* with its daring simplicity offset by the exquisite modulation at the 18th bar; of *Waly Waly*, where the poignant ostinato of the accompaniment so exactly matches the mood; of *The Ploughboy*, in which the perky little tune accentuates the song's cynical nonchalance. His usual method in these arrangements is to take some phrase from the tune itself and use it either rhythmically, as in *Newcastle*, or contrapuntally, as in *The Ash Grove*[1]. In *Polly Oliver*, the entire melody is made to run in canon, first at the octave, and later at the fourth. Time-honoured devices, but here applied with such sureness of touch, such tact and delicacy, that they in no way complicate the simplicity, or tarnish the freshness, of the tunes themselves. We find the same technique applied in the orchestral Suite of Catalan dance tunes called *Mont Juic*, in which I had the very enjoyable experience of collaboration with Britten. A similar approach to the problem of composition made such an association possible, and though, after agreeing upon the general shape of the movements, we worked at the different parts more or less independently, I hope I may claim that a reasonably homogeneous Suite emerged. Working with him, as I then did, I was able to observe one aspect in particular of his attitude towards composition. This is his extraordinary flair for what 'comes off' in actual performance, and his readiness to subordinate other considerations to it. I mention this quality here because it has enormous importance in light music. Where the actual material is of slight or limited significance, the manner of its presentation is everything; because Britten realizes this so well, and carries it out so brilliantly, his light music is worthy of serious study.

In this connection it is interesting to recall that among the earliest works to attract attention were the two Suites based on melodies by Rossini[2]—the *Soirées Musicales* and the *Matinées Musicales*. The interest of these Suites lies almost entirely in their orchestration. Britten has not attempted to transform the music into something that might have been composed by himself as, for instance, Strawinsky has done in *Pulcinella*; the harmonies are those that Rossini might have used. All Britten has done is to arrange and score them for medium sized orchestra. But what scoring! It is the exact opposite of that which was in vogue thirty years ago, when a composer's object seemed to be

[1] See pp. 47f. and Ex. 44 in *The Musical Atmosphere*, p. 48.—EDS.
[2] See also *The Incidental Music*, p. 299.—EDS.

to make every instrument sound as strange and unlike itself as possible. One listened to orchestras in which trumpets were never unmuted and clarinets and bassoons made to hiccough and wheeze at the extremities of their compass. These grimaces are now less admired, and it is true to Britten's character that he instinctively avoids them, giving his instruments the kind of music that suits them best, in such a way that the same phrase passing from one to the other will be modified accordingly. This causes them all to have the utmost resonance, and produces the brilliance of sound and purity of orchestral colour that characterize all Britten's instrumental works.

Other light music of the early period includes some excellent incidental music, such as that written for the documentary film *Night Mail*, or for the plays of Auden and Isherwood that were produced in the late 'thirties. Nor must we forget the lively and imaginative *Canadian Carnival*. But it is not until we reach *Albert Herring* that Britten emerges as a composer capable of sustaining a light idiom throughout an entire opera.

Herring, produced at Glyndebourne in the summer of 1947, is one of the rare comic operas that combine qualities belonging essentially to light music with a valid and interesting contemporary idiom, a combination which does not, as it might so easily, detract from the unity of style. One cannot compare this work with the earlier light music which we have been considering because here we have entirely original composition, whereas we were previously concerned with arrangements; but one sign of the great advance which has been made is that though the virtuosity of the scoring is even greater, the listener is less conscious of it. It is difficult to believe that such variety (and occasionally such force, as in Act III where the village worthies enter with the crown of orange blossom) is possible with an orchestra of only twelve. But more interesting than this is the actual language and style of the opera itself. The themes are of the simplest kind—ordinary even, if it were not that one is quickly made aware of their implications and possibilities. Moreover the very individual manner in which they are harmonized lends them a colour that makes them unexpectedly significant. A good instance of this is the tune (Ex. 1) sung by the three children:

Ex.1

This is not merely a matter of technique. The harmony is part of the tune itself and one feels certain that both must have taken shape together in the composer's mind. Another example of this unity is the duet "Come along, darling" which begins thus (Ex. 2):

Ex.2

The emotional subtlety and suppressed excitement of this piece are quite extraordinary; the accompaniment, with its continual hovering between B flat and B natural,[1] is scored, in the first verse, for bass flute, horn and bass clarinet (the same combination which is used with such effect in *The Rape of Lucretia*) and subsequently taken up by the strings an octave higher for the second verse. Though the feeling in this duet is more sensuous than passionate, it has a genuine breath of romance—a thing that is very rare in present-day music and could not have been achieved without a thoroughly integrated style. Other examples of this unity could be found on almost every page.

Herring has both gaiety and humour; the former quality is often found in light music, the latter rarely. Here the humour, sometimes broad, sometimes subtle, is essentially part of the characterization. The tone of voice of each character is admirably translated into music: the rich, flamboyant vocalises of Lady Billows—not without a certain dignity—the refined twitterings, occasionally converted into real coloratura, of Miss Wordsworth, the mellifluous platitudes of the Vicar, the Mayor's almost hysterical eloquence, and the sepulchral gruntings of Superintendent Budd, are all welded with great skill into a whole. No dramatic point is ever made that is not expressed in strictly musical terms, with the result that each movement of the work would still have a musical validity even if divorced from the action. This, I imagine, is a characteristic of good opera in whatever idiom it may be conceived.

The most recent work falling into the category that we are considering is *The Little Sweep*—the musical part of the entertainment called *Let's Make an Opera*. This, I think, is the summit of Britten's achievement in the realms of light music—all his gifts for it are gathered together in this little masterpiece, as brilliant and accomplished as it is touching and human. The tunes, as simple as they well could be, are treated with originality, but with an originality that immediately compels acceptance, and the extreme skill with which the music is written is combined with such directness that the listener is unaware of it. In so much contemporary music the composer's technique seems an end in itself (perhaps because there is so little else to admire), but here

---

[1] It is really an alternation between a major seventh on B flat and a minor seventh on G, the latter implying the dominant seventh of C, to which key, however, the music never goes.

it is unobtrusive. Witness the ease with which the parts in the quartet between Rowan, Miss Baggott and the two sweeps are first heard singly and then combined (Ex. 3):

Or the deceptive simplicity of "Help! help! she's collapsed!" which is really a passacaglia with contrapuntal treatment of the voices, as in Ex. 3 above. The audience songs are easy to sing and to remember, yet each has in abundance those little touches that make it so new and alive. The delightful *Sammy's Bath* (see Ex. 4), once learnt, is never forgotten.

The catchy tune is given a tremendous swing by the cross-rhythm in the first two bars, and is further enhanced by the brilliant sparkle of the superimposed quaver passage. Equally unforgettable are the pathos of "O why do you weep through the working day?" and the gaiety of the final coaching song.

In *The Little Sweep*, perhaps more than in any other work, one is aware of the extreme Englishness of Britten's music. It is not what has come to be accepted as an English musical idiom—indeed it could hardly be further removed from the style that is based on English folk music. It is more an emotional atmosphere, a state of mind, that pervades his music, which is intensely English. It makes itself very clearly felt in *Peter Grimes*, and I often think I feel it in his purely instrumental music, but perhaps that is my imagination. Certainly *Let's Make an Opera* could only have been devised in England; the cosy nursery atmosphere, the Dickensian sweeps, and the very unsophisticated approach to the story have an immensely English flavour. How far there is anything specifically English in Britten's choice of subjects, or how far his preoccupation with the persecution and betrayal of innocence (the underlying theme of all his operas) is a purely personal thing, one cannot say. In either case it can only spring from an unusually compassionate heart.

WILLIAM MANN

The Incidental Music

IN the formation of Britten's mature vocabulary and style his incidental music has been of much importance; as a corpus of creative work it is not so significant. One film score has won huge popularity outside the cinema—the variations and fugue on a theme by Purcell originally written as *The Young Person's Guide to the Orchestra* for the film *Instruments of the Orchestra*. Among connoisseurs of the cinema, the scores of *Night Mail* and *Coal Face* are admired for their ingenuity and integration[1]; and the masterly musical part of *The Rescue*, a radio melodrama which Britten wrote with Edward Sackville-West, owes its mastery to a little swarm of film scores, not in themselves especially memorable, and known only to the staff of the Central Office of Information which houses them, and to a few students of film.

Britten has often made it plain that he takes a workman's view of his art; in writings and speeches he has almost been at pains to impress on the world the view of composition as a craft, not merely a calling[2]. The composer can be grateful for commissions offered by the theatre, cinema or radio, not only because they help him to live, but because they enable him to give birth to ideas that may have been gestating for some time but were not in themselves suitable for extended composition. The essence of incidental music is mood-painting, ensurance of continuity, and provision of extra-visual (or in broadcasting extra-auditory) detail. The ideas do not have to be objectively good ones, and the cuts, imposed almost invariably by time-considerations, see to the excisions of padding except where padding is necessary as a means of marking time—a musical device as useful in accompanying neighbour arts as it is useless in pure music.

[1] Cf. also [158].—EDS.
[2] See *The Musical Atmosphere*, p. 53, and [345].—EDS.

It is not to be expected that every one of these scores should contain fine material; their purpose was ephemeral. But looking at them, or hearing them again, the ideas are right ideas, even when not musically sublime; and they are economically and rightly used. Above all the modest scoring required in many of these works paid its dividend when Britten came, not only to the economy of his chamber operas, but to his full-scale orchestrations, where every constituent of the score was to make a valuable effect.

From 1934–1936 Britten was in the employ of the G.P.O. Film Unit, arranging, and occasionally composing, music for documentary films. The first films with scores to his credit were *C.T.O.* and *Conquering Space* (both 1935). Funds were small and the instrumentation had to be minuscule—three or four instruments. This was a useful discipline, and a stimulus to Britten's resourceful invention—a stimulus enhanced by his preoccupation with musical parallels for sound effects.

The King's Stamp (1935), for example, is scored for flute (doubling piccolo), clarinet, percussion and piano (four hands). Music is a junior partner in this piece which, under William Coldstream's direction, described the making of the Silver Jubilee stamp. The impression is of music spatchcocked into the sound track to liven up the less interesting moments, of a lack of musical integration into the seen and spoken elements of the film. The idiom of the music is an assertive, neo-classic diatonicism touched with Gallicisms (e.g. the persistent figure in sevenths for piano and flute near the end). As Barnett Freedman conceives the design for the stamp, Britten offers a cool, limpid cantabile for clarinet and piano that looks forward to the melodies of his later chamber operas; the printing office scene is accompanied by an invention for piano duet whose four note theme with inversion is an early symptom of the careful symmetrician.

It was with *Coal Face* (1935), in which Grierson joined Coldstream, that Britten achieved his first film score of distinction. Music is not here a background; indeed, the correspondence of incident and musical image is a constant revelation. A Welsh subject naturally suggested the co-option of voices and these could not but awake the musical sympathies and exploratory colour-sense of the man who had composed *A Boy was Born*. The most striking are the underground sequences—the procession of miners, with rhythmic accompaniment of listed categories of employment punctuated by side drum and bass drum; the choral glissando that depicts a falling shower of coal and the

miners' apprehension; the humming and whistling at break-time; the
voices, quickly rhythmical, which imitate the action of the electric coal-
cutter and juxtapose man with machine; and finally the female chorus,
heard as the lift ascends, with its pungent Italianate modulation through
the flattened leading-note. Flowing melody and keen rhythm are the
memorable qualities of the music *per se.*

In *Night Mail* (1936), Britten was working with Auden and Cavalcanti. Music is more sparingly used but still properly integrated. A
modest orchestra of clarinet, trumpet and strings aspires to functional
sound effects. The most extended and impactive musical sequence comes
near the end. The train climbs a long hill to rhythmic instrumental
accompaniment; as it reaches the top a broad tune covers the rhythm,
and on the downward slope a 4/4 *Allegro,* in which a tiny and exuberant
figure (Ex. 1) has prominence, assumes control:

Ex. 1
(Allegro)

To this same year belong *Banking for Millions, Message from
Geneva* and *Men of the Alps.* The type of film music to which these last
two and the remaining scores of 1935 belong may be most satisfactorily
studied in Britten's work for *The Line to the Tschierva Hut* (1937). One
could almost sum up these scores as "Alpine and telephone music".
B♭, a favourite outdoor key for Britten, dominates *Tschierva Hut*[1];
the orchestra is of café size; and the introduction and epilogue allude
to the folk song *Von Luzern auf Wäggis zu.* Trumpet is prominent at
the start. When we see the telephone line being fixed in position along
the mountainous way, a rocking accompaniment figure in triplets begins
to make itself felt on harp and flute. As the work progresses a melody
of quasi-Alpine character (Ex. 2) is heard on viola and 'cello:

Ex. 2 *(Moderato)*

etc.

The triplet figure returns and persists up to the coda, so that the
whole is in box-form: ABCBA. It is a charming score to a charming
film.

Calendar of the Year, another G.P.O. film of 1937, deals with

[1] The name of the Swiss Alpine Club's hut at Pontresina.

scenes of English life through the four seasons. Britten's workaday score inevitably falls into sections. Not all the music is original. Rossini is called in to help for one scene; Chopin rightly accompanies a shot of *Les Sylphides* (but not the right bit of Chopin); and a summer fair-ground supplies its own pipe organ music. But the harvest sequence and the initial panorama are pleasantly set, and the spring episode contains a characteristic harmonic procedure: tonic triad over tonic moving to dominant seventh on supertonic over dominant. The appearance of W. H. Auden as Father Christmas in the Christmas toyshop sequence may be noticed.

Also to 1937 belong two or three documentary films not made for the G.P.O.: Britten's one feature film score, for *Love from a Stranger*, of which no complete copy seems to have been preserved, and the incidental music to Auden's and Isherwood's *The Ascent of F6*.

Scored for piano (four hands) and percussion, the music for *F6* consists of nine numbers; like the play, it combines a sharp vein of satire with a wistful simplicity. Satire commands the entractes for Mr. and Mrs. A., a slow one in G minor and a quick one in C, framed in a complacent jazz idiom; Gunn's "A date with Love" number which solemnly repeats its one melodic phrase in C, C minor, D minor and D major (with added sixth) in the best commercial manner; and the *Caberet* (sic) *Jazz Song* "Forget the Dead" which is more elaborately wrought, with harmonic roots in I.S.C.M. fourths instead of Tin Pan Alley thirds. As in Auden, irony sometimes blends with heart-felt emotion and the tongue forgets its place in the cheek; for example, in the E♭ minor Blues "Stop all the clocks", the treatment of a conventional figure (Ex. 3)

Ex.3

BASS: E♭

and the scoring of the piece leave *Kitsch*-land for the reaches of music.

The Mother's two songs "Michael, you shall be renowned" and "Still the dark forest" exploit a soothing mood. Mrs. Ransom is a Freudian figure, not a person, and her hold over Michael is perhaps expressed by the emphasis on the mediant in these numbers, i.e. the modulation from E into G♯ in the first, and the shifting harmonization, C major, E minor, of the second, whose melody hovers on E. The strophic tune of "Still the dark forest" is set with a variety that looks forward to Britten's folk-song arrangements and the *Dirge* of the *Serenade*. The other numbers are descriptive. A chant for the monks contrasts first the bottom octave of the bass voice F-F, then the octave above it; the final nonsense words are spoken very low. Both of the two bits of 'climbing music' have a heavy ostinato bass and a high melismatic treble in tenths, but in the second, the treble is slightly simpler. After Gunn's death, beneath the spoken chorus, the two sections are joined together.

The overture begins with the théme of Gunn's song in C which is briefly developed to lead into part of the *Caberet Jazz Song* in E. The Mother's second song follows, and after it the Waltz to which she dances in the Pantomime (Act I, Sc. 3). "Still the dark forest" returns with a different last line, suggesting a coda in 4/4 which reappears at the very end of the play. It is dominated by a phrase in the right hand of the bass that proves to be the basis of "Stop all the clocks" (see Ex. 3).

1938 saw *Hadrian's Wall*[1], Britten's first radio score for a feature programme. His music for G.P.O. films included the arrangements of Rossini (later revised as *Soirées Musicales*) for Lotte Reiniger's silhouette cartoon *The Tocher*; "tocher" is the Scots word for 'dowry', the dowry in this case being a Post Office Savings Book. In this score, Britten used voices, notably in the nocturne where they sing in unison against piano and woodwind, and in the lover's ride which is set to Rossini's song *La Danza*. Britten also wrote music to a G.P.O. documentary called *Four Barriers*; he collaborated with Montagu Slater in two puppet-plays, *The Seven Ages of Man* and *Old Spain*, and with W. H. Auden and Christopher Isherwood in *On the Frontier*.

Three documentaries were the cinematic fruit of 1939: *Advance Democracy* (which figures elsewhere in Britten's catalogue as a part-song), *God's Chillun*, and *H.P.O., or 6d. Telegram*. This last was an abstract film by Donald Taylor, a delightful affair to which Britten responded with a gay, childlike score for children's voices, oboe, trumpet, percussion and piano (if there are other instruments the sound track must have worn badly with the years). To 1939 also belongs the music to J. B. Priestley's *Johnson over Jordan*.

[1] Like several other 'ephemeral' scores, this has vanished. The records of its performance, and all material, are believed to have been destroyed during air-raids in the last war. To this year also belongs *The Sword in the Stone*, whose music was rediscovered and re-broadcast in 1952.

The score of *On the Frontier* (1938) was for piano (four hands) and percussion (as for *F6*), but has not, apparently, survived. *Johnson over Jordan* uses small full orchestra. The sinister passages—in the nightmares of office and nightclub—are well realized with a minimum of complexity; one particularly remembers a sequence of slowly changing tremolo string chords under a persistent cowbell rhythm. The music for the ballet of secretaries was later incorporated in the *Diversions on a Theme* for piano (left hand) and orchestra.

Since 1939, Britten has composed only one other film score, *Instruments of the Orchestra* (1946), which is discussed elsewhere[1]. I will only add that the music oddly contrives to mirror the *visual* aspect of each instrument as well as its technical personality. How appropriate, for instance, is the matching of the mighty double basses with their elephantine phrases, and the intent expression of the tuba-player with a portentous broken arpeggio.

Britten wrote nothing for screen or radio while he was in America and only one work for the stage—the (withdrawn) opera *Paul Bunyan*. Soon after his return to England in 1942 he turned his creative attention to radio again. With it we come to Britten's most considerable work in the incidental field.

The Rescue was conceived by Edward Sackville-West, who wrote the text, as a radio opera; Britten's collaboration was acknowledged as that of an equal. A dramatic version of the closing books of the *Odyssey*, starting with Odysseus's arrival on the shores of Ithaca and ending with peace in the palace, *The Rescue* was written in 1943. It was given on the Home Service in two parts, on successive evenings in November of that year. Two complete performances were broadcast in the Third Programme during the summer of 1951.

The Rescue is an epic piece. Sackville-West's essentially romantic approach—but there are romantic elements in Homer, for example in his use of the formal epithet and in his observation of detail—Britten matches with the large scale of his emotional approach to the subject. The score strikes by its sweeping effects, by its strong, deliberate diatonicism, by its economical treatment of material, and by its musically satisfying design.

Since radio is a non-visual medium, and not every actor has an unmistakably individual voice, characterization is all-important; Britten, by associating themes and instruments with certain characters,

[1] As *The Young Person's Guide to the Orchestra*; see *Britten and the Young*, pp. 276f.—EDS.

points the characterizations. Athene is represented by a trumpet in D, and by a soaring, syncopated theme (Ex. 4) that features Britten's favourite Lydian fourth and launches the play with a sense of voyaging adventure:

This music is also suitable as a background to singing voices, as when Athene calls to Hermes in Part I; the texture remains beautifully airy. Irus, the pimp and Quisling, is vividly portrayed on the xylophone, whose incisive timbre enables us to sense his stealthy approach as surely as must the people of Ithaca. Odysseus's theme (Ex. 5) belongs to the strings:

Its value is not so much intrinsic—the sequential tune and somewhat prosaic bass line are almost pompously heroic—as suggestive; it is extremely susceptible of transformation and development. Nevertheless it is the most persistently memorable tune in the score. To Penelope falls the most arresting theme (Ex. 6); her grief and her glimmering hope for Odysseus's return are evoked by thickly sonorous plucked (no, not so much plucked as ripped) chords for harp and strings, and by the pathetic tones of the saxophone, here divested of all its unctuous or vapid associations:

Like the other themes so far quoted, Ex. 6 appears again and again. At the end it is taken up by triumphant voices, and attains a new tonal basis; for whereas it was, effectively, in D minor harmonized in B♭, now it is strong D major and harmonized so (Ex. 7):

Many of the numbers are built up on tiny figures, one of which (Ex. 8) suggests the tension of the rescue operation itself:

Ex. 8 is later developed and its rhythm underlies the music of other numbers in the episode.

Sea-girt Ithaca is depicted by what might be called an undulating figure (Ex. 9)

which is used as a background, as a scene-setting medium, or as a means of pushing the musical action forward; in Nos. 10 and 52 (the dramatic plan allows for a recapitulation at the start of Part II), flutes with violins, clarinet with violas, and bass clarinet with 'cellos propel the phrase in strict imitation. When Telemachus sets sail from Ithaca, some splendid sea music is heard, whose basic figure (Ex. 10)

has the effect of being evolved from No. 2 (Ex. 9). This exfoliatory thematic usage can be traced elsewhere, in connection with Athene's, Penelope's and Odysseus's themes.

Among the longer numbers, attention should be drawn to the music accompanying Odysseus's arrival at Ithaca—a long chain of melodic sequences in D minor developing into an extended melody for Athene in A major (Britten's Lydian fourth again prominent)—and of the finale Part I, with vocal trio "Far forth" (in 5/4) which includes one of those transparent key-switches (from D into B♭) that Britten knows how to pull out of the hat with such devastating effect[1]; the finale ends with oboes and trumpets repeating the rhythm of "Bide the time", falling a third each time, from G♯ to F to C♯ to B♭, over a D major triad with added major sixth. There is a charming scherzo (No. 52) reminiscent of the recently completed *Hymn to St. Cecilia*, with a modulating refrain; and there is an impressive contrapuntal build-up on a diatonic theme that looks forward to "This is our moment" in Act III, Sc. 1, of *Billy Budd*. I have already referred to the climactic No. 78 in which Penelope's theme rises up triumphant in vocal quartet.

For *The Rescue* Britten had the benefit of full orchestra and solo voices (but not chorus) all of which are used with the sure hand of the master craftsman. *The Rescue* was such an achievement that we looked forward with optimism to Britten's opera *Peter Grimes*, then already being planned.

After the war, Britten returned to incidental music, collaborating with Ronald Duncan in *This Way to the Tomb* (1945), *The Eagle has Two Heads* (1946), and *Stratton* (1949).

This Way to the Tomb is divided into two parts, Masque and Antimasque. The music of the Masque is all vocal, much of it choral. The first *Deus in adjutorium* is an unaccompanied setting of Psalm 69; its sections appear later in the play. Of these, the opening section is in two parts, with a burst of four-part writing at the end. *Confundantur et revereantur* is short and homophonically diatonic. The point of *Avertantur retrorsum* is the ambiguous third (see Ex. 11)

Ex. 11

and its reflection, the sixth, a pleasing device which is deployed at

[1] Cf. the collapse of the shanty in Act I of *Budd* (figure 14) out of its B♭ minor-F♯ minor tonality on to a bland but contextually overwhelming E♭ major triad.

length in two-part imitation. The 'conclusion—E major-E minor triads on the word "Euge"—is serene and relaxed. A *più mosso* passage, *Exsultant et laetentur*, is concerned with conjunct thirds. In the subsequent *tranquillo*, the sopranos, with exquisite effect, cover sustained chords with rosalias based on arpeggios of the seventh. *Ego vero egenus* is busy with the interval of a second (as was *Avertantur* with the third) and achieves a tensely emotional effect through its imitative contrapuntal exploitation; the final climax, a four-part unison shout of "Domine ne moreris" on B, recalls at once the end of Verdi's *Requiem* (though that was *pppp*) and the unison D's in *Noel!* from *A Boy was Born*[1]. The last section *Gloria patri* sets up an ostinato in the bass, and another (? canon at the major tenth) in the alto, and overlays them with canon between soprano and tenor, first at three bars' interval, then at two, then at one and a half, reducing freely to one bar's space. A short quotation (Ex. 12) shows how suspensions between alto and bass give an apt feeling of timelessness to the passage:

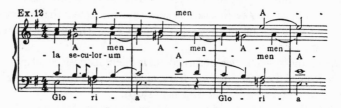

A tiny unaccompanied soprano number, *Oh, proud heart*, makes a point of the diatonic seventh, falling to the tonic through the fifth, with a Scotch snap, again and again (three times actually, but the song is marked *D.C. ad lib*).

St. Anthony's meditation, *Quaerit loca lacrymarum*, is set strophically. The melody consists of a phrase thrice repeated with a cadence at the end, modulating to the key of the next soloist's tessitura. The phrase is characterized by a dropping seventh and by its opening which falls gently from the ninth[2] to the seventh, with plangent effect (*lacrymosa* indeed). The two-part accompaniment devolves upon swaying thirds (see Ex. 13):

---

[1] Ex. 5 in *The Choral Music*, p. 89.—Eds.

[2] This analysis assumes a tonal climate, not easily classified, for the tonality is undeniably ambiguous, as Ex. 13 shows. The first bar could be read as E major, or G♯ minor; the author's aural commonsense tells him the piece is in E, but some listeners might feel that the tonality was fixed by the second bar (F♯ minor or D major). It would be pedantic to quarrel.

Ex.13 *Andante*

Quae - rit lo - ca la - cry-ma - rum,Pro - mit etc.

Quae - rit   Pro -

Quae - rit   Pro -

Alto is the soloist in the first verse; soprano in the second; then tenor between altos and basses; and lastly a bass soloist is accompanied by all four parts.

Also in the Masque are three songs, *Morning, Evening* ("The Red Fox, the Sun") and *Night*, which are sung by the poet Julian. The melodic line of *Morning* plays with a pattern of five notes, while the accompaniment scatters chord clusters rhythmically and in arpeggio (see Ex. 14):

Ex.14   *Poco vivace*

Voice

Morn - ing is   on - ly   a   he - ron   etc.

Piano
or
Harp

Arpegg. sim.

The first verse modulates from G to E, the second from E to the dominant of G; the third repeats the process of the first; the fourth returns to the tonic by a changed ending that emotionally exploits a rising sequence. One might complain that the last vocal phrase (Ex. 15)

Ex.15

Voice

Too ____   hea - vy

Piano
or
Harp

sets the words cumbrously, and involves an unfacile modulation. But this charge can easily be squashed on considerations of textual implications, of the need for strongest tension at the point preceding return to the unfettered accompaniment which closes the song.

Evening "may be sung unaccompanied"; but that would remove its pungent B major-minor character. The piano or harp disperses downward arpeggios, each of which has B as its root and contains a D♯ which bites against the B minor melody. The arpeggios follow a pattern—the upper note falls and rises through three flattened degrees of the major scale from the keynote, then three diatonic degrees from the dominant. The accompaniment to the third verse, dealing with "the old owl, the moon", begins in the bass clef, and, its bass note falling, rises with the vocal line, as does the moon, until the voice reaches E♭, and the piano arpeggios E♭ minor. These latter soar and their upper B♭ rises another semitone to achieve tonic B major for the last verse, where the stars are portrayed in the upper register.

Night is a ground in 5/4. The pattern of the basic phrase descends four times by tone, so that the last bar of the ground occurs on the flattened dominant, lending an individual touch to its structure. The vocal setting is simple—it would be hard to be anything else with this highly allusive verse—and derived largely from the tune of the ground itself. For all the pleasant touches, this is not one of Britten's truly characteristic songs, as are the other two. Yet the three together might profitably figure in recital programmes; certainly *Evening* is a first-rate piece.

Britten's Antimasque for *This Way to the Tomb* hardly bears serious consideration. It is scored, like the *F6* music, for piano (four hands) and percussion, and is deliberately satirical to a point of amiable banality. There is an attractively tart March (bass in F, treble in F♯ major), a Litany that employs beguiling and not always analysable sonorities, and a Trio for mobile worker, girl of leisure and man of culture. This last ingeniously sets three verses in different keys—a quasi-Boogie-Woogie in B minor, a Blues in D, and what I can only call a Stomp in F; on returning to B minor, all the vocal lines, which prove to fit, are simultaneously combined. Although obviously done as a task, this music was, in its context, highly successful.

Those who saw *The Eagle has Two Heads*, Duncan's English version of the play by Jean Cocteau, will remember the impressive ending when Queen and lover lie dead as the band outside plays a fanfare-cum-National Anthem. This is scored for three trumpets, four cornets, three trombones, two tubas, cymbal and side drum. The preliminary flourishes build up from the triad (with added sixth) of Bb to Gb, from C to Ab, and from D to Bb. The National Anthem is harmonically a good deal more adventurous than most, though it consists of only one line repeated—rather on the pattern of a public-school song. Needless to say, the one line furnishes another example of Britten's skill in juxtaposing ordinary chords with extraordinary effect (Ex. 16):

Ex. 16

Apart from these collaborations with Ronald Duncan, Britten's only post-war incidental music for the theatre has been the score for a production of Webster's *The Duchess of Malfi*, mounted at New York in 1946, with Elisabeth Bergner in the title rôle. The score has been lost but I am informed that it used a leading motif for Duke Ferdinand[1], and that Britten introduced material from his setting of the *Lyke-Wake Dirge*, since the producer thought of using this movement from the *Serenade* in the course of the performance.

For the radio, Britten wrote incidental music to Louis MacNeice's *The Dark Tower* (1946), and a score entitled *Men of Goodwill*, to accompany the world survey before the King's speech on Christmas Day, 1947.

The Dark Tower is called a radio parable play. It tells how "Childe Roland to the dark tower came"—Roland the last of the family of heroes, questioning by nature where his brothers and forefathers had accepted their crusade, beguiled on the way by many temptations, recalled by his dying mother, and through that call suddenly made aware of his mission's significance. The story is told in a verse idiom rich in metaphor and symbol. For the first production in January 1946 (it has been re-broadcast on several occasions) Britten wrote special music. The play is dedicated to him; "without his music", says MacNeice in a foreword, "*The Dark Tower* lacks a dimension".

There are sixteen musical numbers, scored for trumpet, percussion and strings; the trumpet's rôle is limited to the playing of the Challenge

[1] Acquaintance with Claggart's music in *Budd* may stimulate the imagination about this.

Call, unaccompanied save in the last number (at the moment when Roland

> "Yet
> Dauntless the slughorn to my lips I set,
> And blew")

which has sustained string and timpani support. Effectively for twenty-six string players and one percussion player, this virtuoso score is of the most brilliant order, richly sonorous, glittering, evocative, highly inventive and, for the players, highly taxing.

The most complex number is that which accompanies Roland's journey through the forest; the speaking inhabitants are a parrot and a raven, cynics both, but Britten suggests a myriad equally caustic brethren on neighbouring branches. These voluble creatures are represented by a solo string quartet against the ripieno strings. The orchestral violins double-trill softly, violas, 'cellos and basses call to one another in very soft glissandi, each of nearly two octaves' span. The solo birds discourse *fortissimo*. The 'cello scoops harsh tenths, the viola executes downward glissandi in double-stoppings, first violin nags away at a soprano B in altissimo or careers madly down from there to middle C, while the second violin utters loud mocking calls on three notes (later the various calls are differently distributed). In the broadcast these fantastic sounds not only suggested many birds, but enhanced the nightmare tension of the scene.

Another effective number suggests the noise of the ship's engines thus (Ex. 17):

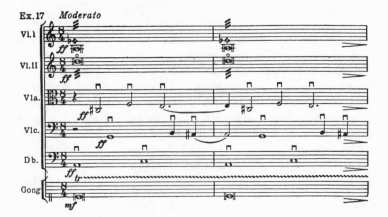

The reader who has heard the play will remember Ex. 17's heavy buzz which, like Honegger's *Pacific 231*, evokes the idea rather than the sound of machinery.

If we isolate the trumpet, we must also specify the solo violin in this score. One of MacNeice's characters is the Siren Neaera, who plays upon her fiddle, calling out not the names of her tunes (she only knows one) but, oddly enough, the tempo at which her whim demands that the tune be played. The basic nature of this melody (see Ex. 18)

displays its intended superficiality—and we notice how much more artistically that dubious quality is achieved here than in the *F6* music of 1937; the artist, always a clever one, had grown up musically in the intervening years. Those who heard the play will recall too the church music for bell and lower strings *divisi*, and the heart-beat sequence in the desert, which begins with a plain rhythm (15/8!) on double basses, and slowly gains textural weight and rhythmic complexity until at last the tower is sighted and the theme connected with it bites its way through the music as Roland's great moment draws near. While *The Rescue* is built on a bigger scale, the music for *The Dark Tower* must have a special place in the recollections of many musicians who heard it—a place that is buttressed, this listener can affirm, by looking at the score.

The Christmas Day music, *Men of Goodwill*, which accompanied the voice of Sir Laurence Olivier, is based on the carol *God rest you merry, Gentlemen*, and scored for full orchestra. Of its six numbers certainly the second and last do not deserve the oblivion unthinkingly bestowed on ephemeral works of art, but the merits of the two depend, properly, on the effect of their surroundings. The second is an *allegro con brio* scherzo of a skittishly Mephistophelean order, where the tune is exposed in canon at the bar, in G minor against an F major accompaniment (see Ex. 19):

The last, the finale, sets the tune in canon (one in four) on the brass, and surrounds it with a dignified counterpoint, itself treated in strict imitation, for strings and woodwind. Beside these, attention could be caught by the neat dovetailing of melody and counter theme in the first number (so that the end of the quasi-ritornello often starts the chorale-line for the trumpets and trombones), the attractive, chime-like, counterpoint in the *andantino* third number, and the virile counter melody (Ex. 20) in the *allegro maestoso* fifth:

Readers may well have noticed the references to non-availability of some of these scores, or to their virtual non-recognition; but even from an enforcedly partial assessment of them, it is plain that Britten's incidental music has served his development to sterling purpose. Any of these scores is likely to have stirred a response in some chance listener, encouraged him to study more closely the music of Britten, or perhaps modern music as a whole, and thus fulfilled one of the greatest functions music knows; that stimulation which puts him who profits in the permanent debt of the artist whose creation has changed the course of another human being's life.

BIBLIOGRAPHY OF

Benjamin Britten's

INCIDENTAL MUSIC

(Compiled by Eric Walter White)

(a) for theatre

TIMON OF ATHENS: verse play by William Shakespeare (Group
 Theatre), Westminster Theatre, London, November, 1935

AGAMEMNON OF AESCHYLUS: translated by Louis MacNeice (Group
 Theatre), Westminster Theatre, London, November, 1936

THE ASCENT OF F6; verse play by W. H. Auden and Christopher
 Isherwood (Group Theatre), Mercury Theatre, London, February, 1937

OUT OF THE PICTURE: verse play by Louis MacNeice (Group Theatre),
 Westminster Theatre, London, December, 1937

THE SEVEN AGES OF MAN: puppet play by Montagu Slater (Binyon
 Puppets), Mercury Theatre, London, 1938

OLD SPAIN: puppet play by Montagu Slater (Binyon Puppets), Mercury
 Theatre, London, 1938

ON THE FRONTIER: verse play by W. H. Auden and Christopher
 Isherwood (Group Theatre), Arts Theatre, Cambridge, 1938

JOHNSON OVER JORDAN: play by J. B. Priestley, New Theatre, London,
 February, 1939

THIS WAY TO THE TOMB: a Masque and Antimasque by Ronald Duncan
 (Pilgrim Players), Mercury Theatre, London, October, 1945

THE EAGLE HAS TWO HEADS: play by Jean Cocteau, translated by
 Ronald Duncan (Company of Four), Lyric Theatre, Hammersmith, London, September, 1946

THE DUCHESS OF MALFI: verse play by John Webster, New York, 1946

STRATTON: verse play by Ronald Duncan, Theatre Royal, Brighton,
 October, 1949

(b) for radio

HADRIAN'S WALL: radio feature with script by W. H. Auden, 1938

THE SWORD IN THE STONE: radio play adapted by Marianne Helwig from T. H. White's novel, 1938

THE RESCUE: radio drama by Edward Sackville-West, 1943.

THE DARK TOWER: radio play by Louis MacNeice, 1946

MEN OF GOODWILL: radio feature, Christmas, 1947

(c) for cinema

CABLE SHIP: documentary film, G.P.O. Film Unit, 1933 [title music only]

C.T.O.: documentary film, G.P.O. Film Unit, 1935

CONQUERING SPACE: documentary film, G.P.O. Film Unit, 1935

THE KING'S STAMP: documentary film, directed by W. Coldstream, G.P.O. Film Unit, 1935

BANKING FOR MILLIONS: documentary film, G.P.O. Film Unit, 1936

COAL FACE: documentary film, directed by J. Grierson, G.P.O. Film Unit, 1936

NIGHT MAIL: documentary film, verses by W. H. Auden, produced by Harry Watt and Basil Wright, G.P.O. Film Unit, 1936

MESSAGE FROM GENEVA: documentary film, G.P.O. Film Unit, 1936

MEN OF THE ALPS: documentary film, G.P.O. Film Unit, 1936 [with original music by Benjamin Britten and music of Rossini arranged by Benjamin Britten and Walter Leigh]

THE SAVINGS OF BILL BLEWITT: documentary film, directed by Harry Watt, G.P.O. Film Unit, 1937

THE LINE TO THE TSCHIERVA HUT: documentary film, directed by A. Cavalcanti, G.P.O. Film Unit, 1937

CALENDAR OF THE YEAR: documentary film, directed by E. Spice, G.P.O. Film Unit, 1937

AROUND THE VILLAGE GREEN (alternative, or discarded, title VILLAGE HARVEST): documentary film, directed by Marion Grierson and E. Spice, Travel and Industrial Development Association, 1937

LOVE FROM A STRANGER: feature film, directed by Rowland V. Lee, Trafalgar Films, 1937

THE WAY TO THE SEA: documentary film, directed by J. B. Holmes, Strand Films, 1937

FOUR BARRIERS: documentary film, G.P.O. Film Unit, 1938 [music by Benjamin Britten and John Foulds]

HOW THE DIAL WORKS: documentary film, G.P.O. Film Unit, 1938

THE TOCHER: silhouette film, produced and devised by Lotte Reiniger, G.P.O. Film Unit, 1938

MONY A PICKLE: documentary film, G.P.O. Film Unit, 1938 [music by Victor Yates, Benjamin Britten and John Foulds]

GOD'S CHILLUN: documentary film, G.P.O. Film Unit, 1939

H.P.O., OR 6D. TELEGRAM: abstract film by Donald Taylor, produced by Lotte Reiniger, G.P.O. Film Unit, 1939

ADVANCE DEMOCRACY: documentary film, directed by Ralph Bond in association with Basil Wright, Realist Film Unit, 1939

INSTRUMENTS OF THE ORCHESTRA: documentary film, directed by Muir Mathieson, Crown Film Unit, 1946

MUSIC FOR BALLET

SOIRÉE MUSICALE: based on *Soirées Musicales* (op. 9), a suite of five movements from Rossini; London Ballet (choreography by Antony Tudor), Palladium Theatre, London, November, 1938

LES SYLPHIDES: Britten orchestrated Chopin's music for the Ballet Theatre, New York, 1940; his version was used by the American company during their season at Covent Garden in 1946

DIVERTIMENTO: based on *Soirées Musicales* (op. 9) and *Matinées Musicales* (op. 24), two suites of five movements each from Rossini; American Ballet Company (choreography by George Balanchine), South America, June, 1941

JINX: based on *Variations on a Theme of Frank Bridge* (op. 10); Dance Players (choreography by Lew Christensen), National Theatre, New York, April, 1942

SIMPLE SYMPHONY: based on *Simple Symphony* (op. 4); Ballet Rambert (choreography by Walter Gore), Theatre Royal, Bristol, November, 1944

FANTAISIE ITALIENNE: based on *Soirées Musicales* (op. 9) and *Matinées Musicales* (op. 24); Théâtre de la Monnaie, Brussels, 1948

OUI OU NON? (*Ballet de la Paix*): based on the *Variations and Fugue on a Theme of Purcell* (*The Young Person's Guide to the Orchestra*) (op. 34); Association des Amis de la Danse, Théâtre National Populaire du Palais de Chaillot, Paris, 1949

LE RÊVE DE LEONOR: based on *Variations on a Theme by Frank Bridge* (op. 10); Ballets de Roland Petit (choreography by Frederick Ashton), Prince's Theatre, London, April, 1949. [Music arranged specially for full orchestra by Arthur Oldham.]

LES ILLUMINATIONS: based on *Les Illuminations* (op. 18); New York City Ballet (choreography by Frederick Ashton), City Centre, New York, March, 1950

DIE VERSUNKENE STADT: based on *Sinfonietta* (op. 1); (choreography by Mara Jovanovits), Stadttheater, St. Gallen, Switzerland, 1950

PAUL HAMBURGER

The Pianist

P IANO-PLAYING composers fall into three
classes: the virtuoso-composers like Chopin and Liszt,
who compose in order to play; the all-rounders, including pretty well everyone capable of handling the instrument, who
play in order to compose; and a minority, such as Mozart, the young
Beethoven, Brahms and Britten, who compose, sometimes, what they
will like to play, and play, sometimes, what a composer ought to like.
These last do not cling to the piano as to their own exclusive Pegasus
that will carry them on high, nor do they shift its keys as the units of a
ready-reckoner that will prepare them for their more ambitious quartets
and symphonies. Their relationship to the piano is affable, easy-going;
they can leave it alone for a while and return to it later. Not that they
underestimate the instrument when they write for it—many new
sonorities are due to them—but the art of music always takes first
place over the art of piano playing. In short, they are not pianist-
composers but composer-pianists.

Britten's place among them is peculiar in that here is a polished
technician and interpreter who has, so far, not written many piano
solos. Indeed, if we except the Concerto, all his piano works are incidental; the by-products of a fertile musical mind. Yet this does not
deprive us of the pleasure of hearing Britten play, nor does it reduce the
importance of his appearances as a pianist. For while there are good
historical reasons for the comparative scarcity of piano music with
serious modern composers, song accompaniment has attained, *via*
Wolf, Debussy and Warlock, such a pitch of variegation and refinement
that its execution asks for most of the technical, and all (and more) of
the musical equipment of a soloist. When Britten plays his own songs
for Peter Pears we not only derive that exhilarating impression of

effortless partnership, of his playing the piano as if it were not a piano, which Schubertians must have derived from hearing Schubert play for Vogl, but we also get a piano recital thrown in for our money. Besides, Britten is readier than any composer ever, old or new, to play the piano music of others. We, the public, the critics, and the performers must be profoundly thankful for this; for if the composer who has no need to distort his judgment of his colleagues is rare, the one who puts this undistorted judgment not into so many words but into so many sounds is even rarer. Indeed, a discussion of Britten's playing of Mozart, Schubert and Schumann may give us a clue to his attitude towards his own music.

What strikes one most forcibly about Britten's approach to other composers is the fact that it is not an approach. Not for him the pious pilgrimage to the shrine of genius, the states and stages of introspection, concentration, castigation and revelation that distinguished a Busoni or a Schnabel on their knight-errantry to musical sainthood. He does not query because he has always known the answer. Born a genius, a man, that is, who by nature acts in accordance with the laws of music, fulfilling their commands at his place in evolution, he has been doubly fortunate in being vouchsafed, in the occasional superabundance of providence, an understanding of the vastly different biddings that have gone out to other geniuses in other times and places. He plays a Mozart concerto (alas, only one or two a year) not merely as if he had written it, but as if he had written it last night (". . . thank God the orchestral parts have come from the copyist in time for this morning's rehearsal . . . good thing I heard the misprint in the second violins . . . trust me to write passages that suit my fingers . . . ah, that's an idea for a cadenza . . ."). Such a state of affairs is inadequately described by the critical labels 'intense insight', 'amazing identification', 'feeling for style'; it is completely misunderstood in the idiotic 'exact recreation of 18th century manner'. On the other hand, a believer might rightly call it 'a state of grace', an agnostic 'a freak of nature', and a benign psychologist 'the strange and happy story of Dr. Britten and Mr. Mozart'. This does not mean that Britten is unaware of what he is doing, but that, however great or small his consciousness of inter-pretative processes, it is incidental to their musical results. Britten as a performer is the *reductio ad absurdum* of the friendly and/or hostile contest of intellect and instinct in recreative art.

A similar relationship obtains between Britten's technique and musicianship. Arthur Benjamin, the composer and pianist, with whom Britten studied the piano at the Royal College of Music, is not the man to press any technical fads on his pupils. Britten would not have accepted them, anyway. His playing looks more normal than that of many a famous virtuoso, and yet his passage-work sparkles, his tone-gradation is in a class by itself, and wrong notes are quite con-spicuously absent. His great control of the keyboard results from what pianists call an 'acute fingertip-sensitivity' (*Fingerspitzengefühl*), supplemented sparingly with wrist and arm movements that free the mechanism of playing while they are in themselves almost invisible. His legato disguises the basically percussive nature of the instrument most successfully, yet he is economical in the use of the 'golden', expressive tone that is so misapplied nowadays: he saves it, most so when he accompanies, for places of real melodic espressivo. This gives his part-playing in particular a chaste, silver-edged quality. His staccato, from the broadest portamento to the shortest finger-staccato, varies not only in length, but in tone-quality, irrespective of volume: a hallmark of a great pianist. Quick repeated chords, as in the second of the *John Donne Sonnets*, he shakes easily out of his sleeve, and his octaves have a steely, resilient quality without ever becoming harsh or bumptious.

Yet we know that Britten does not practise much, and that his technical accomplishment is largely unconscious, a thing he takes for granted. To say that his technique always serves a musical purpose, nice as it sounds about other pianists, is as much an understatement as those quoted above. Just as he does not 'approach' the style of other masters, so he does not 'apply' his technique. Again, while other pianists have a technique as an engineer has a tool-box with which to tackle a difficult job, Britten's hands, in a metaphor that is less strained than it might seem, *become* the hands of other composers in the way they deal with the favourite technical idiosyncrasies of each writer for the piano, as if they had pursued him throughout the course of years in his unguided ramblings over the keyboard. It is not primarily the brilliance of Britten's playing that distinguishes it from other pianists'— this can to a large extent be acquired—but the natural aptness of the little figure, the fall of a series of notes, the lay-out of parts, in short, his mastery of that region where technique borders on musicianship and can hardly be grasped consciously by the performer. It is this com-partment of technique that makes many a player feel at home with a composer from the start but, alternately, thwarts him—however excellent his technique and musicianship—when he tries to reach out to other composers. Not so with Britten: there is hardly a composer who does not make him enter this innermost cell of pianism from which technique and musicianship stem.

A gift such as Britten's for lightly effacing the borderline between technique and musicianship makes not only for great soloists but also for great accompanists, or, to be more precise, 'great chamber-musicians'. Now, while our foremost accompanists, such as Gerald Moore and Ernest Lush, are potential chamber-music players who blossom out into full partnership whenever they find a worthy partner, Britten is privileged to have, all the year round, a 'voice and piano team' with Peter Pears, as others have a 'violin and piano sonata team' or a string quartet. The merits of this duo are so universally recognized that it may suffice here to point to a few of Britten's contributions: how, in an introduction, he sets a strict basic tempo, yet gives a hint or two that the singer may, and should, loosen it up; how, in an interlude, he replies to the singer's last words, not with an echo, but as an intelligent sympathizer; how, in a postlude, he points the moral not only of the story, but of the music (hear how he makes the final cadence a condensation of all the others); how he not only rejoices or suffers with the singer, but occasionally (as in certain Mahler songs) opposes or mocks him; how the very quality and variety of his touch persuades the singer to give the right tone-colour and vary it accordingly. Purcell (in Britten's settings), Schubert's *Die schöne Müllerin* and Schumann's *Dichterliebe* are some of the things for which the Britten-Pears team are most beloved. ('Beloved', I think, is the right word: for such is the moral force of the artists' conviction that the public—and not only the devotees—cease, after a while, to admire uncritically and begin to love critically.) When Britten performs Purcell, the "mixture of clarity, brilliance, tenderness and strangeness" which, as Britten says in the preface to his Purcell realizations, "shines out in all Purcell's music", shines out with equal radiance in his playing. In Schubert, the intimate lyrical situation and the figurative wealth of the nature-poet's musical morphology are suffused with intimations of eternity. In Schumann, the crisis of the subject[1] in a liberal civilization is recreated in Britten's hands with the tenderest impartiality.

This brings us to Britten's playing of his own works. A listener gifted with the most acute perception of music and men, but ignorant

[1] 'Subject' in the philosophical sense.—EDS.

of Britten's compositions, would be unable to divine that the superb pianist up there playing those modern songs in a mixed programme was their composer. Is it because Britten plays the classics equally well, or because he makes no fuss about his own works? Whichever way you look at it, it comes to the same. He plays exactly what is printed, which means of course he plays exactly what is not printed but what would be printed if musical notation were advanced enough, and publishers rich enough, to make possible several editions of the same piece according to a few of the greatest interpreters. The performer Britten treats the composer Britten as an equal. He lets us know that he likes this music, even that he respects it. Its technical difficulties stimulate him. He plays the piece, not only as if he had written it himself, but as if he had written it yesterday. Has he written it himself? Apparently. The programme, anyway, will have it that he has. How, then, can he know it so well? He must have forgotten that he wrote it. Can an actor who is a king act a king? No, because no actor is a king, and a king who is an actor should not need a stage. Can a king amongst composers play a performer? If fortune smiles on us, yes. But he will need a dressing-room wherein to doff his tweeds and don a tail-coat.

[With regard to Hamburger's observations on Britten's undistorted judgments of other composers (first paras. on pp. 315 and 317 respectively), it would seem to us that the composers of whom his judgment *is* distorted (see *The Musical Character*, pp. 323 and 325) Britten the pianist leaves alone.—EDS.]

HANS KELLER

The Musical Character

BRITTEN'S musical character is here considered from two complementary standpoints, the extra-historical and the historical. Needless to say, "extra-historical" does not mean extra-historical, since there isn't such a thing. Rather, it means with reference to more than one particular age or culture. For instance, the historical proposition "Critic Z deems Composer Y an unmitigated X" assumes extra-historical significance as soon as we discover that 150 years ago Critic B deemed Composer A exactly the same unmitigated X. In such logical circumstances, moreover, even a designedly historical judgment can become "extra-historical". The Spanish philosopher of culture, Ortega y Gasset, for example, observes that antique man, before he does something, makes a step back like the toreador about to deliver his death-blow. He slips into the past as into a diving-bell before he plunges into a present problem. True, but not only for antique man[1]. True also for Britten and Mozart. Others, too, have slipped into the diving-bell. But they never proceeded to dive.

I. THE EXTRA-HISTORICAL ASPECT: BRITTEN AND MOZART: A CHALLENGE IN THE FORM OF VARIATIONS ON AN UNFAMILIAR THEME

Ars adeo latet sua. OVID

Written in 1946, the following thesis was first published in 1948 [136], when it aroused comment on the continent as well as in this country. On the whole, the continental response seemed more favourable than home-grown reactions—a state of affairs explainable by the analysis of

[1] The "true-not-only-for", i.e. the extra-historical meaning of history, is really the basic thought of Spengler's *Decline of the West*.

resistances to Britten's music given in [159]. Apart from one or two stylistic changes, the paper is here submitted in its original form, i.e. neither brought up to date (except for such obvious additions as the inclusion of *Budd* in an observation which concerns itself with *Grimes*, *Lucretia*, and *Herring*) nor down to the criticisms it has encountered. Not up to date because, if there are any points in the thesis at all, it is important to realize that, and how, they were recognizable at that fairly early stage in Britten's development. Not down to the criticisms because the criticisms were not up to the paper which had in fact anticipated them. Some commentators even seem to have taken their reading of the title for my content and thus saved themselves proceeding as far as the first sentence:

Remarkable similarities between Benjamin Britten and Mozart obtrude themselves on the suitably prejudiced observer, prejudiced, among other things, in favour of the view that presence of similarities does not imply absence of differences. People are wont to harp on the relation of Britten to Purcell (and to other composers, such as Mahler, whom they know Britten to admire). With Purcell, however, Britten has obviously established what in psychoanalysis one would call a superego identification—Purcell, that is to say, is Britten's father, and there is a limit to one's interest in the continuous pointing out of evident family resemblances.

Yet there is a way in which both comparisons between Purcell and Britten, and between Mozart and Britten, are equally beneficial: they counteract the current over-emphasis on the historical aspect of music, to which, in the case of the comparison with Mozart, is to be added action against the over-emphasis on the ethnological and geographical aspects.

To be sure, the exaggerated importance attached to historical factors has itself to be considered historically, as a sign of our times: the significance of the temporal environment for human activities, mental or otherwise, has once again been discovered, and to discover means to overestimate.

In music, moreover, historical explanations are particularly welcome, for the factors that go to make the individual musical character are a rather mysterious affair, and it is one of the tragedies of the mind that it prefers mysterious explanations to waiting for the facts to become a little less mysterious.

One of those who overdo the historical aspect of Britten's own work is Britten. "It is largely a matter of when one was born. If I had been born in 1813 instead of 1913 I should have been a romantic, primarily concerned to express my personality in music . . ." [322].

I don't think he would. True, he would have been *more* of a romantic, but in the sense in which he uses the word not primarily one: of all romantics he would have been the least romantic. Taking into account everything that depth psychology teaches us about character formation in early childhood, it is fairly safe to assume that, other things being as nearly equal as they can be, a Benjamin Britten born in 1813 would not tend (again in his own words) towards the "point at which the composer would be the only man capable of understanding his own music" [322]. This is not to say that nature is necessarily more important for a man's artistic character than nurture, but rather that there are, not only in nature but also in nurture, character-building elements whose dependence on historical circumstances—given a large cultural frame like 'western civilization'— is negligible. In early childhood (between minus-nine months and six years) contemporary aesthetic trends are not usually of great importance even to a precocious individual such as Britten. To quote two instances cited by him, Picasso and Strawinsky did not just come because history told them to, but because they liked being told. History is of course always clever afterwards: had Picasso and Strawinsky not worked against individualistic art, she would not have betrayed that she had told them to, but would have told us that they behaved according to her previous precepts.

One does not, then, understand Britten as soon as one knows that he belongs to the twentieth century and why, and that he is an Englishman[1] and why. Trying to neutralize the over-stress on historical and also on geographical interpretations (important as these admittedly are) this section will, but for a small exception, disregard them altogether.

Often when another writer's view of either composer approximates to my own, I shall give his instead of or in addition to mine, in order to exclude as far as possible the objection that I am begging the question. And, wherever convenient, I shall, of course, also let the composers speak for themselves.

The most obvious common characteristic of Britten and Mozart is their youthful maturity, which concept has in either case a double meaning: proficiency early attained and maturity retaining a youthful aspect. Busoni on Mozart: "He is young like a youth and wise like an

[1] It may at the same time be worth mentioning that "from his childhood days on. [Mozart] was especially fond of England and the English". (Alfred Einstein, *Mozart— His Character, His Work*, London, 1946, p. 88f.).

aged man—never out of date and never modern . . ." But just because of their immense *talent*, their extreme receptivity and adjustability, their *genius* emerges and matures almost belatedly: their development contrasts sharply with Schubert's and particularly Mendelssohn's, where genius, and mature genius at that, breaks forth at an improbably early stage.

Both composers manifest their maturity in artistic behaviour that is largely classical. To me they seem to be masters in the solution of a paradox inherent in all classical art: the paradox of restrained, yet explicit emotion.

Both have an impeccable sense of form. With Britten this particular asset is even acknowledged by his sternest critics, while Mozart's sense of form can only be called, with Busoni, "extra-human".

Both are liable to be severely misunderstood (yes, *are*, for even in Mozart's case this is not yet a thing of the past), not only by their critics, but also by a great number of the great number of their followers. For their music is approachable on various levels, each seemingly giving a complete picture in itself, so that the superficial listener, moving on the most superficial level, may yet be strongly impressed and may think he knows all about what he hears. In this connection Mozart's attitude towards the 'popular' should be noted. Writing about the first three Vienna piano Concertos he says (letter of 28th December, 1782):

> These concertos are a happy medium between what is too easy and too difficult; they are very brilliant, pleasing to the ear, and natural, without being vapid. There are passages here and there from which connoisseurs alone can derive satisfaction; but these passages are written in such a way that the less learned cannot fail to be pleased, though without knowing why . . .

Are we not here reminded of Britten's popularity, as well as of the fact that he is at times reproached with "making concessions"? In any case, Mozart and Britten are the only two composers I know who strongly and widely attract people who do not understand them.

Both composers are clever, supreme craftsmen, hence both are accused of trying to be clever and of lacking in the deeper emotions:

> It is a pity that in his truly artistic and beautiful compositions [he] should carry his effort after originality too far, to the detriment of the sentiment and heart of his works. His new [compositions] . . . are much too highly spiced to be palatable for any length of time.

One of Britten's more 'favourable' critics? No, one of the most favourable among the then contemporary critics of Mozart's six quartets dedicated to Haydn. "It is perhaps the one work . . . in which he achieved real sublimity." But this, surely, is one of Britten's "favourable" critics, talking, I don't know, of *Grimes* (referring to "Now the Great Bear and Pleiades"), or of the *Donne Sonnets* (referring to the sixth), or of *Lucretia* (referring to the English horn and strings passage at Lucretia's last entry). . . . No, it is a critic of Mozart again, this time one of our own age, a very favourable one; nor is he just a scribe. It is in fact one who often is above criticism—Professor Dent on *The Magic Flute* (1940). "The 'splendid isolation' of Mozartian music from the standpoint of biographical interpretation caused this music to be explained, in a period of romantic afflation, as *academic in form, cold, empty, frivolous, superficial.*"[1] Precisely the same descriptions are not seldom given of Britten's music today, though we are not living in a period of romantic afflation. And if it be objected that Britten, as distinct from Mozart, actually *is* cold and empty and superficial, we who find warmth and a rich and deep content in his music have at least this to be said in our favour: while one does not usually find things that are not there, one often does not find things that are. I would suggest that both composers sublimate not only their depths, but also their heights, i.e. they even sublimate their sublimity. (Richard Strauss, incidentally, calls Mozart "the sublimest of all composers".)

In the music of neither Mozart nor Britten is there a sign of inhibitions (as distinct from restraint). In this respect their exact contrary is Brahms. [*Addendum, 1952*: At that time (1947) I had, of course, no idea of Britten's actual attitude towards Brahms (nor indeed of his ideas about Mozart) as shown in *Harewood*, p. 6, but I think my comparison explains his dislike. That "he once admired" Brahms (*loc. cit.*) must be due to the fact that then his musical character had not yet gained definite form. His eventual aversion to Brahms's genius, while significant for the elucidation of his own, has given rise to an evaluation which, needless to add, is quite incompetent.] It is this freedom from inhibitions that makes a certain type of neurotic listeners belittle their works: we cannot easily bear it if others do not suffer from what we deny suffering from ourselves. Hand in hand with the absence of intra-musical inhibitions goes a delight in accepting,

[1] Einstein, *op. cit.,* p. 109. Italics mine.

and working within, given limitations. With Mozart this point is self-evident. As for Britten, we need not believe him too much when he gives a variety of practical reasons for the scoring of *Lucretia*, *Herring*, and *The Beggar's Opera*; for it is clear that these reasons offer him a welcome excuse for trying what he can do within the limitations of the chamber opera.

Ease, facility, effortless skill—these points are obvious in the case of either composer. Among their admirers both Mozart and Britten are known to be able to "manage anything". I hope there will never be any opportunity of proving that Britten can even manage things that bore him stiff; in Mozart's case such proof is furnished by the F minor *Fantasy* for what is called a barrel-organ (*Orgelwalze*) or clock (*Uhr*), "a kind of composition which I detest", as he writes to his wife. But the general fact that both composers can write on commission as if they did not write on commission is of course established. The essence of such music for a special occasion does not with them betray external compulsion. Here the history of the Mozart *Requiem* is symbolic: an outer impulse is changed into an inner one.

The continued success of such impulse-changing does not depend merely on versatility, but also on deep-reaching agility. Britten is perhaps the most agile composer of our time. Busoni on Mozart: "He is universal through his agility." Universality itself has many aspects with Mozart and Britten. Two of these are particularly significant, both aesthetically and psychologically:

(1) A German writer on music, Carl Gollmick (1796–1866), divides composers into two classes (he would!), i.e. "melodists" and "contrapuntists", and proceeds to show that Mozart satisfies the requirements of both these classes. If one wants to use this objectionable division—as a stenographic makeshift—for showing that it cannot be used in Mozart's case, and why not, one can also apply it, in almost the same way, to Britten.

(2) Both composers have a sense at once of humour and of tragedy which they manifest quite clearly and which yet tends to go unrecognized by many of us because we do not easily permit ourselves to indulge, in our turn, in this double sense, and because we often find it difficult to bear contrary standpoints in the same man or work, or expressed at the same time. Yet, as the psychoanalyst O. Rank has clearly recognized apropos of *Don Giovanni*, music

is uniquely suited "to express, at the same time, different tendencies".

This point merits a little further attention, for which purpose I must, alas, once more differ from Professor Dent. Replying to the time-honoured question whether *Don Giovanni* is a serious or a comic opera, he says: "The simplest plan is to take the opera as its author and composer intended—as an amusing comedy, with a touch of social satire and a great deal of fantastic impossibility." One is all for taking the opera as all this, but Dent wants it to be taken as this alone. The libretto may stand such a one-sided interpretation, but the music does not. The question whether *Don Giovanni* is a serious or a comic opera does not indeed exist: it is both[1]. Similarly, *Così fan tutte* is not just "an elaborate artificial comedy" (Dent). The great E major aria, for instance, or Act II's A major duet, suggests otherwise.

With Britten the whole story started all over again. A prominent and otherwise perspicacious critic remarked, in view of *Lucretia* (which, upon thorough study, I deem a great work), that the composer's bent was not for "tragic or even human feeling", but solely "for artificial comedy". Meanwhile, Britten's first comic opera, *Herring*, had itself shown that he was able, in the words of Charles Stuart, to take "excursions into a rarer world, with the earthiness of comic opera left behind and below". We must recognize that there are two sides to Britten[2]. In fact, I personally think that whenever there is only one side to an artist it is a wrong one.

Both composers create in the same way. Britten: "Usually I have the music complete in my head before putting pen to paper" [322]. In this respect their exact contrary is Beethoven (like Brahms, a composer whom Britten does not fully understand). They also create, if I may say so, on the same way:

> When not flying or sailing to foreign opera houses and concert halls . . . Britten is perpetually rushing off to catch trains for voice-and-piano recitals with Peter Pears in remote provincial towns. The business of musical creation goes on serenely among

[1] The two schools of interpretation, the 'tragic' and the 'comic' both equally one-sided, *can* be roughly located along historical and geographical co-ordinates. As far as the latter magnitude goes, the tragic school is predominantly German, the comic predominantly English.

[2] On the basis of psychological reflections such as I have sketched above *sub* (2), I ventured the prediction in June 1947 [133a] that "the *serious* musical aspect of [*Herring*] will tend to be underestimated, or even neglected". Many reviewers proved me right. Among the exceptions there was Desmond Shawe-Taylor who, writing of the *Threnody* in the last act, pointed out that "it is such moments as these which make it a superficial judgment to write the work off as a farce or a charade" [276a].

the bustle and the baggage. Looking unseeingly through train windows . . . Britten composes as fluently as if he were sitting in a soundproof cell, with quires of manuscript paper before him and a grand piano at his elbow [322].

And travel does not interrupt Mozart's creative activity; it rather stimulates it. When long journeys are out of the question, as for example, during the last ten years in Vienna, he is constantly changing his residence . . . from the town out into the suburbs, and from the suburbs back again into town.[1]

Britten's parallel manœuvres between London and Snape and, later, between Aldeburgh and London, are, of course, well known. (See also *Pears*, p. 60.)

Scoring: strictly speaking, this problem does not appear to be one with Mozart and Britten (except where they are concerned with other composers' works: *The Messiah*, *Matinées Musicales*). "With Mozart", Arthur Hutchings aptly observes[2], "such problems [of balance, tone-colour, variety, etc.] do not seem to exist. He may have been lucky; the band may have been at just the right stage of development to make instrumental thinking but one element in musical thinking as a whole . . ."[3] (Dear old History again, though it is true that Hutchings later rejects her claims.) Compare this with what one of the most discerning critics of Britten, Desmond Shawe-Taylor, says about this composer's "musical thinking as a whole":

One difference between Britten and most of his contemporaries is that, in the process of composition, his imaginative "inner ear" is listening, all the time and at full stretch, to what he is doing; fascinating as his music looks on paper—for he is a master of figuration and every kind of musical device [as Mozart is.—H. K.]—I feel tolerably sure that his ideas never occur to him as anything but sheer sensuous sound, and that it is to this fact that they owe the force and freshness with which they strike the listener's ear.

Thus, for instance, Mozart's and Britten's compositions for orchestra are not orchestrated, but orchestral.

[1] Einstein, *op. cit.*, pp. 4f.
[2] "A Note on the 'Additional Accompaniments'", *The Music Review*, VII. 3, p. 161.
[3] Hutchings's sentence ends thus: ". . . as it is to a composer writing a chamber work". The relevance of this phrase, however, escapes me; surely it needs qualifying. Brahms, for instance, certainly conceived music in an abstract manner even where he was concerned with chamber music, much of which clearly exhibits his surmounting instrumental problems.

Both composers seem to derive much from melodic inspiration. More materially, they are liable to be inspired by the human voice (as also by language, including foreign language), and indeed influenced by individual voices (as well as by instruments and instrumentalists). As regards Mozart, "opera was always composed for a special occasion and for particular singers; the choice of singers influenced the vocal style and other characteristics as well"[1]. The same is true of Britten's operas to varying degrees; even *Grimes* was "considerably influenced" by the Sadler's Wells Opera Company [24]. It would seem to me that when Britten writes for tenor or soprano he is in advance of himself in a similar way as Mozart when writing a piano concerto (in which he can let himself be inspired not only by his piano playing but also, in various ways though indirectly, by vocal ideas). At the same time Britten the pianist has for me some striking similarities to what I picture to be Mozart the pianist; but as I have not heard Mozart I shall not enlarge on this point (see, however, *Hamburger*, pp. 314–318).

In any case Mozart's piano concertos and Britten's tenor compositions are instances of their common love for virtuosity which, together with their common love of the dramatic, is also part of their intense common love for opera. Both, moreover, carry their symphonic thinking into opera, and their operatic thinking into extra-operatic music.

As for the more extra-musical aspects of their operas, the psychological and sociological theme of rebellion plays an important part (see *Harewood*, p. 7). Even *The Magic Flute*, it must be remembered, "was a work of rebellion"[2]; *Grimes* and *Lucretia*, as well as *Herring* and *Budd*, centre on the motive of opposition to (society's) tyranny and *The Beggar's Opera* combines the spirit of social with that of artistic opposition.

Operatic technique (Mozart to his father, 13th October, 1781):

> Why, an opera is sure of success when the plot is well worked out, the words written solely for the music and not shoved in here and there to suit some miserable rhyme . . . I mean, words or even entire verses which ruin the composer's whole idea. Verses are indeed the most indispensable element for music—but rhymes— solely for the sake of rhyming—the most detrimental. These high

---

[1] Einstein, *op. cit.*, p. 109.
[2] Einstein, *op. cit.*, p. 465.

and mighty people who set to work in this pedantic fashion will always come to grief, both they and their music. The best thing of all is when a good composer, who understands the stage and is talented enough to make sound suggestions, meets an able poet, that true phœnix; in that case no fears need be entertained as to the applause, even of the ignorant.

Britten [25] :

> This "working together" of the poet and composer seems to be one of the secrets of writing a good opera. In the general discussion on the shape of the work—the plot, the division into recitatives, arias, ensembles and so on—the musician will have many ideas that may stimulate and influence the poet. Similarly, when the libretto is written and the composer is working on the music, possible alterations may be suggested by the flow of the music, and the libretto altered accordingly. . . . The composer and poet should at all stages be working in the closest contact, from the most preliminary stages right up to the first night.

Joseph Gregor[1] has pointed out that, in spite of what there was before him, Mozart may in some respects be regarded as a founder (a "second founder") of opera. The same can already be said today, as far as the modern British—perhaps not only British—field goes, of Britten.

We cannot leave the subject of opera without quoting a criticism of *Don Giovanni*, or rather of a review of *Don Giovanni*, whose resemblance with various criticisms of allegedly too favourable reactions to Britten's operas is, it will be admitted, almost uncannily striking. Einstein[2] rightly reminds us that

> no biography should fail to reproduce . . . —as evidence of contemporary presumption, especially characteristic of Berlin—the dictum of an anonymous writer who was moved by an enthusiastic description of 'Don Giovanni' by Bernhard Anselm Weber in the 'Musicalisches Wochenblatt' of 1792 to the following reprimand: "His report of Mozart's 'Don Juan' is highly exaggerated and one-sided. No one will misjudge Mozart, the man of great talents and the expert, prolific and pleasing composer. Yet I do not know any well-grounded connoisseur of art who considers him a correct, not to say finished, artist; still less will the critic of sound judgment consider him, in respect to poetry, a proper and fine composer."

[1] *Kulturgeschichte der Oper*, Zürich, 1941.
[2] *Op. cit.*, p. 134.

When they are not accused of striving after originality, Mozart and Britten are accused of lacking originality, of eclecticism. In Mozart's case such an accusation will necessarily be indirect, because unfortunately it isn't done. (If it were, the lack of understanding in many a half-hearted 'admirer' would more easily be seen.) One way of thus indirectly attacking Mozart is to discover too much of him in Christian Bach, and to end up by playing Christian Bach instead of Mozart[1].

With regard to Britten's 'eclecticism', the accusations are of course direct and numerous. Instead of allowing ourselves to be detained by them, let us look at the whole question from the other, understanding side. To begin with, Mozart again. Here is an eminent musicologist on his 'eclecticism'; we shall easily see how this applies to Britten:

> . . . [Mozart] united the musical treasures of all nations of his time. This could easily have led to a mixture without character, but . . . Mozart did not imitate anyone or anything; the external appearance of music was but a means of expression to him, never technique. . . . It is not enough . . . to say that content and form balance each other in Mozart's music, for this unity is style, and while the style is constant the variety of its manifestations is as great as the number of his works. Mozart never created really new forms, but by regarding the existing styles not as unities but as phenomena which contribute towards a general style, he created a universal all-inclusive style. . . .[2]
>
> We must not forget that Mozart was the child of an era customarily called the "golden age" of musical art. Such a golden age . . . offers to the genius the richest treasures of the various artistic forms . . . He simply takes the gifts of his epoch, intact, and, as self-evident matter, utilizes them at his will . . . Mozart shuffled [the creations of the eighteenth century] like a pack of cards and the result was a strikingly original and individual world.[3]

This is all true, I suggest, except for the over-stress on history: Britten is doing a similar shuffling without being the child of a golden age.

Let us now hear Britten's own words on his 'eclecticism'. After implying that he passes from manner to manner "as a bee passes from flower to flower", he declares: "I do not see why I should

---

[1] *Pace* Christian Bach's mastery and all that Mozart owes to it.
[2] P. H. Láng, *Music in Western Civilization*, 1942, p. 636.
[3] *Ibid.*, p. 137.

lock myself inside a purely personal idiom. I write in the manner best suited to the words, theme or dramatic situation which I happen to be handling" [322]. We here remember that Einstein speaks of Mozart's "astonishing capacity for imitation, assimilation and elaboration of whatever suited him"[1], of his being "the greatest master of style, or rather of all musical styles"[2]. Indeed Mozart himself wrote to his father (7th February, 1778): "As you know, I can more or less adopt or imitate any kind and any style of composition." Einstein suggests[3] that this capacity accounts for Mozart's super-nationality, and I would add that it also accounts for Britten's, whose success among foreign musicians in this country and abroad is remarkable. It may be interesting to note in this connection that Britten's solution of the modern sonata problem in his C major Quartet has perhaps been most strongly appreciated by two ex-Austrian musicians: Erwin Stein [288] and the present writer [132]. According to the music critic of *The Times*[4], sonata form "is for all its universal validity an essentially Austrian way of thinking in music" (see also *Keller*, p. 228).

Britten's afore-mentioned remarks on his 'eclecticism' include a reminder that has already been partly quoted at the beginning of this article: "The romantics became so intensely personal that it looked as though we were going to reach a point at which the composer would be the only man capable of understanding his own music."[5] And Mozart writes to his father (28th December, 1782): "The golden mean of truth in all things is no longer either known or appreciated. In order to win applause one must write stuff which is so inane that a cabby could sing it, or so unintelligible that it pleases precisely because no sensible man can understand it. . ." Again, could not the following, too, have been written, *mutatis mutandis*, by Britten?

This is what I think [of a Concerto for two flutes by Friedrich Hartmann Graf, 1727–1795]. It is not at all pleasing to the ear, not a bit natural. He often plunges into a new key far too brusquely and it is all quite devoid of charm. When it was over, I praised him very highly, for he really deserves it. The poor fellow must have taken a great deal of trouble over it and he must have studied hard enough. At last a clavichord, one of Stein's, was brought out of the

[1] Einstein, *op. cit.*, p. 110.
[2] *Op. cit.*, p. 129.
[3] *Op. cit.*, p. 103.
[4] "English Chamber Music", *The Times*, January 17th, 1947.
[5] [322].

inner room, an excellent instrument, but covered with dust and dirt. Herr Graf, who is director here, stood there transfixed, like someone who has always imagined that his wanderings from key to key are quite unusual and now finds that one can be even more unusual and yet not offend the ear.[1]

Reflecting upon Mozart's temperament, Einstein says:

He yielded to an influence quite ingenuously, quite in the feminine fashion. He strove least of all for originality; because he was entirely certain of the Mozartian, personal stamp of his product. *Facile inventis addere* cannot apply to him; this adage applies indeed only to science or technique. What he derived from others was for him a fertilization, which eased the course of the spiritual and musical pregnancy and birth.[2]

And Desmond Shawe-Taylor, after mentioning, *inter alia,* Verdi's and Handel's influence upon *Herring,* remarks that "in spite of such links, the whole score remains immensely characteristic of its composer" [276]. The whole problem of Mozart's and Britten's originality and eclecticism can, I think, be summed up in Einstein's words: "Mozart belongs, like Bach, to the rare species of the conservative revolutionaries, or the revolutionary conservatives."[3]

In a paragraph on the youthful aspects of Mozart, Láng[4] thinks that in the composer lives all the eighteenth century's

youthful delicacy and feminine grace, . . . its brightness and naturalness, . . . its flexibility, its loving care for the little and the fine, its fondness for variation and for the characteristic. . . . But this lovable youthfulness ripens into maturity, and playful freedom and moodiness are harnessed by schooling and discipline, ingenuous feelings are formed by classic measure, ideas are deepened to symbols of universal significance.

Note how very exactly the spiritual tendencies here enumerated apply to Britten, although—neo-classicism apart—one does not find the affinities between our own time and the eighteenth century very striking.

[1] Mozart to his father, 14th October, 1777.
[2] *Op. cit.*, p. 122.
[3] *Op. cit.*, p. 162—see, however, Section II (c), p. 342.
[4] *Op. cit.*, p. 624.

One may at the same time concede that the form in which Britten's fondness for variation quite often manifests itself, i.e. the ostinato, is in part historically determined (see Section II (c), pp. 344f.).

In and beyond the art of variation, the fundamental musical principle of repetition is treated in a similar way by the two composers. Both mechanical reiteration and narcissistic re-citation are absent; thematic relationships, though frequent and really simple, often go unrecognized by the superficial listener because in the process of transformation or transplantation of themes or fragments far-reaching changes of emotional significance are secured, though of course at the same time an underlying emotional identity is preserved.

The strong drive of either composer towards economy (as distinct from poverty) of thematic material is just as obvious as the fact that economy, in either case, also radiates in other directions, e.g. the instrumental.

In an article entitled "Back to Mozart?" Felix von Weingartner once remarked:

> . . . thus I want to give the following answer to the question put in the title: To create, with our modern means of expression, *in Mozart's spirit*—this would perhaps be the right thing . . . But . . . can there be any question of "back"? I think it must much more truly be said: "*Forward* to Mozart!"[1]

Can it be chance that Weingartner was, as far as I know, the first to call Britten (after hearing the oboe Quartet in 1934) a genius?

Before I try to round off my thesis I should like to quote some more of Busoni's aphorisms on Mozart. Their relevance will, I trust, be appreciated at this stage without further comment. "He doesn't risk anything foolhardy." "He is capable of saying very much, but never says too much." "He carries all characters within himself, but only as an exhibitor and portraitist." "Together with the puzzle he gives you the solution." "He can always draw water from any glass because he has emptied none." "His smile is not that of a diplomat or actor, but that of a pure nature—yet that of a man of the world." "He is spirited without any nervousness—idealist without becoming immaterial, realist without ugliness." "It is the architectural that is most closely related to his art."

[1] His italics.

"In respect to universality", writes Einstein, "Mozart may be compared only with other great masters; and in our comparisons we shall limit ourselves to the eighteenth and nineteenth centuries."[1] He would not, I believe, have thus limited himself if he had known Britten's music.

> Nearest [to Mozart], perhaps, is Handel, the master of the cantata, the opera, the oratorio, the concerto grosso, the sonata—but we are stopped short already. Did not all this flow from one unified, mighty source, Italian vocalism, the *bel canto* of the monumental aria?[2]

On the basis of present suggestions, I submit, we cannot be stopped short in this or any other way when we compare Britten with Mozart. Britten, that is to say, is not only immeasurably nearer to Mozart than Handel because his (Britten's) universality does not spring from one unified source, but also because, beneath, above and beyond the sphere of universality, Britten and Mozart have far more in common than Handel and Mozart. "And was Bach universal? To be sure, he left no corner uncultivated in the fields of instrumental and vocal music. . . . Actually, however, all this, too, grows from one root—instrumental music. . ."[3] And so it goes on. Gluck, Einstein's next object of comparison, need not, it will be admitted, detain us. "Both Haydn and Beethoven are cramped by the word, they speak most freely in the instrumental fields."[4] And even putting the question of universality apart again, can it be suggested that Haydn-Mozart comparisons or Beethoven-Mozart comparisons are comparable with a comparison between Britten and Mozart?

> And this would bring us to Schubert, the composer of the "Unfinished" and the D minor Quartet, and of hundreds of perfect songs, the only one who could be compared to Mozart, if it were not that, although he wrote operas too, the dramatic, the scenic, the feeling for the stage, were denied to him.[5]

I submit that Britten stands far nearer to Mozart than does Schubert,

[1] *Op. cit.*, p. 103.
[2] *Ibid.*
[3] *Ibid.*
[4] *Op. cit.*, p. 104.
[5] *Ibid.*

once more not only in respect of universality (cf. particularly "the dramatic, the scenic, the feeling for the stage"), but also—as I hope the present paper tends to show—in almost every other respect. In fact, to me personally it seems that the only deep-rooted musico-characterological difference between Britten and Mozart is that the one is often strongly inspired by nature, while the other is an indoor composer.

Passing, for obvious reasons, over the rest of Einstein's list of composers to be compared, or rather not to be compared, with Mozart, we arrive at this admirable summing-up of Mozart's universality:

> When one considers the somnambulistic surefootedness and grace with which Mozart masters the vocal and the instrumental, mass and opera, quartet and concerto, one's admiration grows immeasurably at the phenomenon of his uniqueness as a universal musician.[1]

This is not the time, and I am not the man, to decide about the relative greatness of Mozart and Britten; to assess how far with Britten, too, "the world-spirit wishes to show that here is pure sound, conforming to a weightless cosmos, triumphant over all chaotic earthliness, spirit of the world-spirit"[2]; but as one who is soaked in the music of both Mozart and Britten I may be allowed to claim that for the first time Mozart, the universal musician who masters everything with a somnambulistic surefootedness and grace, has found a companion. And personally, I regard Britten as the greatest of all living composers whose music I understand.

II. THE HISTORICAL ASPECT: THE CRISIS OF BEAUTY AND MELODY

As soon as we turn to the historical situation in which Britten finds, and many a weaker composer loses himself, the Britten-Mozart parallel ends with more than one bang issuing forth from the twentieth century's powerfully reinforced kitchen department. Since every age considers itself the most critical, the most critical dare not do so, but after our time's arrogant and lazy modesty—"who are we to judge

[1] *Op. cit.*, p. 105.
[2] The concluding sentence of Einstein's book, p. 471.

ourselves"—has evaporated, the fact remains or emerges that Mozart is a child of the golden age (see Section I, p. 329) while Britten is a child of the rotten age. The much-discussed and, in comparison with previous ages, much overestimated cleft between composer and public is one of the least serious symptoms; a far graver sign is the absence of any cleft between bad music and even the good musician. Those who nowadays talk of 'organic' music tend to forget that it is only the organic which rots, and once rotting has become the fashion, devaluation calls itself revaluation, and evaluation becomes a matter of taste, opinion or social utility, while every new organism is felt to be unnatural. At no previous time in our musical history would such sham creations as *The Rake's Progress* or *Die Liebe der Danae* have had a chance; indeed, at no previous time would they have been written by good composers.

What such anthologies, pastiches, pot-pourris and self-imitations are said to possess are melody and beauty—two things which the musical as well as the unmusical man in the street quite rightly finds lacking upon the more self-consciously 'contemporary' scene. On even the most cursory inspection, however, *The Rake*'s and *Danae*'s 'beauty' and 'melody' will be found to be pale and defective copies of their easily recognizable models, so that there is not the faintest reason why one should not rather listen to the models themselves, e.g. *Così fan tutte* (more than *Don Giovanni*) in the case of *The Rake,* or Wagner and the earlier Strauss himself in the case of *Danae*. In other words, that *The Rake* and *Danae* are appreciated is not due to a real sense of melody, but to the loss of any sense of real melody which would get at the models and forget the copies.

The historical facts are that melody, extensive melody in the sense of the second subject (and recapitulation) from the first movement of Mozart's clarinet Quintet, has become impossible within the domain of tonality, while beauty in Mozart's sense has become unnecessary. The decline of melody is directly due and proportionate to the diatonic cadence's loss of potency; the change in creative attitudes towards the never successfully defined[1], but often definite concept of beauty is a problem transcending the sphere of music and even of art altogether, and cannot be understood without reference to the development and the age of our culture. It will be convenient to

---

[1] Even Goethe renounced the task (letters to Friederike Oeser, 13th February, 1769, and Hetzler junior, 14th July, 1770).

examine these complicated and interrelated factors in separation, and to treat the more complex and comprehensive first.

(a) FROM BEAUTY TO TRUTH

*"The beautiful does not
matter to me."* PICASSO

Nor did it to Strawinsky when he heard someone complaining about the beautilessness of his music—an irrelevant criticism, he thought (I am recalling from memory). Thus the two liberators from personal art to whom Britten has drawn attention (see Section I, p. 321, and [322]). Picasso may perhaps be said to occupy a middle position between the objectivist Strawinsky and the other, opposite leader of our time's music, the individualist Schoenberg. But all three seem agreed about the superfluity of the concept of beauty. Schoenberg writes in his *Harmonielehre*: "Beauty comes into being when the uncreative begin to miss it. Before that it does not exist, for the artist does not need it. For him, truthfulness is enough."

This seems a far cry from Mozart, who thought that ". . . music, even in the most terrible situations, must never offend the ear, but must please the hearer, or in other words must never cease to be *music* . . ."[1] A far cry, but not essentially a different cry: no one has insisted more than Schoenberg that music must remain music, not only in the most terrible situations, but even when allied to a text. In fact, Picasso's observation that "art does not mean applying a rule of beauty, but expressing what instinct and intellect are able to grasp of the world" would have received Mozart's unconscious and Beethoven's conscious consent. What, in fact, we have witnessed in the later stages of our culture is not only and simply a development from phantasy to realism, from beauty to truth, but also a change of attitude towards the beauties of the past which have become truer and truer: art has turned out to have not just *created* a world, but *discovered* the mind and its worlds. Conversely and consequently, we have become alive to the beauty of truth; indeed, when beauty is replaced by truth, the ugly must eventually become beautiful.

(i) *The General Cultural Situation*

More sexual than aggressive energies are needed for the creation of

[1] Letter to his father, 26th September, 1781.

beauty; more aggressive than sexual energies are needed for the discovery of truth. Recent times have brought greater sexual freedom and perhaps unprecedented frustration of aggressive tendencies, so that from the standpoint of social psychology alone the development from beauty to truth must be considered inevitable. That far more people are being killed and tortured today than in previous times when there was less talk about humanity does not of course mean anything in terms of psychic economy: it all depends on how you kill them. Our technical advances have unfortunately made it possible for us to kill a maximal number of people at the minimal level of psychic expenditure, whereas formerly even small-scale killings involved the release of powerful amounts of aggression, with the emergence of correspondingly powerful guilts afterwards. In addition, while opportunities for the discharge of aggression are steadily decreasing, aggressive urges themselves are actually on the increase, not only because unreleased aggression makes for further aggression (whether turned against the self or outward), but also because our comparative freedom from sexual restraint increases our intra-psychic inhibitions and anxieties; owing to the infantile Oedipus situation we tend to fight for a freedom we cannot bear—all the less since the loss of religion (no matter whether this means, objectively, the loss of truth, or of illusion, or of both), itself partly the effect and partly the cause of increased aggression, has robbed us of our security which the new and often equally emotional religions, whether Sciences or States, can only very partly restore. Hence unprecedented frustration, hence unprecedented neurosis and aggressiveness. From the concentration camp to the sado-masochistic, percussive double stoppings on what was once the 'singing' instrument of the violin, sadism is liable to manifest itself on every level of barbarity or sublimation.

It even manifests itself in all sweeping reflections on aggressiveness, inasmuch as they concern themselves too much with the contribution to death and too little with the discovery of life for which aggression has been or may be responsible. This is all the more regrettable since every useful channel will have to be found for human aggressiveness if mankind is to survive—a policy whose application will have to start in, indeed concentrate on, the character-forming years of early childhood. Meanwhile, to be sure, it is not even realized that man hates his neighbour as himself, nor that self-hate is as harmful as hate and more harmful than self-love.

In the sphere of conceptual thought, the contribution which sublimated aggression is rendering to our culture can be suggested by a single word—*analysis*. It is no chance that the main usurpers of religion, metaphysics and of the various derivatives of idealist philosophy show this word on their banners: Freud's *psychoanalysis*, as well as *analytic philosophy* and its *linguistic analysis*. (Significantly in our context, Morton White of Harvard University has observed that "the present period of analytic philosophy has still not recovered from the militant charm of this method". Even Jung's psychological system, which cannot—and perhaps does not wish to—claim validity on purely scientific grounds, has felt compelled to neglect its allegedly synthetic aspects in its title and just to reverse the Freudian appellation, calling itself *Analytic Psychology*.

In the political sphere one can hardly yet speak of conceptual thought, nor indeed of much thought altogether, but it remains interesting to observe that what started as, or at least well intended to be, the most realistic movement, i.e. that of scientific socialism, made its influence felt across all political parties in a similar way as the analytical movement pervaded the entire realm of reflective thought[1]. A particularly curious state of affairs was reached in Austria prior to Dollfuss's quasi-dictatorship, when the three parties on which public interest centred—extremist right, unsocialist, and barbaric, conservative right centre, clerical and semi-fascist, and the left—all sailed under the flag of 'socialism': the Nazis ('*National Socialists*'), the *Christian Socialists*, and the actual socialists ('*Social Democrats*').

In fact, the surest sign of our age's aggressive search for 'the real facts' is that every illusion, every perversion and lie which was previously promulgated or enacted in the name of God or Goodness, is nowadays propagated for the sake of truth, realism, or utility. Yet, many as are our illusions about truth, we are beginning to learn the truth about our illusions.

(ii) *The Artistic and Musical Situation*

One of the reasons why we tend to consider Mozart's truths beautiful, and Bartók's full of many other things beside and above and opposed to beauty, is that by this late time in our culture most pleasant truths have been discovered and it remains the unpleasant task of our geniuses to unearth repressed material which the conscious mind

---

[1] The present writer has no political allegiances.

duly regards as ugly. It needs more courage today than ever to be a good artist, and more cowardice than ever to be a bad artist; nor is it surprising that there are so few people left who have the courage not to be artists at all.

The time of the simply beautiful feeling as well as of the simple tragedy is over because we know all about them; the rest is either silence or Hollywood or the Soviet Symphony. At the same time, Soviet 'social realism', Picasso's 'grasping of the world' and Schoenbergian 'truthfulness' and 'factuality' all assert that truth is better than fiction; again, the same idea or pretext inspires the furthest opposites.

From Strawinsky's rediscovery of the past (a testimony of our culture's years: History is a sign of old age) to Schoenberg's discovery of the future, from Hindemith's utility to Britten's social conscience (see *Harewood*, p. 7, and *Mitchell*, p. 53), from Schoenberg's inspired thematicism (to thine own theme be true) to an uninspired remark in the *Oxford Harmony*, Vol. II, which condemns coloratura and suggests that nowadays composers want, and ought, to get on with the job, from Bartók's aggressiveness to Strawinsky's sado-masochism, from Webern's asceticism to Boulez's aggressive narcissism, from the historical reality behind *Wozzeck* to the spiritual topicality of *Il Prigionero* (likewise based on a true story), from the Contemporary Composer's uninspired compositions to his searching programme notes on what he thinks are his compositions, the fight for one or the other aspect of truth and reality is in full if asymmetric swing, criss-crossing and ploughing the field of new music without much regard for the beauties it might, and sometimes still does, yield. At its worst, beauty has become a waste product, at its best a by-product. It is a largely desexualized fight, then, and perhaps Schoenberg is the only one who has begun, despite and in conjunction with his powerful aggression, to resexualize music. But then, Schoenberg is of the future, of a new culture.

(b) THE MELODIC CRISIS

The decline of melody is partly illusory and partly real. Unfortunately, the illusory part has serious consequences too: it isolates the composer from society at least as successfully as Schoenberg's "emancipation of the dissonance". That, in what is doubtless growing into a polyphonic age, melody of all things should be found lacking by even the average musician is ground for alarm.

The average musician has been nurtured on 'classical' music, and he conceives of melody in terms of symmetry and clearly recognizable anti-symmetry (Brahms), but does not identify a melody which is more asymmetric than anti-symmetric (Schoenberg) as a melody at all. Rhythmically speaking, he remains a musical 'poet' in that it never struck him that there may be such a thing as musical 'prose' (Reger's and Schoenberg's independent and identical term) outside the palely musical sphere of loose recitative; hence his illusion that Schoenberg lacks both melody and rhythm. In point of musical fact, the exact opposite is true: Schoenberg's twelve-tone structures have regained extensive melodies by substituting extra-tonal means of large-scale tension and dis-tension for the weakened diatonic cadences.

Within the diatonic and the 'chromatic major and minor' field (Richard Arnell's term[1]), however, the crisis of melody is real. Its history is longer than one would suspect; upon analytic reflection, the late Beethoven started it all, though like Schoenberg he was so far in advance of what could still be done that the crisis did not become apparent for quite a time afterwards. Ironically enough, it became quite manifest in a master whom the musical man in the street nowadays upholds as a shining example of unspoilt melodic virtue, i.e. the Verdi of the *Requiem* and *Otello* who, just because his harmony on the whole remains conservative, begins to mistrust the power of widely-arched cadentiations within and around a melodic line, with the result that he no longer relies on extensive or even extended melodies, but rather compresses rich melodic contents into short phrases (thus creating the illusion of 'long' melodies) and, for the rest, adopts slightly extra-musical (e.g. recitativic) means of extension and transition. This, for me, is the real reason for the superficially 'theatrical' style of the *Requiem*: the intra-musicalization of operatic means of extension and bridging.

Today there are no extensive melodies to speak of outside Schoenberg's work on the one hand and tonal pastiche on the other; how impotent the tonal cadence has become in this respect is indicated by the fact that one of the two leaders of our musical time, Strawinsky, while continuously reminding us of the prime importance of melody,

[1] "A Note on Tonality", *Music Survey*, II. 3, p. 179.

is incapable of producing a single original one. By neo-classical and eclectic routes he has, for a time, achieved the impossible, i.e. a melodic line (say, Jocasta's aria in *Œdipus Rex*) which, though unoriginal in form, accumulates sufficient original content to keep itself on the near side of the Styx and in fact to bear the stamp of inspiration and genius. But the trouble about miracles is that they are not easily repeatable because one cannot practise them (or perhaps because one can), and underlying the melodies of *The Rake's Progress* the listener senses a process less allied to composition than to stamp-collecting.

(c) BRITTEN: SYNTHESES AND SOLUTIONS

The swift decline and rebirth (prosification) of melody, due as they are to the weakening of the diatonic cadence, themselves emerge as an aspect of the development from beauty to truth. For on the harmonic level, this development manifests itself in the whirling speed at which the emancipation of the (psychologically truthful) dissonance and the disruption of tonal unity has taken place—a far quicker pace, that is to say, than would have been necessary technically, i.e. from the purely musico-historical point of view. Schoenberg's future-born mind, by no means the first, but certainly the last and strongest force in this intense acceleration, became entirely aware of it; indeed, he reminded twelve-tone fanatics that plenty of good music remained to be written in C major.

Britten has written it, quite literally: C major has become something of a pet key to this admirer and master of simplicity. He is the greatest synthesist since Mozart, all the greater since his task is so much more difficult. He is synthesizing opposing movements of the past, opposing movements of the present, national with international and present with past tendencies (see *Mitchell*, pp. 37–45). The only force which he virtually excludes from his syntheses is Schoenberg's (as distinct from Berg's) own (cf. *Stein*, p. 247). But then Schoenberg is the future's premature birth, and from the really *musico*-historical (as distinct from the, nowadays, irrelevant chronological) point of view, you might just as well have asked Mozart to include Beethoven's visions in his material for composition.

As a matter of fact, since both the Britten-Mozart and the Schoenberg-Beethoven parallels are pretty close, the relation between Britten and Schoenberg shows many striking parallels with that between

Mozart and Beethoven. Einstein's suggestion (see Section I, p. 331) that "Mozart belongs, like Bach, to the rare species of the conservative revolutionaries, or the revolutionary conservatives" is perhaps a trifle vague if one does not know Mozart so well that one doesn't need the suggestion. For those, that is to say, who refuse to divine Einstein's meaning, every genius may belong to one or the other of what they might well consider these two distinct "rare species". Perhaps it would be clearer to say that with geniuses like Beethoven and Schoenberg, the newly discovered acts in a masculine way upon the traditional which assumes a feminine rôle; whereas with Mozart and Britten, new inventions adopt a more passive, feminine attitude, letting the past and the already-discovered present play the active and masculine part. Thus considered, Mozart and Britten might be called 'revolutionary conservatives', Schoenberg and Beethoven 'conservative revolutionaries'.

The passive attitude of the new makes for a synthesis between beauty and truth, because little is beautiful that hasn't been new for quite a while. Britten lets past beauty act upon new or recent truth, e.g. upon progressive tonality or on raised norms of dissonance and consonance. Where, on the other hand, he is rediscovering archaic means of expression, the known, already-discovered present is likely to assume the active rôle. In a word, it is usually (to the intelligent musician) the more immediately known or feelable which plays the active part.

Towards the modes, for instance, it is Britten's moderate modernism that plays the active rôle of a strong and friendly host: he *naturalizes* modality. That is to say, he might address a newly-created modal theme as the Under-Secretary of State, Home Office, addresses the newly-naturalized British citizen:

> You have acquired to all intents and purposes the status of a natural-born modern subject. . . . You are consequently entitled to all . . . rights, powers and privileges, and are subject to all obligations, duties and liabilities to which a natural-born twentieth-century subject is entitled or subject.

Here, then, newly old truth (accepted modernism, generally comprehensible harmonic standards) acts upon renewed old truth (rediscovered modality), but the result is again a beautification of truth, for re-created modality serves as a strong bridge between the diatonicism of the past and the anti-diatonicism of the present and of the present future: the pre-diatonic is a natural mediator between the diatonic ('beauty') and the post-diatonic ('truth'). This synthesis deserves all the more admiration since British music of the recent past and of the present past is crowded with undesirable modal aliens.

Schoenberg has written that "only two of the remaining four modes [i.e. apart from Ionian and Aeolian] ever played a rôle in the imagination of the composers, Dorian and to a lesser degree Phrygian. Except for a small number of examples, Lydian and Mixolydian failed to have real life." Like every genius (in fact like Schoenberg himself), Britten proves right theory wrong. For his Lydian and Mixolydian inventions are actually full of life, e.g. the opening of *Grimes*'s second act, or *The Birth of Nicolas* (Lydian), or the framing hymn "Whilst we as two observers stand" (Mixolydian) from *Lucretia* (see Ex. 3 on p. 138); in fact he has a predilection for the Lydian fourth (see *Stein*, pp. 130f., *Mann*, p. 301, and *Mitchell*, p. 43). At the same time the truth of Schoenberg's theory shows even in Britten: the children's opera's third and probably best audience song, which is indistinguishable from a natural-born modern—or, should we say, timeless—tune, is dominated throughout by its Phrygian G minor (see Ex. 52a on p. 56). Not often does such a thing happen in contemporary music, where the modes are fond of hiding their artificiality by just dropping in for a moment or two.

Britten's modalities amalgamate his Englishry (see *Mitchell*, pp. 9–58, and *Stein*, pp. 130f.) with our age's originally continental tendency towards (re-)discovery, an achievement for which musical history has to be grateful to him. For two other such international unifications, however, he has to be grateful to historio-geography. For difficult as our age is even for the creative mind, it offers unique opportunities to the unprovincial English composer. In the Austro-German tradition, the development from beauty to truth meant that *thematicism*, musical factuality, assumed an ever-increasing importance. Polythematic structures came to be built on monothematic bases, second subjects grew from first subjects; in a word, one stuck to the point, a phrase which does not work in the plural. The monothematification of the sonata had, after all, allured the masters from the very beginning; not only and obviously Haydn, but even Mozart showed great interest in returning sonata form to a monothematic base. Indeed, polythematicism (as distinct from simply contrasting A–B–A forms which have only one *theme*) with its need for extended integration inevitably yearns for some kind of monothematic approach, whether by thematic relation, thematic subordination, or thematic complementation which welds contrasting ideas into a still fundamental whole. Truth- and faithfulness to the theme reached their last consequences in Schoenberg who, in his own words (letter to Nicolas Slonimsky) "was always occupied with the aim to base the structure of [his] music *consciously* on a unifying idea which produced not only all the ideas, but regulated also the accompaniment and the harmonies". With the introduction of the tone-row which came to assume *sub*-thematic significance, providing as it could the material for contrasting themes, the road was once again free for polythematic (sonata) structures whose different subjects yet remained faithful to the basic creative art, i.e. the row itself.

Leaving the ultimate consequences of the Schoenbergian approach on one side, but fortified on the other hand by the monothematic tendencies in his English tradition, Britten was able to dive into this development towards intra-musical truthfulness with perfect grace. It is not in fact he alone who profited by the recent history of musical form: there is no doubt that the renascence of English music as a whole owes a great deal to the renewed, supra-national significance of mono-thematicism. Britten's synthesis of Central-European thematicism and English monothematicism cum Strawinskian ostinato extends, of course, over his polythematic structures too. He is probably incapable of those dramatic sonata forms (cf. *Chissell*, p. 257, and *Mitchell*, p. 37) which expose extremely contrasting, yet complementary ideas within a narrow space, and of which the first movement of Beethoven's Fifth is a supreme example, though there, too, a 'monothematic' basis is secured by the principal motif. (In general, it seems that supreme operatic dramatists have no burning interest in sonata dramatism, while supreme sonata dramatists are not over-concerned about stage dramatism.) Nor does he incline towards the dramatic sonata development, the intense working-out in the continental sense which Schoenberg has resuscitated. But with the help of his synthesis, he has nevertheless conquered sonata form (see *Hamburger*, pp. 211–233, and *Keller*, p. 228): in fact, the synthesis is clear within less than a third of the exposition in the second Quartet's first movement, where the basic tenth introduces and underlines each of the three subjects (Exx. 9, 10, and 11 on pp. 229f.). And in case this be considered too

English a procedure, unworthy of the great sonata tradition with its uninhibited polythematic varieties, we must remind ourselves that Mozart applied a similar principle in the opening movement of the clarinet Trio, where the second subject starts with a basic variation of the first's opening motif.

As far as Britten's closely integrated forms are concerned, his ostinatos and variation structures represent the climax of his mono-thematic synthesis. Another aspect of the development towards intra-musical truth makes itself felt here, i.e. the freeing of ostinato struc-tures and themes for variations from bar-line or dance-symmetry (see *Pears*, p. 71, *Stein*, p. 128, and *Keller*, pp. 228f.), a process which is of course part and parcel of the general decline of symmetry, whether this manifests itself in prosification of melody, in the decen-tralization of harmony apparent in progressive tonalities (not to speak of atonalities), or indeed in the visual and literary arts. Melville, the author of *Billy Budd, Foretopman*, explains the form of his story in a few simple words which epitomize our whole historical contention: "The symmetry of form attainable in pure fiction cannot so readily be achieved in a narration essentially having less to do with fable than with fact." Nevertheless, even in these anti-symmetries or asymmetries, Britten often lets the past (symmetry) act masculinely upon the new idea, a simple example being the ostinato *Threnody* in *Herring* (see Ex. 7 on p. 139), whereas the corresponding funeral march passacaglia in *Lucretia* (see Ex. 5 on p. 138) goes so far as to let the past triumph completely with its two-bar structure.

The other historio-geographical synthesis for which Britten has to be grateful to his national character is his 'socialism' (see *Harewood*, p. 7, and *Mitchell*, p. 53) in the widest, unpolitical sense, his love for the common people, ordinary language, common sense and commonplace. The development from beauty to truth was bound to arrive at the discovery of commonplace's uncommonness, particularly at a late cultural stage, when the uncommon had become common-place. And again the Englishman meets this development halfway with his concrete, anti-speculative mind, with his common-sensical character which one can best test in the extreme field of philosophy where—if anywhere—abstract speculation could still find its rightful place. In England, however, the analytic movement, linguistic analysis, is not only overpoweringly successful, but has decided, within its ranks, in favour of the man in the street, of ordinary language, following G. E. Moore (and Ludwig Wittgenstein) rather than Bertrand Russell.

Grimes (like its father *Wozzeck*) and *Budd* are based on historical common-life subjects, the children's opera is a children's 'Grimes', *Herring*'s is a common problem and the piece even employs common language. *Grimes* rightly renounces the beautification (i.e. musical expression) of the simple tragedy, of the boy's death and Peter's death: Britten's English tendency towards understatement (see *Keller*, footnote on p. 226) helps him to suppress the no longer statable (see (a) (ii) above). Yet *Grimes* is more beautiful than *Wozzeck* (which does not necessarily mean better, though I think it is too). Why?

Primarily, I submit, because of Britten's melodic invention, which "is one of his gifts to be most thankful for" (*Pears*, p. 62) Pears's observation is yet more important than its formulation might lead one to suspect. Britten stands or falls with his melodic invention, just as one of his unofficial masters, Strawinsky, eventually stumbled over his lack of melodism. In fact, the pedal and the Strawinskian ostinato, the curse of so much contemporary music, immediately assume positive significance under a rich melodic invention (see *Keller*, pp. 226f., and *Pears*, p. 72) which thus receives support in place of the outworn harmonic dance schemes. Curious as it may seem to partisans as distinct from musicians on either side, Britten's melodic inventiveness can, among our age's composers, only be compared to Schoenberg's: like Schoenberg he is essentially a melodist.

It is his melodic gift which beautifies his discoveries of the common; and as we have already seen (p. 345), he does not hesitate at times to let the past overwhelm the present. Albert Herring's refrain "And I'm more than grateful to you all for kindly providing the where-withal!" (see Ex. 28 on p. 33), for instance, contents itself with traditional harmony and symmetrical rhythmic structure. I have suggested elsewhere [131] that "the whole point of the opera, Albert's emancipation, is summed up" in these four bars which are "thrice repeated to different words, between shouts of 'Preposterous', etc., and an ineffective tirade from Lady Billows. Both the opera's humour and its warmth are compressed into Albert's little song."

Song? Four bars! We have arrived at an elementary instance of Britten's resolution of the melodic crisis itself. It is the compression of content in this tune which immediately removes it from any suspicion of pastiche: here, as often elsewhere, the content of an aria is expressed in a phrase or two (cf. also *Pears*, p. 70). Extended melodies are few in Britten; rather, he follows Verdi's reactions to the weakening of the diatonic cadence, including what we have called the intra-musicalization of operatic means of extension and bridging (see (b) above), e.g. the above-quoted intermezzi between the repetitions of Albert's refrain or, in Act I, Sc. 2, the two interruptions of Albert's monologue (see Ex. 16 on p. 22) which spare him the problem of extending the inspired melody. (The positive significance of the first interruption is explained by *Holst* on p. 282.) Fundamentally, the cadence's loss of potency has left two melodic possibilities and one necessity within the realm of tonality. The necessity is extreme compression: the possibilities are (1) 'open' motifs or phrases which leave out the cadence and lend themselves, *inter alia,* to sequential repetitions, and (2) cadential motifs or phrases which avail themselves of the remaining potency of the diatonic cadence—enough for a short phrase—and can be used, *inter alia,* as ostinatos and/or as receptacles into which looser structures can discharge themselves. Both possibilities have been exploited by the two opposites, Wagner and Britten, but while Wagner, according to the requirements of his "eternal melody" (which, of course, isn't anything of the sort, but rather an eternal development [287]), has concentrated on the first, Britten, following his classical tendencies, has found undreamt-of riches in the cadential phrase, as a glance through the music examples of this book will readily show.

Naturally, the abundance of Britten's melodic ideas cannot be classified under one or two heads, but it can certainly be said that every single one of his mature ideas is somnambulistically alive to, yet not over-conscious of, the melodic crisis: aware of what can no longer be done, his active past remains perpetually sensitive to what can still be done. After not only the *Oxford Harmony,* but most time-conscious composers have condemned the coloratura to death, he has the face to revive it, keeping it at the same time so functional (cf., e.g., the *Serenade*'s *Hymn*) that the sternest seeker for the truth is satisfied alongside the softest yearner for beauty. With the beginning of *Lucretia* (see *Del Mar,* p. 140), he pushes unprecedentedly far ahead into the sphere of factuality, reversing the traditional operatic scheme so far as to replace the most intra-musical operatic form, the overture, by the most extra-musical informality, i.e. the recitative;

but at the same time his musicalization of the recitative, which has started, as with Verdi, by making a virtue of melodic necessity, and which has already borne ripe fruit as early as the *Serenade* and *Grimes*, assumes ever stronger structural meaning; the recitative is eaten up by the music, until in *Budd*, which foolish newspaper critics thought recitativic, it is almost entirely resolved into a flexible musical prose (see *Stein*, pp. 199f.) of definite thematic and structural functions which formalizes the prose text and has, for the moment, remained as misunderstood as Schoenberg's atonal prose (see (b) above), the critics' principle being that every shape which they did not identify as a shape could only be a recitative. As so often, there is a point to their stupidity, in that Britten could never have gained his melodic freedom without divesting the recitative of its formal freedom and independence (nor perhaps, without the 'asymmetric' inspirations of the English language: see *Stein*, p. 131). Only, they start to notice the recitative at the very moment when it is vanishing, thinking that he is making music recitativic just when he has musicalized the recitative out of existence. In fact, *Budd* seems to show capacities for a tonal prose, for functional and unrepetitive melodic extension which may one day give the lie to at least part of my death certificate on extensive tonal melody. I think I have good reason to hope for the worst, for Britten has already proved one right theory wrong (see p. 343 above), and his sensitivity to what can still be done by tonal means, or what can't except by him, is naturally stronger than a critic's.

One would not, for instance, have blamed an (imaginary) contemporary critic of Mozart's *Sinfonia Concertante* for wind quartet, K. 297, for declaring the identical (E flat) tonality of the three movements a mitigated bore, and for pronouncing, on the basis of this experience, that since not even a composer of Mozart's calibre could write three movements in the same tonality with complete success, the time for that sort of thing was surely over. Yet, a considerable time afterwards, Britten built his *Sinfonia da Requiem* on the same principle, developing all three movements in the key of D and, moreover, largely in triple time. While it is true that by this time "D" meant something different from what "E flat" meant for Mozart, the fact remains that Mozart's problem was easier than Britten's who, nevertheless, composed the piece as if the problem did not exist, furnishing what is probably our time's only fully successful example of such a continous central tonality. The few other forms of the kind one has heard, of which Blacher's *Partita* for strings and percussion seems the best, either run the repeated risk of being as monotonous as they are, horizontally, monotonal, or else do not really use their home tonality as a functional basis; a C major near the beginning and a C major chord at the end of each movement, with sly implications of G major somewhere in each middle and unfunctional tonal chaos elsewhere, are not enough.

To be sure, we find chaos, newly discovered chaos in the *Sinfonia da Requiem* too; "it is", as *Stein* (p. 250) says, "chaos painted somewhat differently from the opening of Haydn's *Creation*." And in the recapitulation of this (*Dies Irae*) movement, deeply felt disintegration ensues, which prompts *Stein* (p. 251) to the telling observation: "I do not think that disorder has ever before been conveyed in so convincing a musical form". Not before, but afterwards, i.e. in the rhapsodic 'Mad' Interlude in *Grimes*, where Britten's psychic realism once more investigates this deep and unexplored province of the mind. Perhaps it was the very newness of the venture in the *Sinfonia da Requiem*, and the fact that disintegration had to be integrated, that necessitated the active intervention of a very past principle of tonal integration. In *Grimes* (see *Keller*, p. 122), there is the guarantee of the constant dominant seventh on D, as well as of the very strictest thematic integration with the rest of the opera, some of which has escaped an analyst (see [264] and, as corrective, [166a], as well as *Keller*, p. 119).

The question remains how, psychologically speaking, Britten contrives to make his truths 'beautiful' or at least—in the case of such repressed, 'ugly' material as emerges in these scenes of disintegration—un-ugly, 'fascinating' and indeed 'well-sounding' to even the conservative, 'beauty'-starved listener. In other words, what makes his past act upon his present? What makes him always synthesize beauty with truth? Why does he bother? But he does not merely bother; he wants to, he *needs* to, he spontaneously *does*. As far as his recovery of infantile surface layers of the mind is concerned (see *Mitchell*, p. 54), the reply is simple, simpler even than it would be in the case of what, I suggest, is Wagner's corresponding recovery of adolescence. It is not only that the more pleasant aspects of the child's mind have so far remained musically undiscovered (as had the adolescent emotionality and spirituality which Wagner reclaimed), and that therefore there is at least one psychic territory left which is both new and potentially 'beautiful' (see (a) (ii) above), but also that the child's voice—used as it is as a new and functional instrument of immediate appeal (see *Holst*, pp. 279ff.)—establishes a frame both beautiful and realistic, in fact *real,* for what the composer has to say in the way of childhood feelings.

The less beautiful aspects of the preconscious and unconscious mind, however, have no voice that can be used as an instrument; they can only make themselves understood by way of high degrees of intervallic or formal tension (relative to the norms of consonance and of structural equilibrium within a given mode of expression). And here the miracle happens again: the 'ugly' is beautified, the strident is mollified; what is being discovered is not only the unconscious, but as it were a tactful and, as far as sensitivity to sound goes, a tradition-ful way of putting it across. What is discovered is, amongst other sounds, 'the sonority of the second' (see *Stein*, p. 249). "Composers before him have indulged in the exploitation of the interval, but Bartók and others used it mostly for its stridency. In Britten's music the second has become beautiful [*sic*] and tender—'a new sound symbolizing a new personality', as Schoenberg, in his *Harmonielehre*, defined similar events of the past" (*ibid.*).

What is this new personality? It does not show Bartók's straightforward sadism. It does not show Strawinsky's equally uncomplicated sado-masochism. It does not manifest much interest in the re-sexualization of music, such as has been achieved by Schoenberg (see (a) (ii) above), whose ear, it must be incidentally remarked, would never have tolerated (for instance) the kind of exposed, consecutive minor seconds which the more naïve and barbaric Bartók could allow himself.

Britten is a pacifist (see *Harewood*, p. 5). It is an established fact[1] that strong and heavily repressed sadism underlies pacifistic attitudes. About the vital aggressive element in Britten's music (as distinct from his extra-musical character) there cannot indeed be the faintest doubt, and those whose ears are not sensitive enough to recognize the sadistic component at least in his treatment of the percussion, will still be able to confirm our observation upon an inspection of his libretti, children's opera included. So far, so unenlightening: almost all our age's important minds tend to be unusually aggressive in one way or another (cf. (a) (i) above). What distinguishes Britten's musical personality is the violent repressive counter-force against his sadism:

---

[1] See E. Glover, *War, Sadism and Pacifism,* George Allen, London, 1947.

by dint of character, musical history and environment, he has become a *musical pacifist* too. This, I think, is the solution to the manifold solutions he has effected upon our war-worn and war-weary musical scene, to the paradox of his ruthless, yet beauty-conscious search for the truth.

In 'real' life, pacifism (as distinct from scientific research into, and consequent peaceful organization of, aggression) is an illusion. In art, and especially in our art, pacifism is realism *par excellence,* producing as it can the quickest possible communicability of new discoveries. The only guarantee, to be sure, that pacification will not degenerate into compromise is genius.

Discography

THE following discography is believed to include all commercial recordings of Benjamin Britten's music issued up to September 1952. It does not include such items as B.B.C. transcriptions (e.g. of the piano Concerto) which are not available to the public. The English recording company and numbers are given first, followed (in brackets) by American or other equivalents *of the same recording*; alternative recordings, if they exist, are clearly shown as such. Long Playing recordings, or LP versions of standard sets, are shown in bold type; all other entries are 78 r.p.m. The coupling (or the "fill-up" of a set of records) is printed beneath the record entry in italics and in square brackets. Most of the Decca records in the AX and AK series (automatic couplings) were first issued in manual couplings with the same numbers preceded by X or K. 10-inch discs are indicated by having prefix and number in italics.

Victor is the American equivalent of English H.M.V.; Columbia has the same name in both countries. English Decca recordings formerly appeared on the American Decca label; since 1949 a new company, called "London", has handled the English Decca catalogue in America. It has unfortunately proved impossible to hear several valuable LP additions to the Britten repertory recently issued in America.

In addition to the records of his own music listed below, Benjamin Britten is also to be heard as accompanist to Peter Pears in the following records of music by other composers:

HMV   DB 6763 The Queen's Epicedium (Purcell, arr. Britten)
            DB 21423 Im Frühling *and* Auf der Bruck (Schubert)
            DA 7038–9 Five Old American Songs (arr. Copland)
Decca   *AM 585–7* On Wenlock Edge (Vaughan Williams)

I am greatly indebted for help in preparing this discography to Messrs. F. F. Clough and G. J. Cuming, authors of the *World's Encyclopædia of Recorded Music,* and to Messrs. Sidgwick and Jackson, its publishers.

OPERAS

PETER GRIMES, Op. 33, Three Acts, 1945

Four Sea Interludes, Op. 33a ⎱ Concertgebouw Orch/Van Beinum.
Passacaglia, Op. 33b . .⎰ Decca AK 1702–4
(Amer. Decca set EDA 50)
(London set LA 201)

Interludes only . . . LSO/Sargent. Col. DX 1441–2
(Italian Col. GQX 11191–2)
(Amer. Col. 72677–8, set MX 303)

Ditto (LP) . . . **(Amer. Col. ML 2145)**
[*Lambert: Rio Grande*]

Peter Grimes is the work with which Britten established his fame, and one which he has not yet surpassed in power and imaginative intensity. It is a pity that no substantial extracts should yet have been recorded from this opera. Some day, no doubt, a more or less complete version will become available in Long Playing form; meanwhile we must be content with the orchestral excerpts which are often played in the concert hall. Of the two quoted versions, the Decca is easily the superior; not only because it includes the great *Passacaglia,* but because both recording and performance reach a higher level. Indeed it is unlikely that any English audience, whether in the theatre or the concert hall, has heard certain passages so splendidly realized as in this recording by the Concertgebouw Orchestra under Van Beinum; among its more notable features are the strong, resonant tone of the high unaccompanied violins at the opening of the first interlude, and the frenzied, yet controlled, brass outbursts at the climax of the *Passacaglia.*

THE RAPE OF LUCRETIA, Op. 37, Two Acts, 1946

Abridged Recording
Male Chorus . . Peter Pears (T)
Female Chorus . . Joan Cross (S)
Collatinus . . Norman Lumsden (B)
Junius . . . Denis Dowling (Bar.)
Tarquinius . . Frederick Sharp (Bar.)

Lucretia .   .   .   Nancy Evans (C)
Bianca   .   .   .   Flora Nielsen (MS)
Lucia   .   .   .   Margaret Ritchie (S)
Chamber Orch./Reginald Goodall. HMV C 3699–3706 (Auto C 7706–13)
(Victor set M–1288).

In abridged opera sets, each listener is sure to find some of his
favourite passages omitted. Perhaps the most serious loss in the
Lucretia set is the imaginative music which paints the hot, sultry night
at the beginning of the first scene. On the whole, however, the selection
does justice to the score: and it is particularly fortunate that the most
continuously lyrical stretch of music (Act I, Scene 1: Lucretia with her
women) has been included in full. The recording balance is inclined
at first to favour the voices against the small chamber orchestra; but
the fault becomes less perceptible on the later sides. The cast, which
is that of the first production, could hardly be surpassed.

ORCHESTRAL MUSIC
(See also under Operas, Film Music and Transcriptions)

Simple Symphony, Op. 4. Boyd Neel String Orch. Decca AX 245–7
[*Bach: Fugue in A minor*]

Variations on a Theme of Frank Bridge, Op. 10 (1950 recording). Boyd Neel
String Orch. Decca AK 2307–9 (London set LA 100)
Ditto (1938 recording). Boyd Neel String Orch. Decca X 226–8

The Young Person's Guide to the Orchestra, Op. 34 (Variations and Fugue
on a Theme of Purcell). Liverpool Phil. Orch./Sargent. Col. DX 1307–9s
(Amer. Col. 72228/30, set MM 703). (Fr. Col. GFX 168–170s)
[In England, last side blank; in America, last side contains *Bach: Suite
No. 3, Air*]
Same recording (LP)   .   .   .   **(Amer. Col. ML 4197)**
[*Handel: Fireworks Music*]

The *Simple Symphony* and the earlier of the two versions of the
Frank Bridge Variations are pre-war recordings by the Boyd Neel
ensemble: very satisfactory in their day, but without the upper fre-
quencies to which the best post-war recording has accustomed us.
In this respect both the other sets quoted above are outstanding. Boyd
Neel's re-recording of Opus 10, besides unusually faithful reproduction
of string tone, displays brilliant attack and clean phrasing. Equally
worthy of recommendation is the Columbia *Young Person's Guide*,

in which the dazzling showmanship of Britten's score has called forth answering qualities in the conductor.

CHAMBER MUSIC

Fantasy-Quartet, Oboe & Strings, Op. 2. H. Gomberg/Galimir Trio.
Esoteric ES 504
[*Britten: String Quartet No. 1*]
String Quartet No. 1, D major, Op. 25. Galimir Quartet. **Esoteric ES 504**
[*Britten: Fantasy-Quartet, Op. 2*]
String Quartet No. 2, C major, Op. 36. Zorian Quartet. HMV C 3536–9
(Auto C 7651–4)
[*Purcell: Fantasia upon one note*]

The Esoteric Long Playing disc is a valuable coupling which I have been unable to hear. The Zorian Quartet's authoritative performance of the second string Quartet is a capital recording, which was unthinkably scheduled for deletion in mid-1951; fortunately it has been reprieved by transfer to the Special List, where, however, it is obtainable in automatic couplings only. In the Purcell fill-up, the second viola part (the 'one note') is played by Benjamin Britten.

MUSIC FOR TWO PIANOS

Introduction and Rondo alla Burlesca, Op. 23, No. 1. Clifford Curzon/
Benjamin Britten. Decca K 1117 (London T 5269)
Mazurka Elegiaca, Op. 23, No. 2. Clifford Curzon/Benjamin Britten. Decca
K 1118
(Both the above were issued together as Amer. Decca set ED 17)

These two records were made before Decca had introduced their *ffrr* technique, and the piano tone is rather shallow and tubby. But the performance is as fine as the names of the players would lead one to expect, and the records are well worth attention, since the music is seldom given, and the *Mazurka Elegiaca*, in particular, is a piece of considerable charm.

CHORAL MUSIC

Hymn to St. Cecilia, Op. 27 (Auden)
Fleet Street Choir/Lawrence   Decca AK 1088–9
[*Holst: This have I done*]

Another recording:

Chamber chorus of Washington/Calloway   **WCFM LP-11**
[*Britten: Ceremony of Carols, Te Deum in C*]

Another recording:

Augustana Choir/Veld   **Key Records LP 14**
[*Brahms: Der bücklichte Fiedler, Op. 93a, No. 1;
Vaughan Williams: Lord, Thou hast been our refuge*]

A Ceremony of Carols, Op. 28

M. Korchinska (harp)/Morriston Boys' Choir/Sims   Decca AK 1155–7
[*Kodály: Ave Maria; Bartók:*   (Amer. Decca set EDA 86)
Enchanting Song]

Same recording (LP)   **London LPS 57**

Another recording:

L. Newell (harp)/Victor Female Choir/Shaw
                                    Victor 12–1011–3 (set M–1324)
Same recording (LP)   **Victor LM-1088**

Another recording:

S. Meyer (harp)/Boys of Washington
Cathedral Choir/Calloway   **WCFM LP-11**
[*Britten: Te Deum in C, Hymn to St. Cecilia*]

Rejoice in the Lamb, Op. 30 (Smart)

Washington Presbyterian Church Choir/Schaefer
[*Kodály: Missa Brevis*]   **WCFM LP-4**

Te Deum in C Major (for choir and organ)

Washington Cathedral Choir/Calloway   **WCFM LP-11**
[*Britten: Ceremony of Carols, Hymn to St. Cecilia*]

Hymn to the Virgin

Choir of St. John's Church, Upper Norwood/Betteridge
[*Spicer: The Birds; Piggot: Come my way,
my truth, my life*]   *CC 1*

The *Hymn to the Virgin*, an early anthem, is a semi-private issue
by the "Croydon Celebrity Recording Society", obtainable (for
9s. 6d.) from 38, Norbury Avenue, Thornton Heath, Surrey. The
Te Deum in C major (not to be confused with the later *Festival Te
Deum*) is included in one of several American issues of the choral
music which I have been unable to hear.

The *Hymn to St. Cecilia*, one of the composer's most fresh and airy works, deserves a new English recording. Not only is the existing set dated from a technical point of view, but the performance, to which in a rash moment the composer once gave his blessing, is tentative and insecure. On the other hand, the Decca set of the *Ceremony of Carols* by the Welsh boys' choir, in spite of some patches of dubious intonation, is an enchanting performance, precisely in key with the innocent gaiety and tenderness of the music.

MUSIC FOR SOLO VOICE AND ORCHESTRA

Les Illuminations, Op. 18 (Rimbaud). A. Mock (S)/La Jolla Orch./Sokoloff.
                                                            Alco Y–1211
[*Martinu: Sinfonietta La Jolla*]
Serenade, Op. 31 (Various authors). P. Pears (T)/D. Brain (Horn)/
    Boyd Neel String Orch./Britten.   Decca AK 1151–3

Among Britten's more established and popular works, *Les Illuminations* is by far the most serious omission from our gramophone repertoire; it is strange indeed that Peter Pears and the Boyd Neel Orchestra should not have recorded their incomparable interpretation of this lovely score. I have not heard the recent American LP; the soloist, Alice Mock, used to sing such parts as Gilda some 20 years ago with the Chicago Opera Company.

On the other hand, the *Serenade,* one of the composer's most lovable works, is available in a fine recording by the artists for whom it was written. It is very much to be hoped that this set will soon be transferred to LP, where the awkward breaks in the first and last of the songs would be avoided, and the distant horn in the Epilogue could make its magical effect undisturbed by surface scratch.

MUSIC FOR SOLO VOICE AND PIANO
(See also under Folk Song Arrangements)

The Birds (Belloc), no opus number. B. Neely (Tr.)/G. Moore HMV *B10041*
    [*Mozart: Alleluia*]
Seven Sonnets of Michelangelo, Op. 22. P. Pears (T)/B. Britten. HMV
    B 9302, C 3312 (Australian HMV *EA 3124*, EB 219)
The Holy Sonnets of John Donne, Op. 35. P. Pears (T)/B. Britten. HMV
    DB 6689–91 (Auto DB 9348–50)

The Birds is an attractive early composition, but Master Billy Neely's performance demands our indulgence.

The *Michelangelo Sonnets* were the first records to be made by the Pears-Britten duo; they date from 1942. It is understandable that both music and performance should have created a sensation at the time, but there are patches of over-recording, especially in the 10-inch disc, which now sound uncomfortable to the ear; a fresh recording, with the benefit of LP, would be highly desirable. On the other hand, the set of the *Donne Sonnets* (issued in 1949) does full justice to the burning intensity of Pears's declamation and the virtuosity of Britten's accompaniment.

FILM MUSIC

Irish Reel (from film *Village Harvest*). Charles Brill Orch. Decca AK 873
[*Britten: Soirées Musicales, side 1*]

TRANSCRIPTIONS

Soirées Musicales, Op. 9 (after Rossini). Charles Brill Orch. Decca AK 873–4
[*Britten: Irish Reel*]
    Ditto, *Tarantella* only. Boston Prom/Fiedler. Victor *10–1401* in set
    M–1204
[*Britten: Matinées Musicales*]
Matinées Musicales, Op. 24 (after Rossini). Boston Pops/Fiedler. Victor
10–1399–1401 in set *M–1204*
[*Britten: Soirées Musicales—Tarantella*]
Same recording (LP) **LM-1093**
[*Anderson: Irish Suite*]

Britten's Rossini arrangements are less artful, and less brilliant, than those of Respighi[1], so that it does not perhaps greatly matter that the *Soirées* are available only in a rather poor pre-war recording, and the *Matinées* only in America.

FOLK SONG ARRANGEMENTS

Little Sir William; Oliver Cromwell;   ⎱ P. Pears (T)/B. Britten.
The Sally Gardens (Yeats)   ⎰   Decca *M 555* (London *R 10008*)

The Ash Grove   ⎱ P. Pears (T)/B. Britten.
Sweet Polly Oliver ⎰ London *R 10009*

[1] Cf. *The Light Music*, pp. 288–289.—EDS.

Hamburger, P. : Review of 'A Charm of Lullabies', Op. 41, *Music Survey*, Vol. II, No. 4, London, Spring, 1950. 111

"Mainly about Britten", *Music Survey*, Vol. III, No. 2, London, December, 1950. 112

Reviews of 'Albert Herring' and 'The Beggar's Opera' when performed at the Cheltenham Festival and the Lyric Theatre, Hammersmith, 1950, *Music Survey*, Vol. III, No. 2, London, December, 1950. 113

Hapke, W. : " 'Albert Herring' (Hanover)", in BRITTEN ISSUE of *Opera* (see Item No. 115). 114

Harewood, The Earl of, ed. : BRITTEN ISSUE of *Opera* (contributions by: Walter Hapke; Hans Schmidt-Isserstedt; Hans Zimmermann; R. M. Lalande), Vol. II, No. 6, London, May, 1951. (See also Items Nos. 114, 174, 265, and 316.) 115

Harewood, The Earl of: Programme notes on 'Albert Herring' and 'The Rape of Lucretia' in the Programme Book of the Aldeburgh Festival, 1949. 116

"Comment" [English Opera Group], in BRITTEN ISSUE of *Opera* (see Item No. 115). 117

Hind, J. : "Un estudio de la ópera de Benjamin Britten", *Platea*, Nos. 7 and 8, Buenos Aires, July-August, 1951. 118

Holst, I. : "Britten's 'Saint Nicolas' ", *Tempo*, No. 10, London, Winter, 1948–1949. 119

"The Aldeburgh Festival" ['Let's Make an Opera'], *Ballet and Opera*, Vol. VIII, No. 2, London, August, 1949. 120

"Benjamin Britten's 'Saint Nicolas' " (leaflet), Boosey and Hawkes, London, 1949. 121

"Britten's 'Let's Make an Opera' ", *Tempo*, No. 18, London, Winter, 1950–1951. 122

"Benjamin Britten's 'Billy Budd' ", *Foyer*, No. 2, London, 1952. 123

Hope-Wallace, P. : "Britten's 'Billy Budd' ", *Manchester Guardian*, 3rd December, 1951. 124

"Billy Budd", *Picture Post*, London, 22nd December, 1951. 125

Howes, F. S. : "Britten, Edward Benjamin" (see Item No. 42). 125a

Huntley, J. : BRITISH FILM MUSIC (pp. 157 ff.), Skelton Robinson, London, 1947. (See also Item No. 342.) 126

Hürlimann, B. : "Eine Kinderoper von Benjamin Britten", *Schweizerische Musikzeitung*, Zürich, April, 1950. 127

Hussey, D. : "Broadcast Music—'Peter Grimes' ", *Listener*, London, 21st March, 1946. 128

Hussey, D. (cont'd.): "Soft Roes on Toast" ['Albert Herring'], Listener, London, 26th June, 1947.   129

"Broadcast Music" [Britten], Listener, 30th September, 1948.   129a

Jacobs, R. L.: "The Significance of 'Peter Grimes'", Listener, London, 7th March, 1946.   130

Keller, H.: THE RAPE OF LUCRETIA, ALBERT HERRING, Covent Garden Operas, Boosey and Hawkes, London, 1947.   131

"Benjamin Britten's Second Quartet", Tempo (old series), No. 18, London, March, 1947.   132

"A Film Analysis of the Orchestra" ['Instruments of the Orchestra' and 'The Young Person's Guide to the Orchestra'], Sight and Sound (British Film Institute), Vol. XVI, No. 61, London, Spring, 1947.   133

"Glyndebourne Preface" ['Albert Herring'], Sound, London, June, 1947.   133a

Keller, H., and Cameron, K.: Correspondence on 'Instruments of the Orchestra', Sight and Sound (British Film Institute), Vol. XVI, No. 62, London, Summer, 1947.   134

Keller, H. (cont'd.):
"Britten's New Opera in London" ['The Rape of Lucretia'], Reconstruction, Vol. XII, No. 48, New York, (1947 ?).   135

"Britten and Mozart: A Challenge in the Form of Variations on an Unfamiliar Theme", Music and Letters, Vol. XXIX, No. 1, London, January, 1948.   136

" 'Peter Grimes' at Covent Garden" [note on alterations in score], Music Review, Vol. IX, No. 1, Cambridge, February, 1948.   137

"Excerpts from 'The Rape of Lucretia'", H.M.V. Analytical Note No. H.619, E.M.I. Ltd., Middlesex, March, 1948.   138

Reviews of 'Fish in the Unruffled Lakes', 'The Ride' and 'Slumber Song' from 'Lucretia' [supplementary note to Item No. 131], and 'Three Divine Hymns', 'Saul and the Witch at Endor', from Purcell's 'Harmonia Sacra', Music Review, Vol. IX, No. 2, Cambridge, May, 1948.   139

Review of Columbia and Decca records of 'Grimes' Interludes [analytical note on concert version of 'Passacaglia'], Music Review, Vol. IX, No. 2, Cambridge, May, 1948.   140

Review of H.M.V. Folk Song record (DA 1873), Music Review, Vol. IX, No. 2, Cambridge, May, 1948.   141

Review of H.M.V. records of 'Lucretia' [supplementary analysis to Item No. 131], Music Review, Vol. IX, No. 2, Cambridge, May, 1948.   142

Keller, H. (*cont'd.*) : Review of Item No. 293 [supplementary analysis to Item No. 264], *Music Review*, Vol. IX, No. 2, Cambridge, May, 1948. 143

"Benjamin Britten: Film Composer", *British Film Review*, Vol. I, No. 3, May, 1948, and *Film Monthly Review*, Vol. VI, No. 5, June, 1948. 144

"A Britten Festival" [the Aldeburgh Festival], *Everybody's*, London, 5th June, 1948. 145

"Britten's Second String Quartet" [thematic structure and texture of 1st mvt.], letter to *Musical Times*, London, June, 1948. 146

"Britten's 'The Beggar's Opera' ", letter to *Listener*, London, 14th October, 1948. 147

Review of 'Albert Herring' [supplementary analysis to Item No. 131] and Six Songs from Purcell's 'Orpheus Britannicus', *Music Review*, Vol. IX, No. 4, Cambridge, November, 1948. 148

"The English Opera Group", *Music Parade*, Vol. I, No. 7, London, 1948. 149

"Britten's 'Beggar's Opera' ", *Tempo*, No. 10, London, Winter, 1948–1949. 150

Review of Item No. 21 [supplementary analysis to Item No. 131], *Music Review*, Vol. X, No. 2, Cambridge, May, 1949. 151

"Benjamin Britten and the Young", *Listener*, London, 29th September, 1949. 152

"Brittens Kinderoper", *Basler Nachrichten*, No. 451, 22nd October, 1949. 153

"Profile—Benjamin Britten", *Crescendo*, No. 23, London, October, 1949. 154

"First Performances" ['Spring Symphony', 'Let's Make an Opera', 'St. Nicolas'], *Music Review*, Vol. X, No. 4, Cambridge, November, 1949. 155

"Saint Nicolas" [review of vocal score], *Music Survey*, Vol. I, No. 6, London, 1949. 156

"New Music in the Old Year" ['St. Nicolas', 'Beggar's Opera'], *Music Parade*, Vol. I, No. 10, London, 1949. 157

"Benjamin Brittens 'Beggar's Opera' ", *Schweizerische Musikzeitung*, Zürich, 1st January, 1950. 157a

"Film Music: Britten" ['Night Mail'], *Music Survey*, Vol. II, No. 4, London, Spring, 1950. 158

"Resistances to Britten's Music: Their Psychology", in BRITTEN ISSUE of *Music Survey* (see Item No. 160). 159

Keller, H., and Mitchell, D., eds.: BRITTEN ISSUE of *Music Survey* (contributions by: Donald Mitchell; Hans Keller; Benjamin Britten; Hans F. Redlich; Harold Truscott; Charles Stuart), Vol. II, No. 4, London, Spring, 1950. (See also Items Nos. 27, 159, 213, 251, 295, and 305.)   160

Keller, H. (*cont'd.*) : "Britten und Mozart", *Oesterreichische Musikzeitschrift*, Vol. V, Nos. 7/8, Vienna, July/August, 1950. (Unauthorized and partly wrong translation of Item No. 136.)   161

"Zum 'Raub der Lukrezia' ", *Salzburger Nachrichten*, 9th August, 1950.   162

"Musical Self-contempt in Britain" [elaboration of Item No. 159], paper to Social Psychology Section of British Psychological Society, 4th November, 1950.   163

Review of 'Spring Symphony', *Music Review*, Vol. XI, No. 4, Cambridge, November, 1950.   164

" 'Der Raub' und 'The Rape' ", *Blätter der Salzburger Festspiele*, No. 2, Salzburg, 1950.   165

"Festatmosphärische Störungen" [Britten and Aldeburgh Festival], *Salzburger Nachrichten*, 29th August, 1951.   166

"Britten: Thematic Relations and the 'Mad' Interlude's 5th Motif" ['Peter Grimes'], *Music Survey*, Vol. IV, No. 1, London, October, 1951   166a

Kelly, C. : "Henry Purcell—A Performing Edition" (leaflet), Boosey and Hawkes, London, n.d. (See also item No. 348.)   167

King, W. G. : "New Opera in New York" ['Peter Grimes'], *Cue*, New York, 7th February, 1948.   168

Klein, J. W. : "The Rape of Lucretia", *Musical Opinion*, London, September, 1946.   169

" 'Albert Herring'—Britten's Third Opera", *Musical Opinion*, London, August, 1947.   170

"Britten and English Opera", *Musical Opinion*, London, July, 1949.   171

"Britten's Advance to Mastery", *Musical Opinion*, London, March, 1952.   172

Knyvett, G. : "Benjamin Britten", *Dansk Musiktidsskrift*, Copenhagen, 27th February, 1952.   173

Lalande, R. M. : " 'The Rape of Lucretia' (Mulhouse)", in BRITTEN ISSUE of *Opera* (see Item No. 115).   174

Lambert, C. : "Britten's New Concerto" [Concerto No. 1, for piano and orchestra], *Listener*, London, 25th August, 1938.   175

Lavauden, T. : " 'Peter Grimes', L'Œuvre Géniale du Compositeur Anglais Benjamin Britten", *La Tribune de Genève*, 11th July, 1945.   176

Lindgren, E. : THE ART OF THE FILM (p. 146), Allen & Unwin, London, 1948.   177

Linstead, G. F. : "Benjamin Britten and the 'Spring Symphony' ", *Hallé*, No. 30, Manchester, November, 1950.   178

Lonchampt, J. : "Les Variations sur un thème de Purcell de Benjamin Britten" ['The Young Person's Guide to the Orchestra'], *Journal des Jeunesses Musicales de France*, 3è année, No. 3, Paris, 21st November, 1950.   179

Mann, W. : "Britten's 'Lachrymae' ", *London Musical Events*, Vol. VI, No. 12, December, 1951.   180

"Britten's 'Billy Budd' ", *London Musical Events*, Vol. VII, No. 2, February, 1952.   180a

Manning, R. : FROM HOLST TO BRITTEN: A STUDY OF MODERN CHORAL MUSIC, Workers' Music Association, London, 1949.   181

"Benjamin Britten", *Monthly Musical Record*, Vol. 73, No. 847, London, June, 1943.   182

Manvell, R. : FILM ['Night Mail', 'Coalface', pp. 100 ff.], revised edition, Pelican Books, Harmondsworth (Middlesex), November, 1946.   183

Mason, C. : "Britten: Another View", *Monthly Musical Record*, Vol. 73, No. 849, London, September, 1943.   184

"Benjamin Britten", *Musical Times*, London, February, March, April, 1948.   185

"Britten's 'Sinfonia da Requiem' ", *Manchester Guardian*, 17th May, 1951.   186

"Britten's 'Spring Symphony' ", *Manchester Guardian*, 26th May, 1951.   187

"Britten's 'Spring Symphony' ", *Manchester Guardian*, 23rd July, 1951.   188

"Modern British Music" ['Sinfonia da Requiem'], *Manchester Guardian*, 28th September, 1951.   189

"Opera" ['Billy Budd'], *Spectator*, London, 8th December, 1951.   190

"English Opera Group: Britten's New Work" ['Abraham and Isaac—Canticle II'], *Manchester Guardian*, 26th January, 1952.   191

Mason, C. (*cont'd.*) : "Lettera da Londra" ['Billy Budd'], *La Rassegna Musicale*, Rome, January, 1952.   192

"'Billy Budd' Comes to Manchester", *Manchester Guardian*, 15th March, 1952.   193

"Hallé Orchestra:'Sinfonia da Requiem'",*Manchester Guardian*, 4th April, 1952.   194

Mason, R. : "Herman Melville and 'Billy Budd'", in BRITTEN ISSUE of *Tempo* (see Item No. 95).   195

Mayer, Dr. L. K. : "Lasst uns eine Oper machen", *Oberösterreichische Nachrichten*, Linz, 8th February, 1952.   196

McDonald, O. H. : "The Semantics of Music" ['Serenade' and 'On This Island'], *Music Survey*, Vol. I, No. 4, London, September, 1948.   197

McNaught, W. : "Broadcast Music—Mainly about Britten", *Listener*, London, 30th July, 1942.   198

"Peter Grimes", *Musical Times*, London, July, 1945.   199

"Opera at Glyndebourne" ['Albert Herring'], *Musical Times*, London, July, 1947.   200

"Britten's 'Billy Budd'", *Musical Times*, London, January, 1952.   201

Mellers, W. H. : MUSIC AND SOCIETY (pp. 178–182), 2nd edn., Dobson, London, 1950.   202

"Stylization in Contemporary British Music", *Horizon*, Vol. XVII, No. 101, London, May, 1948.   203

"The Beggar's Opera" [review of vocal score], *Music Survey*, Vol. II, No. 1, London, 1949.   204

"Recent Trends in British Music", *Musical Quarterly*, Vol. XXXVIII, No. 2, New York, 1952.   205

Mengelberg, K. : "Brittens Nieuwe Opera" ['The Rape of Lucretia'], *Nederland*, 3rd August, 1946.   206

"De Opera 'Albert Herring' van Benjamin Britten", *Mens en Melodie*, Utrecht, September, 1947.   207

Michel, A. : "'Albert Herring' et 'Peter Grimes'", *Le Phare*, 3rd June, 1948.   208

Mila, M. : "Posizione di Britten nella musica inglese", *La Rassegna Musicale*, Rome, October, 1948.   209

"Musica per il consumatore", *La Fiera Litteraria*, Rome, 28th February, 1950.   210

Milner, A. : "Billy Budd", *Score*, London, May, 1952.   211

Mitchell, D. : "Britten's 'Let's Make an Opera', Op. 45", *Music Survey*, Vol. II, No. 2, London, Autumn, 1949.   212

Mitchell, D. (*cont'd.*) : "A Note on 'St. Nicolas': Some Points of Britten's Style", in BRITTEN ISSUE of *Music Survey* (see Item No. 160).   213

Mitchell, D., and Keller, H., eds. : BRITTEN ISSUE of *Music Survey*, Vol. II, No. 4, Spring, 1950 (see Item No. 160).   214

Mitchell, D. (*cont'd.*) :

"So They Said" [review of reviews of first English performance of the 'Spring Symphony'], *Music Survey*, Vol. II, No. 4, London, Spring, 1950.   215

"Let's Make an Opera", *Making Music*, No. 12, Hitchin (Herts), Spring, 1950.   216

"The Cheltenham Festival—Britten Operas" ['The Beggar's Opera' and 'Albert Herring'], *Manchester Guardian*, 14th July, 1950.   217

"Aldeburgh, England", *Opera News*, Vol. XV, No. 1, New York, 16th October, 1950.   218

"A Note on the 'Flower Aria' and 'Passacaglia' in 'Lucretia' ", *Music Survey*, Vol. III, No. 4, London, June, 1951.   219

"The Lyric, Hammersmith: Britten Season" ['Albert Herring'], *Music Survey*, Vol. III, No. 4, London, June, 1951.   220

"Britten on Records", *Disc*, Vol. V, No. 18, Bristol, Autumn, 1951.   221

"The Young Person's Composer", *Making Music*, No. 17, Hitchin (Herts), Autumn, 1951.   222

"The Brilliance of Mr. Britten", *Disc*, Vol. IV, No. 16, Bristol, Winter, 1951.   223

"Britten's Latest Opera Opens at Covent Garden" ['Billy Budd'], *Eastern Daily Press*, Norwich, 3rd December, 1951.   224

"Billy Budd", *Tribune*, London, 14th December, 1951.   225

"More Off than On 'Billy Budd' ", *Music Survey*, Vol. IV, No. 2, London, February, 1952.   226

"Benjamin Britten and the English Tradition", an illustrated talk given in the B.B.C. Third Programme, London, 17th July, 1952.   227

"The Later Development of Benjamin Britten: Texture, Instrumentation, and Structure", *Chesterian*, London, July, October, 1952.   228

Moor, E. L. : "Introduction à la Musique de Benjamin Britten", *L'Age Nouveau*, Paris, 1948.   229

Mullen, E., Franey, E., and Franey, N. : "A Children's Symposium on Britten's Children's Opera", *Music Survey*, Vol. II, No. 4, London, Spring, 1950.   230

Murrill, H. : "Purcell Britten—A Challenge, discussed by Herbert Murrill", *Music Lover*, London, April, 1947.   231

Newman, E. : "Peter Grimes", *Sunday Times*, London, 10th, 17th, 24th June, 1945.   232

" 'Peter Grimes' and After", *Sunday Times*, London, 24th, 31st March, 1946.   233

"The Rape of Lucretia", *Sunday Times*, London, 21st, 28th July, 1946.   234

"Mr. Britten and 'Albert Herring'—I", *Sunday Times*, London, 29th June, 1947.   235

" 'Albert Herring'—II", *Sunday Times*, London, 6th July, 1947.   236

"Strauss, Britten and Gounod", *Sunday Times*, London, 19th October, 1947.   237

"Billy Budd", *Sunday Times*, London, 9th December, 1951.   238

Ottoway, D. H. : "Serge Prokoviev and Benjamin Britten", *Musical Opinion*, London, July, 1950.   239

"A Note on Britten", *Monthly Musical Record*, Vol. 81, No. 930, London, October, 1951.   240

Paap, W. : "The Beggar's Qpera", *Mens en Melodie*, Jaargang III, No. 8, Utrecht, 1948.   241

"Een Kinder-opera van Benjamin Britten", *Mens en Melodie*, Utrecht, 7th July, 1951.   242

Pears, P. : "Neither a Hero nor a Villain" ['Peter Grimes'], *Radio Times*, London, 8th March, 1946.   243

Petersen, F. S. ; "Benjamin Britten og 'The Rape of Lucretia' ", *Dansk Musiktidsskrift*, No. 8, Copenhagen, 24th August, 1949.   244

"Omkring 'The Rape of Lucretia' " [reviews of Item No. 21 and H.M.V. 'Lucretia' set], *Dansk Musiktidsskrift*, No. 8, Copenhagen, 24th August, 1949.   245

Piper, J. : "The Design of Lucretia", in THE RAPE OF LUCRETIA (see Item No. 21).   246

Piper, J., and Coleman, B.: " 'Billy Budd' on the Stage" in BRITTEN ISSUE of *Tempo* (see Item No. 95).   247

Poot, M. : "La Création de 'Albert Herring' ", *Nation Belge*, 2nd June, 1948.   248

Porter, A. : "Britten's 'Billy Budd' ", *Music and Letters*, Vol. XXXIII, No. 2, London, April, 1952.   249

Redlich, H. F. : Review of 'The Holy Sonnets of John Donne', *Music Review*, Vol. IX, No. 2, Cambridge, May, 1948.   250

Redlich, H. F. (*cont'd.*): "The significance of Britten's Operatic Style", in BRITTEN ISSUE of *Music Survey* (see Item No. 160).   251

"New English Song" [review of 'Canticle I'], *Music Review*, Cambridge, Vol. XI, No. 4, November, 1950.   252

Rees, C. B.: "Benjamin Britten", *London Musical Events*, Vol. VI, No. 4, April, 1951.   253

Reid, C.: "Britten Makes It Seven . . .", *Evening Standard*, London, 29th November, 1951.   254

Reinhart, T.: "Ein deutsches Buch über Benjamin Britten" [review of Item No. 308], *Melos*, Heft 9, Mainz, September, 1950.   255

Robertson, A.: Review of H.M.V. records of 'Lucretia', *Gramophone*, London, March, 1948.   256

Rosenberg, H.: "Peter Grimes", *Dansk Musiktidsskrift*, Copenhagen, 1947.   257

Rubsamen, W.: "Current Chronicle" [reviews of Los Angeles performances of 'Albert Herring', 'St. Nicolas', 'The Beggar's Opera'], *Musical Quarterly*, Vol. XXXVI, No. 4, New York, 1950.   258

Russell, T.: Programme note on 'Spring Symphony' for L.P.O. concert, Royal Albert Hall, London, 9th March, 1950.   259

Rutz, H.: "Das moderne Musiktheater" ['Rape of Lucretia' and Boris Blacher's chamber opera 'Romeo und Julia'], *Salzburger Nachrichten*, 10th August, 1950.   260

"Benjamin Brittens 'Billy Budd' ", *Melos*, Mainz, January, 1952.   261

Sackville-West, E., and Shawe-Taylor, D.: THE RECORD GUIDE (pp. 142–148), Collins, London, 1951.   262

Sackville-West, E.: "Music: Some Aspects of the Contemporary Problem", *Horizon*, Vol. X, Nos. 54, 55 and 56, London, June, July, August, 1944.   263

"The Musical and Dramatic Structure", in PETER GRIMES (see Item No. 47).   264

Schmidt-Isserstedt, H.: " 'The Beggar's Opera' (Hamburg)", in BRITTEN ISSUE of *Opera* (see Item No. 115).   265

Schuh, W.: ZEITGENÖSSISCHE MUSIK [contains reviews of Swiss performances of the 'Serenade', 'Peter Grimes', 'The Rape of Lucretia' and 'Albert Herring'], Atlantis-Verlag, Zürich, 1947.   266

"Benjamin Brittens neue Oper 'Billy Budd' ", *Schweizerische Musikzeitung*, Zürich, 1st January, 1952.   267

Scott, M. M.: "Benjamin Britten och 'Peter Grimes'", *Musik-Varlden*, Stockholm, March, 1946. 268

"Benjamin Brittens Andrea Opera" ['The Rape of Lucretia'], *Musik-Varlden*, Stockholm, March, 1947. 269

Shaffer, P.: "Benjamin Britten", *Panorama*, No. 6, London, Spring, 1952. 270

Shawe-Taylor, D., and Sackville-West, E.: THE RECORD GUIDE (pp. 142–148), Collins, London, 1951. 271

Shawe-Taylor, D.: "Peter Grimes", *New Statesman and Nation*, London, 9th, 16th June, 1945. 272

"The Rape of Lucretia", *New Statesman and Nation*, London, 20th July, 1946. 273

"'Peter Grimes' in Stockholm", *The Arts*, London, 1946. 274

"Instruments of the Orchestra", *New Statesman and Nation*, London, 1st February, 1947. 275

"Britten's Comic Opera", *Listener*, London, 12th June, 1947. 276

"Glyndebourne" ['Albert Herring'], *New Statesman and Nation*, London, 28th June, 1947. 276a

"Britten's 'Spring Symphony'", *New Statesman and Nation*, London, 18th March, 1950. 277

"Billy Budd", *New Statesman and Nation*, London, 1st, 8th December, 1951. 278

Slater, M.: PETER GRIMES (libretto), Boosey and Hawkes, London, 1945. 279

PETER GRIMES AND OTHER POEMS, John Lane The Bodley Head, London, 1946. 280

"The Plot of 'Peter Grimes'", *Tempo* (old series), No. 9, London, December, 1944. 281

"The Story of the Opera", in PETER GRIMES (see Item No. 47). 282

Smith, L. G.: "'Donald of the Burthens' and 'Billy Budd'", *Music Parade*, Vol. II, No. 10, London, 1952. 283

Squire, W. H. Haddon: "The Aesthetic Hypothesis and 'The Rape of Lucretia'", *Tempo* (new series), No. 1, London, September, 1946. 284

Stedman, J. W.: "Grimes Against The Borough", *Opera News*, New York, 7th February, 1949. 285

Stein, E.: "Benjamin Britten", in THE BOOK OF MODERN COMPOSERS (see Item No. 78). 286

"Opera and 'Peter Grimes'", *Tempo* (old series), No. 12, London, September, 1945. 287

Stein, E. (*cont'd.*) : Analysis of string Quartet No. 2, Hawkes Pocket
    Scores, Boosey and Hawkes, London, 1946.   288

    "Form in Opera: 'Albert Herring' Examined", *Tempo*, No. 5,
    London, Autumn, 1947.   289

    "Benjamin Britten's Operas", *Opera*, Vol. I, No. 1, London,
    February, 1950.   290

    "Britten's 'Spring Symphony' ", *Tempo*, No. 15, London,
    Spring, 1950.   291

    "The Music of 'Billy Budd' ", *Opera*, Vol. III, No. 4, London,
    April, 1952.   292

Stuart, C. : PETER GRIMES, Covent Garden Operas, Boosey and
    Hawkes, London, 1947.   293

    "Maupassant Reversed" ['Albert Herring'], *Observer*, London,
    21st June, 1947.   294

    "Britten 'The Eclectic' ", in BRITTEN ISSUE of *Music Survey*
    (see Item No. 160).   295

    " 'Billy Budd'—The Music", *Hallé*, No. 44, Manchester,
    January, 1952.   296

    " 'Billy Budd': The Score by Benjamin Britten", *World Review*,
    London, January, 1952.   297

Stuckenschmidt, H. H. : " 'Peter Grimes' in Berlin", *Die Neue
    Zeitung*, Munich, 24th May, 1947.   298

    "Heiteres Opernspiel" ['Albert Herring'], *Die Neue Zeitung*
    (Berlin edition), Munich, 5th November, 1950.   299

Terry, A. : " 'Peter Grimes' as anti-British propaganda", *Sunday
    Times*, London, 6th January, 1952.   300

Thomson, V. : "Music" ['Peter Grimes'], *New York Herald Tribune*,
    13th February, 1948.   301

    "The Theaters" ['The Rape of Lucretia'], *New York Herald
    Tribune*, 30th December, 1948.   302

Tinel, P. : "Albert Herring", *Le Soir*, Brussels, 3rd June, 1948.   303

Truscott, H. : "Serenade, Op. 31" [review of vocal score], *Music
    Survey*, Vol. I, No. 5, London, 1949.   304

    "Britten's Sinfonietta, Op. 1", in BRITTEN ISSUE of *Music
    Survey* (see Item No. 160).   305

Vernes, Y. : " 'Billy Budd' de Benjamin Britten", *Le Journal Musical
    Français*, Paris, 1st May, 1952.   306

Walker, E., ed. by Westrup, J. A. : A HISTORY OF MUSIC
    IN ENGLAND (pp. 357–359), Oxford University Press,
    1952.   306a

Westrup, J.A., ed.: See Item No. 306a.

Westrup, J. A.: "The Virtuosity of Benjamin Britten", *Listener*, London, 16th July, 1942.   307

White, E. W.: BENJAMIN BRITTEN, Eine Skizze von Leben und Werk, Atlantis-Verlag, Zürich, 1948.   308

BENJAMIN BRITTEN, A Sketch of His Life and Works, Boosey and Hawkes, London, 1948 (English version of Item No. 308).   309

THE RISE OF ENGLISH OPERA, John Lehmann, London, 1951. (See also Item No. 346.)   310

"A Musician of the People", *Life and Letters Today*, London, April, 1939.   311

"Peter Grimes", *Penguin New Writing*, No. 26, Harmondsworth (Middlesex), Autumn, 1945.   312

"Billy Budd", *Listener*, London, 22nd November, 1951.   313

"Billy Budd", *Adelphi*, Vol. XXVIII, No. 2, London, First Quarter, 1952.   314

Programme note on 'Spring Symphony' for B.B.C. concert, Royal Festival Hall, London, 28th May, 1952.   315

Zimmerman, H.: " 'Let's Make an Opera' (Zürich)", in BRITTEN ISSUE of *Opera* (see Item No. 115).   316

Anon.: "A Conversation with Benjamin Britten", *Tempo*, No. 5, London, August, 1941.   317

"Sadler's Wells Opera—'Peter Grimes' ", *The Times*, London, 8th June, 1945.   318

" 'Peter Grimes'—Second Thoughts", *The Times*, London, 15th June, 1945.   319

"Britten's Dramatic Music—'Peter Grimes' ", *The Times*, London, 26th October, 1945.   320

"Glyndebourne Opera—'The Rape of Lucretia' ", *The Times*, London, 13th July, 1946.   321

"Profile—Benjamin Britten", *Observer*, London, 27th October, 1946.   322

"Notes of the Day" ['Albert Herring'], *Monthly Musical Record*, Vol. 77, No. 889, London, September, 1947.   323

"Young People's Guide to the Orchestra", *Music Teacher and Piano Student*, London, September, 1947.   324

"Covent Garden—'Peter Grimes' ", *The Times*, London, 7th November, 1947.   325

Anon. (cont'd.): "Opera's New Face", *Time*, New York, 16th
February, 1948.   326

"The Critics on 'Peter Grimes'" [a compilation of American
critical views on the opera], *Opera News*, New York, 8th
March, 1948.   327

"Benjamin Britten's 'Spring Symphony'—Form and Content",
The Times, London, 22nd July, 1949.   328

"Benjamin Britten" [reviews of 'The Holy Sonnets of John
Donne'; 'Canticle I'; 'A Charm of Lullabies'; 'St. Nicolas'],
La Rassegna Musicale, Rome, Spring, 1950.   329

"The 'Spring Symphony'—Britten's New Work", *The Times*,
London, 10th March, 1950.   330

"Benjamin Britten's 'Spring Symphony'" [review of vocal
score], *Musical Opinion*, London, April, 1950.   331

"'The Sleeping Children': An Inquest" [a review of Brian
Easdale's opera, which discusses the validity of the chamber
operatic style, Britten's particularly], *The Times*, London,
13th July, 1951.   332

"A Modern Programme" ['Sinfonia da Requiem'], *The Times*,
London, 27th September, 1951.   333

"'Billy Budd': A Synopsis", in BRITTEN ISSUE of *Tempo*
(see Item No. 95).   334

"Britten's New Opera—'Billy Budd' at Covent Garden",
The Times, 3rd December, 1951.   335

"'Billy Budd'—The Interval of the Second", *The Times*,
London, 7th December, 1951.   336

"'Elizabeth and Essex': Mr. Britten's Plans" [the 'Coronation'
opera], *Manchester Guardian*, 30th May, 1952.   337

ARTICLES, ETC.,
BY BENJAMIN BRITTEN

(*Writings by Benjamin Britten on his own music are included
in the bibliography above*)

"An English Composer Sees America", *Tempo* (American edn.),
Vol. I, No. 2, New York, April, 1940.   338

"On Behalf of Gustav Mahler", *Tempo* (American edn.), Vol. II,
No. 2, New York, February, 1942.   339

"How a Musical Work Originates", *Listener*, London, 30th July,
1942.   340

"How to become a Composer" [partial reprint of a broadcast talk entitled "The Composer and the Audience"], *Listener*, London, 7th November, 1946.   341

Paragraph on Film Music, in Huntley. (See also Item No. 126.)   342

Programme notes in the Programme Book of the Aldeburgh Festival, 1949. [These notes are, of course, very brief, but they comment on an interesting range of composers: Pergolesi, Chopin, Fauré, Haydn and Frank Bridge.]   343

Contribution to "Verdi—A Symposium", *Opera*, Vol. 2, No. 3, London, February, 1951.   344

Address on being made an honorary freeman of Lowestoft, 28th July, 1951, in *Tempo*, No. 21, London, Autumn, 1951.   345

Introduction to THE RISE OF ENGLISH OPERA (see Item No. 310).   346

Contribution to "Obituary: Arnold Schoenberg", *Music Survey*, Vol. IV, No. 1, London, October, 1951.   347

Introduction (with Peter Pears) to "Henry Purcell—A Performing Edition" (leaflet), Boosey and Hawkes, London, n.d. (See also Item No. 167.)   348

"Variations on a Critical Theme", *Opera*, Vol. III, No. 3, London, March, 1952.   349

"The Marriage of Figaro" [review of Covent Garden performance], *Opera*, Vol. III, No. 5, London, May, 1952.   350

"A Composer in Our Time" [partial combined reprint of Items Nos. 341 and 345], *Adam*, Year XX, Nos. 224–225–226, London, 1952.   351

ADDENDA

Bradbury, E.: "Iris Lemare" [see p. 445 of this article for mention of an early work by Britten, an 'Alla quartetto serioso' (1933), three movements of which were performed at a Lemare Concert], *Musical Times*, London, October, 1952.   352

Britten, B.: Programme note for second string Quartet's first performance, Wigmore Hall, London, 21st November, 1945.   353

Keller, H.: "Peter Pears" X ['Herring'], *Opera*, Vol. II, No. 6, London, May, 1951.   354

Raynor, H.: "Britten, Stravinsky and the Future of Opera", *Musical Opinion*, London, October, November, 1952.   355

Rubbra, E.: Review (full score) of 'Variations on a Theme of Frank Bridge' (Op. 10), *Music and Letters*, Vol. XIX, No. 3, London, July, 1938.   356

Stein, E.: ORPHEUS IN NEW GUISES, Rockliff, London, 1953.   357

Tranchell, P.: Review of 'Six Metamorphoses after Ovid' (Op. 49), *Music and Letters*, Vol. XXXIII, No. 4, London, October, 1952.   358

Index to Britten's Music

Abraham and Isaac, 72n., 360, 367
Adagio, 264. See also *Diversions on a Theme.*
Advance Democracy, 30, 97, 363. See also Incidental Music.
Agamemnon of Aeschylus. See Incidental Music.
"Ah, Belinda, I am prest with torment", 192. See also *Dido and Aeneas.*
Albert Herring, 13, 22, 23, 24, 26, 30, 33, 34–6, 38, 40, 41, 45, 46, 50n., 52, 55, 56, 69, 71, 115, 123, 140, 143, 146–62, 163, 282, 289–91, 320, 324, 325, 327, 331, 346, 360, 366
All people that on earth do dwell, 52. See also *Saint Nicolas.*
"Alla Quartetto Serioso", 388
"Among the men, coquets we find", 169, 183. See also *Beggar's Opera.*
"And I'm more than grateful to you all", 32. See also *Albert Herring.*
Antique, 32, 65, 66, 363. See also *Illuminations.*
Aria Italiana, 12, 241. See also *Variations on a Theme of Frank Bridge.*
Around the Village Green. See Incidental Music.
As dew in Aprille, 364. See also *Ceremony of Carols.*
As it is, plenty, 18, 64, 363. See also *On this Island.*
Ascent of F6, The. See Incidental Music.
Ash Grove, The, 47–8, 288, 358, 359, 364. See also *Folk Songs.*
At the round Earth's imagined corners, 365. See also *Holy Sonnets of John Donne.*
"At the tree I shall suffer", 168, 171. See also *Beggar's Opera.*
Avertantur retrorsum, 303–4. See also *This Way to the Tomb.*

Badinerie, 263. See also *Diversions on a Theme.*

Ballad of Green Broom, 366. See also *Five Flower Songs.*
Ballad of Heroes, 3, 13, 30, 97–8, 363
Ballad of Little Musgrave and Lady Barnard, 90, 96, 365
Ballet de la Paix. See Incidental Music.
Ballet music. See Incidental Music.
Balulalow, 364. See also *Ceremony of Carols.*
Banking for Millions. See Incidental Music.
Batter my Heart, 365. See also *Holy Sonnets of John Donne.*
"Before the barn-door crowing", 168. See also *Beggar's Opera.*
Beggar's Opera, The, 47, 53, 133n., 163–85, 324, 327, 366
Begone Dull Care, 362. See also *Friday Afternoons.*
Being Beauteous, 33n., 34, 363. See also *Illuminations.*
Belle est au jardin d'amour, La, 359, 364. See also *Folk Songs.*
Beware, 60
"Bide the time", 303. See also *Rescue.*
Billy Budd, 5n., 13n., 15n., 23, 26, 27ff., 36n., 40n., 50n., 53, 56, 58n., 69, 123, 133n., 142n., 143, 156n., 198–210, 211n., 303, 320, 327, 345, 346, 348, 360, 367
"Billy Budd, king of the birds!", 40n. See also *Billy Budd.*
"Billy in the Darbies", 198, 209. See also *Billy Budd.*
Birds, The, 60, 357, 358, 362
Birth of Nicolas, The, 99, 343. See also *Saint Nicolas.*
Blessed Virgin's Expostulation, The, 76, 367
Boisterous Bourrée, 237–8, 246, 362. See also *Simple Symphony.*
Bolero, 363. See also *Soirées Musicales.*
Bonny Earl o' Moray, The, 359, 364. See also *Folk Songs.*

Bourrée Classique, 12, 241. See also *Variations on a Theme of Frank Bridge*.

Boy was Born, A, 2, 9–11, 12, 14, 31, 55, 67, 69, 84, 85, 86–9, 90, 94, 99, 100, 280, 296, 362

"But ah! what language can I try", 187, 195. See also *Dido and Aeneas*.

"But can I leave", 170. See also *Beggar's Opera*.

"But now again my spirits", 170. See also *Beggar's Opera*.

"But valour the stronger", 170. See also *Beggar's Opera*.

Caberet Jazz-Song, 298, 299. See also *Ascent of F6*.

Cable Ship. See Incidental Music.

Calendar of the Year, The. See Incidental Music.

"Can love be controll'd", 167. See also *Beggar's Opera*.

Canadian Carnival, 84, 289, 363

Canticle I, 50, 71, 72, 360, 366

Canticle II, 360, 367

Canzonetta, 363. See also *Soirées Musicales*.

"Cease your funning", 169, 175. See also *Beggar's Opera*.

Ceremony of Carols, A, 23, 46, 62, 67, 84, 85, 94–5, 280, 356, 357, 364

Chant, 12, 242. See also *Variations on a Theme of Frank Bridge*.

"Charge is prepared, The", 170, 178, 184. See also *Beggar's Opera*.

Charm, A, 366. See also *Charm of Lullabies*.

Charm of Lullabies, A, 71, 72–3, 279, 366

"Child you're not too young to know", 118. See also *Peter Grimes*.

Chorale, 263. See also *Diversions on a Theme*.

Coal Face. See Incidental Music.

"Come along, darling", 290. See also *Albert Herring*.

"Come, sweet lass", 169, 174, 183. See also *Beggar's Opera*.

Come you not from Newcastle?, 48, 288, 359, 365. See also *Folk Songs*.

Concertos:
    Diversions on a Theme, 263–4, 300, 363
    Piano Concerto (No. 1), 72, 257–60, 314, 352, 363
    Scottish Ballad, 264–5, 364
    Violin Concerto (No. 2), 4, 14n., 260–3, 360, 363

Confundantur et revereantur, 303. See also *This Way to the Tomb*.

Conquering Space. See Incidental Music.

Cradle Song, A, 366. See also *Charm of Lullabies*.

C.T.O. See Incidental Music.

Cuckoo, 362. See also *Friday Afternoons*.

"Curse attends a woman's love, A", 169, 183. See also *Beggar's Opera*.

Dance of Death, 62, 97, 362. See also *Our Hunting Fathers*.

Dark Tower, The. See Incidental Music.

"Date with Love, A", 298. See *Ascent of F6*.

Dawn Interlude, 53, 112, 365. See also *Peter Grimes*.

Death, be not proud, 71, 265. See also *Holy Sonnets of John Donne*.

Death of Nicolas, The, 99. See also *Saint Nicolas*.

Deo Gracias, 364. See also *Ceremony of Carols*.

Départ, 33, 66, 363. See also *Illuminations*.

Deus in adjutorium, 303. See also *This Way to the Tomb*.

Dido and Aeneas, 47, 74–5, 77, 186–97, 367

Dies Irae, 37, 62, 249, 250, 349. See also *Sinfonia da Requiem*.

Dirge, 50, 68, 71, 150, 299, 307, 365. See also *Serenade*.

Diversions on a Theme. See Concertos.

Divertimento. See Incidental Music.

Donne Sonnets. See *Holy Sonnets of John Donne*.

Driving Boy, The, 55, 100, 366. See also *Spring Symphony*.

Duchess of Malfi, The. See Incidental Music.

Eagle has Two Heads, The. See Incidental Music.

Early Morning Bathe, 269, 270, 362. See also *Holiday Diary*.

Ee-Oh!, 362. See also *Friday Afternoons*.

Ego vero egenus, 304. See also *This Way to the Tomb*.

Eho! Eho!, 364. See also *Folk Songs*.

Elegy, 68, 365. See also *Serenade*.

"Embroidery in childhood was a luxury of idleness", 121. See also *Peter Grimes*.

En nymphas! en pastores!, 81. See also *Queen's Epicedium.*
Epilogue, 209. See also *Billy Budd.*
Epilogue, 60, 63, 362. See also *Our Hunting Fathers.*
Epilogue, 68. See also *Serenade.*
Evening, 305, 306. See also *This Way to the Tomb.*
Evening Hymn, 77, 367. See also *Three Divine Hymns.*
Evening Primrose, The, 366. See also *Five Flower Songs.*
Exsultant et laetentur, 304. See also *This Way to the Tomb.*

Fair and fair, 19, 23, 366. See also *Spring Symphony.*
Fairest Isle, 80, 367. See also *Seven Songs.*
Fanfare, 363. See also *Illuminations.*
Fantaisie Italienne. See *Incidental Music.*
Fantasy Quartet. See *Quartets.*
"Far forth", 303. See also *Rescue.*
Festival Te Deum, 93, 94, 356, 365
Fileuse, 364. See also *Folk Songs.*
"Fill ev'ry glass", 168, 176. See also *Beggar's Opera.*
Film Music. See *Incidental Music.*
"First time at the looking-glass, The", 168. See also *Beggar's Opera.*
Fish in the Unruffled Lakes, 64, 363
Fishing Song, 362. See also *Friday Afternoons.*
Five Flower Songs, 10, 90, 366
Flow, O my tears, 234. See also *Lachrymae.*
"Flowers bring to every year", 136. See also *Rape of Lucretia.*
Foggy, Foggy Dew, The, 359, 365. See also *Folk Songs.*
Folk Songs, 47–9, 287–8, 364, 365
"Forget the Dead", 298, 299. See also *Ascent of F6.*
Four Barriers. See *Incidental Music.*
Four Sea Interludes, 53, 365. See also *Peter Grimes.*
"Fox may steal your hens, A", 167, 171. See also *Beggar's Opera.*
Frank Bridge Variations. See *Variations on a Theme of Frank Bridge.*
Friday Afternoons, 69, 94, 279, 280, 362
Frolicsome Finale, 239, 362. See also *Simple Symphony.*
Fugue and Finale, 242. See also *Variations on a Theme of Frank Bridge.*
Fun-fair, 269, 270–1, 362. See also *Holiday Diary.*

Funeral March, 97. See also *Ballad of Heroes.*
Funeral March, 63. See also *Our Hunting Fathers.*
Funeral March, 12n., 142n., 242. See also *Variations on a Theme of Frank Bridge.*

"Gamesters and lawyers, The", 168 See also *Beggar's Opera.*
"Glitter of waves and glitter of sunlight", 117. See also *Peter Grimes.*
Gloria patri, 304. See also *This Way to the Tomb.*
God's Children. See *Incidental Music.*
Golden Sonata. See *Sonatas.*
"Good night!", 26. See also *Rape of Lucretia.*

Hadrian's Wall. See *Incidental Music.*
Heigh-ho! Heigh-hi!, 359
"Help! help! she's collapsed!", 285, 292. See also *Little Sweep.*
Here's to you, Fuzzy Wuzzy, 60
"He's mad or drunk!", 117. See also *Peter Grimes.*
Herod, 362. See also *Boy was Born.*
Highland Balou, The, 73, 366. See also *Charm of Lullabies.*
"Hither, dear husband", 169. See also *Beggar's Opera.*
Holiday Diary, 267, 268, 269–71, 362
Holiday Tales. See *Holiday Diary.*
Holy Sonnets of John Donne, The, 30, 50, 69–71, 72, 73, 84, 316, 323, 357, 358, 360, 365
"Horay in Amborah", 166, 169. See also *Beggar's Opera.*
"How cruel are the traytors", 168. See also *Beggar's Opera.*
"How cruel men are", 135. See also *Rape of Lucretia.*
"How happy could I be with either", 168, 179. See also *Beggar's Opera.*
"How quiet it is to-night", 71. See also *Rape of Lucretia.*
"How shall my Soul its Motions guide", 76. See also *Blessed Virgin's Expostulations.*
How the Dial Works. See *Incidental Music.*
H.P.O., or 6d. Telegram. See *Incidental Music.*
Hymn, 68, 347, 365. See also *Serenade.*

Hymn to St. Cecilia, 4, 46, 61, 67, 68, 85,
    89, 90, 279–80, 303, 355, 356–7, 364
Hymn to the Virgin, A, 85, 89, 356, 362
Hymns, 51–3

"I accept their verdict", 40n. See also
    Billy Budd.
"I, like a ship in storms", 167. See also
    Beggar's Opera.
I Lov'd a Lass, 92, 362. See also *Two
    Part Songs*.
I Must be Married on Sunday, 362. See also
    Friday Afternoons.
"I often wonder", 136. See also *Rape
    of Lucretia*.
"I remember", 136. See also *Rape of
    Lucretia*.
If my complaint could passion move, 233–4.
    See also *Lachrymae*.
"If any wench Venus' girdle wear", 167,
    178. See also *Beggar's Opera*.
"If love the virgin's heart invade", 167,
    171. See also *Beggar's Opera*.
If Music be the food of love, 367. See also
    Seven Songs and *Six Songs*.
"If the heart of a man", 168. See also
    Beggar's Opera.
"If thus a man can die", 170. See also
    Beggar's Opera.
Il est quelqu'un sur terre, 364. See also
    Folk Songs.
I'll sail upon the Dog Star, 367. See also
    Seven Songs.
Illuminations, Les, 4, 13, 30ff., 37, 41,
    65–6, 67, 72, 84, 237, 313, 357, 360,
    363. See also Incidental Music.
"I'm bubbled", 168. See also *Beggar's
    Opera*.
"I'm like a skiff", 169. See also *Beggar's
    Opera*.
Impromptu, 259–60. See also Piano
    Concerto.
In freezing Winter Night, 364. See also
    Ceremony of Carols.
In the bleak Midwinter, 280, 362. See
    also *Boy was Born*.
"In the days of my youth", 169. See also
    Beggar's Opera.
Incidental Music:
    Advance Democracy, 299, 313.
    Agamemnon of Aeschylus, 311
    Around the Village Green, 312, 358
    Ascent of F6, The, 3, 298–9, 300, 311
    Ballet de la Paix, 313
    Banking for Millions, 297, 312
    Cable Ship, 312

Incidental Music:—*contd.*
    Calendar of the Year, 297–8, 312
    Coal Face, 3, 295, 296, 312
    Conquering Space, 296, 312
    C.T.O., 296, 312
    Dark Tower, The, 307–10, 312
    Divertimento, 313
    Duchess of Malfi, The, 307, 311
    Eagle has Two Heads, The, 303, 306–7,
        311
    Fantasie Italienne, 313
    Four Barriers, 299, 312
    God's Chillun, 299, 312
    Hadrian's Wall, 299, 311
    How the Dial Works, 312
    H.P.O., or *6d. Telegram*, 279n., 299,
        313
    Illuminations, Les, 313
    Instruments of the Orchestra, 276, 300,
        312
    Jinx, 313
    Johnson over Jordan, 299, 311
    King's Stamp, The, 296, 312
    Line to the Tschierva Hut, The, 297,
        312
    Love from a Stranger, 298, 312
    Men of Goodwill, 307, 309–10, 312
    Men of the Alps, 297, 312
    Message from Geneva, 297, 312
    Mony a Pickle, 312
    Night Mail, 3, 289, 295, 297, 312
    Old Spain, 299, 311
    On the Frontier, 3, 299, 300, 311
    Oui Ou Non?, 313
    Out of the Picture, 311
    Rescue, The, 300–3, 309, 312
    Rêve de Leonor, Le, 313
    Savings of Bill Blewitt, The, 312
    Seven Ages of Man, The, 299, 311
    Simple Symphony, 313
    Soirée Musicale, 313
    Stratton, 303, 311
    Sword in the Stone, The, 299, 312
    Sylphides, Les, 313
    This Way to the Tomb, 26n., 303–6,
        311
    Timon of Athens, 311
    Tocher, The, 299, 312
    Versunkene Stadt, Die, 313
    Village Harvest, 312, 358
    Way to the Sea, The, 312
Instruments of the Orchestra. See Inci-
    dental Music.
Interlude, 95, 364. See *Ceremony of Carols*.
Interlude, 363. See *Illuminations*.
Interludes. See *Four Sea Interludes*.
Introduction, 240. See also *Variations on
    a Theme of Frank Bridge*.

Introduction and Rondo Alla Burlesca, 268, 272–3, 355, 364
Irish Reel, 358
"Is Albert virtuous, yes or no?", 147. See also *Albert Herring*.
'Is then his fate", 168, 179. See also *Beggar's Opera*.

*J*azz-man, 362. See also *Friday Afternoons*.
Jazz Song, 298, 299. See also *Ascent of F6*.
Jesu, as Thou art our Saviour, 362. See also *Boy was Born*.
Jinx. See Incidental Music.
Job's Curse, 76, 78, 367
John Donne Sonnets. See *Holy Sonnets of John Donne*.
'John you may have heard the story", 118. See also *Peter Grimes*.
Johnson over Jordan. See Incidental Music.

*K*ermesse Canadienne. See *Canadian Carnival*.
King's Stamp, The. See Incidental Music.

*L*achrymae, 211, 233–5, 366
Lacrymosa, 37, 249, 250–1. See also *Sinfonia da Requiem*.
"Let her among you without fault", 113. See also *Peter Grimes*.
Let Sullen Discord Smile, 367. See also *Suite of Songs*.
Let the florid music praise!, 16, 17, 63, 363. See also *On This Island*.
"Let us take the road", 168. See also *Beggar's Opera*.
Let's make an Opera, 40, 52, 282–6, 291–3, 366
Lift Boy, 91–2, 362. See also *Two Part Songs*.
"Lilliburlero", 165, 166, 169. See also *Beggar's Opera*.
Line to the Tschierva Hut, The. See Incidental Music.
Little Sir William, 358, 364. See also *Folk Songs*.
Little Sweep, The, 13, 17, 25, 53, 55, 56, 57, 85, 98, 150, 282–3, 291–3, 366. See also *Let's make an Opera*.
London, to thee I do present, 366. See also *Spring Symphony*.

Lord, what is man?, 76, 367. See *Three Divine Hymns*.
Love from a Stranger. See Incidental Music.
"Lucretia!", 134, 140. See also *Rape of Lucretia*.
Lullaby, 219. See also *Suite* for violin and piano.
Lullay, Jesu, 362. See also *Boy was Born*.
Lyke-Wake Dirge, 307. See also *Dirge*.

*M*ad Bess, 80, 367. See also *Six Songs*.
"Maid is like the golden ore, A", 167. See also *Beggar's Opera*.
Man is for woman made, 367. See also *Six Songs*.
"Man may escape from rope and gun", 168, 173. See also *Beggar's Opera*.
March, 263. See also *Diversions on a Theme*.
March, 364. See also *Matinées Musicales*.
March, 260. See also Piano Concerto.
March, 363. See also *Soirées Musicales*.
March, 362. See also *Suite* for violin and piano.
March, 240–1. See also *Variations on a Theme of Frank Bridge*.
Marine, 33, 66, 363. See also *Illuminations*.
Marsh Flowers, 366. See also *Five Flower Songs*.
Matinées Musicales, 288, 313, 326, 358, 364. See also *Divertimento*.
May, 362
Mazurka Elegiaca, 268, 273–5, 355, 364
"Me Judah's Daughters once Caress'd", 76. See also *Blessed Virgin's Expostulation*.
Men of Goodwill. See Incidental Music.
Men of the Alps. See Incidental Music.
Merry Cuckoo, The, 366. See also *Spring Symphony*.
Message from Geneva. See Incidental Music.
Messalina, 61, 62. See also *Our Hunting Fathers*.
"Michael, you shall be renowned", 298. See also *Ascent of F6*.
Michelangelo Sonnets. See *Seven Sonnets of Michelangelo*.
Miller of Dee, The, 365. See also *Folk Songs*.
"Miser thus a shilling sees, The," 168, 177. See also *Beggar's Opera*.
"Moods of the court, The," 163, 169. See also *Beggar's Opera*.

Mont Juic, 288, 363
Mony a Pickle. See Incidental Music.
Moonlight Interlude, 121, 222, 365. See also *Peter Grimes*.
Morning, 305–6. See also *This Way to the Tomb*.
Morning Star, The, 50n., 366. See also *Spring Symphony*.
Mother Comfort, 363. See also *Two Ballads*.
Moto Perpetuo, 364. See also *Matinées Musicales*.
Moto Perpetuo, 219, 362. See also *Suite* for violin and piano.
Moto Perpetuo, 241–2. See also *Variations on a Theme of Frank Bridge*.
Music for a While, 80, 81, 367. See also *Seven Songs*.
"My love is all madness", 169, 174. See also *Beggar's Opera*.
"My only hope depends on you", 123. See also *Peter Grimes*.

New Year Carol, A, 362. See also *Friday Afternoons*.
Nicolas and the Pickled Boys, 98. See also *Saint Nicolas*.
Nicolas comes to Myra and is chosen Bishop, 52. See also *Saint Nicolas*.
Night, 268, 270, 271, 362. See also *Holiday Diary*.
Night, 305, 306. See also *This Way to the Tomb*.
Night Mail. See Incidental Music.
Night Song, 25, 285. See also *Little Sweep*.
"No power on earth", 166, 169. See also *Beggar's Opera*.
Nocturne, 263. See also *Diversions on a Theme*.
Nocturne, 364. See also *Matinées Musicales*.
Nocturne, 64, 66, 363. See also *On This Island*.
Nocturne, 365. See also *Serenade*.
Noel!, 304, 362. See also *Boy was Born*.
Noël passée, La, 364. See also *Folk Songs*.
Not all my torments, 367. See also *Six Songs*.
"Now little fish on tender stone", 23. See also *Spring Symphony*.
"Now the Great Bear and Pleiades", 23, 116, 323. See also *Peter Grimes*.
Now the leaves are falling fast, 20, 64, 363. See also *On This Island*.
Now thro' Night's caressing grip, 363. See also *On This Island*.

"Nunc dimittis", 99. See also *Saint Nicolas*.
Nurse's Song, The, 366. See also *Charm of Lullabies*.

O Can ye Sew Cushions, 364. See also *Folk Songs*.
"O cruel, cruel case", 170, 184. See also *Beggar's Opera*.
"O hideous Flower", 136. See also *Rape of Lucretia*.
O might those sighes and teares, 50, 365. See also *Holy Sonnets of John Donne*.
"O Polly, you might have toy'd", 167, 175. See also *Beggar's Opera*.
"O, ponder well!", 167, 183. See also *Beggar's Opera*.
O that I'd ne'er been married, 60
O Waly, Waly, 288, 359, 365. See also *Folk Songs*.
"O what a lovely day", 136, 139. See also *Rape of Lucretia*.
"O what pain it is to part!", 168. See also *Beggar's Opera*.
"O why do you weep through the working day?", 293. See also *Little Sweep*.
Odes and Elegies, 81–2
"Of all the friends", 170. See also *Beggar's Opera*.
"Oh! for a quill drawn from your wing", 76. See also *Lord, what is man?*
Oh my blacke Soule, 365. See also *Holy Sonnets of John Donne*.
Oh, proud heart, 304. See also *This Way to the Tomb*.
Oh, to vex me, 365. See also *Holy Sonnets of John Donne*.
Old Abram Brown, 94, 279, 362. See also *Friday Afternoons*.
Old Joe has gone Fishing, 49. See also *Peter Grimes*.
Old Spain. See Incidental Music.
Oliver Cromwell, 359, 364. See also *Folk Songs*.
On the brow of Richmond Hill, 367. See also *Seven Songs*.
On the Frontier. See Incidental Music.
On This Island, 3, 16–20, 30, 31, 33, 63–4, 363
Oui Ou Non? See Incidental Music.
Our Hunting Fathers, 3, 12, 13, 15–16, 30, 60–3, 69, 140, 142n., 362
"Our Polly is a sad slut!", 167. See also *Beggar's Opera*.
"Ourselves like the great", 169, 176. See also *Beggar's Opera*.

Out of the Picture. See Incidental Music.
Out on the lawn I lie in bed, 99, 366. See also *Spring Symphony*.
"Over the hills and far away", 167, 175. See also *Beggar's Opera*.

*P*antomime, 364. See also *Matinées Musicales*.
Parade, 66, 363. See also *Illuminations*.
Passacaglio, 353, 365. See also *Peter Grimes*.
Pastorale, 67, 365. See also *Serenade*.
Paul Bunyan, 4, 300
"Per vitam Domini", 97. See also *Wedding Anthem*.
Peter Grimes, 1, 5, 13, 23, 30, 38*n*., 40, 49, 50, 52, 69, 71, 85, 101–31, 132, 140, 146, 200, 222, 268, 283, 293, 303, 320, 323, 327, 343, 346, 348, 349, 353, 360, 365
Phantasy Quartet. See Quartets.
Phrase, 65, 363. See also *Illuminations*.
Piano Concerto. See Concerto.
Pious Celinda, 367. See also *Seven Songs*.
Playful Pizzicato, 238, 362. See also *Simple Symphony*.
Ploughboy, The, 288, 359, 365. See also *Folk Songs*.
Polacca, 277. See also *Young Person's Guide to the Orchestra*.
Polly Oliver, 288
Prelude and Fugue, 237, 242–4, 365
Prelude and Fugue on a Theme of Vittoria, 366
"Pretty Polly, say", 167, 178. See also *Beggar's Opera*.
Procession, 46, 95, 364. See also *Ceremony of Carols*.
Prologue, 198, 201–2, 205. See also *Billy Budd*.
Prologue, 60, 61, 362. See also *Our Hunting Fathers*.
Prologue, 69, 102, 123, 127. See also *Peter Grimes*.
Prologue, 68. See also *Serenade*.
Purcell Realizations. See under various titles.

*Q*uaerit loca lacrymarum, 304–5. See also *This Way to the Tomb*.
Quand j'étais chez mon père, 364. See also *Folk Songs*.
Quartets:
    Phantasy Quartet, 2, 11, 37*n*., 211, 218, 219, 355, 362

Quartets:—*contd.*
    String Quartet No. 1, 4, 37*n*., 211, 219–25, 355, 364
    String Quartet No. 2, 37, 211, 219, 222, 224, 225–33, 249, 330, 355, 365
Queen's Epicedium, The, 81, 352, 367
"Quel che nel tuo bel volto bramo e 'mparo", 21. See also *Seven Sonnets of Michelangelo*.

*R*adio music. See Incidental Music.
Rainbow, The, 91, 362. See also *Three Two-part Songs*.
Rape of Lucretia, The, 1, 5, 26, 36*n*., 38, 53–4, 69, 71, 96, 115, 123, 132–45, 146, 149, 154, 156, 160*n*., 279, 291, 320, 323, 324, 325, 327, 345, 347, 353–4, 365
Rats Away!, 61, 362. See also *Our Hunting Fathers*
Recession, 46, 95, 364. See also *Ceremony of Carols*.
Recitative, 263. See also *Diversions on a Theme*.
Recitative and Aria, 257, 259. See Piano Concerto.
Recorded music, 352–60
"The Red Fox, the Sun", 305, 306. See also *This Way to the Tomb*.
Rejoice in the Lamb, 19, 46, 57, 95, 280, 356, 360, 365
Requiem Aeternam, 37, 249–50, 251–2, See also *Sinfonia da Requiem*.
Rescue, The. See Incidental Music.
Rêve de Leonor, Le. See Incidental Music.
Ride-by-Nights, The, 91, 362. See also *Three Two-part Songs*.
Ritmico, 263. See also *Diversions on a Theme*.
Roi s'en va- t'en chasse, Le, 359, 364. See also *Folk Songs*.
Romance, 263. See also *Diversions on a Theme*.
Romance, 12, 32, 241. See also *Variations on a Theme of Frank Bridge*.
Royauté, 33, 66, 363. See also *Illuminations*.
Rubato, 263. See also *Diversions on a Theme*.

*S*ailing, 268, 269, 270, 362. See also *Holiday Diary*.
St. Cecilia. See *Hymn to St. Cecilia*.
Saint Nicolas, 38, 50, 52, 53, 55, 69, 98, 150, 280–1, 343, 360, 366

Sally Gardens, The, 288, 358, 364
Sammy's Bath, 292. See also *Little Sweep.*
Saul and the Witch at Endor, 76, 79–80, 367
Savings of Bill Blewitt, The. See Incidental Music.
Scottish Ballad. See Concertos.
Seascape, 18, 64, 363. See also *On This Island.*
Sentimental Saraband, 237, 238, 246, 279, 362. See also *Simple Symphony.*
Sephestia's Lullaby, 366. See also *Charm of Lullabies.*
Serenade, 10, 13, 45, 46, 50, 67–8, 69, 71, 84, 110, 150, 237, 278, 347, 348, 357, 365
Seven Ages of Man. See Incidental Music.
Seven Songs, 80–1, 367
Seven Sonnets of Michelangelo, 4, 21, 30, 31, 37, 41–5, 46, 48, 50, 65, 66–7, 69, 70, 71, 73, 84, 115, 357, 358, 364
Shine out, fair sun, 100, 366. See also *Spring Symphony.*
Ship of Rio, The, 91, 362. See also *Three Two-part Songs.*
Simple Symphony. See Symphonies.
"Since I must swing", 170. See also *Beggar's Opera.*
"Since laws were made", 170. See also *Beggar's Opera.*
Since she whom I loved, 70, 365. See also *Holy Sonnets of John Donne.*
Sinfonia da Requiem. See Symphonies.
Sinfonietta. See Symphonies.
Six Metamorphoses after Ovid, 211n., 367
Six Songs, 80–1, 367
"So I drink off this bumper", 170. See also *Beggar's Opera.*
So when the glittering Queen of Night, 267. See also *Suite of Songs.*
Soirée Musicale. See Incidental Music.
Soirées Musicales, 84, 288, 299, 313, 358, 363. See also *Divertimento* and *Fantasie Italienne.*

Sonata:
    Golden Sonata, 82, 235–6, 367
Sonetto XVI, 42, 364; *XXIV,* 44, 67, 364; *XXX,* 42–3, 67, 364; *XXXI,* 44–5, 364; *XXXII,* 42, 364; *XXXVIII,* 44, 67, 364; *LV,* 21, 364. See also *Seven Sonnets of Michelangelo.*
Sonnet, 68, 365. See also *Serenade.*
"Soomer is icoomen in", 47, 99, 100, 281. See also *Spring Symphony.*
Sound, Fame, thy brazen trumpet, 81, 367. See also *Suite of Songs.*

Sound the Flute, 366. See also *Spring Symphony.*
"Spirto ben nato", 71, 364. See also *Seven Sonnets of Michelangelo.*
Spring Carol, 364. See also *Ceremony of Carols.*
Spring Symphony. See Symphonies.
Spring, the Sweet Spring, 366. See also *Spring Symphony.*
"Starry Vere, God bless you", 209. See also *Billy Budd.*
"Still the dark forest", 298–9. See also *Ascent of F6.*
"Stop all clocks", 298, 299. See also *Ascent of F6.*
Storm Interlude, 109, 115, 122, 365. See also *Peter Grimes.*
Stratton. See Incidental Music.
Succession of the Four Sweet Months, The, 90, 366. See also *Five Flower Songs.*
Suite for violin and piano, 211, 219, 237, 362
Suite of Songs, 367
Sunday Morning Interlude, 109, 117, 365. See also *Peter Grimes.*
Sweet Polly Oliver, 358, 359, 365. See also *Folk Songs.*
Sweeter than Roses, 80, 367. See also *Six Songs.*
Sword in the Stone, The. See Incidental Music.
Sylphides, Les. See Incidental Music.
Symphonies:
    Simple Symphony, 60, 98, 237–9, 246, 279, 313, 354, 362. See also Incidental Music.
    Sinfonia da Requiem, 4, 13, 31, 37–8, 62, 84, 249–52, 348, 349, 360, 363
    Sinfonietta, 2, 10, 11, 63, 86, 247–9, 313, 362. See also *Versunkene Stadt.*
    Spring Symphony, 5n., 10, 12, 19, 23, 30, 38, 45, 47, 49, 50, 55–6, 62, 84, 85, 94, 99–100, 143, 184n., 198, 218–19, 229n., 252–6, 281–2, 360, 366

Tarantella, 264. See also *Diversions on a Theme.*
Te Deum in C Major, 93, 356, 362
"That is the sort of weak politeness", 69. See also *Peter Grimes.*
That Yongë Child, 364. See also *Ceremony of Carols.*
Theatre music. See Incidental Music.
"Their eyes, their lips", 170. See also *Beggar's Opera.*

There is no Rose, 62, 364. See also *Ceremony of Carols*.
There was a Man of Newington, 362. See also *Friday Afternoons*.
There was a Monkey, 362. See also *Friday Afternoons*.
There's none to soothe, 359, 365. See also *Folk Songs*.
"They listen to money", 114, 122. See also *Peter Grimes*.
"This is our moment", 303. See also *Billy Budd*.
This Little Babe, 23, 364. See also *Ceremony of Carols*.
This Way to the Tomb. See Incidental Music.
Thou hast made me, 365. See also *Holy Sonnets of John Donne*.
Thou tunest the world, 367. See also *Suite of Songs*.
Three Divine Hymns, 76–8, 367
Three Two-part Songs, 90–1, 279n., 362
Three Kings, The, 362. See also *Boy was Born*.
Threnody, 26, 148, 154, 325n., 345. See also *Albert Herring*.
"Through all the employments of life", 167, 171. See also *Beggar's Opera*.
'Thus gamesters united", 169, 171. See also *Beggar's Opera*.
"Thus I stand like the Turk", 170. See also *Beggar's Opera*.
"Thus sleeps Lucretia", 136, 143. See also *Rape of Lucretia*.
"Thus when a good housewife", 168, 173. See also *Beggar's Opera*.
"Thus when the swallow", 168. See also *Beggar's Opera*.
Timon of Athens. See Incidental Music.
Tirolese, 363. See also *Soirées Musicales*.
'*Tis Holiday*, 367. See also *Suite of Songs*.
" 'Tis woman that seduces", 167, 171. See also *Beggar's Opera*.
To Daffodils, 366. See *Five Flower Songs*.
Toccato I, 264; *II*, 264. See also *Diversions on a Theme*.
Toccata in D, 258. See also Piano Concerto.
Tocher, The. See Incidental Music.
Tragic Story, A, 362. See also *Friday Afternoons*.
Trees they grow so high, 364. See also *Folk Songs*.
Turn then thine eyes, 367. See also *Seven Songs*.
"Turtle thus with plaintive crying, The", 167, 183. See also *Beggar's Opera*.
Two Ballads, 363.
Two Part Songs, 362

Underneath the Abject Willow, 363. See also *Two Ballads*.
Useful Plough, The, 362. See also *Friday Afternoons*.

Variations and Fugue on a Theme of Purcell, 84, 313, 354, 365. See also *Oui Ou Non?*
Variations on a Theme of Frank Bridge, 11–15, 16, 84, 142n., 237, 239–42, 264, 313, 354, 360, 363. See also *Jinx* and *Rêve de Leonor*.
Versunkene Stadt, Die. See Incidental Music.
Village Harvest. See Incidental Music.
Villes, 65, 363. See also *Illuminations*.
Violin Concerto. See Concertos.
"Virgins are like the fair flower", 167, 178. See also *Beggar's Opera*.
Voici le printemps, 364. See also *Folk Songs*.

Waltz, 364. See also *Matinées Musicales*.
Waltz in D, 258–9. See also Piano Concerto.
Waltz, 362. See also *Suite* for violin and piano.
Waters Above, 366. See also *Spring Symphony*.
Way to the Sea, The. See Incidental Music.
We sing to Him, 77, 367. See also *Three Divine Hymns*.
Wedding Anthem, 23, 96, 366.
Welcome Maids of Honour, 366. See also *Spring Symphony*.
Welcome Odes, 190. See also *Dido and Aeneas*.
"We'll walk to the spinney", 23, 153. See also *Albert Herring*.
"Were I laid", 167. See also *Beggar's Opera*.
"We've made our own investigations", 24. See also *Albert Herring*.
"What gudgeons are we men!", 169. See also *Beggar's Opera*.
"What harbour shelters peace?", 114. See also *Peter Grimes*.
What if the present, 365. See also *Holy Sonnets of John Donne*.
"What would Missus Herring say?", 160. See also *Albert Herring*.
"When he holds up his hand", 169, 172. See also *Beggar's Opera*.

"When my hero in court appears", 169, 172. See also *Beggar's Opera*.

When will my May come, 47, 366. See also *Spring Symphony*.

"When you censure the age", 168, 174. See also *Beggar's Opera*.

"When young at the bar", 169, 178n. See also *Beggar's Opera*.

"Which way shall I turn me?", 169. See also *Beggar's Opera*.

"Whilst we two observers stand", 343. See also *Rape of Lucretia*.

"Why did she stare", 160. See also *Albert Herring*.

"Why does the Nubian", 134. See also *Rape of Lucretia*.

"Why how now, Madam Flirt!", 169, 176. See also *Beggar's Opera*.

Why should men quarrel?, 367. See also *Suite of Songs*.

Wiener Walzer, 12, 239. See also *Variations on a Theme of Frank Bridge*.

Wolcum Yole!, 364. See also *Ceremony of Carols*.

"Would I might be hanged", 170, 176. See also *Beggar's Opera*.

Young Person's Guide to the Orchestra, The, 24, 53, 55, 84, 276–9, 282, 300, 313, 354, 365

"You'll think e'er many days ensue", 168, 179. See also *Beggar's Opera*.

"Your counsel all is urged in vain", 195. See also *Dido and Aeneas*.

"Youth's the season made for joys", 168. See also *Beggar's Opera*.

Index of Works Other than Britten's

General references to composers will be found in the Index of Names and
Places, pp. 402ff.—EDS.

Anderson
Irish Suite, 358

Bach, J. S.
Passacaglia, 231
Suite No. 3, Air, 354
Barnett, J. F.
Ancient Mariner, The, 59
Bartók, Béla
Enchanting Song, 356
Beethoven
32 Variations in C minor, 231
Eroica, 232
Eighth Symphony, 226n.
Fifth Symphony, 344
Berg, Alban
Wozzeck, 38n., 106, 144, 339, 346
Berkeley, Lennox
Mont Juic, 288, 363
Berlioz
Nuits d'été, Les, 13n.
Blacher, Boris
Partita, 349
Brahms
Bücklichte Fiedler, Der, 356
Fourth Symphony, 231
Haydn Variations, 233
Bridge, Frank
Idyll No. 2, 240

Chopin
Sylphides, Les, 298, 313
Coleridge-Taylor, Samuel
Hiawatha, 59
Tale of Old Japan, 59
Copland, Aaron
Five Old American Songs, 352

Dallapiccola, Luigi
Il Prigionero, 339
Dowland, John
Flow, O my Tears, 234–5
If my complaints could passion move,
233–4

Elgar, Edward
Dream of Gerontius, The, 59
King Olaf, 59

Folk Songs
Keys of Heaven, The, 59
Oh no, John, 59
Foulds, John
Four Barriers, 299, 312
Mony a Pickle, 312

Gay, John
Beggar's Opera, The, 133n., 163–85,
366
Graf, Friedrich Hartmann
Concerto for two flutes, 330

Handel
Fireworks Music, 354
Joshua, 245
Messiah, The, 59, 245, 326
Rinaldo, 175
Haydn
Creation, The, 59, 250, 349

399

Holst, Gustav
  Miniature operas, 132
  This have I done, 355
Honegger, Arthur
  Pacific, 231, 309
Hymns
  London New, 99
  Old Hundredth, 98

Kodály, Zoltán
  Ave Maria, 356
  Missa Brevis, 356

Lassus
  Lagrime di San Pietro, 84
  Psalmi Penitentiales, 85
Leigh, Walter
  Men of the Alps, 312
Liddle
  Abide with me, 59

Mahler, Gustav
  Eighth Symphony, 85, 99, 246, 252
  Fifth Symphony, 115n.
  First Symphony, 245–6
  Kindertotenlieder, 13, 43, 50
  Lied von der Erde, Das, 246, 252
  Lieder eines fahrenden Gesellen, 13
  Nun will die Sonn' so hell aufgeh'n!, 50
  Third Symphony, 13
Martinu, Bohuslav
  Sinfonietta La Jolla, 357
Mendelssohn
  Elijah, 59
Milhaud, Darius
  Choëphores, Les, 144
  Christophe Colomb, 144
Monteverdi
  Madrigals, 85
  Sestina, 84
Mozart
  Alleluia, 357
  Clarinet Quintet, 335
  Clarinet Trio, 345
  Così fan tutte, 132, 325, 335
  Don Giovanni, 324–5, 328, 335
  Fantasy in F minor, 324
  Magic Flute, The, 323, 327
  Marriage of Figaro, The, 129
  Sinfonia Concertante, 348

Palestrina
  Masses, 85
  Vergini, 84

Parry, Hubert
  Judith, 59
Piggot
  Come my way, my truth, my life, 356
Purcell
  Abdelazar, or The Moor's Revenge, 276
  Blessed Virgin's Expostulation, The, 76, 367
  Dido and Aeneas, 187–97, 367
  Divine Hymns, 71
  En nymphas! en pastores!, 81
  Evening Hymn, 76, 367
  Fairest Isle, 80, 367
  Fantasia upon one note, 355
  Golden Sonata, 235–6, 367
  Harmonia Sacra, 74, 76, 80, 82, 367
  If music be the food of love, 367
  I'll sail upon the Dog-Star, 367
  Indian Queen, The, 189
  Job's Curse, 76, 78, 367
  Let Sullen Discord Smile, 367
  Lord, what is man?, 72, 76, 367
  Mad Bess, 80, 367
  Man is for woman made, 367
  Music for a while, 80, 81, 367
  Not all my torments, 367
  On the brow of Richmond Hill, 367
  Orpheus Britannicus, 74, 80, 81, 82, 367
  Pious Celinda, 367
  Queen's Epicedium, The, 81, 352, 367
  Saul and the Witch at Endor, 76, 79, 367
  Sir Anthony Love, 190
  So when the glittering Queen of Night, 367
  Sound, Fame, thy brazen trumpet, 81, 367
  Sweeter than Roses, 80, 367
  Three Divine Hymns, 76, 367
  Thou tunest this world, 367
  'Tis Holiday, 367
  Turn then thine eyes, 367
  We sing to Him, 76, 367
  Why should men quarrel?, 367

Ravel, Maurice
  Concerto for piano (left hand), 263
  Heure espagnole, L', 132
Rossini
  Danza, La, 299
  Matinées Musicales, 288, 313, 326, 358, 364
  Soirées Musicales, 288, 289, 313, 358, 363

INDEX OF WORKS OTHER THAN BRITTEN'S 401

Scheidt, Samuel
  Chorale Preludes, 83
Schoenberg, Arnold
  Changing Chord, The, 89n.
  Erwartung, 132
  First Chamber Symphony, 247
  Five Orchestral Pieces, 89
  Ode to Napoleon, 144n.
  Pierrot lunaire, 2, 144
  Psalm "O du mein Gott: alle Völker preisen Dich", Op. 50c, 144n.
  Survivor from Warsaw, A, 144n.
Schubert
  Auf der Bruck, 352
  Im Frühling, 352
  Schöne Müllerin, Die, 317
  Unfinished Symphony, 333
Schumann
  Dichterliebe, 317
Spicer
  Birds, The, 356
Strauss, Richard
  Liebe der Danae, Die, 335
Strawinsky, Igor
  Apollon Musagète, 64
  Œdipus Rex, 64, 341
  Persephone, 64
  Pulcinella, 288
  Rake's Progress, The, 39n., 335, 341
  Symphony of Psalms, 38, 66

Vaughan Williams, Ralph
  Fifth Symphony, 15
  Lord, Thou hast been our refuge, 356
  On Wenlock Edge, 352
Verdi
  Falstaff, 40, 130
  Otello, 40, 109, 130, 340
  Requiem, 304, 340

Wagner
  Liebestod, 188
  Meistersinger, Die, 146
  Parsifal, 267
  Rienzi, 267
  Tristan und Isolde, 146, 156, 188
Walton, William
  Viola Concerto, 229
Wolf, Hugo
  Italian Serenade, 45
  Italienisches Liederbuch, 45

Yates, Victor
  Mony a Pickle, 312

Index of Names and Places

Advance Democracy (film), 299, 313
Aeschylus, 311
Agamemnon of Aeschylus (play), 311
Alamein, 4
Albert Hall, 360
Aldeburgh, 4, 5, 6, 7–8, 211*n*., 233;
 Festival, 5, 6, 7, 211*n*., 233, 365
Alston, Audrey, 239
Amityville, L.I., 4, 260
Amsterdam, 281
Anderson, 358
Arne, 62, 83
Arnell, Richard, 340
Around the Village Green (film), 312
Ascent of F6, The (play), 3, 298, 300,
 311
Ashton, Frederick, 313
Auden, W. H., 3, 4, 12, 13, 16, 20, 31,
 60, 63, 64, 65, 66, 67, 90, 97, 99,
 100, 254, 289, 296, 298, 299, 311,
 312, 355, 362, 363, 364, 366
Augustana Choir, 356
Austria, 228, 239, 241

*B*ach, J. C., 329
Bach, J. S., 7, 59, 73, 75, 191, 231, 275,
 333, 342, 354
Balanchine, George, 313
Balfe, 67
Ballet de la Paix (ballet), 313
Banking for Millions (film), 297, 312
Barbirolli, Sir John, 260
Barcelona, 219
Barnefield, Richard, 255, 366
Barnett, J. F., 59
Bartlett, Ethel, 257, 264
Bartók, 249, 338, 339, 350, 356
Bax, Arnold, 49, 275
B.B.C., 86, 300, 352; Symphony Orchestra,
 257

Beaumont and Fletcher, 255
Beecham, Sir Thomas, 260
Beethoven, 13, 84, 226*n*., 231, 232, 245,
 267, 314, 325, 333, 336, 340, 341,
 342, 344
Beinum, Van, 353
Belloc, Hilaire, 60, 357, 362
Belsen, 70
Benjamin, Arthur, 2, 271, 316
Benjamin Britten (White), 96
Berg, Alban, 7, 14, 38*n*., 39*n*., 73, 106,
 110, 144, 339, 341
Bergner, Eliasbeth, 307
Berkeley, Lennox, 219, 257, 288, 363
Berlioz, 13, 92
Betteridge, 356
Beware (Longfellow), 60
Billy Budd, Foretopman (Melville), 198–
 210, 345, 367
Birds, The (Belloc), 60
Blacher, Boris, 349
Blake, William, 60, 72, 255, 365, 366
Bond, Ralph, 313
Boston, 4
Boughton, Joy, 211*n*.
Boulez, 339
Bournemouth Municipal Orchestra, 263
Boyce, 83
Boyd Neel String Orchestra, 239, 242,
 354, 357
Boyes, Henry, 260
Brahms, 59, 219, 231, 233, 314, 323, 325,
 340, 356
Brain, D., 357
Bridge, Frank, 2, 32, 59, 60, 239, 240, 271
Brighton, 311
Bristol, 313
Britten, Benjamin, a melodist, 346; a
 professional musician, 6; and chil-
 dren's voices, 10; and John Ireland,
 11; and Mozart, 319–34, 348; and
 Schoenberg, 341–7; and Strawinsky,
 346; and Vaughan Williams, 11; and
 Verdi, 331, and young people, 276-86;

Britten, Benjamin—contd.
approach to other composers, 315–16; as a parodist, 11 *ff.*; as a pianist, 267–9, 314–18; as choral composer, 83–100; at Aldeburgh, 7–8; at R.C.M., 2–3, 60; attempts to found English operatic tradition, 110; attitude towards music, 6–7; birth, 1; Bridge's influence, 2; childhood, 1–3, 59; childlike spirit, 54–6; chromaticism, 35*f.*; classicism, 36; compared with Mozart, 319–34, 341, 348, 342; compared with other pianists, 315; compared with Schoenberg, 341*ff.*; compared with Wagner, 347; contemplates emigration, 3; continuos, 74*ff.*; contrapuntal art, 24; devotional music, 92–6; early compositions, 60; economy of form, 21; effect of Belsen and Buchenwald on, 70, 71; effect of his pacifism, 350–1; Elizabethanism, 50–1; Englishry, 9–11, 15–16, 39, 45, 46–52, 54*ff.*, 130–1, 293, 343, 346; Europeanism, 10; 11–15, 30–5, 37–45, 49, 50–1, 58; exemption from military service, 5; firmly rooted in vocal element, 83–4; folk songs, 47–52; gift for creating dramatic situations, 108; gift for satire, 11*ff.*; gift of the vernacular, 56–8; Handel's influence, 331; handling of mixed voices, 85*f.*; harmonic assurance, 34*f.*; his family's encouragement, 1; homesickness, 265; in Canada, 4, 260; in U.S.A., 3–5, 7, 41, 219, 257, 260, 263, 264, 265, 271, 300; in Vienna, 219; influenced by Strawinsky, 38*f.*; innocence of spirit, 54–6; Italianism, 41*ff.*; likes and dislikes, 6–7; love of East Anglia, 52–4; love of the common people, 345; Mahler's influence on, 13–14; melodic freedom, 347*f.*; melodic invention, 62, 346*f.*; musical character, 319–51; musical imagery, 18; musicianship, 316*f.*; not an innovator, 73; on eclecticism, 329–30; orchestral experiments, 133; passion for Elizabethan music, 7; personality of, 266; political beliefs, 3, 7; recovery of adolescence, 349–50; regional influences, 54; relation to English tradition, 9*ff.*; relation to other composers, 320*ff.*; Schoenberg's influence on, 247; social conscience, 7, 339; treatment of vocal music, 59–73, 184, 199–200; understanding for poetry, 4; use of children's

Britten, Benjamin—contd.
voices, 280*ff.*; use of dotted rhythm, 18–19; use of human voice, 68–9; Verdi's influence on, 40–1, 331
Britten, Mrs., 1, 5, 59
Brooklyn, 4
Brosa, Antonio, 219, 260
Bruckner, 92
Bruckner, Mahler, Schoenberg (Newlin), 212*n.*
Buchenwald, 71
Burns, Robert, 60, 366
Busoni, 321, 322, 332
Byrd, William, 83

Cable Ship (film), 312
Calendar of the Year (film), 297, 312
California, 264, 271
Calloway, 356
Cambridge, 311
Cameron, Basil, 260, 264
Canada, 4, 260
Carnegie Hall (New York), 260
Carner, Mosco, 15*n.*
Cavalcanti, A., 296, 312
C.E.M.A., 5
Central Office of Information, 295
Charles Brill Orchestra, 358
Cheltenham Festival, 257
Chesterian, The, 34*n.*
Chicago Opera Company, 357
Chopin, 275, 298, 313, 314
Christensen, Lew, 313
Cincinatti Symphony Orchestra, 264
Clare, John, 90, 253, 366
Clough, F. F., 353
Coal Face (film), 3, 295, 296–7, 312
Coates, Eric, 59
Cocteau, Jean, 306, 311
Coldstream, William, 296, 312
Coleridge, 7
Coleridge-Taylor Samuel, 59
Concertgebouw Orchestra, 353
Conquering Space (film), 296, 312
Coolidge Quartet, 219
Copland, 352
Coprario, 67
Cornish, William, 364
"Corpus Christi" carol, 280
Crabbe, George, 4, 90, 111, 365, 366
Cross, Joan, 353
Crozier, Eric, 98, 146, 177, 365, 366, 367
C.T.O. (film), 296, 312
Cuming, G. J., 353
Cummings, Dr. W. H., 187
Curzon, Clifford, 264, 355

Dallapiccola, Luigi, 339
Dark Tower, The (radio play), 307–9, 312
de la Mare, Walter, 60, 91, 94, 362
Debussy, 267, 275, 314
Decline of the West (Spengler), 319n.
Delius, 271
Dent, Professor, 187, 323, 325
Dickens, Charles, 294
Dido and Aeneas (Dent), 187
Disc, 11
Divertimento (ballet), 313
Dollfuss, 338
Donne, John, 30, 70, 84
Dowland, John, 62, 211, 233–4, 366
Dowling, Denis, 353
Driving Boy, The (Clare), 253
Duchess of Malfi, The (play), 307, 311
Duncan, Ronald, 133–4, 136n., 300, 306, 307, 311, 365, 366
Dundee, 264
Dunne, J. W., 133
Dvořák, 92

Eagle has Two Heads, The (play), 300, 306–7, 311
East Anglia, 1, 4, 52–5, 71
Edinburgh, 99
Eichstaett, 96
Einstein, Alfred, 321n., 323, 326, 327, 330, 331, 333, 334, 342
Eisler, Hanns, 97
Elgar, Sir Edward, 49, 59, 83, 85, 275
Eliot, T. S., 38n.
English Opera Group, 5, 186
Evans, Nancy, 72, 354
Experimental Theatre Group, 12

Fair and Fair (Peele), 255
Fantaisie Italienne (ballet), 313
Festival Hall (London), 260, 360
Festival of Music for the People, 3
Fiedler, 358
Fingerspitzengefühl, 317
Fleet Street Choir, 355
Florence, 212
Flowers of the Forest, 264
Forster, E. M., 4, 53n., 55n., 367
Foulds, John, 312
Four Barriers (film), 299, 312
Freedman, Barnett, 296
Freud, 298, 337
Foxe's Book of Martyrs, 156

Galimir Quartet, 355; Trio, 355
Gasset, Ortega y, 319
Gay, John, 163–85, 327, 366
German, Sir Edward, 59
Germany, 69–70, 96
Gimpel, 260
Glover, E., 350n.
Gluck, 7, 333
Glyndebourne, 289
God's Chillun (film), 299, 312
God rest you merry, Gentlemen, 309
Godard, 59
Goddard, Scott, 13
Goethe, 91, 99, 335n.
Gollmick, Carl, 324
Gomberg, H., 355
Goodall, Reginald, 354
Goossens, Eugene, 264; Leon, 212
Gore, Walter, 313
Gounod, 59
G.P.O. Film Unit, 296–8, 299
Graf, Friedrich Hartmann, 330–1
Graves, Robert, 91, 362
Greenaway, Kate, 285
Greene, 83
Greene, Plunket, 62
"Greensleeves", 181
Gregor, Joseph, 328
Gresham's School, Holt, 2
Grierson, J., 296, 312; Marion, 312
Guarini, 92
Guthrie, Tyrone, 164, 166, 366

Hadrian's Wall (radio feature), 299, 311
Hamburger, P., 212n.
Handel, 59, 62, 75, 166, 175, 191, 326, 331, 333, 354
Harewood, Earl of, 96
Harmonielehre (Schoenberg), 89n., 249, 336, 350
Harrison, Julius, 184
Harvey, Trevor, 263
Hawkes, Ralph, 3
Hadyn, 59, 73, 245, 246, 250, 252, 323, 333, 343, 349
Helwig, Marianne, 312
Herrick, George, 95; Robert, 90, 254, 366
Hetzler, jnr., 335n.
Hindemith, 339
Hollywood, 339
Holmes, J. B., 312
Holst, Gustav, 49, 132, 275, 355; Imogen, 365n.
Holt, 2

Honegger, 309
How the Dial Works (film), 312
Howells, 49
H.P.O., or 6d. Telegram (film), 299, 313
Hutchings, Arthur, 326

"In the bleak midwinter", 280
Instruments of the Orchestra (film), 295, 300, 313
International String Quartet, 212
Interpretation in Song (Greene), 62
Ireland, John, 2, 11, 59, 271, 275
I.S.C.M. Festivals, 60, 212, 219
Isherwood, Christopher, 12, 289, 298, 299, 311

Jinx (ballet), 313
Johnson over Jordan (play), 299, 300, 311
Jolla Orchestra, La, 357
Jonson, Ben, 67, 68, 365
Jovanovits, Mara, 313
Jung, 338

Keats, 365
Keller, Hans, 184n., 226–9, 231
King's Stamp, The (film), 296, 312
Kipling, Rudyard, 60
Knight of the Burning Pestle, The, 255
Kodály, 356
Koppel, H. D., 359
Korchinska, M., 356
Koussevitzky, 4; Music Foundation, 4
Kulturgeschichte der Oper (Gregor), 328

Lambert, 353
Lancing College, 98
Láng, P. H., 329, 331
Lassus, 84, 85
Lawes, 67
Lawrence, 355
Lee, Rowland V., 312
Lehmann, Liza, 59
Leigh, Walter, 312
Lemare, Iris, 2
Lewis, Wyndham, 61
Liddle, 59
Line to the Tschierva Hut, The (film), 297, 312
Listener, The, 4
Liszt, 275, 314

Liverpool Philharmonic Orchestra, 354
London, 2, 7, 219, 257, 260, 264, 311, 313; Philharmonic Orchestra, 260
Long Island, 4, 260
Longfellow, 60
Los Angeles, 219
Los Angeles Times, 46n.
Love from a Stranger (film), 298, 312
Lowestoft, 1, 59; Choral Society, 1, 59
Lumsden, Norman, 353
Lush, Ernest, 317

*MacNeice, Louis, 307, 309, 311, 312
Mahler, 6, 11, 13, 14, 38, 39, 40, 43, 50, 73, 85, 89n., 97, 99, 115n., 245–6, 252, 317
Maine, 263
Martinu, 357
Mathieson, Muir, 313
Matthews, Thomas, 260
Maupassant, Guy de, 146, 147ff., 366
Mellers, W. H., 10, 13, 14, 15, 51, 55
Melville, Herman, 198ff., 345, 367
Men of Goodwill (radio feature), 307, 309–10, 312
Men of the Alps (film), 297, 312
Mendelssohn, 59, 140n., 212, 322
Menuhin, Yehudi, 70
Merrill, R., 359
Merry Cuckoo, The (Spenser), 253
Message from Geneva (film), 297, 312
Meyer, S., 356
Michelangelo, 65, 66, 84
Milhaud, 144
Milton, 253, 366
Mock, Alice, 357
Monteverdi, 7, 72, 73, 83, 84, 85
Mony a Pickle (film), 312
Moore, G. E., 346
Moore, Gerald, 317, 357
Morning Star, The (Milton), 253
Morriston Boys' Choir, 356
Mozart, 6, 59, 73, 86, 112, 129, 132, 140n., 233, 245, 267, 314, 315, 319–34, 335, 336, 338, 341, 342, 343, 345, 348
Mozart—His Character, His Work (Einstein), 321n., 323, 326, 327, 330, 331, 333, 334, 342
Music and Society (Mellers), 10–11, 13, 14, 15, 55
Music in Western Civilization (Láng), 329, 331
Music Review, The, 326
Music Survey, 30, 320, 340, 349
Musical Antiquarian Society, 187, 188
Musicalisches Wochenblatt, 328

Nashe, Thomas, 253, 366
Neely, B., 357, 358
New Statesman and Nation, 325n., 326
New York, 4, 260, 311, 313; Philharmonic
    Orchestra, 260
Newell, L., 356
Newlin, Dika, 212n.
Nicholls, Agnes, 59
Nielsen, Flora, 354
Nietzsche, 65
Night Mail (film), 3, 295, 296, 312
North Sea, 53
Norwich, 60; Festival, 13

Obey, André, 133, 136n.
Observer, The, 228n., 320, 321, 325, 326,
    330, 365
Odyssey, 300
Oeser, Friederike, 335n.
Old Spain (play), 299, 311
Olivier, Sir Laurence, 309
On the Frontier (play), 3, 299, 300, 311
Orwell, George, 55n.
Oui Ou Non? (ballet), 313
Out of the Picture (play), 311
Out on the lawn I lie in bed (Auden), 254
Ovid, 211n., 319, 367
Oxford Harmony, 339, 347

Paderewski, 273
Palestrina, 83, 84, 85
Paris, 313
Parry, 10, 59, 83
Paul Bunyan, 300
Pears, Peter, 4, 7, 74, 111, 267, 314, 317,
    325, 352, 353, 357, 358, 359
Peele, George, 253, 255, 366
Pepusch, Dr., 166, 170n.
Petit, Roland, 313
Philip, John, 366
Picasso, 321, 336, 339, 356
Playford, Henry, 76, 80
Priestley, J. B., 299, 311
Primrose, William, 233
Promenade Concerts, 257, 264
Prout, 75
Pontresina, 297n.
Puccini, 59, 110
Purcell, 6, 7, 47, 51, 62, 64, 67, 71-2,
    73, 74-82, 101, 186-97, 223, 225,
    235-6, 276, 295, 317, 320, 352, 354,
    355, 361, 365, 367; Society, 186, 187

Quarles, Francis, 72, 86, 95, 362, 366
Quebec, 260

Radio Times, The, 111
Randolph, Thomas, 73, 366
Rank, O., 324
Ravel, 132, 263, 267
Ravenscroft, T., 362
Rawsthorne, A., 275n.
Record, The, 53
Redlich, H. F., 84n.
Reger, 340
Reiniger, Lotte, 299, 312, 313
Rejoice in the Lamb (Smart), 95
Rescue, The (radio drama), 295, 300-3,
    309, 312
Rêve de Leonor, Le, 313
Rilke, Rainer Maria, 31
Rimbaud, 31, 65, 66, 84, 357, 363
Ritchie, Margaret, 354
Robertson, Alec, 46n.; Rae, 257, 264
Rome, 133
Rosier de Madame Husson, Le (Mau-
    passant), 146, 366
Rossetti, Christina, 362
Rossini, 12, 288, 298, 299, 312, 313, 358,
    363, 364
Royal College of Music, 2, 11, 186, 316
Royal Philharmonic Orchestra, 260
Rubbra, 49
Russel, Bertrand, 346

Sackville-West, Edward, 53, 295, 300,
    312
Sadler's Wells Opera Company, 327;
    Theatre, 101
St. Gallen, 313
St. John of the Cross, 36n.
St. John's Church Choir (Upper Nor-
    wood), 356
St. Jorite (Quebec), 260
St. Michael's College, Tenbury, 186
St. Nicolas, Bishop of Myra, 99
Salzburg Festival, 239
Sargent, Sir Malcolm, 354
Savings of Bill Blewitt, The (film), 312
Scarlatti, 275
Schaefer, 356
Scheidt, Samuel, 83
Schiötz, Aksel, 359
Schnabel, Artur, 6, 315

Schoenberg, 2, 61n., 88, 89n., 110, 132, 144, 144n., 247, 249, 267, 336, 339, 340, 341, 342, 343, 344, 346, 348, 350
Schubert, 13, 59, 60, 73, 83, 84, 85, 86, 212, 216, 245, 315, 317, 322, 333, 352
Schumann, 59, 315, 317
Schütz, 83
Selected Essays (Eliot), 38n.
Seven Ages of Man, The (puppet play), 299, 311
Shakespeare, 65, 311
Sharp, Frederick, 353
Shaw, 356
Shawe-Taylor, Desmond, 53, 325n., 326, 331
Shine out, fair sun, 253
Simple Symphony (ballet), 313
Sims, 356
Slater, Montagu, 111, 299, 311, 365
Slonimsky, Nicolas, 344
Smart, Christopher, 95, 365
Snape, 5, 257
Soirée Musicale (ballet), 313
Sokoloff, 357
"Soomer is icoomen in", 256, 281
Sound, 325n.
Sound the Flute (Blake), 255
South America, 313
Southwell, Robert, 364
Soviet Symphony, 339
Spanish Civil War, 3, 7, 97
Spengler, 319n.
Spenser, 253, 366
Sprechstimme, 144, 144n.
Spice, E., 312
Spicer, 356
Spring, the Sweet Spring (Nashe), 253
Stainer, 75
Stanford, 10, 92
Stein, Erwin, 226, 330; Miss Marion, 96
Sterne, Lawrence, 165n.
Stiles-Allen, 59
Stratton (play), 300, 311
Strauss, 323, 335
Strawinsky, 7, 38–40, 64, 66, 73, 110, 219, 267, 288, 321, 335, 336, 339, 340–1, 344, 346, 350
Structural Functions of Harmony (Schoenberg), 270n.
Stuart, Charles, 228, 325
Style and Idea (Schoenberg), 61n.
Suffolk, 1, 5, 6, 7–8, 55, 130, 283
Sullivan, Sir Arthur, 59
Swingler, Randall, 3, 97, 363
Swiss Alpine Club, 297n.
Switzerland, 313
Sword in the Stone, The (play), 299n., 312
Sylphides, Les (ballet), 313

Taylor, Donald, 299, 313
Tchaikovsky, 6
Tempo, 184n., 226, 330
Tenbury, 186; MS. of Dido and Aeneas, 186–7
Tennyson, 60, 67, 365
Terzverwandtschaft, 217n.
This Way to the Tomb (radio play), 303–6, 311
Thorpeness, 211n.
Three Choirs Festival, 83
Thurber, 73
Time and Tide, 15n.
Times, The, 58n., 228n., 330
Timon of Athens (play), 311
Tocher, The (film), 299, 312
Tom Tiddler's Ground (de la Mare), 94
Tristam Shandy, 165n.
Tudor, Antony, 313
Turn Ye to Me, 264
Tusser, Thomas, 362
Two Cheers for Democracy (Forster), 53n., 55n.

U.S.A., 4–6, 7, 41, 55, 146

Vaughan Williams, 10, 11, 14, 15, 49, 92, 254, 275, 352, 356
Veld, 356
Verdi, 6, 31n., 40–1, 73, 92, 109, 110, 129, 130, 140n., 304, 331, 340, 347, 348
Verlaine, 60
Versunkene Stadt, Der (ballet), 313
Victor Female Choir, 356
Vienna, 2, 11, 14, 112, 219
Viennese school, 39
Village Harvest (film), 312
Vogl, 315
Von Luzern auf Wäggis zu, 297

Wagner, 59, 109, 125, 129, 130, 146, 156, 267, 335, 347, 349
Walton, William, 49, 229, 275
War, Sadism and Pacifism (Glover), 350n.
Warlock, Peter, 92, 314
Washington Cathedral Choir, 356; Chamber Chorus, 356; Presbyterian Church Choir, 356
Waters Above (Vaughan), 254
Watt, Harry, 312

Way to the Sea, The (film), 312
Weber, 7, 328
Webern, 339
Webster, John, 307, 311
Wedderburn, James, 364; John, 364; Robert, 364
Weingartner, Felix von, 332
Welcome, Maids of Honour (Herrick), 254
When-as the rye reach to the chin (Peele), 253
When will my May come? (Barnefield), 255
White, E. W., 96; Morton, 338; T. H., 312
Wigmore Hall (London), 243

Wither, George, 92, 95, 362
Wittgenstein, Ludwig, 346; Paul, 257, 263, 264
Wolf, Hugo, 45, 314
Wood, Haydn, 59; Richard, 96; Sir Henry, 257
Woodforde-Finden, Amy, 59
World's Encyclopædia of Recorded Music, 353
Wright, Basil, 312, 313
Wyss, Sophie, 63, 359

Zorian Quartet, 225, 355

Index of Music Examples

Albert Herring
  Act I, Sc. 1, 25, 33, 41, 156, 152, 157
  Act I, Sc. 2, 22, 23, 56, 149, 153, 156, 290
  Act II, Sc. 1, 46, 47, 149, 157, 176n.
  Act II, Interlude, 153, 158
  Act II, Sc. 2, 155
  Act III, 33, 35, 36, 150–2, 154, 159, 161–2
All people that on earth do dwell, 52
Antique, 32
Ash Grove, The, 48
As it is, plenty, 19

Beggar's Opera, The
  Act I, Sc. 1, 183
  Act I, Sc. 2, 171, 175–6
  Act II, 174, 180
  Act III, 172, 173, 177, 179, 181–2
Billy Budd
  Prologue, 29n., 201, 202
  Act I, 28, 29, 202, 203, 204, 205
  Act II, Sc. 1, 202, 203
  Act II, Sc. 2, 203, 204, 206
  Act III, Sc. 1, 27, 207
  Act III, Sc. 2, 208
  Act IV, Sc. 1, 57
  Act IV, Sc. 2, 27, 208
Boy was Born, A, 11, 86, 87, 88, 89

Canticle I, 50
Ceremony of Carols, A, 46, 95
Come you not from Newcastle?, 48

Dawn Interlude, 53
Death of Nicolas, The, 99
Départ, 34

Dido and Aeneas. See Purcell Realizations.
Driving Boy, The, 100

Fair and fair, 20
Falstaff (Verdi), Act I, Sc. 2, 40
Funeral March, 142n.

Holiday Tales, 270, 271
Holy Sonnets of John Donne, 51
Hymn to St. Cecilia, 90

I Lov'd a Lass, 92
Illuminations, Les, 32, 33, 34
Incidental Music
  Ascent of F6, The, 298
  Dark Tower, The, 308, 309
  Eagle has Two Heads, The, 307
  Instruments of the Orchestra, 276, 277, 278
  Line to the Tschierva Hut, The, 297
  Men of Goodwill, 310
  Morning, 305
  Night Mail, 297
  Rescue, The, 301, 302
  This Way to the Tomb, 303, 304, 305
Introduction and Rondo alla Burlesca, 273

Kindertotenlieder (Mahler), 44, 51

Lacrymosa, 251
Let the florid music praise!, 16, 17

Let's make an Opera, 18, 26, 56, 283, 284, 285, 286, 292, 293
Little Sweep, The, 18, 26, 56, 283, 284, 285, 286, 292, 293

Mazurka Elegiaca, 273, 274

Nicolas and the Pickled Boys, 98
Nicolas comes to Myra and is chosen Bishop, 52
Night, 271
Night Song, 26, 285
Now the leaves are falling fast, 20, 21

On This Island, 16, 17, 18, 19, 20, 21

Peter Grimes
    Prologue, 102, 127
    Act I, Sc. 1, 53, 103, 105, 106, 115, 126
    Act I, Sc. 2, 23, 126
    Act II, Sc. 1, 107, 108, 109, 119, 126, 128
    Act II, Interlude, 110, 128
    Act II, Sc. 2, 103, 104, 107, 126
    Act III, Sc. 1, 106, 127
    Act III, Sc. 2, 105, 123
Piano Concerto, 258, 259, 260
Purcell Realizations
    Abdelazar, or The Moor's Revenge, 276, 277
    Blessed Virgin's Expostulation, The, 76
    Dido and Aeneas, Act I, 190, 192, 193, 194; Act II, 195, 196; Act III, 196
    En nymphas! en pastores!, 81
    Evening Hymn, 77–8
    Job's Curse, 79
    Lord, what is man?, 77
    Mad Bess, 80
    Orpheus Britannicus, 80
    Queen's Epicedium, The, 81
    Saul and the Witch at Endor, 79
    Sweeter than Roses, 80
    Three Divine Hymns, 77, 78

Rape of Lucretia, The
    Act I, Sc. 1, 138, 141
    Act I, Sc. 2, 116, 141, 145
    Act II, Sc. 1, 143, 144
    Act II, Sc. 2, 54, 137n., 138, 139, 141, 142, 143
Rejoice in the Lamb, 19
Requiem Aeternam, 251, 252
Royauté, 33

Saint Nicolas, 52, 98, 99, 280
Seascape, 18
Seven Sonnets of Michelangelo, 22, 42, 43, 44, 45, 115n., 116
Sinfonia da Requiem, 250, 251, 252
Sinfonietta, 247, 248, 249
Sir Anthony Love (Purcell), 190
Six Songs, 80
Spring Symphony
    Part II, 12, 255
    Part III, 20, 48
    Part IV (Finale), 57, 100, 281

Te Deum in C major, 93
Three Two-part Songs, 91

Variations on a Theme of Frank Bridge, 14, 32, 142n.
Violin Concerto, 261, 262

Wedding Anthem, 96
Welcome Odes, 190
When will my May come?, 48

Young Person's Guide to the Orchestra, The, 276, 277, 278